Lecture Notes in Computer Science 1045

Edited by G. Goos, J. Hartmanis and J. van Leeuwen

Advisory Board: W. Brauer   D. Gries   J. Stoer

Springer
Berlin
Heidelberg
New York
Barcelona
Budapest
Hong Kong
London
Milan
Paris
Santa Clara
Singapore
Tokyo

Berthold Butscher Eckhard Moeller
Herwart Pusch (Eds.)

Interactive Distributed Multimedia Systems and Services

European Workshop IDMS'96
Berlin, Germany, March 4-6, 1996
Proceedings

Springer

Series Editors

Gerhard Goos, Karlsruhe University, Germany

Juris Hartmanis, Cornell University, NY, USA

Jan van Leeuwen, Utrecht University, The Netherlands

Volume Editors

Berthold Butscher
Eckhard Moeller
Herwart Pusch
GMD FOKUS
Hardenbergplatz 2, D-10623 Berlin, Germany

Cataloging-in-Publication data applied for

Die Deutsche Bibliothek - CIP-Einheitsaufnahme

Interactive distributed multimedia systems and services :
proceedings / European Workshop IDMS '96, Berlin, Germany,
March 1996. Berthold Butscher ... (ed.). - Berlin ; Heidelberg ;
New York ; Barcelona ; Budapest ; Hong Kong ; London ;
Milan ; Paris ; Santa Clara ; Singapore ; Tokyo : Springer, 1996
  (Lecture notes in computer science ; Vol. 1045)
  ISBN 3-540-60938-5
NE: Butscher, Berthold [Hrsg.]; IDMS <1996, Berlin>; GT

CR Subject Classification (1991): H.5.1, H.4.3, C.2, B.4.1, K.6.5, D.4.6, J.1

ISBN 3-540-60938-5 Springer-Verlag Berlin Heidelberg New York

© Springer-Verlag Berlin Heidelberg 1996
Printed in Germany

Typesetting: Camera-ready by author
SPIN 10512619   06/3142 – 5 4 3 2 1 0   Printed on acid-free paper

Preface

To cover the future needs of business and residential customers in the information society, interactive multimedia applications such as Interactive TV, Video-on-Demand, Audio-on-Demand, News-on-Demand, Tele-shopping or Tele-education, are envisaged or being developed and installed. These interactive multimedia applications are based on a number of services which provide facilities for access to e.g. broadcast television, broadcast radio, multimedia storage systems including multiple access of real-time data, interactive hypermedia documents or personal communication services such as electronic mail and fax, on a *single end system* whose capabilities may vary from highly sophisticated workstations to set-top units and mobile end systems.

Key issues in the goal of obtaining an integrated approach for both the business and the residential domains are extensibility, scalability and quality of service. The *European Workshop on Interactive Distributed Multimedia Systems and Services*, IDMS'96, addresses these topics and examines current and new approaches from different perspectives ranging from architecture to technology. This volume contains the papers presented at the workshop held in Berlin, Germany, March 4-6, 1996. IDMS'96, a workshop of the Section "Communication and Distributed Systems" of GI/ITG, is organized by GMD FOKUS with support from DeTeBerkom, ERCIM and Siemens.

The Call For Papers resulted in contributions from eight countries from which the Program Committee selected twenty papers to be presented at the workshop together with one invited paper. Three keynote speakers, Andy Hopper (Olivetti Research Laboratory, UK), Christian Huitema (INRIA, France) and Ralf Guido Herrtwich (RWE Telliance, Germany), were invited to open each workshop day with their stimulating views on the following subjects: the network computer, realtime multimedia over the Internet and interactive television evolving from multimedia systems. For the workshop panel the subject "global multimedia communications: choosing the right platform" was proposed. The nine sessions of the workshop cover:

- application development support;
- multimedia services on demand including formats for multimedia presentation systems;
- multimedia conferencing aspects such as low bandwidth, security and personal mobility;
- multimedia networking and transport covering security and quality of service aspects as well as media scaling in case of lack of resource reservation protocols;
- continuous-media streams including aspects such as scheduling, filtering, control and synchronization;
- multimedia experiments such as the "virtual classroom".

Many people contributed in preparation for the workshop - committee members, authors and reviewers. We would like to thank the Program Committee for producing a well-balanced technical program and the local Organizing Committee for all the supporting activities to make the event happen. Special thanks goes to Herwart Pusch as Chair of the local Organizing Committee.

January 1996   Berthold Butscher and Eckhard Moeller

General Co-Chairmen

Organizations

Sponsored/organized by:

Gesellschaft für Informatik (GI) / Informationstechnische Gesellschaft im VDE (ITG)

GMD - Forschungszentrum Informationstechnik
Forschungsinstitut für Offene Kommunikationssysteme (FOKUS)

Supported by:

DeTeBerkom

European Research Consortium for Informatics and Mathematics (ERCIM)

Siemens

Committees

General Co-Chairmen

Berthold Butscher	GMD FOKUS/DeTeBerkom, Germany
Eckhard Moeller	GMD FOKUS, Germany

Program Committee

Hans Werner Bitzer	DeTeBerkom, Germany
Gerold Blakowski	Deutsche Bank, Germany
Christopher S. Cooper	Rutherford Appleton Laboratory, UK
Walid Dabbous	INRIA, France
André Danthine	University of Liège, Belgium
Wolfgang Effelsberg	University of Mannheim, Germany
David Hutchison	Lancaster University, UK
Winfried Kalfa	TU Chemnitz-Zwickau, Germany
Thomas Magedanz	TU Berlin, Germany
Gisela Maiß	DFN-Verein, Germany
Eckhard Moeller	GMD FOKUS, Germany (Chair)
Bernhard Plattner	ETH Zürich, Switzerland
Kurt Rothermel	University of Stuttgart, Germany
Joachim Schaper	Digital CEC, Germany
Jean Schweitzer	Siemens AG, Germany
Michael Weber	University of Ulm, Germany

Local Organizing Committee

Silke Cords	GMD FOKUS, Germany
Barbara Intelmann	GMD FOKUS, Germany
Christine Passon	GMD FOKUS, Germany
Herwart Pusch	GMD FOKUS, Germany (Chair)

Contents

Contents

Session 4: Enhanced Multimedia Conferencing
Chair: Chris S. Cooper (Rutherford Appleton Lab.,UK)

Session 5: Multimedia Networking & Transport
Chair: Winfried Kalfa (TU Chemnitz-Zwickau, Germany)

Session 6: Continuous-media Streams: Scheduling and Filtering
Chair: Wolfgang Effelsberg (Univ. of Mannheim, Germany)

Heidi-II: A Software Architecture for ATM Network Based Distributed Multimedia Systems

M. Gu, K. Nahrstedt, V. Larsen,
R.H. Sinzia, D. Raychaudhuri

C&C Research Laboratories, NEC USA, Inc.

Abstract: In this document, we describe the architecture of a distributed multimedia software prototype, "Heidi-II," currently under development at our laboratories. This prototype aims to demonstrate a software framework for deployment of efficient, quality-of-service (QoS) based multimedia applications over ATM networks, using a synergistic combination of several novel approaches. In particular, the software architecture incorporates the following key components: Axtkit, a new distributed scripting language for easy-to-use and efficient object-oriented implementation of multimedia applications across networks; EasyInView, a new graphical user interface for intuitive access of multimedia services over a network; ATM bearer MacLayer, an advanced ATM API with automatic service provisioning, range of protocol entities, ABR VBR/CBR services, dynamic bandwidth negotiation and quality-of-service (QoS) support; VibeX, a dynamically negotiated variable bit-rate transport mode in ATM networks for efficient support of under structure with network level flow control and subnetwork Transport Protocol (MTP), a transport service framework protocol control to streamline delivery of real-time applications over an ATM network.

1 Introduction

We consider a fairly general multimedia computing and communications scenario, as illustrated in figure 1. In this environment, a variety of multimedia devices, both fixed and portable, communicate with each other and/or retrieve information from remote multiservers. Observe that the scenario shown is characterized by the coexistence of many application, multiplexes, and services platforms on a single multi-service broadband network. It is desirable that the same applications for multimedia information retrieval, video-on-demand, groupware, etc., will run on some PCs/workstation/set-top boxes, as well as on portable devices such as notebook PCs, PDAs (personal digital assistants) or PICs (personal information appliances).

In the system under consideration, network-based multimedia services are central to the application, and are equally accessible to both static and mobile users. It is recognized that in order to maximize utility and convenience, it is essential to design a seamless networking and software architecture which encompasses both wired and wireless portions of the system. Of course, there may be quantitative differences in the computing

Heidi-II: A Software Architecture for ATM Network Based Distributed Multimedia Systems

M. Ott, D. Reininger, G. Michelitsch, V. Bansal,
R.J. Siracusa, D.Raychaudhuri

C&C Research Laboratories, NEC USA, Inc.

Abstract: In this document, we describe the architecture of a distributed multimedia software prototype ("Heidi-II") currently under development at our laboratories. This prototype aims to demonstrate a software framework for development of efficient, quality-of-service (QoS) based multimedia applications over ATM networks, using a synergistic combination of several novel approaches. In particular, the software architecture incorporates the following key components: *Jodler*, a new distributed scripting language for easy-to-use and efficient object oriented implementation of multimedia applications across the network; *CockpitView*, a new graphical user interface for intuitive access of multimedia services over a network; *ATM Service Manager*, an advanced ATM API with automatic service provisioning, transport protocol options, ABR/ VBR/CBR services, dynamic bandwidth renegotiation and quality-of-service (QoS) support; *VBR+*, a dynamically renegotiated variable bit-rate transport mode in ATM networks for efficient support of media streams with network-level QoS control; and *Multimedia Transport Protocol (MTP)*, a stream-oriented, lightweight media transport protocol customized for delivery of real time video/audio, etc. over ATM networks.

1 Introduction

We consider a fairly general multimedia computing and communication ("C&C") scenario, as illustrated in Figure 1. In this environment, a variety of multimedia computing devices, both fixed and portable, communicate with each other and/or access information from remote media servers. Observe that the scenario shown is characterized by the coexistence of many applications, media types, and service platforms within a single multi-service broadband networking framework. It is desirable that the same applications for multimedia information retrieval, video-on-demand, groupware, etc. will run on static PC/workstation/set-top box, as well as on portable devices such as notebook PCs, PDAs (personal digital assistance), or PIAs (personal information appliance).

In the system under consideration, network-based multimedia services are central to the application, and are equally accessible to both static and mobile users. It is recognized that in order to maximize utility and convenience, it is essential to design a seamless networking and software architecture which incorporates both wired and wireless portion of the system. Of course, there may be quantitative differences in the comput-

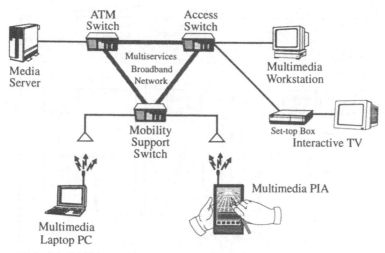

Fig.1. Typical multimedia "C&C" scenario.

ing, media processing/display or communication capabilities of different multimedia terminals in the system, depending on available hardware speed or network bandwidth. The objective is to have a qualitatively uniform system architecture that applies across different platform and network types.

Selected design topics discussed in the following chapters include: a distributed software framework; a new user-interface which emphasizes communication; and an inclusive quality-of-service framework.

2 Software Architecture

Developing applications and services for an environment of terminals with greatly varying capabilities and network resources constitutes a considerable challenge. It will become impractical to specifically provide for every possible resource configuration. Instead we need a software architecture which allows applications to adapt dynamically to changes in available resources. Another important aspect of this work is mobility of both, the physical device, as well as the application. The latter occurs when a user changes devices but wants to maintain context (e.g. moves from a whiteboard to a PDA).

To study these problems, we have developed a software architecture which allows for rapid prototyping of distributed multimedia applications [OCO94, OAM95]. So called "resource objects" in a distributed object space orchestrate the interaction between media processing modules and also expose the capabilities of these modules to other objects. This object space is realized in a new network programming language, called *Jodler* [Ott94].

Figure 2 shows the overall architecture of our prototype system. Jodler engines on every physical node (e.g. terminal, compute/data server, network switch) host objects which

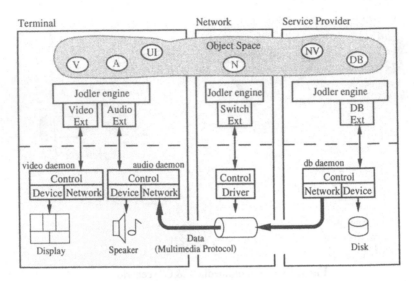

Fig.2. System overview

can send messages to each other. Communication between objects residing within different engines is transparently enabled through dynamically created communication links. Further, an object can easily migrate between engines while all references to other objects as well as from other objects to itself remain valid.

Local resources, such as media storage, displays, or audio speakers are accessed and controlled through daemon processes. The control interface of these daemons is connected to a daemon specific extension of the nearest engine. The aforementioned resource objects represent these daemons and allow other objects to reserve and control the available resources. For instance, a simple network VCR application, represented by the "NV" object in Figure 2, will reserve and coordinate various resources, such as the movie database "DB", a network channel "N", and display resources for video "V" and audio "A", besides a user interface component "UI" to start and stop the movie.

2.1 Jodler: A Network Programming Language

As mentioned above, and shown in Figure 2, a central part of our architecture is a global object space with a single communication mechanism independent of the "physical" location of corresponding objects.

As this work started out with exploring new approaches to user-interfaces for distributed, multimedia centric applications we required a very dynamic programming environment. We initially chose Tcl[Ous94], an embedable scripting language and extended it with the below described media modules. However, the simplicity of Tcl soon became a burden due to the lack of suitable data abstraction mechanisms and difficulties in efficiently programming distributed applications. Therefore, instead of adopting another, existing language we decided to create a new language which gave us the freedom to experiment with a mix of concepts borrowed from existing languages and some new

ideas. The result is Jodler which has the following properties:
- object-oriented
- prototypes
- delegation or module operators
- active objects with migration
- dynamically maintained, global object space
- location independent object ID
- constraint object references
- object verification
- controlled resource access and allocation

In its current implementation, Jodler is an interpreted language employing an object model based on prototypes and delegation [Bor86]. An interpreter is well suited for heterogeneous environments while it also provides a safety cushion between the actual programs and the bare hardware. The object model of prototypes, in turn, provides a very concrete view of what an object needs for execution and who it is communicating with.

Objects in Jodler contain named slots that may store either state or behavior. State slots may contain a literal (string, list) or a pointer to another object. A message sent to a state slot will return its contents. Behavior slots contain blocks with variable arguments. A message sent to a behavior slot will return the result of the block activated with the arguments of the message. However, the type of slot is transparent to the sender of the message. Blending state and behavior makes it easy to implement constructs, such as active variables.

In a prototype based language, new objects are created by cloning existing ones. Objects know of other objects by holding object references and therefore do not require a global registrary on the language level. In practice, we will need some mechanism to "introduce" objects to each other, but this is left to the application domain to provide.

Influenced by Self [USm87], we initially adopted delegation as the inheritance mechanism but found it to lead to overly complex inheritance structures when we designed larger systems. Instead, we recently started to experiment with the concept of module operators [BrL92] which seem to allow for a cleaner design when applied to similar problems. It does, however, place a heavier burden on the run-time system and we need to further investigate if this carries an inherent performance penalty.

2.1.1 Migration

When an object sends a message to another object it is (usually) completely unaware of the location of the receiving object. This means that the placement of objects is largely decoupled from the functionality of these objects. However, sometimes objects do need to know where they are, or we want to employ an application independent "resource" monitor which dynamically and asynchronously migrates objects to optimize resource consumption. To this end, we introduced the guest/host relation into Jodler which ensures that all guests of a host object and the host itself reside in the same engine. Migration can be initiated by changing the host reference of an object to a host residing in another engine. This process will be completely transparent to the object itself and to all other objects.

2.1.2 Service Objects

A unique feature of our object model is that object references can be defined in terms of constraints. This allows the environment to automatically change a reference to another object if the constraint remains satisfied.

Currently, the only constraint supported is an object's request for a specific service. A *service broker* will return a reference to an object providing that service, but the reference will be tagged as a service link. If, for instance, an object migrates to a new engine, a local broker can re-evaluate all service references and may transparently switch some of them to a more "efficient" service objects. This will increase the efficiency of migration as general services can often be provided by local objects. It can also be used for providing "location aware" services. Connecting migrating objects to local service objects will allow for services such as, the "nearest" printer, or the "local" weather.

2.1.3 Secure Execution of Active Objects

As we allow active objects to roam around freely we need to address a range of security issues. Jodler provides language primitives for controlling resource access and consumption. The proposed language abstractions are *access/clearance* and *cost/allowance*.

Each object will be assigned a specific clearance by its host, while slots can set an access level. Currently we assign an integer in a preset range and postulate that for a message being delivered successfully, the clearance level of the sender must be "higher" than the access level of the slot identified by the message.

Besides controlling access to resources we also need a mechanism to bound or at least keep track of the consumption of resources on a per object base. In Jodler, similar to [Whi93], we assign an allowance to every object. When an object sends a message, the receiving object can request that a certain allowance will be transferred from the sender to the receiver. The message will fail if the cost charged by the receiver exceeds the allowance of the sender. Further, an object can be requested to periodically "pay rent" to its host (most often the local interpreter). An object will be destroyed when it runs out of allowance.

2.2 Media Processing Modules

To support the applications currently implemented on our test-bed we developed a collection of media processing modules which are divided into three categories: producers, consumers, and processors. Producer components include cameras, microphones, VCRs, and traffic generators. Consumer components include video display (motion JPEG), image display (optimized for X-ray images), and audio playback. Specialized producer and consumer components have also been developed to support various multimedia data storage formats, such as QuickTime. Processing components include network transfer modules utilizing various protocols (TCP, UDP, MTP), and software-only video decoders for MPEG and Cell-B.

Data streams originate at producer modules, are piped through processing modules, and terminate at consumer modules. We designed a separate unique object called a *wire* which controls the data exchange between connected modules and simplifies the interface design of a module considerably. The following code listing illustrates the use of a wire to display a video clip from a movie file; the multimedia version of "Hello World":

```
movie = [qt.open "helloWorld.moov"]
track = [movie.getTrack -media video]
monitor = [ui.video.copy -newWindow]
wire = [wire.copy $track $monitor]
```

A generic interface allows us to assemble independently developed modules into arbitrary processing pipelines. The wire objects make dynamic reconfiguration possible without requiring any additional support from the modules.

Similar in concept to [TAC94] the media processing modules are divided into two parts, a data-driven *flow* domain, and an event-driven *control* domain. The time sensitive and processing intensive data streams, such as audio and video stream through the flow domain. A generic interface allows the construction of data-flow like processing graphs. The control domain, in turn, controls the parameters of the algorithm in the flow domain, or processes control information generated by the flow domain (e.g. identifying a face in a video stream).

The design criteria for the two domains are obviously quite different, while the main emphasis in the flow domain is on efficiency, in the control domain it is on flexibility.

The flow domain in individual modules is implemented in C or C++. Scheduling of the modules and the transport of data packages between adjacent modules are performed by the wire objects. Each module only needs to register "in" and "out" ports which are supplied with a *container* to either take out, or put in a data chunk whenever the respective port is called. It can also temporarily block if it waits for an external trigger, such as a frame from a digitizer.

The control domain is implemented as an object in the above described, distributed object space. Parameters of the algorithm implemented in the flow domain can be set through messages sent to the object. It should be noted that the capabilities of the object can be extended dynamically. For instance, one can check a request to change internal parameters for validity, or if the sender has the privileges to request the change, before the new parameter settings are accepted and forwarded to the flow domain.

In turn, the flow domain can produce periodic measurements or sporadic signals which are either processed in the object (control domain) itself, or sent as a message to other interested objects (e.g. a graph widget showing the energy of an audio stream).

A more detailed description of the internal structure of the modules and especially the wire can be found in [OHe95].

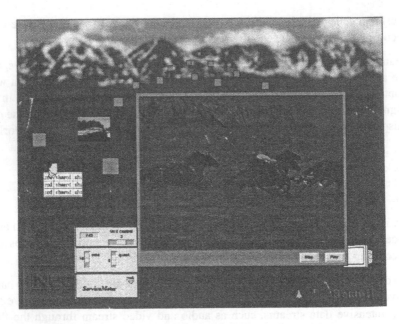

Fig.3. Screen Snapshot

3 CockpitView: A New Graphical User Interface for Accessing Multimedia Services over the Network.

Based on the fact that humans are generally very good at remembering objects by their location, we chose a spatial metaphor for organizing information entities in one global virtual landscape. Recent advances in low-cost 3D graphics hardware make this approach feasible, but in contrast to the video game industry, which emphasis realistic rendering of 3D objects, our goal is to optimize the use of limited screen real estate while allowing the user to keep as much context as possible [Rob93, Sta93].

At the same time we do not believe that ordinary users will want to use special equipment for 3D input and output. We want to be able to manipulate objects directly on a flat screen with either a pen or ones finger. In order to do so we restrict the degrees of freedom an object has in our information landscape and add a 2D work plane, the *dashboard*, at the bottom of the screen. The user looks at the landscape as if through the window of a cockpit (hence the name CockpitView). He can reach out of the cockpit, grab an object on the landscape, move it around, and when he drags it to the dashboard, this object will turn itself into a 2D document which can then be manipulated just as in traditional graphical user interfaces (see Figure 3)

3.1 Shared Virtual Spaces

The concept of a global information landscape does not imply that everything created by a user is automatically visible to all others. By default an object is private and its existence unknown to anyone else. To introduce it to the outside world we create what we call a *Shared Virtual Space*, select one or more participants for it, and associate a private object with that space. At this time this private object will show up at each participant's information landscape [Mic95].

Participants can be active, which means that their every action is immediately reflected on each others screen, or passive, in which case they only observe what is going on within this shared space. The transition between active and passive participation is smooth and natural, allowing users to emulate and combine traditional communication styles, like asynchronous messaging and real-time conferencing, with ease.

We are using a *Coffee Table* metaphor for presenting a shared space to the user. We imagine a coffee table in a coffee house with seats reserved for a group of people. One can sit down at the table and talk to others sitting at the same table. This is an example of synchronous communication. On the other hand, the very same table can be used for asynchronous communication as well. A message put onto the table by one person can be seen by another member and picked up later for reading. We render these tables as 3D table icons on the information landscape. Each participant is represented by a face icon, which is a bitmap rendering of the person's face when he is away from the table, or a live video image when he is sitting at that table. The user pulls a table icon to the dashboard to "sit down" at the table, and pushes the table back into the landscape when he wants to leave. These operations are all the user has to do in order to join or leave a conversation which can include the setup and tear-down of live audio and video feeds, and the loading of shared documents.

3.2 Active Tools

Every object on the screen is an active object that reacts to user generated events as well as to other objects. When the user drops an object onto another one, a compound object will be created. If one of these objects is what we call an *Active Tool,* the attachment will cause the tool object to perform an operation on the other object.

As an example of an active tool we will briefly describe the *ServiceMeter,* shown in Figure 3. This tool, resembling a real world measurement tool, allows the user to adjust the quality of service (QoS) provided by the underlying software and network. The user adjusts the main slider to indicate to the system a level of quality within a scale from 1 to 5. The media software translates this value into a set of parameter values that define a specific service, such as the frame rate of a video source. The ServiceMeter generates slider controls for each of those parameters and hides them under a panel. With the panel opened one can adjust each of these parameters individually within the constraints imposed by the media control software. A small display on the tool keeps a real time update of the amount of cost visible to the user at all time.

3.3 CockpitView Implementation Issues

In our prototype implementation we rely on an object oriented, distributed programming paradigm to provide a transparent mechanism for forwarding messages among remote participants of a shared virtual space. This allows us to share arbitrary objects without requiring any changes made to these objects.

Our user interface framework is built on a *unified structured object model*. Like in structured graphics editors each object of a document is internally represented by a corresponding object in a tree like structure that covers the whole document in case of an editor, or the whole user interface in our system. But in contrast to graphic editors this tree structure also contains user interface widgets essential for operating the system. This way user interaction widgets and application specific data can be treated the same way, allowing for a great deal of flexibility (compare with FRESCO [Tan94]). At the same time each object is also part of an inheritance structure, like in classic object oriented designs. A new object is created by making a clone of an existing object in the inheritance tree of prototype objects and linking this new object into the appropriate place of the tree structure representing the user interface.

The basic graphics operation necessary for implementing the user interface are provided by Tk [Ous94] which has been integrated into the Jodler language environment. The Tk library also provides us with basic event handling. A simple abstraction layer maps these events to messages which are directed to, and understood by objects in the Jodler world.

All 3D effects in our current implementation are based on consistently scaling images of objects placed on the information landscape. In order to improve the responsiveness of our implementation we are making extensive use of caching precomputed images in different scale factors. The use of a full 3D model for rendering objects in the information landscape is planed for the future.

4 ATM Service Manager

The existing transport system architecture is not well suited for multimedia applications which have a diverse range of traffic characteristics and quality of service (QoS) requirements. These new applications, which may be composed of video, audio, image or data, have different traffic characteristics and thus will need call/admission control, different level of QoS guarantees and different underlying transport/adaptation support. In this new environment for multimedia applications, it is essential that QoS is statistically guaranteed system-wide.

An ATM-based framework for QoS control involves two major elements. The first is an ATM network designed to provide a range of transport services with QoS controls [Ram91], while the second is a corresponding software QoS API at servers and terminals [Ban95, Cam94]. ATM networks are being designed to provide various service classes, such as available bit-rate (ABR), variable bit-rate (VBR) and constant bit-rate (CBR), each with its own service parameter list and QoS specification options. In general, ABR is viewed as a packet data service without explicit QoS indication, while CBR is viewed as a circuit-switched service with a pre-specified high QoS requirement. A more continuous form of QoS control is envisioned for the VBR class via specification of a source traffic profile in the form of usage parameter control (UPC) parameters, typically implemented as dual leaky buckets with parameters: peak rate (R_p), sustained rate (R_s), and burst length (B). Statistical QoS guarantees on cell loss rate (CLR) and

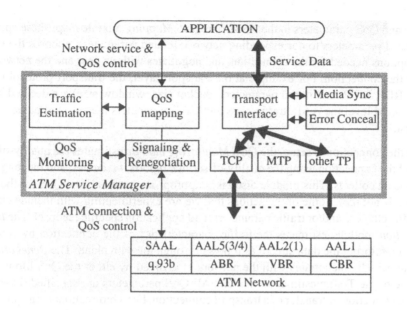

Fig.4. Adaptive QoS-capable API for ATM

cell delay variance (CDV) are then provided by the network, which used an appropriate call admission control process (CAC) to admit new calls.

An appropriate QoS-capable network API is needed to properly utilize ATM network QoS control features such as those discussed above. We are currently investigate a high-level API concept called *ATM Service Manager* (ASM) [Ban95]. In general, an application connected to ATM has a choice of transport protocols (e.g. TCP, UDP, MTP), ATM service class (e.g. ABR, VBR, CBR) and QoS parameters for each media type. Higher layers (media daemons and/or applications) request connection setup to the ASM with desired QoS parameters. The ASM uses those parameters to configure and initialize the service. Typical ASM functions are:

- Map general QoS parameters into appropriate network related parameters like cell loss ratio, cell delay variation and end to end delay. The ATM traffic class and the AAL to be used for the connection is also decided based on the applications requirements.
- Select the transport needed for the connection based on the QoS requirements of the application and the ATM class selected for the connection.
- Negotiate with the peer and the network to setup the connection to ensure the proper exchange of parameters.

Once the service is configured and initialized, the ASM provides statistical guarantees to applications by monitoring and controlling QoS at all architecture levels; any layer not meeting its committed QoS should take some corrective action or inform higher layers. In addition, QoS renegotiation is supported during the connection.

Figure 4 shows the interaction of the various components of the ASM. Higher layers (Media devices and/or applications) send their request for connection setup along with traffic and QoS parameters to the ASM. The *QoS Mapping* module maps these application level parameters to corresponding network related parameters, chooses the transport options needed for the connection, and negotiates with its peer and the network to setup the connection. For example at the transport layer, the transport protocol (TCP, UDP, RDP, MTP) and initial parameters (packet size, window size) are decided while at the ATM level the AAL, traffic class and UPC parameters are selected based on the request.

Once the connection is setup, the *QOS Monitoring module* estimates the quality-of-service of the connection using the quality-of-service reports it receives, and the long term statistics it collects. This module also takes appropriate actions if the QoS for the connection is not met. Some of the actions that we are experimenting with include change of traffic classes, and/or traffic parameters, and application specific feedback The *traffic estimation* module, estimates the traffic characteristics of the connection by continuously monitoring the data stream as it flows through the data plane. The *Renegotiation* module which renegotiates with the network is invoked by either the QoS Monitoring module or the Traffic estimation module. All QoS parameters are specified separately for each direction of transfer of a transport connection. For a bidirectional transport connection two sets of QoS parameters have to be specified, while for a unidirectional transport connection only one set of QoS parameters (for the transfer direction) is necessary.

In addition to the traditional transport protocols and ATM service classes the ASM can also select a new transport protocol called multimedia transport protocol (MTP), and a new ATM service class called VBR+. These additional services are described next.

4.1 Multimedia Transport Protocol (MTP)

A "multimedia transport protocol (MTP)" software prototype for video and multimedia applications over ATM is now being experimentally evaluated on our laboratories' ATM test-bed. MTP is a lightweight stream-oriented transport protocol with a flexible, modular and lightweight implementation based on the use of a hardware ATM AAL. The MTP and supporting AAL facilitate error control after detecting the loss of one or more cells on the channel. Depending upon the error characteristics of the losses due to statistical multiplexing, a standard AAL may not provide optimal error recovery. By identifying specific transport bundling information, MTP can identify losses with cell-level resolution, and then select from appropriate recovery options including retransmission, retransmission with time-limit, delivery with error token, etc. To detect single cell losses, the MTP-AAL provides a continuity counter for loss detection over all cells within a PDU. A map of data loss is optionally provided to the upper layer software so that it can apply appropriate concealment algorithms to the missing data. Also provided is a means to segment an application PDU into a number of transport PDUs (TPDU), and a means of reassembling TPDUs at the decoder. To support decoder concealment in an MPEG video decoder, MTP can emit an error token when a loss is detected.

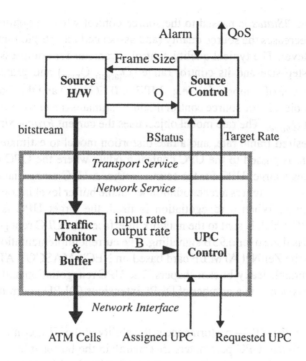

Fig.5. VBR+ modules

4.2 VBR+: A Dynamically Renegotiated VBR Mode for Video

While the VBR service class is potentially more efficient than a static CBR, practical difficulties have been experienced in achieving significant statistical multiplexing gain for video or multimedia calls with conventional fixed UPC parameters [Har93]. Accordingly, we are investigating the feasibility of a new "VBR+" service which supports dynamic bandwidth renegotiation during the course of a call. VBR+ is a feedback enhanced VBR service class that supports dynamic bandwidth renegotiation between the source and the network [Rei95]. VBR+ simultaneously provides QoS guarantees to the user and high utilization through aggressive statistical multiplexing on the network.

The VBR+ implementation combines UPC control at the network service layer with source control at the middleware layer. Figure 5 shows schematically the VBR+ modules. Each module is implemented by a number of software objects. The traffic monitor and buffer module computes the *output rate*[1] and the *input rate* to the module and stores the queued traffic in a buffer. While the *input rate* is source dependent, the *output rate* is determined by the traffic shaper at the ATM I/F and it is dependent on the UPC currently assigned by the network, *Assigned UPC*. The *input rate*, *output rate* and instantaneous buffer occupancy, *B*, are passed to the UPC control module. From the output and input rates a UPC characterization object estimates the current output and source UPC. Also at the UPC control module, a buffer monitor object determines the buffer

---

1. All words in italics indicate parameters shown in Figure 5.

status, *BStatus*. *BStatus* is passed to the source control where a quality control object increases or decreases the source quality (and associated bit-rate) to maintain the buffer at a nominal level. The typical quality control parameter for compression hardware is quantization step-size and its control range (Q_{target}, Q_{max}) and granularity (DeltaQ) depend on the type of compression (e.g., MPEG, JPEG, etc.) and the QoS requirements. A rate model object in the source control module estimates the *target rate*, for the source to be coded at Q_{target}. The rate model object uses the current *Frame Size,* current quantization, Q, desired frame rate, and a rate-distortion model to estimate the *target rate*. The *target rate* is passed to the UPC control module where the UPC characterization object estimates a target UPC for the source traffic. A UPC renegotiation object monitors the *BStatus* and triggers a renegotiation when the buffer level is consistently outside a nominal region. When a renegotiation is fired, the target UPC is mapped to the *Requested UPC* which is sent to the network interface. The UPC renegotiation with the network CAC is done over q.93B signalling. The current implementation of the network interface uses the ZeitNet ATM I/F card based on NEC's MASCOT ATM chip set with UPC-programmable leaky-bucket shapers. The UPC renegotiation and dynamic shaper programming is done via a number of DLPI extensions (DLPI+) currently under development.

An indication of the VBR+ performance is the ability of the UPC control module to successfully renegotiate UPC parameters that maintain the buffer in a nominal region. If the UPC renegotiation is not effective, the buffer level will cause the source control module to be unable to maintain Q in the specified control range. In that case, the source management module will *alarm* the application, which might decide to lower its QoS requirement or increase the cost constraint to allow the ASM to select a service that can provide the desired QoS.

5 Conclusion

Our approach to future, distributed, multimedia application architectures is to take a top-down view of the possible scenarios one can imagine with global and ubiquitous high speed networks available.

In this paper we gave a grand overview of our software architecture, and visited some of the components we have worked on, including a new network programming language, new user interface technologies, and several ATM specific enhancements to network protocols with a focus on QoS support across all layers of software.

The software has been deployed on a variety of terminal/server platforms and operating systems including Sun Sparc workstation (Solaris/ATM), NEC Versa laptop PC (Linux/ wireless ATM), etc., demonstrating that the technical approaches used are both portable and scalable.

We continue to work on our platform to further enlarge the scope of the project by addressing operating system issues and building a wireless ATM networking infrastructure.

References:

[Ban95]   V. Bansal, et. al., "Adaptive QoS-based API for ATM networking", in Proc. NOSSDAV'95, Durham, NH, April 1995.

[Bor86]   A. Borning, "Classes versus prototypes in object-oriented languages", in Proc. ACM/IEEE Fall Joint Computer Conference, pp. 36-40, Dallas, TX, Nov. 86.

[BrL92]   G. Bracha, G. Lindstrom, "Modularity meets inheritance", in Proc. 1992 Int. Conf. on Computer Languages, pp. 282-290., Oakland, CA, April 1992.

[Cam94]   A. Campbell, G. Coulson and D. Hutchinson, "A Quality of Service Architecture", in ACM SIGCOM Vol 24, Number 2, pp. 6-27, April 1994.

[Har93]   H. Harasaki and M. Yano, "A study on VBR coder control under usage parameter control," in Proc. Fifth International Packet Video Workshop, Berlin, Germany, March 1993.

[Mic95]   G. Michelitsch, "Shared virtual spaces as a means for communication and collaboration," to appear in Proc. IEEE International Workshop on Networked Realities, Boston, MA, October 26-18, 1995.

[OAM95] Ott, et. al., "Heidi-II: a testbed for interactive multimedia delivery and communication", in Proc. ACM Multimedia, San Francisco, Nov. 1995.

[OCO95] M. Ott et. al., "A Prototype ATM network based system for multimedia-on-demand", in Proc. IEEE ComSoc Workshop on Multimedia, Kyoto, Japan, May 1994.

[OHe95]   M. Ott, J. Hearn, "Plug-and-play with wires," in Proc. Tcl Workshop, Toronto, July 95.

[Ott94]   M. Ott, "Jodler - a scripting language for distributed applications", in Proc. Tcl Workshop, New Orleans, June 1994.

[Ram91]   G. Ramamurthy and R. Dighe, "A Multidimensional Framework for Congestion Control in BISDN", IEEE J. Selected Areas in Comm., Dec. 1991.

[Rei95]   D. Reininger, G. Ramamurthy and D. Raychaudhuri, "VBR MPEG Video Coding with Dynamic Bandwidth Renegotiation", Proc. ICC'95, pp. 1773-1777, Seattle, WA, June 1995.

[Rob93]   G. G. Robertson, S.K. Card, and J.D. Mackinlay, "Information visualization using 3D interactive animation," in Communication of the ACM, 36(4), 1993.

[Sta93]   L. Staples, "Representation in virtual space: visual convention in the graphical user interface," in Proc. INTERCHI'93, pp. 348-354, ACM, 1993.

[Tan94]   S. H. Tang and M.A. Linton, "Blending structured graphics and layout," in Proc. UIST '94, Marina del Rey, CA, November 2-4, 1994.

[TAC94]   D. Tennenhouse, et. al., "A software-oriented approach to the design of media processing environments," in Proc. IEEE Conf. on Multimedia Computing and Systems, pp. 435-444, Boston, MA, May 1994.

[USm87]   D. Ungar and Randall B. Smith, "Self: the power of simplicity", in Proc. OOPSLA'87, published as SIGPLAN Notices 22(12), Dec 87.

[Whi93]   J.E. White, "Telescript technology: the foundation for the electronic marketplace," White Paper, General Magic, Inc., 1993.

Multimedia Architecture to Support Requirements Analysis

Jeffrey D. Smith and Kenji Takahashi

NTT Software Laboratories

Abstract. Described here is an architecture to support the collaborative creation and elaboration of requirements based on the Inquiry Cycle, a model of requirements analysis. The Inquiry Cycle is also generally applicable to group document production because of its contribution to effectiveness in refining documents and providing traceability. Both synchronous and asynchronous collaborations extended over geographical areas and organizations may be involved, thus the recording, indexing, and playback of conference media streams are considered as a requirement. The implementation and integration of conferencing tools, media servers, and Inquiry Cycle based tools are discussed in terms of architecture and actual experience as it relates to this domain and is extended for general application.

1   Background

Generally, collaborative systems assume that discussions are somewhat unstructured and therefore recording and indexing the discussions is a difficult task at best. Many of the systems based on these assumptions provide generic tools applicable to many tasks, but few make provisions for archiving the interactions and integrating them into the artifacts of the collaboration. In fact, there are already numerous tools for video conferencing, whiteboard drawing, and text editing. Some of these tools are integrated to exchange data or interoperate with each other, and there are methods of recording and replaying the sessions.

In the case of requirements analysis there have been several field studies and experiments [3, 10, 14, 23] that indicate communication, agreement, and traceability management are key activities in requirements analysis. Traceability management would seem to pose a problem in the generic collaboration environment while being a key component of group document production. The Inquiry Cycle [17, 16, 18, 19, 15] was designed to address these problems. The Inquiry Cycle (figure 1) is a cyclical model of requirements analysis consisting of three activities: expression, discussion and commitment. The Inquiry Cycle is an artifact-based model providing two advantages for collaborative work that do not exist explicitly in generic collaboration: 1) changes are traceable, and 2) participant awareness is shared by the fact that the artifact being discussed is visible and explicit.

There are three possible views of the Inquiry Cycle model that have direct application to collaborative efforts: as a rhetoric for explaining one's ideas and

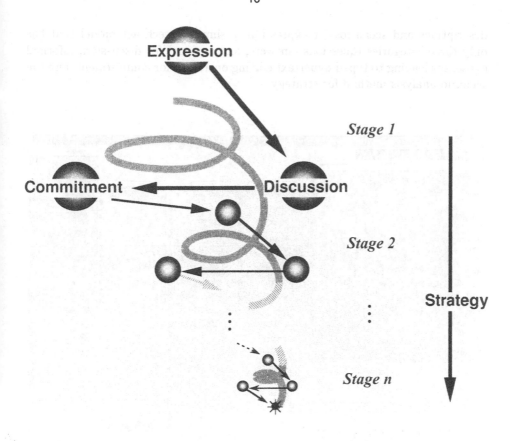

Fig. 1. Inquiry Cycle

persuading others it contributes to effective communication and agreement, as a representation method of requirements analysis history it contributes to traceability, and as a process model it coordinates and guides participants toward an agreed specification. These three views create a collaborative environment which is much more focused, thereby relaxing some of the assumptions of generalization in collaborative tools, but raising the ante on traceability. The view of the Inquiry Cycle as a rhetoric or argument structure, because of the limits set on the range of discussions that take place, aids in the ability to index the multimedia records of sessions. Likewise, the artifact-based discussions give points on which to attach hypermedia objects and organize the media space that would otherwise be impossible in a generic situation.

The Inquiry Cycle model is a general model, thus as a single user tool we have developed Tuiqiao[21], a hypertext tool for requirements analysis based on an instantiation of the Inquiry Cycle model. It allows users to keep track of textual requirements and their related information by linking them in a nonlinear manner. The instantiation of the Inquiry Cycle model consists of textual descriptions and scenarios for expression, a simple speech act model that has only three categories (questions, answers, and reasons) for discussion, informal consensus leading to typed hypertext editing operation for commitment, and the scenario analysis method for strategy.

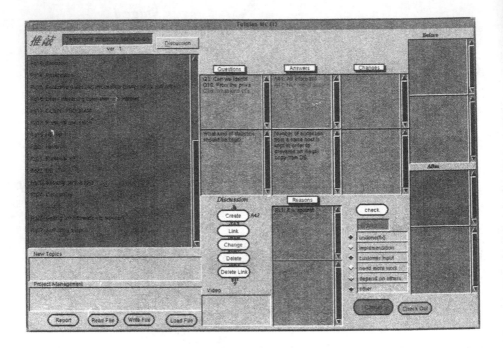

Fig. 2. Tuiqiao

Tuiqiao is being used as the core client software for navigating through the artifacts associated with the requirements analysis process. Versions of the requirements document and the discussion notes are maintained in this system and users can navigate through these.

Other than the organization of data and use of an argument structure we have also determined that a different matrix from the traditional same/different time/place matrix is needed to describe collaborative work. We call our matrix the modes of interaction. The axes of the matrix are syncronicity, locality, and number of participants. Any collaborative effort can range from synchronous to asynchronous, geographically collocated or disperse, with participants either in a group or working individually. As such, this model describes the traditional time and place facets of collaboration with two significant additions: isochronous collaboration and the complex integration of individual work spaces with group collaborations.

2 Bootstrapping and System Requirements

Without going into to great detail concerning requirements analysis and the way the Tuiqiao client is used, this section describes the experience of using Tuiqiao in early implementations for a collaborative project spanning Japan and the US. We have also used the early versions of Tuiqiao in a bootstrapping method to discuss the requirements of the architecture described in this paper and reflect on the features that need to be expanded in Tuiqiao itself to work in such an environment. The conclusions of that experience as they bear on the requirements of a full collaborative multimedia system are reviewed and the general requirements of such a system are introduced both for creation (note-taking) and presentation (browsing) of the requirements artifacts and supporting media.

Tuiqiao was used in a collaborative setting in conjunction with Cogent, which is an electronic meeting room developed at NTT[5]. Cogent is designed such that every participant has his/her own display and can project the screen image to others. In this way the single-user Tuiqiao client could be shared among the participants for sessions held in the Cogent room. Our experience using Tuiqiao for the development of an Internet-based telephone directory service[19] consisted of three teams located in different locations (two in different locations in Tokyo, Japan and one in Palo Alto, California); some using Tuiqiao with and without Cogent, e-mail, and word processors in outline mode. The analysis of these experiences is in[19] and those points relevant to the requirements for a multimedia support system can be summarized as follows:

- Challenge to the original assumptions made in the Tuiqiao instantiation of Inquiry Cycle that: 1) requirements documents to be discussed already exist before a requirements sessions, and 2) all the discussions correspond exactly to specific parts of the requirements drafts.
- "Volatile" information such as whiteboard drawings or brainstorming lists or discussions of sketches drawn on a whiteboard or paper was difficult to record and organize, but was the primary method of discussion at the beginning of the requirements phase and reappeared often in face-to-face discussion. These discussions and sketches contribute significantly to the requirements document and indicate that we need a method of transition from unstructured, volatile information to structured, solid documents.
- Work styles shifted during the requirements analysis process from synchronous collaboration to asynchronous and individual works as we progressed. Following the Inquiry Cycle model our sessions shifted from expression and discussion to commitment, with much of the discussion carried out via e-mail as time progressed. Conclusion - we needed a framework to integrate existing tools for synchronous, asynchronous, and individual work.

2.1 Usage Scenario

The system being designed in response to the above findings is called EColabor (elaboration plus collaboration thus "ecolaboration"). This paper, while it describes many of the core components of EColabor, is intended to present a more generic solution to providing multimedia services to requirements analysis or group document production. Here a typical requirements session using Tuiqiao and EColabor in a Cogent room is described in the following scenario, followed by a continuation of the first session, where an individual augments notes and reviews previous sessions. This scenario illustrates how group document production could proceed in a well developed system. These scenarios are used to introduce the requirements of such a system. (Note that the number of components Q12, A6, etc. is done automatically and not by the user of the system.)

A group is working on the requirements for Project A in a Cogent room in Japan. The requirements document exists in some state of revision and the analysis to be performed on this day is pertaining to requirement item Rq5. There are already two questions (Q12, Q13) that were introduced at the last meeting. Q12 has one answer (A6), Q13 has not been answered. At the beginning of the session one of the participants requests a review of the last session's discussion about Rq5, including Q12 and Q13. The audio and video segments for that session are replayed along with A6 and the whiteboard sketch made to explain A6. An alternative answer to Q12, A7, is proposed. One participant asks a question, Q14, about Q13 attempting to clarify what is being asked. It is decided that Q13 requires more research and is postponed. A change, C2, to Rq5 based on Q12 and associated answers A6 and A7 is proposed and agreed upon. The session ends with a reminder to follow up on Q13.

Sometime after this session the leader of Project A sits down at her workstation to review the session and augment the notes. First, she plays back the meeting from the beginning and stops the playback when Q14 is introduced. She realizes what is probably a better way to ask Q13 and proposes that Q13 be reworded to a new question (Q15) hoping that this will assist in the further research for that question. She adds an audio/video message to Q15 to explain it even further and give some ideas of where to find more information. The change proposed by C2 are also made to the requirements document.

While the merits of such a structured conversational model as shown in the this scenario may be debated, the research [19] has shown the Inquiry Cycle to be effective. More importantly, a focused discussion, the majority of the conversation based on the artifact of the requirements document, allows the system (and users) to categorize discussions. This would be quite cumbersome if the indexing was required to be performed after the meeting, but our system is designed to circumvent the problems of the person doing the work not receiving direct benefit[7]. The EColabor system built around Tuiqiao utilizes "selection triggered segmentation" similar to Synthesis, a video-based collaborative writing tool[17].

Navigation by selecting a given topic and then being shown a limited scope presentation of related data is intrinsic to the design of Tuiqiao. We call this the ring-metaphor. The ring-metaphor provides a sort of "turtle's eye view" of the information by only showing the currently selected data and the data related to that selection in the other windows. In essence, the ring-metaphor provides a filter to the data and allows the user(s) to focus more effectively on the topic being discussed. Selection triggered segmentation is based on the premise that recording is taking place continuously and that index points are added according to what is being selected or entered into the Tuiqiao windows. This combination of the use of the ring-metaphor and selection triggered segmentation allows for a more effective discussion and an efficient interface for indexing.

2.2 Requirements of the Multimedia Architecture

Based on our experiences with Tuiqiao in the Cogent environment and the above scenarios our requirements are detailed below.
Recording and indexing:

- the user doing the work (indexing) has direct benefit
- indexing is done "on-the-fly" and does not require an interface separate from Tuiqiao
- can be used to index any multimedia stream used in collaboration

Playback requirements:

- Time-based navigation (rewind, forward and other VCR-like controls)
- Topic-based navigation by ring-metaphor in Tuiqiao
- Playback of time-based segments (start to finish) provide indication of link relation to requirements artifact.
- Multiple users can access simultaneously (different or same segments)
- Synchronization among users (playback same segment under specified users control)
- Does not require separate interface to "setup" playback sessions (i.e. sd or other session manager)

General requirements:

- Extensible (can utilize future media types)
- Generic browser can be used - web, TV set type viewer
- Reliability (acknowledgment that at least one server received and processed an index request)
- Can be built using standard client tools and network protocols requiring limited modifications

3 Architecture

In order to collaborate effectively across the modes of interaction the users' tools and the data in the EColabor system needs to be managed and presented as seamlessly as possible. For the purpose of this paper the primary discussion is focused on the use of multimedia data which is largely used in synchronous, group situations and sometimes accessed by individuals working asynchronously. The isochronous usage case, where individual groups work separately and synchronize at given times also may make significant use of multimedia conferencing and data.

Following the requirements introduced above the architecture that integrates common tools, the Tuiqiao client, and can utilize the Internet is shown in figure 3. This architecture assumes the continued use of generic tools integrated into the EColabor system. The "multimedia" components of a system that meets the requirements presented above can be broken into four categories: conferencing tools, the Tuiqiao client, the media system, and the control bus.

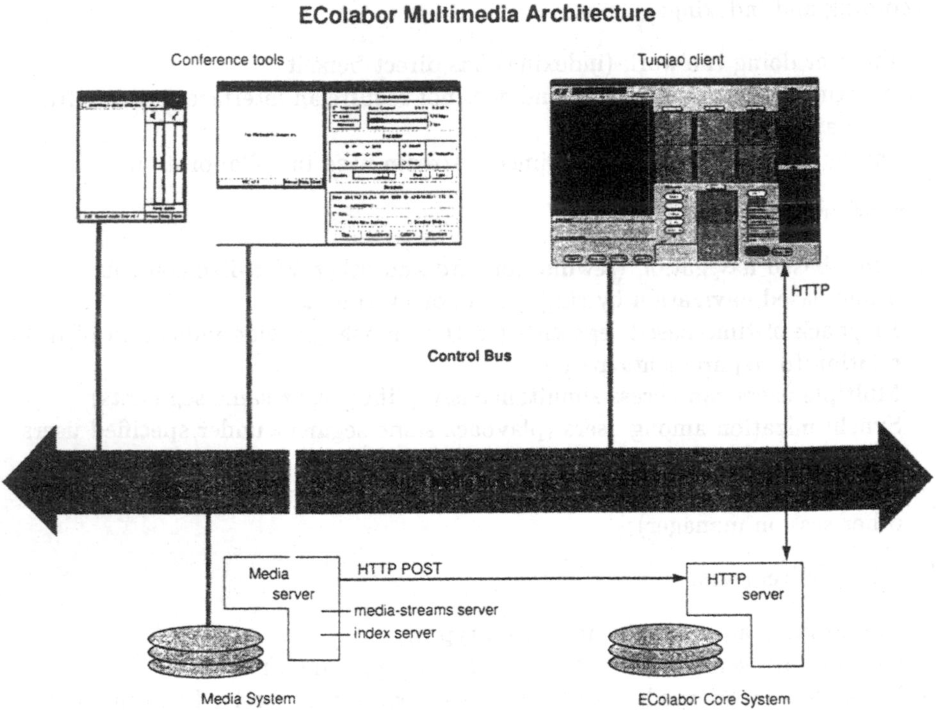

EColabor Multimedia Architecture

Fig. 3. Multimedia Architecture

The figure shows the EColabor system which is built on an OODB with an HTTP[20] interface. The mechanism for the creation of objects that make up the EColabor hypermedia is being defined as a separate sub-project. For the purpose of the multimedia support architecture discussed in this paper it is sufficient to know that an object in the database consist of a URL and a MIME[1] content-type and that these are submitted to the hypermedia structure via HTTP POST. In most cases, questions, answers, etc. will be textual types and included directly in the OODB, on the other hand multimedia objects will contain a MIME external reference that will be used by clients to elicit playback from the multimedia server.

Clearly, a number of the tools must be extended to operate effectively within this architecture, but the basic interfaces users are accustomed to will not change significantly. Because the conference tools, and to a large extent the Tuiqiao client already exist, both requiring only modification to operate in the EColabor environment, the remainder of this section focuses on the media server and the control bus. Once these are described, the interaction of the conferencing tools and the Tuiqiao client is described.

Referring to figure 3 we see a control bus and a media bus. The media bus is assumed to consist of RTPv2 (Real-time Transport Protocol)[21] based media streams. The RTCP (RTP Control Protocol) packets are considered part of the media bus because RTCP is used to control a specific RTP stream or streams in a session whereas the control bus is used to communicate among RTP and non-RTP "participants." The control bus is a predetermined multicast group used as a bus with addressing similar to CCCP (Conference Control Channel Protocol)[8]. The control bus is used to communicate among all clients and servers utilizing a naming tuple that is based on CCCP. Using the control bus Tuiqiao clients can indicate indexing points to the media server, browser clients can utilize VCR-like commands, and multicast group addresses for conferencing or playback can be distributed to active participants.

3.1 Media System

The media system is composed of a database that is front-ended by the media server. The media server contains two subsystems, or servers: the media-streams server and the index server. The media-streams server provides media stream recording and playback based on RTP streams. Control requests (e.g. rewind, pause, etc.) are also processed by the media-streams server. The index server manages incoming index requests and executes HTTP POST requests to the EColabor system.

Conceptually, the media system as a whole is similar to the VuSystem[4] or the work of Gibbs[6] consisting of source, filters, and sinks. At the time of writing this paper we are gathering information about the VuSystem, VCR[2], MediaKit[12], and a high-end video server application developed by NTT to evaluate the suitability of various systems.

The name for a specified media segment is composed of session-name, media-type, start-of-segment, end-of-segment. The session name is a unique identifier of the session the media represents, media-type indicates the media encoding (H.261, nv, ulaw, pcm, etc.), start-of-segment and end-of-segment are the calculated start and end times of the segment based on universal (NTP) timestamps. We propose a URL for accessing the media server of the form:

```
rtp://<host>:<port>/<session-name>/<media-type>/\
<start-of-segment>/<end-of-segment>
```

Based on these identifiers indexes are created by the index server as described in the following section.

3.2 Recording and Indexing

The recording of all active media streams for a session is required by EColabor. Thus by starting a session via Tuiqiao, any conferencing tools that are subsequently initiated will result in their media streams being recorded to the media system.

Accepting and processing index requests is fundamental to the EColabor system, and a request for an index point is generated and processed as follows (referring to the usage scenario):

After the participants review the previous session the discussion proceeds to Q12 and the subsequent answer (A7). A note-taker or the participant who wishes to discuss Q12 clicks on that question in the Tuiqiao window. In doing so "awareness" is shared among the participants, all of the participants can see the topic of discussion, and an index request is sent addressed to the index server. To enter the proposed answer (A7), using the Tuiqiao interface, the question is selected and then an operation to add an answer is selected via the "create" button after which the text of the answer can be entered. By doing this another index request is sent to the index server, this time indicating that the topic of discussion is A7 (which also is related to Q12, which is related to Rq5). When the next question (Q13) is selected, so that Q14 can be asked, an index request (index end-point for both Q12 and A7, and index start-point for Q13) is sent. In this fashion index requests based on selection are sent to start an index and the end-point of the previous discussion is assumed.

Each Tuiqiao client is responsible to maintain the start/end state information for index points that itself has submitted and send end-point requests as appropriate. The index server will set end-points to the end of the session in the case of failure of a Tuiqiao client.

The index requests are of two types start-point and end-point as describe in figure 4.

Once the index end-point has been received the index server creates an index submission to the EColabor system indicating the link information (relative to the Tuiqiao Inquiry Cycle structure), the id of the creator of the link, and a URL for obtaining that media stream from the media server. This will be submitted to the OODB via an HTTP POST request. Specific to our implementation, each submission also contains HTTP LINK information, the forward and backward linking of the object relevant to the Tuiqiao structure, so that a user may later navigate through the discussion topics using Tuiqiao. One can see the generic

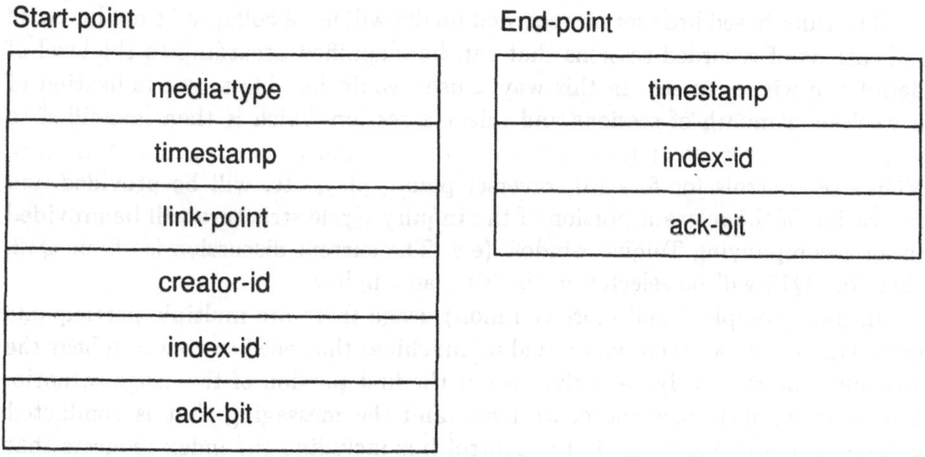

Start-point

media-type
timestamp
link-point
creator-id
index-id
ack-bit

End-point

timestamp
index-id
ack-bit

Fig. 4. Index requests

application of this mechanism whereby the links are collected on a WWW page or an existing page is updated with the appropriate multimedia links via HTTP POST requests.

The Entity-Header and Entity-Body portions of the HTTP POST are as follows:

```
Content-Type: message/external-body;
name=''/session-name/media-type/start-of-segment/end-of-segment'';
site=''media-server.ecolabor.net:port'';
access-type=X-rtp;
Content-Length: n;
Link: <URI>; rel=''supporting media'';

Content-Type: application/x-rtp;
```

3.3 Playback

The playback mechanism is far more dependent on the instantiation of the Inquiry Cycle we have chosen with Tuiqiao and the interaction of the Tuiqiao client and the EColabor server. In its simplest form, topic-based playback consists of requesting the video segment for a specific item, as in the scenario above. The Tuiqiao client places this request via HTTP to the EColabor server and the contents of the returned object include the MIME external type which is the URL for the appropriate video segment. The Tuiqiao client starts a viewer that is compatible with the media-type of the video stream and the video segment is streamed via RTP to a negotiated port on client which submitted the request.

The time-based browser for recorded media will use a collapsed time-line with indications of recorded sessions that can be magnified according to the level of detail one wishes to see. In this way a user would be able to see indication of a week or a month of sessions and select a session which is then magnified to indicate the finer grain time structure for that individual session. With this, VCR-like controls for forward, reverse, pause, play, etc. will be provided and indication of the relevant portion of the Inquiry Cycle structure will be provided in an accompanying Tuiqiao window (e.g. The current discussion is about Q12, therefore Q12 will be selected in the Tuiqiao window.)

In more complex (and more common) usage there are multiple participants each with a Tuiqiao client on individual machines that need to view and hear the streams simultaneously, as is the case in the first portion of the usage scenario. It is here we introduce the control bus and the messaging that is conducted among clients and servers via the control bus including the index requests that are processed by the index server of the media system.

3.4 Control Bus

The control bus, as described in the beginning of this section, utilizes a predetermined multicast address among all the clients for a session. Different sessions may use the same or different multicast group. The control bus messages are based on CCCP which uses a naming tuple of

```
(instantiation, type, address, conf-id),
```

with the conf-id being the session name described earlier as part of the URL for a media stream. There are several extensions including a new application registration for Tuiqiao and timestamping in messages for archiving purposes. Also messages including the VCR-like controls will be available.

Messages on the control bus for this system are messages among clients and messages from clients to servers. Messaging among clients (particularly the Tuiqiao clients) creates an environment similar to Shared Mosaic where the selection actions of one client are reflected in updates to other clients. Clients' messages to servers, such as the index requests, being sent on a bus, allow distributed servers both for recording and playback. Messages can also be archived so that entire sessions can be replayed if desired. The functionality of the control bus and the types of messages can be best illustrated by continuing the elaboration of the scenario presented above.

We have not yet extensively diagrammed the message sequences for complete scenarios across all of the modes of interaction, but here we look at a portion of the first scenario, this time as the goal of an action, the specific user action, and the messages sent as a result (of the form "receiver:message"), as summarized in table 1 to help illustrate the types and sequence of messages.

A user may view previous discussions based on topic by selecting the topic (Q, A, etc.) and noting that there is a media clip available. By clicking on the media clip indication the user is presented with information concerning that

Goal	User action	Message(s) sent
Display previous session	Click previous version in Tuiqiao window	Tuiqiao: change to previous version
Display Rq5	Click on Rq5	Tuiqiao: select Rq5
Indication of a/v segment in Tuiqiao window	none	none
Select a/v segment	Click on a/v segment icon	Tuiqiao: select a/v segment EColabor (http): get segment
Start up a/v tool	none - Launched by Tuiqiao client when a/v segment information was received	Tuiqiao: start a/v tools
Play a/v segment	Click on play button in a/v tool	Media server and A/V tool: negotiate address,port Media server: rtp play request

Table 1. Scenario 1 (topic-based video review) messaging

clip including when that clip was created (during what session) and has the opportunity to "play" that clip.

The messages sent are to other Tuiqiao clients to provide synchronization of views, an http request (not on the control bus) to retrieve a segment (which actually contains the URL for the RTP stream), a negotiation of address and port for the media playback, and a request to the media server to start the indicated RTP stream. The negotiation of address and port for the session is transacted on the control bus thus other active a/v tools will learn of the negotiated address and port. Once the play request is submitted the subsequent media streams are sent on the media bus.

Referring to the usage scenario table 2 summarizes the actions taken and the subsequent messages sent on the control bus during a portion of the group session after the video review.

Complete and rather complex message sequence charts are necessary to understand the flow of messages on the control bus and optimize the messaging protocol. A simple sequence chart for a portion of the messages described in table 2 is shown in figure 5.

Goal	User action	Message(s) sent
Propose answer to Q12	Click on Q12 in Tuiqiao window	Tuiqiao:select Q12 Media server: index start-point Q12
Create answer	Click on "create" button then click on answer area	Tuiqiao: create Answer ref:Q12 Media server: index start point A7
Input answer	Enter text of answer	
Commit answer	Click on "end" button	EColabor (http): submit answer Tuiqiao: A7 created
Ask new question about Q13	Click on Q13	Media server: index end-point A7 Media server: index end-point Q12 Media server: index start-point Q13 Tuiqiao: select Q13
Create question	Click on "create" button then click on question area	Tuiqiao: create Question ref:Q13 Media server: index start-point Q14
Input question	Discuss question. Enter text of question	
Commit question	Click on "end" button	EColabor (http): submit question Tuiqiao: Q14 created
Discuss Rq5	Click on Rq5	Media server: index end-point Q14 Media server: index end-point Q13 Media server: index start-point Rq5

Table 2. Scenario 1 (group review) messaging

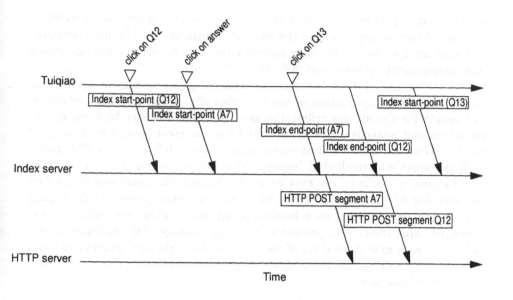

Fig. 5. Sequence chart of index requests

4 Discussion

The integration of the above described components within an architecture that supports structured argumentation, recording and indexing of sessions and subsequent playback via a time-based or topic-based browser, and the management of the interaction of clients used for "ecolaborative" sessions across the various combinations of the modes of interaction is the first step in a fully functional multimedia system for requirements analysis and more generally for collaborative document production. Our work is based on components derived from software engineering research, CSCW, Internet/data communications research, and human-computer interaction. The work of the MICE[11] project in particular has been inspirational and educational, as much has been done to integrate various tools and provide an infrastructure for wide-area collaboration for generic consumption. The future work of the CommerceNet Collaborative Tools Working Group will serve as a test bed for our system in the hands of both engineers and business people.

4.1 Status

What we currently have implemented is the Tuiqiao client and a "traditional" web-based interface for video and audio using the MediaKit. The MediaKit-based web system is being used as a test for audio/video annotation (currently indexed by hand) onto an Inquiry Cycle based HyperNews[13] discussion. The benefits of using the Tuiqiao interface with its "ring-metaphor" navigation is not present in the current test implementation. The web-based browsing, though, will be a part of the final EColabor system and may look very similar to our current output. Our experience, described earlier in the paper, along with a more recent use of the Inquiry Cycle on the web for translation work[9] have indicated that such an approach is desirable and effective. Our experience has also shown that management overhead and tasks related to organizing the data, as opposed to proceeding with the requirements analysis or group document production, constitute a too large portion of the activities of a group and our current requirements for the system reflect the need to allow the user to focus on the discussion and analysis of the artifact and not the creation and referencing of notes. Furthermore, the efficient exploitation of time difference in collaborative work has provided a method of "pipelining" activities with a group in one timezone passing on tasks to the next group in the next timezone and picking up the next day where the other group finished. Our entire process of developing this environment is based on a bootstrapping model where we build the next prototype using the current prototype, taking advantage of the facilities we can include in each new generation of the system. As a globally distributed team ourselves, the tools we are building are essential to continuing our research and have proven invaluable.

4.2   Future work

At this time, RTPv2 tools are not yet widely available. MediaKit in its more recent incarnations is being adapted to take advantage of RTPv2 streams and may also be extended to work with our control bus scheme. We have not yet approached the issues of performance and scalability. Distributed, multiple media systems may provide a solution but will introduce new challenges for naming and control among index servers. The use of our architecture with the control bus will simplify the control of the distributed systems.

Video and audio segments which are linked to particular components of the requirements artifact (question, answer, etc.) are saved in the OODB with an HTTP LINK header. The resolution of meta-relationships of media segments in terms of these links which are part of the Tuiqiao instantiation of the Inquiry Cycle is necessary to allow a user to perform a topic-based browsing of media segments in a coherent way. For example, a user requesting A7 (back to the usage scenario again) should be able to quickly switch to viewing the media segment(s) relating to Q12 as one segment of media. This segment is actually composed of general discussion concerning Q12 and the segment relating to A7. Likewise, the user should be able to view the Rq5 segment as a whole (which is again composed of other segments including Q12 and A7 segments) and navigate among the segments that together form Rq5. We intend to implement this using video algebra[24].

Our current task is to diagram complete scenarios and analyze the messaging sequences to that end. While CCCP and the extensions we are including reflect our current conception of the system, building a prototype based on this model and our analysis of more complete sequence diagrams will give us the data necessary to determine an optimal method. This will also provide input as to the possible amount of overhead for processing messages and the general scalability of the entire architecture.

References

1. N. Borenstein. MIME (Multiple Internet Mail Extensions)Part One: Mechanism for Specifying and Describing the Format of Internet Message Bodies. RFC1251, 1993.

2. S. Clayman. The Video Conference Recorder - A Summary. http://www.cs.ucl.ac.uk/dragon/vcr-summary.ps, 1995.

3. B. Curtis, H. Krasner, and N. Iscoe. A Field Study of the Software Design Process for Large Teams. *Communications of the ACM*, 31(11):1268–1287, 1988.

4. D.L. Tennenhouse, et al. A Software-Oriented Approach to the Design of Media Processing Environments. In *Proc. IEEE Int'l Conf. on Multimedia Computing and Systems*, 1994.

5. E. Kuwana, et al. Computer-Supported Meeting Environment for Collaborative Software Development. to appear.

6. S. Gibbs, C. Breiteneder, and D. Tsichritzis. Audio/Video Databases: An Object-Oriented Approach. In *Proc. 9th IEEEE Int'l Data Engineering Conference*, pages 381–390, 1993.

7. J. Grudin. Why Groupware Applications Fail: Problems in the design and evaluation of organizational interfaces. In *Proc. CSCW '88*, pages 85–93, 1988.

8. M. Handley, I. Wakeman, and J. Crowcroft. The Conference Control Channel Protocol (CCCP): A scalable base for building conference control applications. In *Proc. of ACM SIGCOMM '95*, pages 275–287, 1995.

9. M. Higuchi and K. Takahashi. World Wide Collaborative Writing: A Case Study. In *Proc. Conf. on Asian-Pacific World Wide Web*, 1995. to appear.

10. H. Kaiya and M. Saeki. A Supporting Tool for Face-to-face Meetings to Develop Software Specifications. Technical Report KBSE93-13, IEICE, 1993. in Japanese.

11. Kirstein, et al. Recent Activities in the MICE Conferencing Project. In *Proc. Inet '95*, pages 445–454, 1995.

12. Developed by Vinay Kumar at M/Cast Communications, Inc. No reference available.

13. D. LaLiberte. What is HyperNews? http://union.ncsa.uiuc.edu:80/HyperNews/get/hypernews/about.html, 1995.

14. M. Lubars, C. Potts, and C. Richter. A Review of the State of Practice in Requirements Modeling. In *Proc. RE'93*, pages 2–14, 1993.

15. C. Potts. Using Schematic Scenarios to Understand User Needs. In *Proc. Symposium on Designing Interactive Systems (DIS '95)*, 1995. to appear.

16. C. Potts, J.D. Bolter, and A. Badre. Collaborative Pre-Writing with a Video-Based Group Working Memory. Technical report, Graphics Visualization and Usability Center, Georgia Institute of Technology, 1993.

17. C. Potts and K. Takahashi. An Active Hypertext for System Requirements. In *Proc. 7th Int'l Workshop on Software Specification and Design*, pages 62–68, 1993.

18. C. Potts, K. Takahashi, and A.I. Anton. Inquiry-based Scenario Analysis of System Requirements. *IEEE Software*, 11(2):21–32, 1994.

19. C. Potts, K. Takahashi, J.D. Smith, and K. Ota. An Evaluation of Inquiry-Based Requirements Analysis for an Internet Service. In *Proc. RE'95*, pages 172–180, 1995.
20. R. Fielding and H. Frystyk and T. Berners-Lee. Hypertext Transfer Protocol - HTTP/1.1. Internet draft, 1995.
21. Shulzrinne, et al. RTP: A Transport Protocol for Real-Time Applications. Internet draft, 1995.
22. K. Takahashi and C. Potts. Tuiqiao: A Hypertext Tool for Requirements Analysis. Technical Report GIT-CC-94107, Georgia Institute of Technology, 1994.
23. K. Takahashi and S. Yamamoto. An Analysis of Traceability in Requirements Documents. *IEICE Transaction on Information and Systems*, E78-D(4):394–402, 1994.
24. R. Weiss, A. Duda, and D. Gifford. Composition and Search with a Video Algebra. In *IEEE Multimedia*, pages 12–25, 1995.

MHEG 5 - Standardized Presentation Objects for the Set Top Unit Environment

Klaus Hofrichter - GMD FOKUS

Abstract: The rapid development of multimedia services such as video-on-demand, tele-shopping or personal communication for residential use require the development of standards to ensure interoperability between service providers and customers at several levels: Physical network connection, protocols, management, application and content encoding. This paper introduces the MHEG 5 standard, which addresses the encoding of behavior and layout of multimedia applications. MHEG 5 is designed for low-resource environments such as Set Top Units.

Keywords: Multimedia, MHEG, ISO, Encoding, Services, Set Top Unit

1 Introduction

The vision of MHEG[1] is the interchange of portable information in the MHEG format between independent multimedia data production and execution environments. Due to the variety of information presentation systems, ranging from professional high-performance workstations to low-end personal Set Top Units, the portability of information addressed by MHEG might become a key issue for success of information producers and providers.

The interchange process is not effected by the formats internally used by the systems: Only the export and the import format of data is standardized by MHEG. The systems using MHEG have to define a mapping from their internal data representation to the facilities provided by MHEG, but they gain access to a potentially large variety of multimedia applications in their domain.

The MHEG standardization is carried out by SC29/WG12, a subgroup of the International Standardization Organization (ISO). Currently the group develops five parts of the standard. This paper concentrates on MHEG concepts and in particular on MHEG 5 application. The MHEG standard only deals with encoding of multimedia and hypermedia information. That means the scope of MHEG concentrates on interchange process of data, not the production or execution process. This fact is often not fully recognized and leads to certain misunderstandings of the concepts and mechanisms of MHEG.

The fundamental concept of MHEG is to provide a generic and extensible framework for multimedia and hypermedia object encoding without application or platform spe-

---

1. MHEG is an acronym for Multimedia and Hypermedia Experts Group. This acronym is also used to refer to the standards developed by this group. The official title of the standard suite is 'Coding of Multimedia and Hypermedia Objects'.

cific assumptions for production, handling and execution of the multimedia objects. There are some models of these processes, but the models are not in the scope of MHEG; they are only used to clarify and validate the MHEG facilities. The idea of MHEG-based interchange is, that independent of the production environment the resulting objects may be downloaded and used by different runtime systems. The figure below illustrates this process:

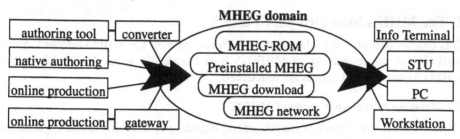

Fig.1.: The MHEG-Object Interchange Process

Depending on the interchange mechanism different production facilities may be used: Off-line production by converting from existing formats (e.g. ToolBook[2]) to MHEG representation or on-line encoding on demand by the presentation system. The communication protocols are not defined by MHEG. Other standards like DSM-CC[3] cover this area.

Since different application areas introduce different requirements on MHEG object functionality, it is not possible to define right now one encoding format which covers all requirements for all cases. MHEG 1 therefore provides certain facilities to extend the standard for the needs of a particular application domain. Such an extension is MHEG 5 for the application domain of video-on-demand and similar applications.

MHEG 5 provides additional functionality for this application area and also restricts the use of further MHEG extensibility to nearly zero which is required for low resource environments.

This paper introduces the important aspects of MHEG 5. Concepts and facilities of MHEG 1 and 5 are described in section 2. Section 3 presents an architecture model for use of MHEG 5 objects, and section 4 covers MHEG 5 related components for production and execution. Section 5 concludes and refers to other information sources related to MHEG.

Note:

This paper was written during MHEG 5 CD[4] ballot and reviewed during DIS ballot. It is possible (actually: it is quite sure) that the MHEG 5 document will be reviewed

---

2. Toolbook is a multimedia authoring system from Asymetrix Corporation

3. DSM-CC is an acronym for Digital Storage Media Commands and Control. This standard is at CD level and developed by SC29 WG11 (MPEG).

4. CD is an acronym for Committee Draft and refers to a certain state in the standardization process. The order of states is WD (Working Draft), CD, DIS (Draft International Standard) and IS (International Standard).

and certain changes will have to be applied. This is a normal process for CD and DIS documents, the reader should be aware of this fact while reading. Nevertheless, it can be expected that the general concept of MHEG 5 remains unchanged and the content of the paper remains in principle valid. Please refer to the on-line information sources at the end of this paper for up-to date information.

2 The MHEG Standard part 1 and 5

This chapter describes the relation of the different parts of the MHEG standard. Since MHEG 1 is the foundation of MHEG 5 it is covered in more detail. Afterwards MHEG 5 concepts and classes are introduced.

2.1 Relation to the other parts of MHEG

MHEG 1 deals with a quite powerful generic encoding of multimedia and hypermedia information. It provides concepts and mechanisms used by the other parts. Therefore, MHEG 1 is the foundation document for all other parts of MHEG. Both MHEG 1 and 5 utilize ASN.1/BER[5] encoding for data representation.

MHEG 2 defines an alternative encoding for MHEG 1 using SGML[6] instead of ASN.1 with the same functionality. However, MHEG 2 is not very well developed, and it is quite unclear if it ever will be. SGML is also used in the WWW[7] environment. MHEG 2 might provide for a simple opportunity to integrate seamless MHEG to the WWW.

MHEG 3 covers extensions of MHEG for scripting language support. This may be used to integrate system independent executable code to the runtime environment, eventually comparable to Sun's JAVA[8] language, which is widely known as an extensions to the WWW environment.

MHEG 4 describes the procedure to register extensions to other MHEG parts.

MHEG 5 uses extensibility features of MHEG 1 and provides a specific subset of functionality for use in the area of video-on-demand and other retrieval oriented client-server applications. The communication between the server and the client is asymmetric; i.e. the client requires only a channel with small bandwidth back to the server for interactivity, while the major amount of data is transferred from the server to the client.

---

5. ASN.1 is an acronym for Abstract Syntax Notation Number One, BER is an acronym for Basic Encoding Rules. ASN.1 provides a system independent notation for data structures, BER is a set of rules which allow to produce a concrete bitstring from an object, specified using ASN.1.
6. SGML is a acronym for Standardized General Markup Language.
7. WWW is an acronym for World Wide Web, an Internet based distributed hypermedia information system.
8. JAVA is a scripting language developed by Sun Microsystems with bytecode representation, running on a virtual (and therefore portable) machine.

2.2 Concepts, Functionality and Classes of MHEG 1

MHEG 1 defines a set of classes which are able to encode multimedia application behavior for presentation. Focussing on layout and logical relationship between multimedia objects. The content data representation of MHEG relies on other standards like JPEG or MPEG. For the description of the relationship in time and space between the content data, some mechanisms are introduced, which fulfil the needs of most multimedia and hypermedia presentations and documents. Of most relevance is the generic mechanism to define interactive behavior and real-time presentation synchronization between separate content data portions.

As described before, the scope of MHEG standardization is the encoding and interchange of multimedia and hypermedia objects. There are only a few basic assumptions on the MHEG runtime system. A minimal MHEG runtime system has to provide an entity for the decoding of ASN.1 data structures and an entity called MHEG engine, which parses and interprets the MHEG objects. The MHEG engine also communicates with the local presentation facilities and the MHEG objects. It responds to the events initiated by an application or the user (e.g.'button pressed') in the specified way. The interpretation process is sketched below:

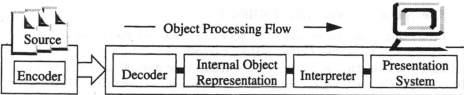

Fig.2.: MHEG Object Processing System

A set of classes has been developed for interchange of information. The inheritance tree is displayed below. Abstract classes are indicated with an italic font. All other classes allow the creation of objects.

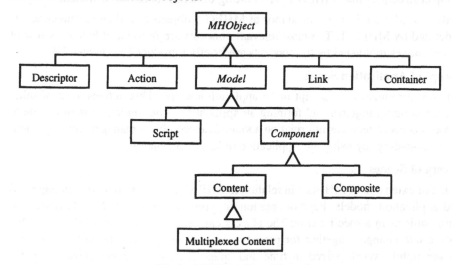

Fig.3.: MHEG 1 Class Hierarchy

A short characterization of the classes which can be instantiated follows:

- Descriptor Class: Includes information about other MHEG objects and the required resources for presentation and processing. It is needed for negotiation and adoption of system resources prior to interpretation.
- Action Class: Specifies parameters and synchronization information of methods to be executed on other MHEG objects.
- Link Class: Specifies events which trigger the execution of action objects.
- Container Class: Used to create groups of objects for interchange.
- Script Class: Represents complex behavior definitions, usually in the form of scripting languages.
- Content Class: Includes or references content data, it's definition of the media type and other content related attributes.
- Multiplexed Content Class: Same as above, plus support for multiplexed content data, e.g. MPEG systems content with multiple data streams.
- Composite Class: Logical grouping of objects, e.g. menus, pages, dialogs etc.

2.3 Concepts and Functionality of MHEG 5

MHEG 5 extends the functionality of MHEG 1 by reuse and modification of existing classes (e.g. Content, Link). Certain MHEG 1 features are restricted. The general idea behind this is related to conformance issues: It should be possible to implement a *complete* MHEG 5 conforming system, even in a low resource environment. This impacts on various MHEG 1 facilities:

- Parallel Execution: MHEG 5 does not support parallel execution of actions. This eases the MHEG engine implementation.
- Restrictions on object structure: MHEG 5 enforces the production of much simpler object structures than MHEG 1: The nesting of data structure is restricted.

Beside this, MHEG 5 forces the author of MHEG 5 objects to follow certain concepts not defined by MHEG 1. The most relevant concepts are introduced below. A few of the new classes motivated by the concepts are briefly introduced in chapter 2.4.

Concept of Application Scope

MHEG 5 introduces the concept of an application scope. This defines a set of other objects belonging together and forming an application. The runtime system is able to preload objects or receives information about advanced object management (e.g. caching, or preloading) by using the Application objects information.

Concept of Scenes

The major extension of MHEG 5 in relation to MHEG 1 is the introduction of page-oriented application models. Page-orientation supports the author of MHEG objects in relating objects in a specific way: The objects can rely on each other in the sense that they are interchanged together for presentation, they may share the I/O devices and they are tightly synchronized in time and space (i.e. they are presented together). Within MHEG 5 a so-called Scene object represents a single page. The page-orientation also influences the interchange process and the granularity of access to objects: MHEG 5 only allows the interchange of Scene and Application objects, other types of objects have to be aggregated for interchange within a Scene or Application.

MHEG 1 does not include the concept of pages, therefore no implicit page-behavior is defined. The introduction of pages specifies implicit behavior, which reduces encoding overhead. For example, transitions from one page to another are much simpler to encode.

Interactive Elements

MHEG 5 also defines explicit interaction classes for simple applications instead of generic facilities provided by MHEG 1. These are Sliders for numeric value selection, Entry-Fields for textual input and different kinds of buttons: Hotspot, Switch Button, Push Button. The buttons support different graphical representations and different behavior.

The MHEG 5 Class tree is shown below. Again, abstract classes are indicated by italic font. Differing from MHEG 1, the Content and Composite classes are abstract classes as well. Multiple inheritance is used within this description.

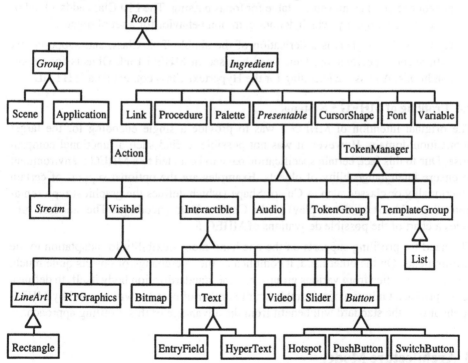

Fig.4.: MHEG 5 Class hierarchy

The next section characterizes the functionality of some classes of MHEG 5:

- Root Class: This class defines to common functionality of nearly all MHEG defined objects. This is in particular addressing and referencing support.
- Scene Class: This class aggregates all objects belonging to a single page. In partic-

ular, this includes Content objects and Link objects.

- Application Class: A group of Scenes may form an application, which is indicated by a list of references to the related Scenes. These Scenes may share content data, e.g. a common background image. The Application Class provides a list of references to Scenes and some initialization facilities for the application.
- Presentable Class: The Presentable Class is inherited by objects, which are visible or audible. This provides more specialization than it is available in MHEG 1 (see Content Class), e.g. the possibility to attach a Font to a Text. There are also special classes for audio and video streams, and for images.
- Action Class: This class is a so-called Mix-In class. The Action Class does not inherit from any other class, but is aggregated by other classes, such as Link and Group. This design allows to restrict certain MHEG 1 functionality: For example, MHEG 5 Action Objects can not be referenced, since they do not inherit the functionality related to addressing.
- Navigation and List Classes: These classes realize a more advanced behavior for navigation with a remote-control like device for a group of objects. These objects are connected via a movement table for focus passing. The List Class adds a kind of template functionality, which defines common behavior for a set of objects.
- Hypertext Class: This is a derivation of the simple Text Class, and supports text with anchor specification, which can be used in MHEG Link Objects for trigger conditions. A possible encoding for the Hypertext Class content data is HTML.

2.4 Profiling of MHEG 5 Systems

The original intention of MHEG 5 was to provide a single encoding for the target application domain. However, it was not possible to find such a functional compromise. Due to this fact, certain specification have to be added to a MHEG 5 environment to ensure interchangeability of objects. Examples are the optional support of certain functionality or classes such as Cursor Shape (which defines the graphical representation of the Cursor on the display) or the Content Data encodings. The standard provides a chart of the possible derivations of MHEG 5.

The need for profiling supports on the one hand more flexibility for adaptation to the requirements. On the other hand, it complicates the interchange of objects quite much. There are activities from various groups, e.g. the standardization body itself, to define a set of profiles. Only if a considerable small number of profiles will be used by MHEG applications, the standard will benefit from the advantage of this profiling approach.

3 Architecture Model

MHEG 5 is designed for the STU environment. This kind of device is typically used for intensive client-server or broadcast applications, where very few providers serve a large number of clients. The dataflow is asymmetric, i.e. the clients do not require much bandwidth to the server, whereas the server typically transmits large amounts of data (e.g. continuous video streams) to the clients.

STU devices are usually equipped with a special hardware to handle audio/video streams. Beside this, other system resources are low-level: Small amount of main-memory and a weak CPU. Network and I/O adapters depend on the application field: STU's are available with ATM connectors, but also with serial modem connectivity only.

This chapter presents a model architecture for such an application environment, with special attention on the use of MHEG 5. Prototypes of these components have been partly implemented and demonstrated by the GLASS[9] project.

3.1 Client-Server Architecture

This sample architecture can be mapped to a video-on-demand service: The user con-nects the STU-based endsystem to a provider system, selects some video-data to be displayed on the STU, and receives the video real-time data stream, which is controlled by the client. A simplified layout of such a system for a single user is sketched below:

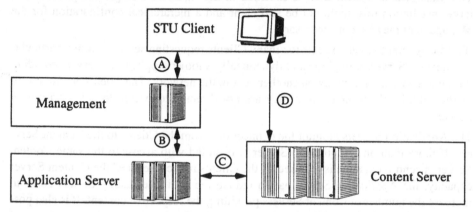

Fig.5.: Configuration of a MHEG using system

Network issues are not covered in this description. The STU client is connected (A) to a Management system, which is responsible for authorization, accounting and applica-tion selection. A local MHEG engine on the client renders an application selection list on the screen, the user chooses an appropriate application, for example a video-on-demand service. The Management system forwards the users request to the selected Application Server (B). The Application Server is running in the responsibility domain of the service provider. In this example the Application Server controls (C) one or more Content Servers, which store the video data. The presentation and layout of the table of contents of the Content Server is encoded by MHEG objects, which are send to the STU client and rendered by the MHEG engine. After some negotiation (price of the video, accounting policy, quality of service, etc.) the Client receives a certain key

---

9. GLASS is an acronym for GLobally Accessible ServiceS. GLASS is a MHEG related project funded by DeTeBerkom. GLASS did not use MHEG 5 (since it was not available at this time), but defines a certain MHEG 1 profile similar to MHEG 5 functionality. Please refer to the WWW resources for further information.

which allows the establishment of a connection to the Content Server via (D). The data is send directly from the Content Server to the Client in order to avoid routing overhead.

3.2 Scalability

The example above is described for a single client only. However, in the real world the system is required to handle multiple clients simultaneously. This chapter gives an overview of the scalability facilities of such a system without going into the details.

In case of multiple clients the most relevant issue is a dynamic system resource adaptation and the reduction of response times between the server and the client. The server system has to respond to a virtually arbitrary number of requests within an acceptable time-frame. In the architecture above, the Management system monitors the users requests. In case of a component overload additional resources may be allocated.

The Management system itself is sketched in the figure as a single component. In a large installation this might not be sufficient and a hierarchical configuration for the Management may become necessary.

If a Management system detects too many Clients requesting services from a particular Application Server, it might install dynamically another Application Server providing the same service, but running on another host in the network. The Clients are not aware of this additional resource, since they are not directly connected to any Application Server.

The Application Servers monitor the connections from the Clients to the Content Servers. If more than one Application Server is installed with access to the same Content Server, a central database is required. If the Clients requests exceed the Content Server capacity, the Application Server has to reduce the available quality of service or to increase the number of Content Servers providing the respective content. It is also possible to move both the Application Server and the Content Server close (in terms of network distance) to the Clients.

3.3 Use of MHEG 5

MHEG 5 objects are handled twofold in the example: They have to be created by the Application Server and the Management System[10], and they have to be interpreted by the Client. Both aspects (Authoring and Interpretation) are covered in more detail in chapter 4.

The role of MHEG 5 objects in this example is the system independent encoding of layout and behavior of small multimedia applications. The Management Server creates MHEG objects which are rendered on the display of the Client using an MHEG Engine. The rendering process not only includes the display of certain content (e.g. the list of available applications), it also includes the interpretation of the interactive behavior of this application: How long the selection box is displayed, what should happen in case of a selection, which kind of confirmation of the selection is required, is there a selection feedback (e.g. highlight effect of buttons or acoustic feedback). The

---

10. The Management System might utilize a special Application Server for this task.

same applies to the Application Server. Using MHEG it is possible to encode in a single object the complete interactive behavior of multiple related pages of an application, which can be processed by the Client without further interaction with the Server. Via the use of Script objects, more complex behavior can be interchanged as well. However, in this case the Client requires an appropriate script interpreter.

4 MHEG 5 related components

In the example two components with a relation to MHEG 5 have been identified: The dynamic MHEG object production by the Application Server and the MHEG Engine running on the Client. Both components are discussed in this chapter. Since these components are part of the runtime system, they are not specified by the MHEG standard. The components realization below are only examples, other approaches or designs are possible.

4.1 Authoring

MHEG objects may be produced off-line by compiling a specification in a certain description language to MHEG objects, or on-line by a dynamic MHEG object generator. MHEG 5 has defined it's own description language, but conversion from other formats is possible as well.

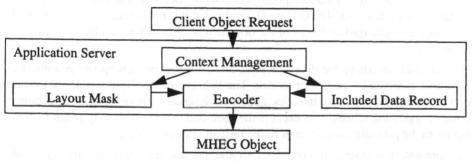

Fig.6.: Application Server Components

The example features dynamic object production, since the intended presentation (e.g. the list of available videos) may change over the time. If a certain page is requested by the Client, the Application Server requires after considering the context of the request two kinds of input data for MHEG object production: The layout mask and the included data records.

The layout mask specifies the general look of a page, e.g. default buttons for navigation to other pages, the background image, sounds, etc. The included data records are created dynamically (e.g. by asking the Content Server for the directory of video data). The data records are added to the layout specification of the page. An appropriate encoder maps the description to MHEG data structures and produces a BER encoded MHEG representation of the requested page.

4.2 MHEG Engine

The MHEG Engine has to handle and execute MHEG objects. A sample design of such an engine is suggested by an annex of MHEG 1, but the Engine is not in the scope of MHEG standardization. However, the classical design approach includes a decoder, a scheduler, a link-processor and a presentation system.

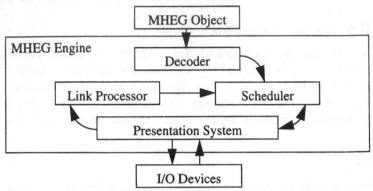

Fig.7.: MHEG Engine Components

The MHEG Engine receives objects created by the production facilities. The objects are translated to an internal data representation by the decoder. The internal data representation may reflect the MHEG class hierarchy, but it is not required to do so. In addition to the interchanged attributes of the objects it is necessary to handle some runtime parameters.

The scheduler interprets the data structures and performs the appropriate actions. The scheduler is driven by the link-processor. The link-processor is responsible for evaluation of conditions, which are interchanged by Link objects. This evaluation (e.g. button down) triggers the scheduler to execute the specified actions. This may result in commands to the presentation system or in the upload of other objects.

The presentation system is connected to the presentation devices (display, loudspeaker). It performs the decoding of content data, renders them on demand by the scheduler of the presentation devices and receives user input. The user input is send to the link processor for further evaluation.

5 Conclusion

In this paper the use of MHEG 5 objects in a client server architecture for a video-on-demand application has been introduced. The functionality of MHEG and the relation to the system components was discussed. The presented concepts have been proved by various projects, e.g. the GLASS project.

The need for standards in this area of development is only partially proven by the actually implemented solutions: On the one hand, it is quite obvious that an approach which integrates multiple different application domains and interchange media (both online and off-line) is an advantage for all involved parties. Nevertheless, the marketplace requires also distinguishable solutions. Established competitors, who have a quite dominant position in a special application area, may not be willing to move to a open solution.

MHEG is not the only solution answering to the requirements in the discussed application domain. There are a lot of proprietary developments, and the use of WWW facilities is currently under evaluation as well. Most prominent is the Internet/WWW approach, which is quite popular in this moment of time. In particular, the approach followed by the JAVA extensions to HTML seems to be successful, even in the STU environment. But in the STU environment, the application designers have to face a complete different customer group as the Internet community is.

MHEG enables portable interchange of multimedia application presentation. This topic might get more importance in the near future, since multimedia content and application production and maintenance becomes more and more expensive in relation to hardware development. The migration from local installations to networked open systems for application distribution supports this trend. Such requirements have driven the MHEG development.

The MHEG 5 standardization has not been finished up-to now. The evolution of the competing solutions and the acceptance of MHEG by system manufacturers and application designers are the relevant checkpoints for the MHEG future.

5.1 Timetable

At the time of writing, MHEG 1 IS is expected to be published early 1996. MHEG 5 DIS ballot will close in April 1996, the corresponding IS can be expected in late 1996.

5.2 On-line Resources

Up to now there is not very much documentation in the bookstores. However, there are several Internet/WWW sites with more detailed information available. The list below covers only resources at GMD FOKUS, additional links to other information and latest development are available there.

http://www.fokus.gmd.de/ovma/mheg/entry.html: MHEG related information
http://www.fokus.gmd.de/ovma/mheg/mheg5/verification: MHEG Verification Group
http://www.fokus.gmd.de/ovma/berglass/entry.html: GLASS project information

5.3 References

ISO 13522.1: MHEG 1 IS: MHEG Object Representation, Base Notation
ISO 13522.2: not available
ISO 13522.3: MHEG 3 CD: Extensions for scripting language support
ISO 13522.4: MHEG 4 CD: Registration Procedure for Format Identifier
ISO 13522.5: MHEG 5 DIS: Support for Base-Level Interactive Applications
ISO 8825.4: ASN.1: Abstract Syntax Notation Number One
ISO 8897: SGML: Standardized General Markup Language

GLASS-Studio: An Open Authoring Environment for Distributed Multimedia Applications

Brian Heumann[1], Torsten Leidig[2] and Peter Rösch[3]

[1] Softadweis AG
[2] Digital Equipment, CEC Karlsruhe
[3] Fraunhofer Institute for Experimental Software Engineering

Abstract: Distributed multimedia applications recently gain a large attraction to the multimedia industry. The MHEG (Multimedia Hypermedia Expert Group) is developing an open international standard for the exchange of multimedia presentations and their work has become quite advanced now. This paper describes the MHEG standard and its implementation in the Berkom GLASS project and presents an open authoring environment for distributed multimedia applications in the MHEG context. Our so-called GLASS-Studio is an authoring environment employing the WYSIWYG (What You See Is What You Get) technique. The environment provides abstractions from the authoring domain and the underlying technical infrastructure of the GLASS system. GLASS-Studio supports rapid-prototyping and simulation capabilities, enabling an incremental and iterative design process. Real-world metaphors like direct manipulation and drag&drop provide an easy-to-learn user interface. We present a flexible cooperation scheme based on the blackboard methaphor and show how guidance and assistance for the author can be incorporated. Finally we give an overview of our generic tool named TNO which has been used for the implementation of GLASS-Studio.

Keywords: Multimedia interfaces, authoring, MHEG, human computer interaction, direct manipulation

1 Distributed Multimedia Applications

Distributed multimedia applications have recently become aroused strong interest with attraction to the multimedia industry. With multimedia services large potential is assumed for the consumer market such as Video-on-Demand, Pay-per-View, Tele-Shopping, Tele-Teaching and Entertainment. The technology for storing, compression and transmission seems mature enough to be put on the market. However, the most important problem of standardization has not yet been solved. Standardization is considered a key factor for success of multimedia applications. A lack of standardization leads to a delayed development of multimedia applications (and devices) because of the potential risk of huge investments in case of failure. The MHEG (Multimedia Hypermedia Expert Group) is developing open international standards for distributed multimedia applications and their work has become quite advanced now [7].

1.1 The forthcoming MHEG-Standard

The upcoming MHEG standard addresses the encoded representation of final-form multimedia and hypermedia objects that will be interchanged across services and applications. The objects are encoded in a binary format, which is specified by using ASN.1 (Abstract Syntax Notation, [4]). This allows the platform-independent exchange of multimedia data in heterogeneous environments. MHEG does not redefine exchange formats for content media types. Instead, existing standards like JPEG and MPEG are integrated and can be referenced when declaring content data types.

Fig. 1. MHEG object interchange

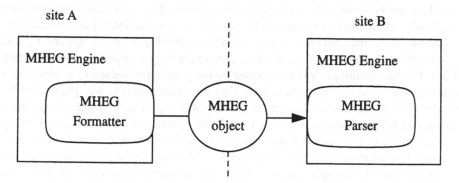

MHEG is not just a binary format, it also defines features for real-time interchange and behavior. The so-called *MHEG engine* interprets the interchanged objects and performs actions (see Fig. 1).

MHEG concepts

The encoding of MHEG is based on the architecture of the ISO/OSI presentation layer. Part of the future MHEG standard is a formal specification of all basic data structures. The *abstract syntax* (ASN.1) describes the data elements and data structures. The *transfer syntax* (Basic Encoding Rules, BER) describes the encoding of the data structures and enables the transfer and processing of the MHEG objects in heterogeneous environments. These definitions, together with the associated behavior are the so-called *MHEG classes*. The MHEG classes are used for the object-oriented design of multimedia presentations. At runtime, instances of the MHEG classes (MHEG objects) are created and interpreted by the MHEG engine. More MHEG objects are created at interpretation time or are retrieved by using the MHEG request/response protocol (MRP).

The basic MHEG classes provide all means for describing kind of content, behavior, user interaction style and composition.

Content

The *content class* is used to define the particular medium type and spatial or temporal attributes of the objects to be presented. The digital data (e.g. text, image, audio or video) can either be included in the object (e.g. for a small text) or be referenced using unique, hierachical identifiers. The *hook* attribute describes the encoding type (e.g. JPEG, MPEG) and optional parameters (e.g. quality of service). Spatial attributes are specified using device-independent *virtual coordinates* on the x, y and z axes. Once a content object has been created at runtime, several views representing this object can be derived. These runtime objects are controlled by the presentation system and the MHEG engine, but they are not exchanged between other components.

Behaviour

One of the most important features of MHEG is the possibility to exchange data describing the behaviour of a multimedia presentation. The behaviour is described by simple rules as „if condition evaluates to true, then execute action". These rules define a network, with links between objects, which the condition can be applied to, and action objects. Instances of the *link class* associate a trigger condition with an action object. Trigger conditions can be expressed by temporal relationships (e.g. after 2 seconds), by transition of object states (e.g. after an audio-sequence was played), or by changes of object attributes. Trigger conditions can be combined by logical operators. The actions to be executed, if a trigger condition evaluates to true, are described by instances of the *action class*. Action objects can create or destroy runtime objects, activate state transitions or change object attributes. The concurrency of different actions can be specified by grouping action objects into nested groups, each group is then attributed with a *synchro indicator* (serial or parallel).

Interaction

Users can influence the course of presentation through certain events. There are two basic types of events that can be triggered by user interaction: *selection* and *modification*. E.g. selection may mean pressing a button changes the status of the runtime object from not-selected to selected. Link objects can refer to this change of state and trigger further actions. Modification is the general form of interaction. Certain types of objects can be changed by user input (e.g. input text fields). Their state then changes to modified and the object attributes contain the new data. Similar to selection, link objects can now trigger further actions.

Composition

The *composite class* helps to group objects of an MHEG application into fewer, larger parts. Beside their container-like functionality, composite objects specify, which objects must be available at the time-point of start-up and close-down. As with the content class, objects can be included or referenced in a composite object.

1.2 The GLASS project

The aim of the Berkom GLASS project (GLobally Accessible ServiceS) is to define an architecture and realize a pre-product implementation of an open system for multimedia services for professional users and consumers. The project was funded by the DeTeBerkom and jointly conducted by the partners GMD Fokus, Digital Equipment,

IBM, Grundig, and the Univesity of Berlin. The envisaged services comprise facilities for access to broadcast services (e.g. TV, radio, interactive program guides), retrieval services (e.g. Video-On-Demand), information services (e.g. hypermedia documents, World-Wide Web) and communication services (e.g. Multimedia-Mail, Fax). All these services are accessible on a single end system in a distributed environment. GLASS is based on the forthcoming MHEG standard.

The GLASS architecture and the tools developed do not only comprehend nice-looking interfaces for MHEG presentations, they also include efficient stores, gateways to other systems (e.g. WWW) and support for the authoring of MHEG applications.

Fig. 2. GLASS components

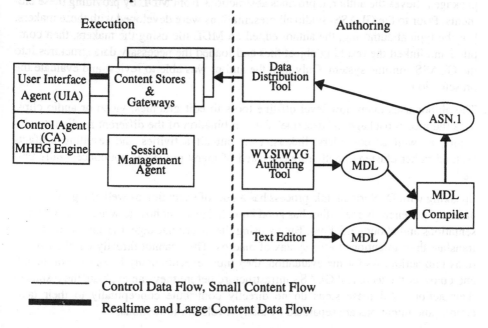

Fig. 2 shows a simplified picture of the different components of the GLASS system at authoring and execution time. The GLASS-specific MHEG Description Language (MDL) enables the author to create MHEG objects without any knowledge about the ASN.1 notation. The MDL source can be created either with a simple text editor or by our WYSIWYG (What You See Is What You Get) tool named GLASS-Studio. The latter will be presented in detail in the next sections of this paper. After the MDL compiler has created the binary MHEG objects, they can be downloaded to the content stores for later retrieval.

The left part of Fig. 2 shows the components which reside at the user's presentation terminal (UIA, CA and MHEG engine). The UIA can have multiple data connections to different content stores at the same time. The gateways (e.g. WWW, TV, Fax gateway) provide the same interfaces as the content stores and can be accessed with the same UIA. Thus, all services are integrated on a single end system. The session management agent (SMA) handles information for accounting, authorization and object location. Only small objects are retrieved from the SMA, while large content data are transferred directly from the store to the UIA. The SMA cooperates with the content stores and grants or disables connections for content data.

1.3 Authoring MHEG Presentations

The GLASS project has developed an internal representation of the MHEG format, the MHEG Description Language (MDL). It is on the same abstraction level as MHEG itself and developing multimedia applications on this level very much resembles assembler programming; MDL does not directly support elements for authoring multimedia applications, such as buttons or scrollbars, well known from GUIs. A macro package relieves the author, it provides abstractions from MDL by providing these elements. Prior to the GLASS-Studio all presentations were developed with these makers. For the typical authoring, the author edited an MDL file using the makers, then compiled and linked the resulting object files and loaded the necessary data structures into the GLASS runtime system. Only then the author was able to review and evaluate the presentation.

The author uses many low-level off-line tools to edit graphics, video or audio clips, uses the macro package to "describe" the combination of the different media into elements, as well as compilers, linkers, etc.; but all activities and resulting artifacts seemed rather clustered, authoring consisted of many processes not conceptually unified.

Speaking with D. Norman, this process has a gulf of execution as well as a gulf of evaluation [8]. Generally the author has good knowledge about how to write appealing presentations and about guidelines. But by using the macro package, the authors must first translate their intentions to the syntax of macros. They cannot directly put their intentions into action. As for the evaluation, they must execute many low-level commands and consider the technical GLASS infrastructure before they can evaluate the results of their actions. All these steps do no directly contribute conceptually to their task; actions and intentions are separated by many levels of indirections.

Before this background we envisaged an environment providing support for the author of multimedia applications for the GLASS runtime system. This environment is called GLASS-Studio.

2 GLASS-Studio

The GLASS-Studio transparently integrates authoring into the GLASS environment, providing abstractions for the functionality. It maps tasks and processes contributing to the author's work onto processes and functions of the underlying system. In this section, we will first quickly introduce the aims that we had in mind when we started to build the GLASS-Studio. Then, in each of the following subsections (2.1 -2.3) we introduce principles which help to fulfill these aims. An example (subsection 2.4) shows how the principles are applied successfully in an authoring session.

The overall aims of the GLASS-Studio are quickly summarized by the following phrases:

a.) Abstraction from the authoring domain

b.) Abstraction from the underlying technical infrastructure of the GLASS environment

c.) Support of methodical, incremental and iterative design

d.) User-friendly interface

e.) Openness and extensibility

Our first aim was to provide abstraction from MDL macros. The author should not necessarily know about MHEG. Therefore user interface elements and mechanisms must be introduced, which hide the technical background. Next, we wanted to shield the author from the underlying technical infrastructure by transparent administration of necessary data and processes not conceptually contributing to the task of authoring. Once a technically advised person has set up the configuration definitions, the design process should continue without any further technical information requested.

Whether or not the multimedia applications that are designed by the author are suitable for the end-users can only be evaluated by practical experience. Therefore the GLASS-Studio should support rapid-prototyping techniques. While the application is built stepwise, it must already be possible to run the preliminary product. By this way early feedback can be incorporated and a better multimedia application will result. Therefore the support of incremental and iterative design techniques was another aim that we have satisfied our list. One of the most important goals of the GLASS-Studio was to provide an easy-to-use graphical user interface. We are convinced, that this goal can best be achieved by employing a WYSIWYG (What You See Is What You Get) interface and well proved user interaction techniques like direct-manipulation and drag&drop [9]. The envisaged environment is also open, providing an interface for external tools and applications that contribute to the authoring or use the resulting multimedia presentation. With such a choice of tools, the author can scale the environment.

2.1 Abstraction of MHEG elements

Development with MDL is a task, which can be done by MHEG specialists only. The abstractions provided by MDL or macro extensions are not suitable for persons coming from other domains. But usually, authoring is done by different persons with intensive knowledge about the specific authoring domain. The abstractions of MDL (resp. MHEG) are not appropriate in this case, because they need to be translated into abstractions from the author's domain. For a better support of the author's task, the author should be able to think "her way", e.g. she uses abstractions and operations like "hang image here", "move button there" and so forth. Thus, it was our primary task to identify the key abstractions of the author's domain.

Because the development of a multimedia presentation is very much like one of multimedia interfaces, it strongly resembles the development of conventional graphical user interfaces. Because of the expertise and knowledge in this field, we wanted to profit from and draw on these. In the field of GUIs (Graphical User Interfaces) there are many frameworks for programming user interfaces and all have similar elements for the interaction and differ only on the actual implementation or design [6]. With multi-media user interfaces we identified similar elements beside integration of the audio and video medias.

We identified the following user interface elements:

- Push and 3 state buttons
- Text fields
- Audio clips
- Video clips
- Images

These user interface elements are very common and almost every GUI supports them, though the actual implementation varies. A lot of design and programming are available for the use of these abstractions. The MHEG model does not support these elements directly, so our abstractions combine multiple MHEG objects into an element which appears to the user as a single. User interface elements are already quite common in the software development, so the author can build upon the expertise in this field.

Because the above listed user interface elements are so well understood, we provided support for the generation of data structures and information for the states of each element. For example, most user think of an image they want to transform into a button element. So the editor provides facilities to extract images for the buttons's states from the original image. Since the author in the GLASS project produces commercial presentations, the editor offers special effects for the image generation, such as transparency, image blending, shadows and others. The tools for image manipulation are transparently integrated in the editor.

For new applications, *metaphors* reduce the knowledge burden on the user: by using a proper metaphor the user can transfer knowledge from well known domains to new ones. Most user-friendly interfaces use this principle of knowledge transfer. Metaphors also strongly influence the representation on the user interface and determine the look&feel of the application. Thus, the choice of a proper metaphor is important, since in applications for GUI systems about half of the code contribute to the man machine interaction! In our case we used the hypertext metaphor. It lends itself very well for a flexible and structured organization of text and other media. The editor uses this metaphor and guides the author in structuring multimedia applications. The author himself can exploit it by providing hypertext links and transitions for the user.

2.2 Presentation structure

For the organization of multimedia presentations, we designed a hierarchy. The *document* represents the presentation itself and contains several *pages* (see Fig. 3). The page provides the user with information and in turn contains multiple *elements*. In MHEG, the concept of pages has not been introduced. Instead, usually one large background image exists with images and buttons inside. In the GLASS project, we experienced, that authors prefer to think of pages instead of a set of currently presentable objects.

All elements or pages can be linked. *Links* provide conditional actions on other elements or transitions to other pages. A link can exist between a page and an element or between two elements. Links are created simply by dragging a rubberband from the source of the link to it's destination. Then a dialog box pops up, which shows all possible actions, that can be executed on the destination object. After the user has selected the desired action, an action object is created implicitly. By this way, the user can think of links connecting presentation objects instead of connecting presentation objects with action objects (which is the case in MHEG).

Note that the HTML model is very different from our model since its based on documents that are usually larger than a page and links that only containt the address of a new document (URL).

Fig. 3. Hypertext Hierarchy

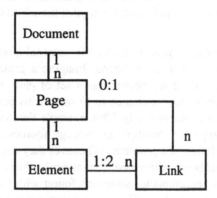

The model described above captures all relevant information and data for the generation of MHEG code in the GLASS environment. We used direct manipulation with WYSIWYG representation of the model's components to provide better support for the author's interaction with the model. The external representations map 1:1 onto the internal model, forming a similar strict hierarchy. Every class of the internal model has an equivalent in the representation.

Throughout the authoring process, all elements can be reused and modified using direct-manipulation techniques [9]. The hypertext metaphor [2] is employed to guide the author structuring his multimedia presentation. At each stage of the design the user can initiate an interactive simulation of the presentation. By this way, the environment also bridges the gulfs of execution and evaluation, speeding up the whole process and giving the author the sense of control over the complete process. Finally, it results in an incremental and iterative process.

2.3 A model and architecture for an open authoring environment

We divided the editor into two main parts: one realizing the internal model, the other for the representation (view) of the user interface. The internal model comprises all objects for the resulting multimedia presentation as well as all processes and data structures for transparent administration and integration into the GLASS environment. The external representation provides a direct manipulation interface with objects faithfully representing the underlying model. The user manipulates only the representations, and they propagate the user actions to the underlying model (see Fig. 4). By this one-way propagation, the state of the representation depends only on the internal model and the internal model is decupled from the interface.

The GLASS-studio not only raises the level of abstraction in the problem domain but also "hides" the underlying technical infrastructure. It shields the author from very technical and GLASS-unique details by transparent administration and integration into the GLASS environment. All necessary data structures are administrated or generated by the studio. From the internal model the editor extracts the information to identify all the data references for the presentation and compiles them into GLASS-conform references.

The editor uses a blackboard approach to share its internal model [3]. The blackboard metaphor is best explained with an example: Imagine a group of persons trying to jointly solve a jigsaw puzzle. Each person has a set of parts he wants to fit into the overall jigsaw. Whenever he sees a chance to fit one of his parts, he does so without asking, independently and autonomously. This example demonstrates the characteristics of the blackboard approach. Multiple knowledge sources observe the blackboard containing the actual solution of a problem. Whenever they can contribute to the solution, they act on the blackboard without conferring with other contributors, this behaviour is independent and opportunistic. Solutions found with the blackboard approach are not deterministic and it lends itself well to heterogenous problem domains with many orthogonal subproblems.

Fig. 4. Internal and external representation in GLASS-Studio

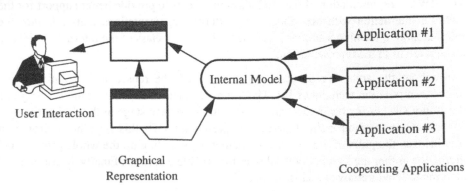

Our blackboard is based upon shared memory, which we realized by using a so-called tuple space. The tuple space connects applications which use it to share data. All data in the tuple space is represented by tuples. Tuples are very easy to manipulate and all data structures can be expressed by using tuple representation. The objects of the model all have methods to convert their data structures into and from the tuple representation.

Via the tuple space the editor cooperates with other applications. These applications have their own representations of the shared model, designed and suitable for their specific purposes. Building on the model, new applications can be developed independently from the editor for which we originally developed the internal model. The applications can be remote and be developed with any programming paradigm or language as long as they have operations that can convert the model's tuple representation into their own.

Fig. 5. Example session

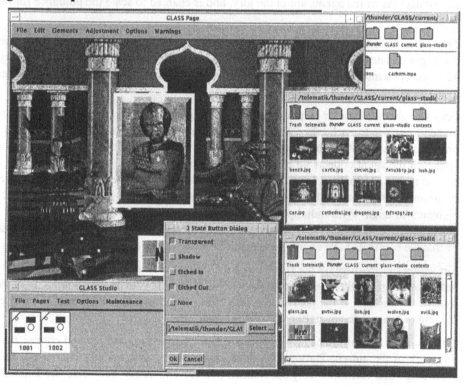

The editor can be easily extended to support modification of the internal model by distributed agents. One approach uses symbolic names and references to identify the operation and the objects on which it is to be performed. The other approach combines symbolic names for the objects with objects denoting "functors": the agent transmits code for the editor which applies the functor object to referenced objects into the model. This approach is more general, since it allows the editor to perform special operations it does not support.

Beside the studio other applications are available in the GLASS environment, e.g. file manager, video and audio editors. The file manager represents the files according to their type, e.g. JPEG files are represented by a small picture of the content. From the file manager the author can easily detect pictures and drag it onto an element of a presentation. The editor uses this picture to generate the corresponding picture of the element's states and updates the internal model (see Fig. 5).

2.4 An example: Guidance

As an example we will demonstrate how applications cooperate through the shared internal model. Many authors use guidelines for the development of multimedia presentations. We tried to group knowledge and guideline topics into "agents" which are each responsible for a small field only. The agents act as critiques and form a jury. The author decides which agents are in the jury, and is enabled to scale the guidance for his work.

The author uses the editor to build a presentation, and for every change in the model the editor updates the shared internal model and activates the waiting agents in the jury. The agents themselves all have their own window representations and only give advice to the author, i. e. they do not change the model.

For example, one agent is responsible for detecting intersections or elements which are placed too close to each other. Another agent comments on the alignment of elements on a page, using either the block approach or the radial placement. With the block approach the agent collects all elements aligned horizontally or vertically in blocks. It tries to merge all blocks as long as possible and if the blocks have only a single element or are too close to each other, the agent comments this fact and gives advice on which elements to align. With radial placement, the agent assumes that the elements form a circle and observes angles and distance of the elements to ensure no intersections occur or that the elements have enough space and distance from each other.

Yet another agent displays the structure of the presentation through a graph. By examination of the graph the agent tries to detect circles and to evaluate the complexity of the hypertext structure. If the presentation has many possible paths, the agent can advice the author to include navigation aids for the user.

This example demonstrates how agents can be developed to criticize and comment on the work of the author. Through the modularization the programmer can encapsulate knowledge and rules into very specialized agents. The author can scale the guidance and form the jury according to his needs. Many other applications are planned, including code generators for other representations.

3 Implementation

Because of our good experience with user interface programming using dynamic languages and rapid prototyping tools, we decided to employ such a tool for building of GLASS-Studio. Our preferred choice was a tool named TNO [5], which we had used very successfully before in many other projects. TNO is our generic tool for graphical editing and generation of graphical front ends for other systems. Application domains are graphical editors for various graphical techniques, cooperative work, CASE environments, and "intelligent" users interfaces in the broad sense. The main goals in the design of TNO was extensibility, ability to customize, easy use and efficient execution. TNO achieves this goal by the use of a high-level user interface language, called EXL.

3.1 EXL: A language for graphical user interfaces

EXL is based on Scheme [1] and added a prototype-based object model, generic functions, relations, and constraints to the language, which we felt are necessary to make user interface programming and conceptual modelling much easier. Although the language is for programming, it's strength lies in conceptual modelling of applications.

Scheme for itself is a big win for user interface programming, namely because it has closures, continuations and automatic storage reclamation. Closures can provide callback functions with the whole environment of the establishing procedure. This is a very natural way of sharing information over distinct functions. Moreover continuations can solve the problem of fragmenting the sequential control flow and make the code more readable by keeping local things together. Additionally they solve concurrency problems, a callback function doesn't have to return as soon as possible because the application has multiple threads. Last not least it enables transparent error handling and recovery.

The Motif toolkit is integrated tightly into the object system, which means widget classes are prototypes and widget resources are virtual slots of prototypes. Resource conversion from Scheme types to toolkit types are done automatically. Any procedure, also continuations, can serve as a callback function. No main loop has to be called. Event dispatching is done via the built-in dispatcher of the runtime system.

Besides the Motif toolkit, the standard library of TNO contains additional widgets for digital video and audio.

The following steps describe the method how we built the GLASS-Studio application:

a.) Design of a semantic model of the application domain using prototypes, generic functions, relations and constraints, (e.g. what is a page, what is a button, how can links from one page to another be modelled, what is an animation).

b.) Make visible representations of parts of the model. These so-called views can be constructed from existing view parts such as list views, graph views, etc.

c.) Put a framework around (e.g. menus and additional dialogs).

d.) Supply additional functions for reading, saving and conversion of data.

These steps are typically needed for graphical applications in general. Additional steps are necessary for larger cooperative applications where the user interface is only one part of the problem.

3.2 Cooperation with TNO

The application designer has to care about communication and coordination within a set of application components. Often components are separated processes which are distributed over a network. Also the components can be heterogeneous in the choice of their implementation language.

A communication scheme based on message passing would be too low-level for complex applications. RPC (Remote Procedure Call), from which CORBA and OLE descents, rely on the procedure call paradigm, which is even too inflexible for loosely coupled cooperation and not suitable for heterogeneous applications.

TNO provides a communication mechanism for distributed heterogeneous components, which is based on a so-called tuple space [3], a kind of distributed shared memory where data is organized in the application independent representation of tuples. This communication mechanism allows address- and time-decupled anonymous communication. Besides the usual client/server cooperation also *m:n* cooperation patterns are possible. API's for C and C++ and even the UNIX shell are provided, so you can choose the implementation language for each separate component.

The GLASS-Studio blackboard methaphor is implemented with the tuple space. The various specialized components are autonomous, separated (sometimes distributed) programs, which are implemented with EXL and C, are connected to the tuple space and watch for certain interesting events on which they react. They provide their results via tuple space vice versa.

Now we can identify the following additional steps for designing a cooperative graphical application:

a.) Identify the cooperation data space and put this part of your application model into the shared data space (make shared data structures).

b.) Choose a mechanism of control and coordination. This may vary from absolutely no control (self-organizing system) to centralized algorithmic control. In between there is a spectrum of control mechanisms. For the GLASS-Studio we used a blackboard model of control with priority-based activation.

c.) Specify the trigger conditions and actions of all components (application components and control components).

4 Conclusion and Lessons learned

In this paper we presented an authoring environment for multimedia applications based on MHEG. We identified the right abstraction and metaphors as crucial for authoring. Although we decided to use a special metaphor, MHEG does not imply any of them. Another abstraction could have been also appropriate. Therefore an open architecture of the authoring system has been essential.

The iterative and incremental way the GLASS-Studio is used, helps to get user feedback in a very early design stage of the multimedia application. The authoring process using the GLASS-Studio is essential faster than the previous process and tools that was employed before.

Because of the large application domain of MHEG, we also needed to use other heterogeneous autonomous tools for various tasks in the authoring environment such as image processing, archiving, etc. On the other hand the author should have more support and interactive guidance while doing his job. In our authoring environment we developed a cooperation infrastructure based on shared data structures which is simpler and more flexible than RPC and event dispatching systems.

The use of a dedicated simple high-level programming language, which is rich in sense of programming concepts (but not too complex) and does not bother the programmer with implementation details (such as storage management) was a good decision for the implementation of the GLASS-Studio. The programming productivity was very high. Programs in EXL were substantially smaller as programs in C or C++ with the same functionality. The prototypical character of the project was supported well.

References

1. W. Clinger, J. Rees: *Revised⁴ Report on the Algorithmic Language Scheme*, Nov. 1991.
2. J. Conklin: Hypertext: An Introduction and Survey, *IEEE Computer*, Sept. 1987.
3. D. Gelernter: Generative Communication in Linda, *ACM Transactions on Programming Languages and Systems*, Vol. 7, No. 1, pp. 80-112, 1985.
4. ISO/IEC IS 8824: *Information Processing Systems Interconnection Specification of Abstract Syntax Notation One (ASN.1)*, 1987.
5. T. Leidig: *Development of Cooperative Graphical Interactive Applications*, Ph.D. Thesis, University of Kaiserslautern, 1994.
6. B.A. Myers: User Interface Software Tools. *ACM Transactions on Computer Human Interaction*, Vol. 2, No. 1, March 1995.
7. T. Meyer-Boudnik und W. Effelsberg: MHEG Explained, *IEEE Multimedia*, Spring 1995.
8. D. Norman: *Design Principles for Human-Computer Interfaces*, in „Readings in Human Computer Interaction", Ed. R. Baecker and W. Buxton, Morgan Kaufman, Los Altos, CA, 1987.
9. B. Shneiderman: DirectManipulation: A Step Beyond Programming Languages. *IEEE Computer*, Aug. 1983.

Television Information Filtering
Through Speech Recognition

ir. Arjen P. de Vries *

Centre for Telematics and Information Technology
University of Twente

Abstract: The problem of *information overload* can be solved by
the application of information filtering to the huge amount of data.
Information on radio and television can be filtered using speech
recognition of the audio track. A prototype system using closed
captions has been developed on top of the *INQUERY* information
access system. The challange of integrating speech recognition and
information retrieval into a working system is a big one. The open
problems are the selection of a document representation model, the
recognition and selection of indexing features for speech retrieval
and dealing with the erroneous output of recognition processes.

Keywords: multimedia, multimedia representation, content-based
retrieval, information filtering, automatic indexing, speech recognition, content analysis, probabilistic information retrieval.

1 Introduction

The *Indexing a Sea of Audio* project forms a foundation for multimedia information filtering projects at the *Cambridge Research Laboratory (CRL)* in
Boston [dV95]. CRL is a research laboratory of *Digital Equipment Coorporation
(DEC)*. One of the strong points of CRL is the audio group. Interesting applications have been developed to ease the incorporation of audio into today's working
environment [LPG+93]. It is believed that audio will play an important role in
computing in the next decades. This particular project addresses the problem of
information overload in multimedia environments.

2 Problem Statement

The achievements in communication systems result in a society where everybody
can publish information. However, we do not have the time and capabilities to
process all these data. People easily get lost in large information spaces [Les89].
A lot of information exists that people would be interested in, if they only knew
that it was available.

---

* This research has been conducted at the Digital Cambridge Research Lab, Massachusetts, United States of America

Since the early sixties, people have investigated the storage and retrieval of automatically indexed documents [vR79], [Sal89]. This research has been restricted to text processing. Little research has been done to investigate the information system solution for information overload applied to multimedia data. However, a lot of television and radio channels are broadcasting thousands of programs a day. How to deal with all this multimedia information is still an open problem.

A lot of expectations have been raised by speech recognition research. Laboratories reported 95% recognition rates on 5,000 word vocabularies [RHL94] and products can be found on the market [vS95]. This puts the development of a multimedia information access system for radio and television within reach. If you could transform audio into descriptive text, it would be possible to index the text representing the audio. Most information on television is *also* captured in the audio track. Of course, somebody looking for a red car crossing the railroad in some movie would not be helped. However, somebody looking for information on cars made by *Renault* would probably find an appropriate documentary.

An audio retrieval system can be used for many purposes. Of course, secret services of all countries would like to pay a lot of money for a system that can keep track of many audio channels. We could archive all meetings of a board of a large company. The formal decision process could be tracked afterwards, to study how mistakes and good decisions are made. An application in health services was suggested by a children's psychiatrist. A system storing recorded sessions can help evaluation of applied therapy to determine optimal treatment. At present, only a logbook kept by the psychiatrist can be used.

3 Research Background

3.1 Information Filtering

An *information retrieval* or *information access* system has the function of leading the user to those documents that will best enable him to satisfy his need for information. Over the years, information retrieval systems have moved from storing relatively short abstracts towards storing large collections of documents of varying size.

The terms *information dissemination* and *information filtering* refer to the delivery of information to users who submitted a profile describing their interests. The dissemination model has become increasingly more important due to the rapid advances in wide-area information systems. The simplest form of such a system is the mailing list. Examples of more advanced information filtering systems are SIFT [YGM] and NRT [SvR91]. Both systems provide dissemination of articles in USENET news.

In [BC92], the authors recognized the fact that information access and information dissemination are basically identical processes. The major difference is that information filtering usually works on a dynamic stream of input data whereas information access deals with relatively static databases. For the retrieval and filtering processes, the same ideas can be applied to both environments. A filtering application can be built on top of a traditional information access system. A common trick is to treat the user profiles as documents and the incoming news documents as queries. The same approach is taken by SIFT and *INROUTE*, the filtering system of the *INQUERY* information retrieval engine.

3.2 Automatic Analysis

Manually indexing will not be possible for all information sources that we want to follow. We definitely need automatic analysis of multimedia data. This section discusses currently available techniques that can be applied in real-time. The collection of techniques implemented in the system limits the capabilities of retrieval by content. An agent-based approach seems suitable to easily extend retrieval systems with emerging analysis techniques [Mae94]. The level up to which analysis has been achieved determines the system characteristics to a large account.

Segmentation or partitioning is necessary to split the incoming continuous stream of multimedia data in a sequence of *documents*. A document is a collection of data that belongs together in a higher semantical level. A news report on CNN and a commercial selling coke are two examples of such documents. A document can contain different types of media. Content analysis focuses on the analysis of information content of these documents. It should be noticed that segmentation information can be viewed as a special type of content information. If segmentation of an audio track identifies a three minute fragment as a song, this fact reveals more than just the borders.

In [Hea94], the text segmentation algorithm *TextTiling* is described. Term repetition is used as a feature to find topic changes. The algorithm is found to produce segmentation that corresponds well to human judgment of the major subtopic boundaries. For the segmentation of audio, several information sources can be used. People have developed speaker change detection and speech emphasis detection [Aro94], [CW92]. In [dV95], a segmentation algorithm in silence, speech and music is described. For the segmentation of video, it is also possible to use the sizes of the compressed frames. In [DLM+94], a real-time algorithm is described that can be applied to produce *storyboards* of a video [LAF+93].

An even harder problem is to index the content information of the parts in the partitioned stream. In case of a text-based environment, full-text indexing can be applied. If a perfect speech recognizer were available, the same would hold for speech data. Algorithms for content analysis of audio are speaker identification [RS78], word spotting [WB91] and speech recognition [RHL94]. Most image analysis algorithms are not real-time. For example, it is almost impossible to recognize a car in arbitrary images. For video, this implies that the only content information we will have available are closed captions. Speech recognition of the audio track seems the solution to get content information when closed captions are not available.

3.3 Filtering Speech

One of the best speech recognition systems is the *SPHINX-II* system, developed at Carnegie Mellon University. This large vocabulary continuous speech recognition system has achieved a 95% success rate on generalized tests for a 5000 word general dictation task. Speech recognition is viewed as a pattern recognition process. Phonetic units are modeled during training and used during recognition. *Hidden Markov Models (HMM)* are the most common approach to model phonetic units [SBG94], [Cox90]. For speech recognition, this tool seems to work well. However, a speech recognizer built with this technology has a restricted *preknown* vocabulary. If the word model is not known by the recognizer, the model of another word will be chosen as the best fit.

Unfortunately, with a restricted vocabulary, speech recognition is not very interesting for the purpose of automatic indexing. Typical queries we would want to perform on radio and television data refer to names and places. We can never anticipate the vocabulary for all possible search terms. Therefore, we have to use another approach to indexing speech.

Speech recognition based on phoneme models alone would not have a restricted vocabulary. The influence of the context on some of the phonemes makes recognition of phonemes as indexing features an impossible task though. In [GS92], an information retrieval model of speech documents is introduced that is in principle vocabulary independent. The key idea is that a small number of *indexing features* consisting of phoneme sequences was identified. These indexing features can be identified in text files as well. Only two different classes of phonemes are used: vowels (V) and consonants (C). The indexing features they proposed are V^+, V^+C^+, C^+V^+ and $C^+V^+C^{+2}$. The letters A, E, I, O, U and Y were denoted as vowels, the other letters are consonants.

The reason why this idea can be used to index speech data with an unlimited vocabulary is that it is not the purpose to recognize the words correctly (which would not be possible yet). The speech recognizer only has to identify the features that occur in the text. These features are only parts of the words. The idea is similar to text retrieval experiments with digrams and trigrams [Wil79]. However, in speech data it is not possible to detect word boundaries. It has been shown that this approach to indexing speech data is indeed feasible on a relatively small data set [SW].

4 INQUERY

INQUERY is a probabilistic information retrieval system [TC91], [CCH92]. It is based on inference networks [Pea89] and capable of dealing with Gigabyte collections. It has shown to be among the best information retrieval systems in the world [CC93]. Information retrieval is viewed as an inference process in which we estimate $\mathcal{P}(\mathcal{I} \mid \text{document})$, the probability that a user's information

---

[2] V^+ means one or more vowels

need is met given a document as evidence. Of course, uncertainness has to be taken into account.

The retrieval model supports multiple *representation schemes*, allows combination of results of different queries and query types and facilitates flexible matching between the terms or concepts used in the queries and those assigned to documents. The notion of multiple representation schemes refers to the fact that documents can be represented in different ways. Information from the abstract of a paper should be treated differently from information that is only given in the complete paper. A given query will retrieve different documents when applied to different representations.

The main tasks performed by INQUERY are building the collection, interpreting the query and using the inference networks to retrieve documents. During collection building, documents are parsed and representation terms are identified. The standard parser relies on a subset of SGML to identify the parts of the document to index like title and text. This parser can be extended or even completely replaced with another parser. The parser can be changed easily since it has been implemented with the standard Unix utilities *lex* and *yacc*.

Although the INQUERY system has been built for text representations, nothing limits the underlying mechanisms to be applied to other representation concepts. For terms that can be expressed in ASCII representation, the original system can be used without a problem. Therefore, the speech documents can be indexed with INQUERY using the features mentioned in section 3.3.

A drawback of using INQUERY for our project was the fact that the system could not deal with incremental indexing. Fortunately, the new version of INQUERY has solved this problem. Instead of using flat inverted files in a custom build system, the system was rebuilt on top of the persistent object store Mneme [BCCM94]. The new technique permits incremental indexing in a fast and efficient way [BCC94].

A more serious problem is that the performance of INQUERY on imprecise data is not known. The formula used to calculate the probability of usefulness of a document is based on term frequencies. These frequencies will have wrong values if the recognition process is not errorfree. This can result in a degradation on recall and precision. [TBCE94], [TBC94] and [CHTB92] report about information retrieval on texts that have been generated using *Optical Character Recognition (OCR)*. This way, the effects of noisy data on the retrieval process have been studied. The retrieval performance was measured on the scanned collection and compared with the results on a manually edited version of the database. [CHTB92] found that high quality OCR devices cause almost no degradation of the accuracy of retrieval, but low quality devices applied to collections of short documents can result in significant degradation of performance. The use of a speech recognizer to produce descriptive text is analogous to the use of OCR devices in these experiments. The results seem to predict that speech recognition should be of high quality to make good information retrieval possible.

Research has to be done whether speech recognition performs well enough to produce output that can be used reliably in a retrieval system. Knowledge of common mistakes by the recognition process could help improve retrieval. Experience with preprocessing the input data on scanned documents in INQUERY is reported in [TBC94]. The results were promising. The inference network model may be a good candidate to deal with these error models. Another level of representation nodes could be added to model the probability of correct recognition. The mathematical implications of this idea for the correctness and the computational complexity still have to be analyzed thoroughly.

5 The Prototype System

So far, a speech recognizer has not been used. We did have a *closed caption decoder* [Fed] though. Closed captions are like subtitles, but may contain slightly more information, eg. 'music' or 'knock knock'. Closed captions are primarily focused on hearing-impaired people. They are added to the television signal manually. These closed captions can be thought of as the output of an almost perfect speech recognizer. Some of the television companies broadcast closed captions together with their audio and video signal. Example broadcasters are the Public Broadcasting System and CNN Headline News.

The application *store-24* is build on top of the *audiofile (AF)* toolbox and was implemented using *Tcl* and *Tk* [Ous94]. Store-24 is a ringbuffer that stores the last twentyfour hours of a radio channel. Because this application is implemented on top of audiofile [LPG+93], everybody in the laboratory (and in principle in the whole world) can listen to this radio. You never miss the news because you can just reposition the audio in time.

5.1 Architecture

The abstract design of the prototype is shown in Fig. 1. It is based on a dual architecture. The incoming data is split in an information content stream and a raw data stream by the automatic segmentation and recognition unit. In the prototype, the information content stream contains the closed-captions of the television data. The storage unit dealing with the raw data is implemented using the *store-24* application. The prototype system only deals with audio.

The output of the automatic segmentation unit is stored separately from the raw audio data. A neural network, used to produce segmentation information, is described in [dV95]. The output of the content analysis unit is stored in an INQUERY data collection. The information content stream only contains the closed captions of the television signal because a speech recognizer was not available yet.

The different versions of the data are linked by {date, time, channel}-tuples. The user of the prototype system can search the data collection by content. INQUERY accepts natural language queries and returns a list of documents. The user interface of the prototype system is implemented on the *World Wide Web*.

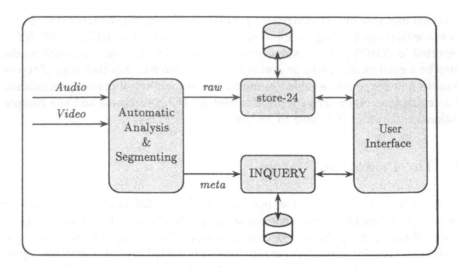

Fig. 1. The prototype framework

As result of a query, the system presents both the information content version and the original audio version of the document. It redirects the playback point of the user's active *store-24* application to the correct channel at the time the document started. A better approach than directly positioning store-24 would be to return a list of links that will position the audio after pressing. If the ringbuffer contained a longer time of audio, eg. a full month, these links could be automatically included in other documents like a user's homepage.

5.2 Implementation

The prototype has been realized on a UNIX platform. The system was implemented using C and Tcl/Tk [Ous94]. Using Tcl simplifies the handling of user input and the integration of different building blocks in one environment.

Because an audio document can be arbitrarily long and the recognition process will make mistakes, fast browsing through the retrieved audio document has to be implemented. The user does not want to listen to ten minutes of audio to find out that the speech recognizer did mix up two words. To enable jumping to retrieved representation concepts, an index of {timestamp, representation concept}-tuples has to be stored within the document. For implementation purposes I chose to store this information in a table containing {line, word, seconds} format, where seconds stores the time relative to the beginning of the document. I chose a word oriented approach of referring to locations within the document because this is the representation that is used within INQUERY. If we would use the indexing features of section 3.3, such a 'word' would be a phoneme sequence. Of course, if we want to store real multimedia documents with the audio at the same location as the text, this representation cannot work any more.

The software accessing the closed caption decoder board does not output documents but just a long, unreadable list of {timestamp, caption}-tuples. These tuples are read by my software and segmented into documents whenever it takes longer than a treshold time for new captions to come in. On CNN Headline News, the only documents that are captioned are news reports approximately between 6 pm and 10 am and most of the commercials. An algorithm segmenting the incoming captions based on a time treshold of twelve seconds turned out to make little mistakes. Of course, this segmentation strategy would not have worked if all information were captioned. In a real application, the segmentation information from different sources mentioned in section 3.2 has to be combined. This is a very hard problem that has received very little attention at present.

The standard parser that comes with the INQUERY package deals with documents marked up in a subset of SGML. I decided to use this parser for my system as I believe that SGML and HyTime will be commonly used to describe (multimedia) documents in the near future [VB95]. An example of a document that I composed automatically from the incoming closed captions is shown in Fig. 2.

```
<DOC>
<DOCNO> CNN-04/04/95-02:00:03 <\DOCNO>
<DATE> 04/04/95 </DATE>
<TIME> 02:00:03 </TIME>
<SOURCE> CNN <\SOURCE>
<TIMES>
{1 1 2}{2 1 3}{3 1 13}{4 1 14}
{5 1 17}{6 1 19}{7 1 20}{8 1 22}
        ...
</TIMES>
<TEXT>
captions paid for by
the us department of education
live from atlanta
headline news
david goodnow reporting
texas authorities are trying
to figure out what caused
        ...
</TEXT>
</DOC>
```

Fig. 2. An example document

To enable the use of INQUERY, the parser of the indexing subsystem had to be extended and the interfacing between retrieval subsystem and user interface had to be implemented. With the help of the INQUERY people from University of Massachussetts at Amherst[3] I managed to make the INQUERY system deal with the document layout explained in the previous paragraph. I added a TIME field to the parser that contains the start time of a document. Using field indexing options from INQUERY, this enables the user to formulate queries for documents of 'this morning'.

I added a TIMES field to the parser to store the index table of {timestamp, caption}-tuples. Although INQUERY has been developed as a general retrieval engine, it is impossible to retrieve non-indexed parts of the documents. However, the best place to keep information that belongs to a document is within the document itself. Therefore, I had to use the undocumented get_raw_doc function call that retrieves the original unparsed document and reparse the retrieved document in my own code.

I will finish this section with an example of how the system should process a query. If the user queries for 'david goodnow', the closed caption documents stored in the INQUERY database collection are searched and INQUERY returns a list of documents ordered by decreasing probability of usefulness to the user. One of the documents that would be retrieved, is the example document given before. The system then reads the index table in the TIMES field for line 5 of the text and adds the 17 seconds to the document time stamp. Segment-24 is tuned to CNN and starts playing at 2:00:20, 17 seconds after the start of the document.

6 Conclusions and Further Work

The prototype application is a nice tool to experiment with. The implementation based on small building blocks realizes extendibility of the system. New approaches to automatic segmentation and analysis of the input data can easily be added and the improvements for retrieval can be studied. Once a standard test set has been defined, precision and recall measures can be used to find good representations of multimedia data from the viewpoint of information access.

A better document model is needed to store the documents. The segmentation information should be stored within the document. The same holds for the different representations of the data. The SGML/HyTime standard seems to be a good candidate for this purpose [VB95], [Erf93].

In theory, hooking up a speech recognizer with the prototype should be a fairly easy task. However, too many factors are unknown to predict whether this approach will result into a working product. It does not seem necessary to develop a new retrieval paradigm for speech data since we can use phoneme sequences.

Speech recognizers make mistakes. Erroneous data can confuse the information retrieval process. Intuitively, I think it is possible to extend the inference network model with knowledge about the probability that a word was recognized

---

[3] I want to thank Michelle LaMar for answering the many mail messages with questions and giving me the code of the Tcl interpreter extended with the INQUERY API calls.

correctly and the alternatives suggested by the recognizer. However, this still has to be proven. Implications of this idea for correctness of the inference network model have to be studied.

References

[Aro94]   B.M. Arons. *Interactively skimming recorded speech*. PhD thesis, Massachusetts Institute of Technology, February 1994.

[BC92]   N.J. Belkin and W.B. Croft. Information filtering and information retrieval: Two sides of the same coin? *Communications of the ACM*, 35(12):29–38, 1992.

[BCC94]   E.W. Brown, J.P. Callan, and W.B. Croft. Fast incremental indexing for full-text information retrieval. In *Proceedings of the 20th International Conference on Very Large Databases (VLDB)*, Santiago, Chile, 1994.

[BCCM94] E.W. Brown, J.P. Callan, W.B. Croft, and J.E.B. Moss. Supporting full-text information retrieval with a persistent object store. In *EDBT '94*, 1994.

[CC93]   J.P. Callan and W.B. Croft. An evaluation of query processing strategies using the TIPSTER collection. In *Proceedings of the sixteenth annual international ACM SIGIR conference on research and development in information retrieval*, pages 347–356, 1993.

[CCH92]   J.P. Callan, W.B. Croft, and S.M. Harding. The INQUERY retrieval system. In *Proceedings of the 3rd international conference on database and expert systems applications*, pages 78–83, 1992.

[CHTB92] W.B. Croft, S.M. Harding, K. Taghva, and J. Borsack. An evaluation of information retrieval accuracy with simulated OCR output. In *Symposium of Document Analysis and Information Retrieval*, 1992.

[Cox90]   S.J. Cox. *Speech and language processing*, chapter Hidden Markov Models for automatic speech recognition: theory and application, pages 209–230. Chapman and Hall, 1990.

[CW92]   F.R. Chen and M.M. Withgott. The use of emphasis to automatically summarize a spoken discourse. In *Proceedings of the International Conference on Acoustics, Speech and Signal Processing*, San Fransisco, CA, March 1992.

[DLM+94] E. Deardorff, T.D.C. Little, J.D. Marshall, D. Venkatesh, and R. Walzer. Video scene decomposition with the motion picture parser. In *IS&T/SPIE Symposium on Electronic Imaging Science and Technology*, San Jose, 1994.

[dV95]   A.P. de Vries. Multimedia information access. Master's thesis, University of Twente, August 1995.

[Erf93]   R. Erfle. Specification of temporal constraints in multimedia documents using HyTime. *Electronic publishing*, 6(4):397–411, 1993.

[Fed]   Federal Communications Commission. *15.119 Closed caption decoder requirements for television receivers*.

[GS92]   U. Glavitsch and P. Schäuble. A system for retrieving speech documents. In *Proceedings of the 15th annual international SIGIR*, pages 168–176, Denmark, 6 1992.

[Hea94]   M.A. Hearst. Multi-paragraph segmentation of expository text. In *ACL '94*, Las Cruces, 1994.

[LAF+93] T.D.C. Little, G. Ahanger, R.J. Folz, J.F. Gibbon, F.W. Reeve, D.H. Schelleng, and D. Venkatesh. A digital on-demand video service supporting content- based queries. In *Proceedings of the first ACM international conference on multimedia*, pages 427–436, Anaheim California, 1993.

[Les89] M. Lesk. What to do when there's too much information. In *Hypertext '89 Proceedings*, pages 305–318, New York, 1989. ACM.

[LPG+93] Levergood, Payne, Gettys, Treese, and Stewart. AudioFile: a network-transparent system for distributed audio applications. In *USENIX Summer Conference*, June 1993.

[Mae94] P. Maes. Agents that reduce work and information overload. *Communications of the ACM*, 37(7):31–42, July 1994.

[Ous94] J.K. Ousterhout. *Tcl and the Tk toolkit*. Addison-Wesley Publishing, 1994.

[Pea89] J. Pearl. *Probabilistic reasoning in intelligent systems*. Morgan Kaufmann, California, 1989.

[RHL94] Rudnicky, Hauptmann, and Lee. Survey of current speech technology. *Communications of the ACM*, 37(3):52–57, 1994.

[RS78] L.R. Rabiner and R.W. Schafer. *Digital processing of speech*. Prentice-Hall, New-Jersey, 1978.

[Sal89] G. Salton. *Automatic Text Processing: The Transformation, Analysis, and Retrieval of Information by Computer*. Addison Wesley Publishing, 1989.

[SBG94] A. Syrdal, R. Bennett, and S. Greenspan. *Applied speech technology*. CRC Press, Inc., Florida, 1994.

[SvR91] M. Sanderson and C.J. van Rijsbergen. NRT: news retrieval tool. *Electronic Publishing*, 4(4):205–217, 1991.

[SW] P. Schäuble and M. Wechsler. First experiences with a system for content based retrieval of information from speech recordings. http://www-ir.inf.ethz.ch/.

[TBC94] K. Taghva, J. Borsack, and A. Condit. Results of applying probabilistic IR to OCR text. In *Proceedings of the seventeenth annual international ACM SIGIR Conference on research and development in information retrieval*, Dublin, Ireland, 1994.

[TBCE94] K. Taghva, J. Borsack, A. Condit, and S. Erva. The effects of noisy data on text retrieval. *Journal of the American Society for Information Science*, 45(1):50–58, 1994.

[TC91] H. Turtle and W.B. Croft. Evaluation of an inference network-based retrieval model. *ACM Transactions of information systems*, 9(3), 1991.

[VB95] P.A.C. Verkoulen and H.M. Blanken. SGML/HyTime for supporting cooperative authoring of multimedia applications. In *Advanced Course: Multimedia Databases in Perspective*, pages 179–212. Center for Telematics and Information Technology of the University of Twente, 1995.

[vR79] C.J. van Rijsbergen. *Information retrieval*. Butterworths, London, 2nd edition, 1979.

[vS95] Hein van Steenis. Spraakherkenning levert eindelijk produkten op. *Automatiseringsgids*, May 26 1995.

[WB91] L.D. Wilcox and M.A. Bush. HMM-based wordspotting for voice editing and indexing. In *Proceedings of the Second European Conference on Speech Communication and Technology*, Genova, Italy, September 1991.

[Wil79] P. Willet. Document retrieval experiments using indexing vocabularies of varying size. II. Hashing, truncation, digram and trigram encoding of indexing terms. *Journal of Documentation*, 35(4):296–305, 1979.

[YGM] T.W. Yan and H. Garcia-Molina. SIFT - a tool for wide-area information dissemination. http://sift.stanford.edu/.

Event and Action Representation and Composition for Multimedia Application Scenario Modelling

Michalis Vazirgiannis, ...

Department of Electrical Engineering
Division of Computer Science
National Technical University of Athens, Greece

ABSTRACT. In this paper we present a model for the representation of multimedia applications based on the scenario concept. The scenario is described in terms of events and actions. The proposed model represents all the events that may occur in a multimedia application (originated from the system, the applications or the user). As regards actions, we propose a rich substrate for spatial and temporal composition representation based on operators that cover all the spatial and temporal relationships among multimedia objects. Finally the scenario of the application is represented as a set of scenario tuples that consist of two (or more) sets of actions originated by the same event (per event).

Keywords: Interactive Multimedia Applications, Events, Scenario, Temporal Composition, Spatio-temporal Modelling

1. Introduction

Multimedia applications can be very complex as regards the relations of the involved objects, transformations of the objects in the scope of the application and relationships among them. We regard a multimedia application as a scenario that includes scenes (configurations of objects in a thematic domain) where the involved objects that are incorporated and interrelated for the purpose of the application. It is obvious that in a complex multimedia application it may be hard, if not impossible, to incorporate the semantic dynamically, and parts that are in the application interrelate. Thus an author (i.e. a multimedia based person) needs tools not high level but complex descriptions of all aspects of a multimedia application.

A key issue in the representation of multimedia applications is the description of spatial and temporal composition of objects' presentation in the application. Moreover, the relationships (synchronisation) among objects must be represented. Thus, for instance, think of a multimedia application in an event based environment in which there is a rich set of events that may occur and define the flow of application features, such as a video sequence, the spatial coincidence of two objects in the application window, the occurrence of a pattern in a media object are events that may be generated by the

Event and Action Representation and Composition for Multimedia Application Scenario Modelling

M. Vazirgiannis, T. Sellis

Department of Electrical Engineering
Division of Computer Science
National Technical University of Athens, Greece

Abstract: In this paper we present a model for the representation of multimedia applications based on the scenario concept. The scenario is described in terms of events and actions. The proposed model represents all the events that may occur in a multimedia application (originated from the system, the application or the user). As regards actions we propose a rich scheme for spatial and temporal composition representation based on operators that cover all the spatial and temporal relationships among multimedia objects. Finally the scenario of the application is represented as a set of scenario tuples that correspond to fundamental sets of actions originated by the same event (or events).

Keywords: Interactive Multimedia Applications, Events, Temporal Composition, Scenario Modelling

1. Introduction

Multimedia applications can be very complex as regards the number of involved objects, transformations of the objects in the scope of an application and relationships among them. We regard a multimedia application as a container that includes scenes (aggregations of objects in a thematic domain) which in turn include objects that are transformed and interrelated for the purpose of the application. It is obvious that in a complex multimedia application it may be very difficult to describe all the possible functionality and paths the user or the application may follow. Thus an authors (who is usually a non-technical person) needs tools for high level but complete description of all aspects of a multimedia application.

A key issue in the representation of multimedia applications is the description of spatial and temporal composition of objects participating in the application. Moreover the relationships (synchronisation) among objects must be represented. Therefore, one can think of a multimedia application as an event based environment in which there is a rich set of events that may occur and define the flow of application. For instance, the end of a video sequence, the spatial coincidence of two objects in the application window, the occurrence of a pattern in a media object are events that may be exploited to trigger other actions in an application. The events may further be composed in order to express richer and more complex conditions.

Complete representation of interactive multimedia applications is an open research issue. A multimedia application description consists of the following modules:

- the media objects that participate in the application along with the presentation specifications and transformations, and

- the description of the application functionality (i.e. the flow of the application and the response to occurring system, application or user events)

An important issue, that arises in the above context, is the composition of media in space and time. Current commercial systems do not adequately cover these issues especially those related to temporal synchronisation and communication between objects participating in the application using events. Therefore there is a need to study

- support for complex events: in an interactive multimedia application there may be situations that are highly complex in terms of events that are interrelated with respect to the functionality of the application.

- spatial composition, i.e. the topological relationships among multimedia objects as they are placed in an application window in the framework of a multimedia application.

In this paper we present a model for the representation of multimedia applications based on the scenario concept. The scenario is described in terms of events and actions. The events in a multimedia application cover a wide range of actions that may occur (originating from the system, the application, or the user). We derive a rich scheme for representing of simple and complex events regarding temporal, spatial and content based issues. We exploit ideas from the active databases area [GAT94] for modelling and composition of events. Moreover we define a scheme for representing actions in the framework of multimedia applications. The scheme supports composition of actions in the spatial and temporal domains. Finally, we present an integrated mechanism for description of application scenaria in terms of scenario tuples. A scenario tuple defines the application response to an event (simple or complex).

The proposed model is based on previous work on an object oriented framework that represents multimedia objects and applications [VAZ93][VAZ95]. This framework is extended towards the direction of

- the representation of simple and complex events
- the representation of spatial and temporal composition of multimedia objects, and
- more complete scenario definition.

2. Event modelling and classification

Events in the context of multimedia information systems widen the context of events, as used in the domain of active databases, since events convey either spatial and/or temporal information. Moreover the presentation of multimedia objects is a read-only action that has no delete or update actions to the multimedia database.

In an interactive multimedia application the various events that occur may be classified in external and internal. External events occur out of the application scope, are related to time and space and are due to changes happening independently of the application. External events may be time instances, time intervals, etc.

Internal events are raised from the application, either by objects participating in the application or by user events in the context of the application or by the system, and are functionally related to the application. Internal events are further classified into:

- state events: these events indicate values that denote the state an object is in (e.g. object A is active)
- condition events: In the context of an application we need to represent conditions that relate to the content of a media objects. These conditions raise events that may be consumed to trigger other actions. The condition may be of the form: (pattern, obj_id) where pattern is a pattern that is detected in the media object identified by obj_id.
- transitional: such events represent continuous changes in object properties or inter-object relationships (e.g. object A goes_away_from object B, audio A1 fades_out, image A1 wipes in image A2)
- method events: Method events relate to the behaviour of entities participating in the application and correspond to the execution of a method, i.e. some user-defined operation on an object.

2.1. Event Modelling

An initial hierarchy that represents the aforementioned classification of events appears in fig. 1. The following is the definition of the class that represents generic events

```
class event
          string            name
          object_id         subject
          object_id_list    object
          action_list       actions
end
```

The attribute name is the string indicating the semantics of the event. The attribute subject denotes the object that raises the event while the attribute object denotes the list of objects that are related to the event, and that are affected by the occurrence of the event. When there are no affected (related objects) a null value is attached. The attribute actions indicates the actions that raise this event. These actions may be class methods, conditions that are fulfilled etc.

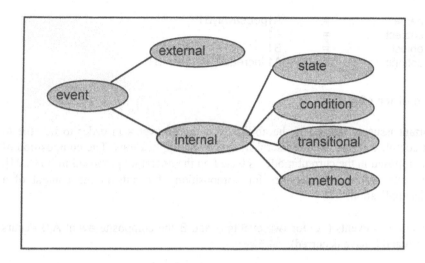

Fig. 1. An initial class hierarchy for representation of events

Examples of event definitions follow. Assume we want to represent the event e1 that is being raised when the time instance 7:42pm comes. We assume that there is a class timer that represents time intervals and has the method time_instance(t) that returns true when value t comes. Then the event e1, according to the aforementioned class is as follows:

```
name        =    e1
subject     =    timer1
object      =    null
actions     =    time_instance(7:42pm)
```

Assume that we want to represent the event that object A1 is active in an application window. According to [VAZ93] for an object that is active the method get_status returns TRUE. The corresponding state event instance (A1isActive) follows:

```
name        =    A1isActive
subject     =    A1
object      =    null
actions     =    (get_status = TRUE)
```

Another example demonstrating method events follows: assume we want to trap the invocation of the method start() when applied the video object V1. The corresponding event would be:

```
name        =    V1started
subject     =    V1
object      =    null
actions     =    start()
```

Finally the following event models the transitional event that is raised when object A1 goes away from object B1:

name	=	A1goesawayB1
subject	=	A1
object	=	B1
actions	=	A1.increase_distance(B1)

2.2. Composition of Events

An important issue of interest is the ability to compose events in order to be able to represent complex events that are useful in real world applications. The composition of events as proposed in the current model is based on the operators proposed in [GAT94]. We propose the following operators for composition of events in the content of a multimedia application:

";" conjunction of events (i.e. for two events A and B the composite event A;B occurs when both A and B have occurred).

"|" disjunction (i.e. for two events A and B the composite event A|B occurs when A or B has occurred)

":t:" sequential occurrence (i.e. for two events A and B the composite event A:t:B occurs when both A and B have occurred and B has occurred t time units after A)

Moreover we define the following functions:

TIMES (n, e) (which means that the event e has occurred n consecutive times)
IN (e,int) (which means that the event e has occurred during the time interval int)

Based on the above, we can define the temporal interval (according to the EBNF syntax):

```
temporal interval = (start, end)
start     = event |  time
end       =  event | time

event     = STRING | function
event     = event {"|", ";", ":t:" event}
```

In active database systems there is a wider repertoire of functions and operators for events[GAT94]. However, in the case of multimedia applications the above set of operators and functions that manipulate events is considered sufficient.

3. Actions (Spatial and Temporal composition)

In a simple model of operation, the manipulation of multimedia objects is based on the actions that modify the spatial, temporal or storage features of them. Hoepner [HOE91] defines actions as arbitrary acts that are classified into atomic and composed ones. Atomic actions cannot be subdivided into partial actions for the purpose of synchronisation while composed actions consist of atomic or other composed actions whose parts have to be synchronised. This classification is made mainly for synchronisation purposes so that atomic actions are used for synchronisation scenaria. The start and end points of an action are used as synchronisation points. Another classification of actions is attempted by [LIT91] where the actions are classified into unary, that adjust the multimedia objects according to the presentation requirements and binary, that compose the adjusted objects according to the presentation script.

Temporal Relationships
The topic of relations between temporal intervals has been addressed by [ALL83]. In that paper there is a definition of a complete set of temporal relations between two actions. These are: *before, during, overlaps, starts, ends, equal* and the inverse ones (this does not apply to equal). Adding vacant time intervals the set is extended with the sequential, *parallel first* and *parallel last* relations. In [VAZ93] a set of path operators that represent the aforementioned relationships are defined. This set defines the semantics of a synchronisation mechanism and the synchronisation of the presentation of multimedia objects. The operators which are also incorporated in the proposed model are: ∧, ∨, *, -t->. The semantics of the aforementioned operators are the following (see fig. 2.):

- The operators ∨ and ∧ cover the relationships *starts* and *ends* respectively.
- i*: The execution of the action will be repeated i consecutive times.
- A-t->B where A and B are temporal intervals and t is a value that indicates the temporal interval between the end of interval A and the beginning of temporal interval B. This operator covers the relationships *before* (for t>0), *meets* (for t=0), *during* (t<0 and |t|>duration A and duration B > duration A), *overlaps_with* (t<0 and |t|<durationA).

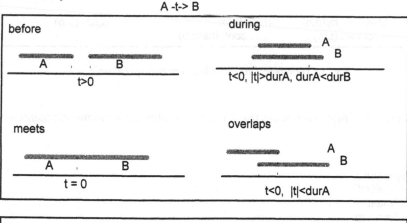

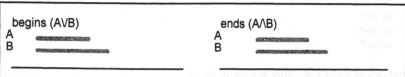

Fig. 2. The temporal operators that are defined and the relationships they represent

The formal definition of the operators based on the EBNF notation follow:

temporal operator
= "∧"
| "∨"
| "-"t"->"
| "i*"

where t is a temporal interval as defined above, and i is an integer.

Spatial Composition
Another aspect of composition is the spatial one, regarding the spatial ordering and overlapping features of the participating objects. There is a complete set of topological relationships describing the spatial relationships between two objects [EGE91]. Thus two objects p, q (see fig. 2.) may coincide (equal), overlap, touch_externally (meet), touch_internally (covers), be inside, lie outside, or be disjoint .

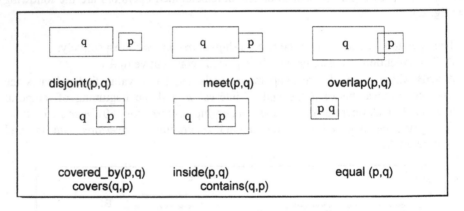

Fig. 3. Topological relations between two spatial objects

We define a set of binary operators that cover the topological relationships mentioned above

spatial operator
= "disjoint"
| "meet"
| "overlap"
| "covers"
| "inside"
| "equal"

The semantics of these operators appear in fig. 3.

4. Scenario Modelling

The scenario of an interactive multimedia application may be represented by a set of tuples indicating the functionality of particular actions. Scenario tuples can be represented by a class having the following attributes:

```
class scenario tuple
          event_expression          start_time
          event_expression          stop_time
          action_expression         action_list
          content_event_expression content_condition
          events                     synch_events
          constraint_expression      constraints
          boolean                    is_active
end
```

start_time: It represents the event expression that triggers the execution of the actions described in the action_list. The attribute stop_time represents the event expression that terminates the execution of this tuple.

action_expression: Represents the list of actions that will take place and their composition in the spatial and temporal domains.

content_condition: an expression that indicates a condition that refers to the content of the multimedia objects included in this scenario tuple. The content condition must be true in order for the particular scenario tuple to be executed. If it is true then an event may be raised. Such an event may be exploited in the start and/or stop events expression; for example one minute after the appearance of the dog in the video start the execution of the tuple.

synch_events: refers to the events generated at the beginning and at the end of the current tuple execution. These events may be exploited for synchronisation.

constraints: this filter represents a set of constraints that must be fulfilled during the execution of the scenario tuple. These constraints refer to either the spatial or the temporal domain. The constraint expression is a spatial and/or temporal constraint that must be true so that the tuple is executed. For example, a constraint would be to start the execution of a tuple not after 13:00pm or to start the tuple only if the application window is big enough for the participating objects to be displayed without cropping.

is_active: this Boolean attribute indicates whether the tuple is active (i.e. the actions described in the tuple are in the execution phase) or not. When the tuple is activated (i.e. when the start_time expression becomes true and the actions in the action_list are executed) this attribute becomes TRUE. Otherwise it is FALSE. This attribute may be used for communication and condition checking purposes among tuples.

4.1. An example of a scenario

We assume a presentation for Western Crete regarding musical and tourist events. There is popular music from the Chania and the Rethimno districts as well as local events that are happening through out the year. The scenario that we would like to capture for such an application (see fig. 4.) is the following:

Starting the application, the images of the two districts are presented while a background music fades in. When the user moves the button FOOD an audio object starts playing (either the music CHANIA_MUS or the music RETHIMNON_MUS depending on which region is closer to the button). Moreover the music volume increases as the button approaches the district while the volume decreases when the button goes away from the district.

When the button EVENTS is entirely in the Chania region, a video starts playing (either the video SUMMER_EVENTS if system time is in the summer season or GENERAL_EVENTS in all other times). Pressing the button EXIT the user ends the application.

This multimedia presentation may be represented according to the proposed model. The representation consists of different modules referring to:

- the events that will be utilised by the application (i.e. start scenario_tuples execution etc.),
- the multimedia objects that participate in the multimedia application, along with their spatial and temporal transformations.
- the scenario tuples that represent the sets of actions that will be triggered by specific events or event expressions.

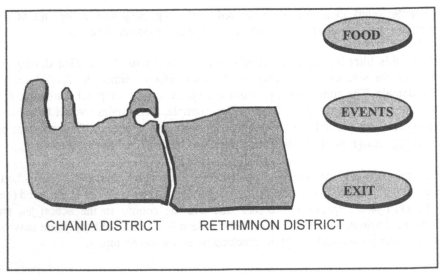

Fig. 4. The multimedia presentation of Western Crete.

The detailed description of the multimedia application follows:

events definition
In this module we represent the events that will trigger actions within the application.
The events are the following:

F_M (this event is raised when the button FOOD is moved by the user):

```
name     = F_M
subject  = b1
object   = NULL
action_list = b1.moving()
```

E_M (raised when the button EVENTS is moved by the user):

```
name     = E_M
subject  = b2
object   = NULL
action_list = b2.moving()
```

E_P (raised when the button EXIT is pressed the user):

```
name     = E_P
subject  = b3
object   = NULL
action_list = b1.button_down()
```

E_I_R (this event is raised when the button EVENTS is spatially in the area of object RETHIMNON_DISTRICT):

```
name     = E_I_R
subject  = b2
object   = NULL
action_list = b2.inside(s2)
```

E_I_C (this event is raised when the button EVENTS is spatially in the area of object CHANIA_DISTRICT):

```
name     = E_I_C
subject  = b2
object   = NULL
action_list = b2.inside(s1)
```

F_C_C (raised when the button FOOD approaches to CHANIA_DISTRICT):
```
name     = F_C_C
subject  = b1
object   = s1
action_list = b1.distance(s1).decreases()
```

F_C_R (raised when the button FOOD approaches to RETHIMNON_DISTRICT).
```
name     = F_C_R
subject  = b1
object   = s2
action_list = b1.distance(s2).decreases()
```

participating object definition:

We next define the objects participating in the application, according to the scheme presented in [VAZ95]. More specifically the media files, the temporal and/or spatial transformations and effects are described, and the spatial positions of the various objects in the application window are defined. According to [VAZ95] the multimedia objects are classified into temporal and spatial ones. The temporal are those that relate to time (sound, video) and spatial are those that relate to space(text, image, video). This classification is represented by the classes t_object and s_objet respectively. Class t_object represents the temporal features of a time dependent media object while the class s_object represents the spatial features of the media objects. In the case of a multimedia application we need to describe the participating media objects. However, in most of the cases the media objects are transformed (either spatially of temporally) in order to fulfil the application requirements. In the model presented in [VAZ95], these transformations are represented by the classes t_media_tuple, s_media_tuple. In the same paper the user interface element button is represented by the respective class as a subclass of class s_object. The objects that participate in the sample application are the following:

- *temporal objects*

The description of the temporal (i.e. audio) objects, along with their temporal transformations, that participate in the scene is following:

a1 (audio object described as background music):

```
t_media_tuple a1
attributes
        m_obj           =       "BACKGROUND MUSIC"
        t_scale_f       =       1
        t_start         =       0
        t_duration      =       null
        direction       =       TRUE
        effect_id       =       fade_in
end
```

a2 (audio object described as CHANIA_MUSIC music):
```
t_media_tuple a2
attributes
        m_obj           =       "CHANIA_MUSIC"
        t_scale_f       =       1
        t_start         =       0
        t_duration      =       null
        direction       =       TRUE
        effect_id       =       null
end
```

a3 (audio object described as RETHIMNON_MUSIC music).

```
t_media_tuple a3
attributes
        m_obj              = "RETHIMNON_MUSIC"
        t_scale_f          =    1
        t_start            =    0
        t_duration         =    null
        direction          =    TRUE
        effect_id          =    null
end
```

- *spatial objects*

The description of the spatial (i.e. text, image, video) objects along with their spatial transformations that participate in the scene is following:

s1 (the image for the Chania district):

```
s_media_tuple s1
attributes
        m_obj            =         "CHANIA_DISTRICT.bmp"
        t_scale_f        =         null
        t_start          =         null
        t_duration       =         null
        direction        =         null
        effect_id =      0
        x_coord          =         50
        y_coord          =         200
        a_width          =
        a_height         =
        effect_id        =         0
        s_scale_f        =         1
end
```

s2 (the image for the Rethimnon district):

```
s_media_tuple s2
attributes
        m_obj            =         "RETHIMNON_DISTRICT.bmp"
        t_scale_f        =         null
        t_start          =         null
        t_duration       =         null
        direction        =         null
        effect_id        =         0
        x_coord          =         350
        y_coord          =         200
        a_width          =
        a_height         =
        effect_id        =         0
        s_scale_f        =         1
end
```

s3 (the video for SUMMER_EVENTS):

```
s_media_tuple s3
attributes
```

```
        m_obj           =       "SUMMER_EVENTS.avi"
        t_scale_f       =       null
        t_start         =       0
        t_duration      =       15
        direction       =       TRUE
        effect_id       =       0
        x_coord         =       200
        y_coord         =       200
        a_width         =
        a_height        =
        effect_id       =       0
        s_scale_f       =       1
end
```

s4 (the video for GENERAL_EVENTS):

```
s_media_tuple s4
attributes
        m_obj           =       "GENERAL_EVENTS.avi"
        t_scale_f       =       1
        t_start         =       0
        t_duration      =       20
        direction       =       TRUE
        effect_id       =       0
        x_coord         =       200
        y_coord         =       200
        a_width         =
        a_height        =
        effect_id       =       0
        s_scale_f       =       1
end
```

b1 (for button FOOD):

```
button B1
attributes
        text            =       "FOOD"
        state           =       FALSE
        enabled         =       FALSE
        object_time     =       0
        t_length        =       0
        t_status        =       0
        t_scale_f       =       1.0
        looping         =       FALSE
        direction       =       TRUE
        m_width         =       100
        m_height        =       50
        plane           =       0
        transparency    =       0
        focus           =       FALSE
end
```

b2 (for button EVENTS):

button B2
attributes

text	=	"EVENTS"
state	=	FALSE
enabled	=	FALSE
object_time	=	0
t_length	=	0
t_status	=	0
t_scale_f	=	1.0
looping	=	FALSE
direction	=	TRUE
m_width	=	100
m_height	=	50
plane	=	0
transparency	=	0
focus	=	FALSE

end

b3 (for button EXIT).

button B3
attributes

text	=	"EXIT"
state	=	FALSE
enabled	=	FALSE
object_time	=	0
t_length	=	0
t_status	=	0
t_scale_f	=	1.0
looping	=	FALSE
direction	=	TRUE
m_width	=	100
m_height	=	50
plane	=	0
transparency	=	0
focus	=	FALSE

end

- *scenario definition*

We now define the application functionality in terms of scenario tuples that define the flow of the application in terms of events, actions and conditions. The first tuple (T1) starts at the start of the application (application_time = 0) and causes display of the CHANIA_DISTRICT and RETHIMNON_DISTRICT images as well playback of the background music:

scenario tuple   T1

start_time	=	0
stop_time	=	E_P
action_list	=	s1.execute() $\wedge$ s2.execute $\wedge$ s3.execute()
content_condition	=	null
synch_events	=	(_,_)
constraints	=	null
is_active	=	

end

The tuple T2(T3) starts playing the music CHANIA_MUS (RETHIMNON_MUS) when the button FOOD starts moving and is coming closer to CHANIA_DISTRICT (RETHIMNON_DISTRICT) than to RETHIMNON_DISTRICT (CHANIA_DISTRICT):

```
scenario tuple    T2
          start_time          =        F_M | (e22 ; F_M)
          stop_time           =        (T3.get_active() = true) | not (F_M) | E_P
          action_list         =        t2.execute()
          content_condition =          null
          synch_events        =        (_, e22)
          constraints         =        null
          is_active           =
end
```

```
scenario tuple    T3
          start_time          =        F_M | (e23 ; F_M)
          stop_time           =        (T2.get_active() = true) |    not (F_M) | E_P
          action_list         =        t3.execute()
          content_condition =          null
          synch_events        = (_, e23)
          constraints         =        null
          is_active           =
end
```

Tuple T4 starts when button EVENTS is entirely in the CHANIA_DISTRICT. Then the video SUMMER_EVENTS starts. The condition for this tuple to be executed is that the system time is in the summer period:

```
scenario tuple    T4
          start_time          =        E_I_C
          stop_time           =        E_P
          action_list         =        s3.execute()
          content_condition =          null
          synch_events        = (_, _)
          constraints         =        IN(sys_time, summer)
          is_active           =
end
```

Tuple T5 starts when button EVENTS is entirely in the CHANIA_DISTRICT. Then the video GENERAL_EVENTS starts. The condition for this tuple to be executed is that the system time is in not the summer period.

```
scenario tuple    T5
          start_time          =        E_I_C
          stop_time           =        E_P
          action_list         =        s4.execute()
          content_condition =          null
          synch_events        = (_, _)
```

```
            constraints     =      NOT(IN(sys_time, summer))
            is_active       =
end
```

Tuple T6 starts when button EXIT is pressed. The execution of this tuple causes the end of the application. The event E_P, described above, triggers the end of all actions in all the tuples that are active.

```
scenario tuple     T6
            start_time        =       E_P
            stop_time         =
            action_list       =       scene.exit()
            content_condition =       null
            synch_events      = (_, _)
            constraints       =       null
            is_active         =
end
```

Tuple T7 increases the volume of CHANIA_MUSIC as the button FOOD approaches to CHANIA district. The tuple is executed if tuple T2 is active (i.e. the CHANIA_MUSIC is being played back). Tuple T8 increases the volume of RETHIMNON_MUSIC as the button FOOD approaches to RETHIMNON district. The tuple is executed if tuple T3 is active (i.e. the RETHIMNON_MUSIC is played back).

```
scenario tuple     T7
            start_time        =       F_M
            stop_time         =       E_P
            action_list       =       t2.increase_volume()
            content_condition =       null
            synch_events      = (_, _)
            constraints       =       T2.get_active()=true
            is_active         =
end

scenario tuple     T8
            start_time        =       F_M
            stop_time         =       E_P
            action_list       =       t3.increase_volume()
            content_condition =       null
            synch_events      = (_, _)
            constraints       =       T3.get_active()=true
            is_active         =
end
```

5. Related Work

Work in the area of active databases and multimedia application modelling is relevant to the work presented here. As regards active databases, we exploited ideas from efforts that aim at modelling and manipulation of events. Previous work that models events and their composition is described in [GAT94]. This model is mainly related to active databases and classifies events in primitive and composite ones. Primitive events are further classified into Time, Method and Abstract events. Composite events are composed of primitive events according to a set of operators (";" conjunction, "|" disjunction, ":" sequential occurrence) and functions [GAT94].

As regards multimedia composition and synchronisation modelling there is a variety of approaches. In [LIT93] a model is presented for the representation and manipulation of relationships among temporal intervals. It introduces the concepts of temporal instant and interval and the actions of temporal access control: start, stop, fast forward, rewind, pause, resume. The innovative features of the proposed model are that it defines a set of n-ary operators for the representation of relationships among many temporal intervals. Moreover the inverse relationships are defined (binary and n-ary). Finally an algorithm for the evaluation of a temporal expression is introduced for calculation of the overall duration, and the time of the temporal composition. This model does not address the scenario concept at all. Moreover it is rather a temporal composition model rather than multimedia application representation scheme.

Another alternative view of synchronisation models is based on Petri Nets. The basic idea in these models is to represent various components of multimedia objects as places and describe their inter-relationships in the form of transitions. Timed Petri Nets have been extended to develop a model that is known as Object Composition Petri Nets [LIT93]. The particularly interesting features of this model are the ability to explicitly capture all the necessary temporal relations and to provide simulation of presentation in both forward and reverse directions. An OCPN can represent all thirteen possible temporal relations between two temporal intervals.

In another model, called Petri-Net-Based-Hypertext (PNBH), higher level browsing semantics can be specified. In this model, information units are treated as net places and links as net arcs. Transitions in a PNBH indicate traversal of a link or the browsing of information fragments. The segments of a PNBH can be played-out in random order, as selected by the user and restricted by the semantics of the net. The disadvantage of the Petri-net based models is that there is no mechanism to specify communication requirements and control functions for distributed composition objects.

Finally, another kind of models are the Object Oriented ones. The basic idea in this approach is to represent a real world thing or concept as an object. An object usually has an identifier, attributes, methods, a pointer to data etc. One such approach is the OMEGA system [CHA94]. In this model a multimedia object has attributes, relationships which are its value reference to other objects, components and methods. To facilitate the presentation of multimedia objects OMEGA uses temporal information associated with each object to calculate precedence and synchronisation between objects.

6. Conclusions and Research Directions

The approach presented in this paper is a first attempt for the description of complex multimedia applications. The formalism proposed is declarative thus facilitating shorter descriptions. More specifically the proposed model defines a framework in which

- complex events,
- complex actions,
- applications scenaria

may be defined in a declarative way.

There are several issues that need to be further investigated in the framework of this model:

Complete set of events
We need to investigate the design of a complete repertoire of events in all the categories mentioned in Section 2. The effort is especially difficult in the area of condition events. As regards transitional events, rich formalisms should be adopted in order to describe transition in a multimedia application adequately.

Spatial and temporal constraint checking at specification time
The scenario tuples indicate actions that will be executed when events occur. Event composition descriptions may not always be consistent with the application state or the system resources, and therefore mechanisms need to be devised for consistency checking.

Scenario execution
An important issue is how scenarios are executed. This is a complex issue since it involves resource allocation, disk management, device characteristics etc. It is to some extent an orthogonal issue to composition specification, but for realistic implementations it has to be taken into account.

References

[ALL83]. J. F. Allen: Maintaining Knowledge about Temporal Intervals, *Communications of the ACM*, Vol. 26, No. 11, November 1983, pp. 832-843.

[CHA94] A. Ghafoor (1994): Multimedia Databases Coursenotes, *ACM Multimedia 94 Conference*.

[EGE91] Egenhofer, M., Franzosa R: Point-Set Topological Spatial Relations, *International Journal of Geographic Information Systems*, Vol 5, No. 2, pp. 160-174.

[GAT94] S. Gatziu, K. Dittrich: Detecting Composite Events in Active Database Systens Using PetriNets, *Proc. of 4th Intl. Workshop on Research Issues in Data Engineering: Active database systems*, Texas, February, 1994

[HOE91] P. Hoepner: Synchronizing the Presentation of Multimedia Objects, *ACM SIGOIS*, January 1991, pp. 19-31.

[LIT91] T.Little, A. Ghafoor: Spatio-temporal Composition of Multimedia, *IEEE Computer*, Vol24, No. 10, October 91, pp. 42-50.

[LIT93] T.Little, A. Ghafoor: Interval-Based Conceptual Models for Tim-Dependent Multimedia Data, *IEEE Transactions on Data and Knowledge Engineering*, Vol. 5, No. 4, pp. 551-563, August 93.

[VAZ93] M. Vazirgiannis, M. Hatzopoulos: A Script Based Approach for Interactive Multimedia Applications, *Proceedings of the MMM (International Conference on Multi-Media Modelling) Conference*, Singapore, (November 9-12, 1993).

[VAZ95] M. Vazirgianis, M. Hatzopoulos: Integrated Multimedia Object And Application Modelling based on events and scenarios, *Proceedings of 1st IEEE International Workshop for MMDBMSs*, 8/1995, Blue Mountain Lake, NY (The Adirondacks).

Interactive Video and Remote Control via the World Wide Web

Klaus H. Wolf
Konrad Froitzheim
Michael Weber

Department of Distributed Systems
University of Ulm

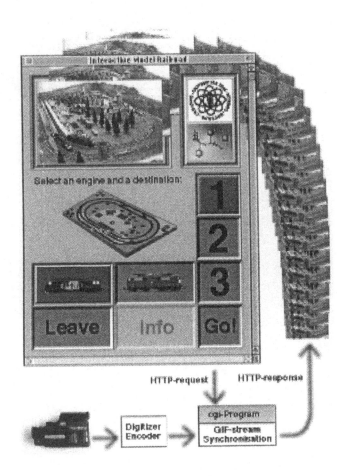

Abstract:

The World Wide Web (WWW) is the most accepted service in the internet providing a globally distributed hypermedia information system. Despite its tremendous growth the WWW lacks functionality beyond its basic request-response resp. download paradigm especially in the area of stream-oriented real-time media. Thus an important development direction for the WWW is the integration of such media into WWW pages. This paper considers methods to include moving images into WWW pages without changing existing standards or protocols. They are based on the multi-image capabilities of many image encoding standards. In combination with dialog elements the system provides interactive video in the World Wide Web. Video as visual feedback to user commands allows for a highly perceptible user interface compared to explicit confirmations. To demonstrate the concept's feasibility a prototype has been implemented and evaluated in an application scenario featuring remote control accompanied by remote visualization.

Keywords:

World Wide Web, remote control, interactive video, GIF

1.   Introduction

1.1   The World Wide Web

The World Wide Web (WWW) [WWW] is a globally distributed hypertext and hypermedia system. Hyperdocuments are non-linear documents containing links to other documents. The hyperdocuments served by the WWW are not restricted to text. Other media such as images, graphics, sounds, and movies can be referenced. A set of documents form the content of a WWW-page. The layout is controlled by an HTML-type document. HTML, the Hypertext Markup Language [HTML], is a text based document description, defined by an SGML document type definition (DTD) [DTD].

From a system architecture point of view the World Wide Web is a client-server system. Documents are exchanged between WWW-clients and WWW-servers using the Hypertext Transfer Protocol (HTTP) [Berne93]. The currently used protocol version, HTTP 1.0, defines a stateless request-response mechanism. To retrieve a WWW-page a transport system connection is established for each document, referenced on this page. The client requests the document by its name and the server responds transferring the document's data. Documents containing non-continuous media are typically downloaded first and presented afterwards. Even interactive elements, such as forms, use the same request-response mechanism. There is no provision of continuous connections between client and server.

The World Wide Web is currently rapidly growing to establish the largest hypertext information system world-wide. Such extensive usage demands advanced features and more flexibility than the system provides today. The system has intentionally been designed as a distributed information system linking locally available documents into a global hypertext document. But many applications, especially in the commercial domain require enhanced features like security, interactivity, transport efficiency, improved layout capabilities, and server-control over the client display. Some of these features, e.g. interactive elements and security, have already been added to the World Wide Web. Others, e.g. HTTP 2.0, are still in the design phase or under discussion. Most enhancements, however, are based on extensions to the used standards or even replacements for them facing a difficult deployment phase.

1.2 Media in the WWW

WWW mechanisms are media independent. Since the HTTP protocol is transparent to the type of documents it is handling, HTTP requests accesse documents by name only. Client and server negotiate media types using the MIME (Multipurpose Internet Mail Extensions) model. The server decides on the document type and returns a MIME type specification with the HTTP response. It is the client's responsibility to select the proper presentation method according to the document type.

WWW pages currently contain text, graphics and dialog elements. Presentation of other data and media is accomplished by external programs, so-called viewers. WWW clients do not directly support synchronous playback of stream oriented media such as audio and video. Audio and video are treated as files which are processed in three phases: retrieve, store in the file system, and present through a viewer. Usually, the presentation of such data begins after the document has been retrieved completely from a server. Thus continuous media cannot be displayed directly (inline) on a WWW-page.

Applications which require continuous updates of the client's view have to force the user to repeatedly retrieve a document [Crocker94]. Discussion on the inclusion of inline media other than graphics, e.g. audio [Uhler94] and video, is currently very lively. How this integration can be achieved is subject to active research. New protocols, protocol elements and extensions to HTML have been proposed [Soo94], [KaasPinTaub94]. However, changes to existing standards widely and intensively used should be done very carefully, and if possible, they should be avoided altogether.

1.3 Image and Movie Formats in the WWW

Although the WWW supports many media formats only a small number of formats is actually used. By far the most widely deployed image format is Compuserve's GIF (Graphics Interchange Format [GIF87]). GIF has been designed for the Compuserve network and has been adopted by the internet community. In the internet not all capabilities of the standard are exploited yet. Software on the internet usually exploits only a subset of the features required to encode images. Other commonly used image formats are JFIF (JPEG File Interchange Format) of the Joint Photographic Experts Group [JPEG] and the X Window system's text-based bitmap encoding (XBM). The JPEG encoding scheme is superior to GIF if applied to continuous-tone images. Its usage is growing fast since the major WWW clients support inline JPEG images.

A standard movie format is the ISO standard MPEG (Moving Pictures Expert Group) [MPEG]. Quicktime and Video for Windows are other movie formats in use, but they are not vendor and platform independent. Nevertheless they can be decoded on nearly all platforms depending on the availability of the proper decoder software on each client system. The decoders are external programs because these data types are not decoded directly by WWW clients. Thus movies are presented off-line after the movie files have been retrieved and stored locally.

2. Pushing the Limits

2.1 Moving Images

All components of the World Wide Web are currently developing. One of the directions is the integration of stream oriented media into WWW pages. Movie delivery via WWW tends to develop towards inline decoding of MPEG within WWW clients. On the one hand it is not foreseen when such clients will become available. On the other hand, realtime encoding of MPEG streams from live sources requires considerable hardware resources at the server sites.

However, there are application scenarios which require moving images based on other formats and mechanisms. Remote control and remote visualization are applications making use of realtime generated animated computer graphics or live video. In contrast to MPEG, still image decoders are readily available in the WWW clients. They can be used to show sequences of images which are perceived as videos if the images replace each other at a reasonable rate.

Regardless of the actually chosen video stream format a client has to support continuous decoding explicitly. The WWW client has to be able to retrieve documents concurrently and present them continuously while successive data arrives. The implementation architecture of the WWW clients must be event and data driven. Clients must not block while retrieving a document.

2.2 Sequence of Still Images

One method for animated graphics or video is the consecutive transmission of individual images. Instead of terminating the transport system connection after transmitting an image, the server continues to send images until the client terminates the connection. Not only images can be animated this way, but also other document types, e.g. text. This leads to a new communication model of the HTTP connection where more than just one document is transferred during the lifetime of a connection.

However this animation method has some disadvantages. Combination of a series of documents to a single structure which fits into an HTTP response requires a description of the contents of the response. This means the addition of a new layer of control structures in between the document layer and the HTTP protocol layer. Existing WWW clients and servers have to be modified in order to deal with streams of documents instead of single documents.

The method allows to exploit the existing decoder software of WWW clients. It supports all image formats including GIF and JPEG. The major disadvantage of such a pseudo animation, if used for moving images, is the fact that always entire images have to be encoded and transmitted. The encoded animation contains considerable redundancy. All images are encoded completely independent from each other. They all contain header information and often encode the same unchanged image parts over and over again.

2.3   Image Streams

Some image formats are not restricted to single images. They describe the encoding of a sequence of consecutive images. Examples are the PNG [PNG95] and GIF formats. Recent specifications of GIF allow for an infinite sequence of images. The images can be of different size and depth within a global rectangle. The possibility to encode differently sized image parts permits simple frame differencing as an optimization method. Of course, the extent of data reduction due to frame differencing depends on the encoded sequence. But a large number of applications, especially in the remote control and process visualization area, rely on animated graphics displays with only slight changes from image to image. Many publicly available GIF-viewers support this multi-image feature. It is indeed possible to present a movie with these viewers.

An image stream encoded in a multi-image format is accessed through hyperlinks as any other document. The WWW client opens the transport system connection, sends the HTTP request and waits for the response. The response contains HTTP header information and the image stream as HTTP body. The HTTP header indicates the document type to the client encoded in a string consisting of type and subtype, e.g. image/gif. This document type description does not have to be changed in order to support multiple images. A GIF encoded image sequence will have the same document type as single images. A single image is regarded as a special case of a sequence containing only one image.

The main advantage of image stream formats compared to sequences of separated images is the possibility to exploit format specific optimization methods like frame differencing. In addition image streams are backward compatible to WWW clients which do not support moving images. Clients, which do not support the multiple image feature of multi-image capable formats but tolerate them, will show the first image of the sequence. They will terminate the connection after having decoded the first image or just stop decoding.

3.   A Prototype Implementation

3.1   Client Software

WWW clients supporting the multi-image option of multi-image graphics formats will automatically present a video when decoding an image sequence. This implies for the most widely used image format, GIF, that clients have to support at least the GIF87a specification. Most WWW clients, however, do not support this specification entirely, i.e. they particularly ignore the multi-image feature. This is due to the fact that GIF has been used in the internet only for the encoding of still images.

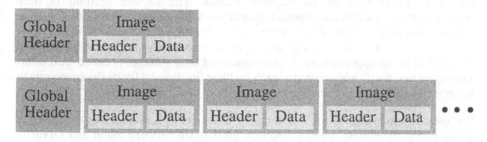

Figure 1: The format of a GIF image (upper) and a GIF stream (lower).

However, treatment of multiple images can easily be added to existing GIF decoder software. A GIF sequence consists of a global header and a series of separately encoded images (Figure 1). The difference between a GIF stream and a GIF image is only the number of images following the global header. There is no additional information or control structure accompanying the existence of more than one image. The global header does not contain information about the number of subsequent images.

An investigation of available GIF image decoder software showed that the required changes for an upgrade from an image decoder to a stream decoder are very small. Thus we modified the GIF decoders of two publicly available WWW clients (Chimera, Mosaic) in such a way that they continue decoding as long as the GIF data stream does not terminate. The modified versions present moving images on a WWW page until the WWW server stops sending images.

3.2   Server Software

A video stream is accessed like any other document via its universal resource identifier or locator (URI/URL). The server transmits documents regardless of type and size. It does not notice if a document is written to disk or directly decoded by the client. Therefore a video stream will be transmitted like any other document. For the simplest case of a pre-recorded video which has been encoded in a multi-image capable format there are no changes required to the server system at all.

Usually WWW servers try to transmit documents as fast as possible. That is the reason why the frame rate at the client display depends on the quality of the transport system connection. The rate may be too high in a local environment and too low over slow links. The first case results in time-compressed presentation of the video. The later creates a backlog of frames, defeating the realtime capabilities. Our experiments showed that some changes to the server system are very useful in order to provide controlled and smooth delivery of image sequences.

We identified three different approaches to show image sequences. In the first approach, called 'best effort' method, transmission and decoding is performed as fast as possible with the assumption that the connection is either slower or just fast enough for realtime display. If a transport system connection is not fast enough for realtime display the frame rate will be low. Anyway such a system will show each image of a sequence. There will be no skipped frames. The second method is time synchronisation. A video transmission system providing time synchronisation tries to transmit only those images of a sequence which fit into the time scale of the video. It will skip images if transmission or display are too slow and it will delay playback at the receiver in the opposite case. A combination of both schemes is called 'best effort with upper rate limit', which tries to reach realtime display and limits the frame rate to an upper bound.

The latter two methods require a component which controls playback at the client. In addition this component needs a feedback mechanism between client and server in order to avoid overflowing of the client's storage space. Synchronization by the client, however, would require a major change to the client's software. We therefore propose time synchronization by the server. A software module in the server controls the transmission speed between video source and the WWW client.

3.3 Server Extension

The World Wide Web software provides a standardized method to include server side extensions called Common Gateway Interface (CGI). It has been designed to allow access to other information systems than WWW, e.g. WAIS or Gopher. But the CGI can be used to feed all kinds of data into the WWW system. In principle the CGI is an extension of the WWW name space of Universal Resource Identifiers to cover not only files but also the output of executable programs (figure 2).

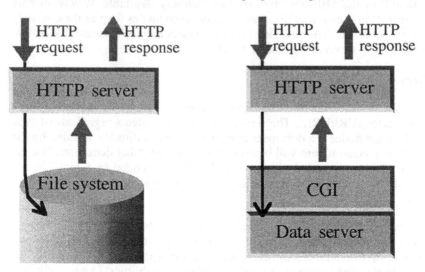

Figure 2:   HTTP servers can be extended via the common gateway interface (CGI). A URI points to an executable program (right) instead of a file.

3.3.1   Solution of Related Projects

Currently the Netscape server-push specification [Netscape95] provides the easiest way to include live video into WWW pages. A CGI program feeds a sequence of single images to the HTTP connection. These images are usually retrieved from the WWW server's file system, i.e. a hard disk. The file system serves as a mediator between the frame grabber and multiple clients. It decouples the transmission rates of the HTTP connections and the data rate of the frame grabber. But the detour through the file system prooves disadvantageous at higher frame rates or higher system load. The number of simultaneous connections is limited by the I/O bandwidth of the file system.

3.3.2   The WebVideo Approach

We designed and implemented a CGI program as video extension to the server, which works entirely in the main memory of the server. It establishes an image database in memory in order to avoid unnecessary file system accesses. This synchronizing CGI program feeds video streams to HTTP servers. It is invoked by the server in response to a request for an image stream from the client. The CGI program is highly flexible by allowing different synchronisation mechanisms, video sources and output formats.

Supported synchronisation mechanisms are:
- best effort, (cf. section 3.2)
- best effort with rate limit, or
- near realtime presentation using frame skipping or delayed transmission.

Synchronisation mechanism, frame rate and upper rate bounds are adjustable by the provider of hypertext documents. They can either be encoded into the URI or be fixed to a certain value. Encoding into the URI allows flexible adjustment for different streams.

Supported video sources are:
- a file,
- a portion of a file addressed by frame numbers,
- a stream from a camera (live source), or
- a single image of an image stream from a camera.

In addition to synchronized playback of pre-recorded sequences the video extension is able to retrieve an image sequence from a system queue. The system queue is a named shared memory space which can be fed by any live video source, e.g. a camera/frame grabber combination. In addition to synchronized streams the system supports extraction of single images. Single images can be used to provide snapshots for directories of streams or to build WWW pages which do not contain stream oriented documents while being up to date though.

Supported output formats are:
- a graphics stream encoded in GIF (cf. section 2.3) or
- sequences of still images encoded in JPEG or GIF (cf. section 2.2).

The encoding of sequences of still images follows the specification of Netscape for server-push animation. The default output format chosen by the server is GIF. However the CGI program automatically recognizes if the connected client supports the JPEG format. In this case the still images contained in the sequence will be encoded in JPEG rather than GIF to save transmission bandwidth due to JPEG's higher compression rates.

For performance and availability reasons the World Wide Web relies on caching at different levels. Clients maintain local caches and institutions use caching WWW servers, called proxies, to reduce remote accesses. In the case of live video and animated graphics caching has to be avoided. Playback of a pre-recorded video stream from file will not be synchronized if the file is retrieved from a cache rather than from the synchronizing server extension. To avoid caching the server marks stream oriented documents as already expired.

3.4   Supporting Multiple Clients

A shared system queue as stream source allows the CGI program to support multiple WWW clients at the same time without significant performance degradation (Figure 3).

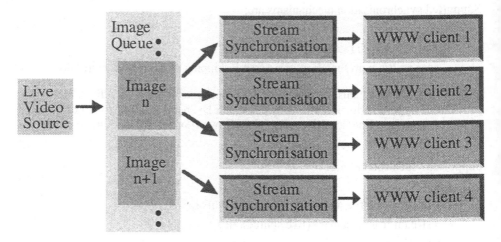

Figure 3:   Many instances of synchronizing CGI programs retrieve the image stream simultaneously. Each of them serves one remote WWW client.

A video stream from a live source is encoded once in one of the supported image or stream formats. Each encoded image of the stream is put into a shared memory space to be accessible for the synchronizing CGI programs. Many instances of stream synchronizers may retrieve the encoded images simultaneously from the shared space of the image queue. They may even retrieve different images at the same time to keep up with the state of their client connections. Encoding the stream only once allows many clients to connect to a live source at the same time without overloading the server computationally.

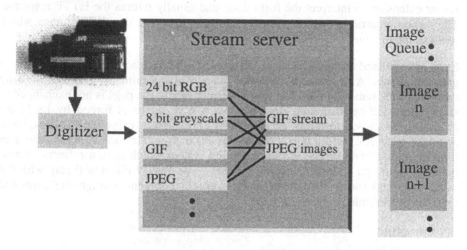

Figure 4: The stream server converts between the image format of a live source and the stream/image format used in the World Wide Web. The converted images are put into a shared memory queue.

An image stream from a live source is encoded by a stream server which fills the shared memory queue for the synchronizing CGI programs (figure 4). The stream server's front-end connects directly to the live video source resp. digitizer. Its back-end serves a number of stream synchronizers via the shared memory queue described above. The main purpose of the stream server is to convert from the image data format of the video source to the target stream format for transmission to the WWW clients. The front-end comprises several image decoder modules which accept different image formats. The back-end is currently equipped with GIF and JPEG encoders.

4. An Interactive Application

Live images are often produced by monitoring systems, either video taken from a camera or computer graphics generated by software. Many remote monitoring systems allow interaction of a user. Such remote control requires a user command channel from the display to the monitored system. The controlled system's feedback is then visually presented as a stream of computer graphics or live video from a camera.

4.1 User Interaction in WWW

The World Wide Web supports user interaction via forms. Forms are encoded as part of the base HTML document. They can contain different user interface elements like buttons, menus and text input fields. User input is not transmitted continuously but is collected by the client and transferred to the server on request of the user. Thus the transmission of user input fits seemlessly into the request-response mechanism of

HTTP. The collected results of user interaction are encoded in a URI and sent with the HTTP request. The server extracts information from the URI, processes it using a server extension to interpret the form data, and usually returns the HTTP response. The response carries a confirmation for the user input as a new WWW page which replaces the old one.

Explicit command confirmations are not necessary if feedback is given visually as a graphics stream. A remote control WWW page contains animated graphics showing the state of the remote system and forms for user input. The page is not exchanged to show command confirmation. Instead, the WWW server is forced by its forms evaluating extension to return an empty HTTP response (using the 'No Response' response code 204) to the client. The form evaluating extension forwards the user input in an adequate format to the controlled system which in turn reflects its new bahaviour through a video or graphics stream. The WWW client will stay with the same page and shows the effect to the controlled system through the animated graphics or live video parts of the page.

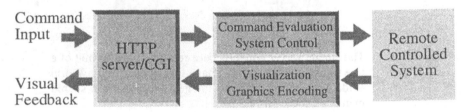

Figure 5:   User commands evaluated by server extensions control system parameters. Visualization of feedback fed into the WWW by another server extension.

4.2   A Sample Scenario

We built a model railroad layout in our laboratory as remote controlled system to serve as an example proving the capabilities of inline video within the proposed WWW environment.

Encoding and decoding of GIF is fast enough to allow about 5 QCIF sized frames per second in our set-up. We tested the performance in a local environment with a Sun workstation as server and Sun and Macintosh clients. Limiting factor in our demonstration scenario are the speed of the available frame grabber and the color conversions (dithering, colormap merging) for 8 bit pseudo color X-Window displays.

We do not exploit the frame differencing capabilities of GIF streams yet. We will add this feature to both the GIF encoder and WWW clients in the near future. We expect higher frame rates because encoder and decoder will have to process only the changed image parts. This will result in a speedup which is proportional to the relation between static and dynamic parts.

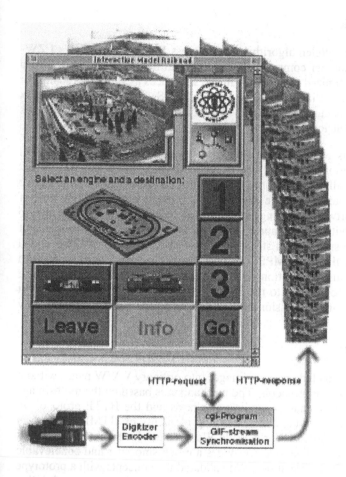

Figure 6: Remote WWW users can operate the model railroad and watch it in realtime.

The HTTP request shown in the picture is issued in order to get the contents of the inline image which is referenced by the base HTML document. The URI points to a stream synchronizing server extension. This server extension gets images from a live camera. The response to the HTTP request is an infinite image stream displayed at the client as video.

An HTML form is used to submit commands to the WWW server. The server forwards the commands to the model railroad controller via a serial interface. After hitting the 'Go!'-button the chosen train begins to move to the selected destination. An additional confirmation is not necessary.

4.3   Real Application

We are currently integrating the system with the World Wide Web front-end of a biochemical synthesis laboratory. Up to now clients of the laboratory have requested synthesis of oligonucleotides from remote via the WWW front-end. The synthesis has been done offline by a robot and the results with printed descriptions have been sent back via the postal service.

Soon clients will operate the robot from remote and watch the synthesis. The status will be displayed as a live video showing the equipment and as a graphics animation of the changing absorption spectrum. A client can dynamically modify synthesis parameters or even stop the process in case of problems. Of course the product has still to be sent with the postal service, but the client knows about its quality instantly.

5. Future Work

GIF uses the Lempel-Ziv-Welch algorithm to compress bitmaps. UNISYS's LZW-copyright may lead to another common image format in the Web. We hope that a successor will support optimized encoding of image sequences as well. Candidates for a replacement of GIF are Planetary Data System (PDS) and Portable Network Graphics (PNG), which is currently developed by Compuserve. Both specifications mention multi-image extensions.

Upcoming WWW clients which support inline presentation of MPEG streams will allow integration of video into the WWW at much lower bandwidth than the current solutions. This is especially true for pre-encoded movies. But transmission of live video from a camera requires realtime encoding. Due to the computational cost of motion compensation software encoding, desktop computers are currently not able to deliver MPEG streams with high compression rates. The bandwidth requirements of such MPEG streams are smaller, but still comparable to a sequence of JPEG coded images. However we will add an MPEG backend to the stream server mentioned above. This means not just integration of available MPEG encoder software. The MPEG software has to be adapted to the stream server system in order to support multiple clients at different transmission rates at the same time while it encodes only once.

6. Conclusions

We presented a scheme to include moving images into ordinary WWW pages without changing existing standards or protocols. The mechanism is based on the multi-image capabilities present in many image encoding standards and the HTTP protocol. In combination with the already standardized dialog elements of HTML the system provides interactive video for the World Wide Web. Visual feedback to commands through animated graphics or live video provides a much smoother and concievable user interface than explicit confirmations. We validated the concepts with a prototype implementation and the successful operation of a remote control scenario with inline video.

References

[Berne93]   Tim Berners-Lee; *Hypertext Transfer Protocol - A Stateless Search, Retrieve and Manipulation Protocol*; 1993; http://www.w3.org/hypertext/WWW/Protocols/Overview.html

[Crocker94]   G. Crocker: web2mush: *Serving Interactive Resources to the Web*, 1994; http://www.ncsa.uiuc.edu/SDG/IT94/Proceedings/DDay/crocker/tech.html

[Uhler94]   S. Uhler: *Incorporating real-time audio on the Web*, 1994; http://www.ncsa.uiuc.edu/SDG/IT94/Proceedings/DDay/uhler/uhler.html

[GIF87]   CompuServe, Incorporated: *CompuServe GIF 87a*, http://icib.igd.fhg.de/icib/it/defacto/company/compuserve/gif87a/gen.html

[Soo94]　　　　　　J. C. Soo: *Live Multimedia over HTTP*, 1994;
http://www.ncsa.uiuc.edu/SDG/IT94/Proceedings/DDay/soo/
www94a.html

[KaasPinTaub94]　　M. F. Kaashoek, T. Pinckney, J. A. Tauber: *Dynamic
Documents: Extensibility and Adaptability in the WWW*, 1994;
http://www.ncsa.uiuc.edu/SDG/IT94/Proceedings/DDay/pinck
ney/dd.html

[JPEG]　　　　　　International Organization for Standardization: *Information
Technology - Digital Compression and Coding of Continous-
tone Still Images*; ISO/IEC DIS 10918-1; ISO 1991.

[MPEG]　　　　　International Organization for Standardization: *Information
Technology - Coding of moving pictures and associated audio
for digital storage up to about 1.5 Mbit/s*; ISO/IEC DIS
11172; ISO 1992.

[PNG95]　　　　　T. Boutell, M. Adler, L. D. Crocker, T. Lane: *PNG (Portable
Network Graphics) Specification*, 1995;
http://sunsite.unc.edu/boutell/png.html

[Netscape95]　　　Netscape Communications Corporation: *An Exploration of
Dynamic Documents*; 1995;
http://home.netscape.com/assist/net_sites/dynamic_docs.html

[WWW]　　　　　*The World Wide Web Consortium*;
http://www.w3.org/hypertext/WWW/

[HTML]　　　　　*Specification of the HyperText Markup Language*;
http://www.w3.org/pub/WWW/MarkUp/MarkUp.html

[DTD]　　　　　　*SGML Document Type Definition of the HyperText Markup
Language*;
http://www.w3.org/pub/WWW/MarkUp/html3/html3.dtd

Radio on Demand

K. Reimann and D. Rüffler

Technical University Berlin

Abstract. This paper describes a petri net inspired interaction specification formalism with an application to a radio on demand service: InfoRadio-on-Demand. A prototype of a Tele Commerce application with a hybrid architecture: www, e-mail and e-cash store.

1 Background

In our workgroup Interactive Information Systems we focus on the following topics: Internet goes Business, WWW Showcases for Newspapers, Banks, Research Institutes, Radio stations. Integration of MultiMedia TeleServices (MMTS) in WWW. One objective of our research activities is the integration of classical media in WWW. We design prototypes of converters, multimedia services and distribution schemes. These are offered to internet aware content providers.

We focus on transformations of old media into new me dia. We are interested in the implications of a transformational trial. Which dimensions are lost and which are new. Will the former content provider or distributer still be able to distribute the new product?

Since may the 12th 1995 we provide the service digiTaz in internet [SM95]. We cooperate with InfoRadio of SFB/ORB [IR]. An overview of the activities of our project is to obtain from our media page [WP].

2 Introduction

Designing multimedia services involves peoples with different roles in a communication between solution provider and content provider. They need a common base of communication. In this paper [RoD] an Interaction Specification Formalism is presented. It offers graphical elements to model an interactive information system with respect of the time dimension. This formalism is not automated. It is bound to notes on a sheet of paper.

InfoRadio-on-Demand is a service which is designed by a small group of developers. In the design phase the form sheets were applied. The documentation of the system contains digitized graphs of this formalism. It is shown how close

* The work discussed in this paper was performed in the context of BERKOM [DTB], where many of the ideas were born. We would like to acknowledge the discussions with our colleagues Stephan Frühauf and Dirk Kuhlmann.

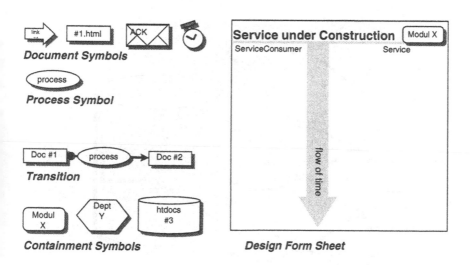

106

structural elements of the formalism and the service constituting windows are correlated.

InfoRadio-on-Demand is a prototype of a Tele Commerce application. Its architecture is hybrid, i.e. it is composed of different internet services. WWW is used as the general platform to present the service. Billing and message handling are important building blocks of this Tele Commerce application.

3 Interaction Specification Formalism

We refer to diagrammatic schemes of structures which offer a representation of states, transitions and tokens as petri net oriented. We leave out the representation of to kens. So the formalism is just petri net inspired. We want to keep the alternating appearance of states and transitions. Any violation of this syntax should be referred to as a weak or inconsistent design.

3.1 Basic Elements and a Form

Fig. 1.: Basic Graphic Elements of the Interaction Specification Formalism

Figure 1 shows the basic graphical elements and a form of the interaction specification formalism. We have rectangles representing documents. We do not distinguish tokens and documents. Transitional processes are represented by circles. Gray circles represent modules of the information system under construction.

A state is a set of documents. In the most cases only one document. A transition is the sequence of one or more documents on the input side transformed by a process into one or more documents on the output side. So far with the petri net metaphor.

We add a design form which motivates the distinction of functional roles and sites as well as some alignment to the flow of time. To avoid an overload of the form we offer some containment symbols. These symbols might be used to refer to refining forms or just to subsume piles of documents. Empty forms are handed out to people involved in the design process. They scribble their process structure in this form respecting the offered elements, syntax and the flow of time. These forms are the basis for discussions with project partners.

3.2 A Simple Sequence

Let's try to find words for the simple example shown in figure 2.

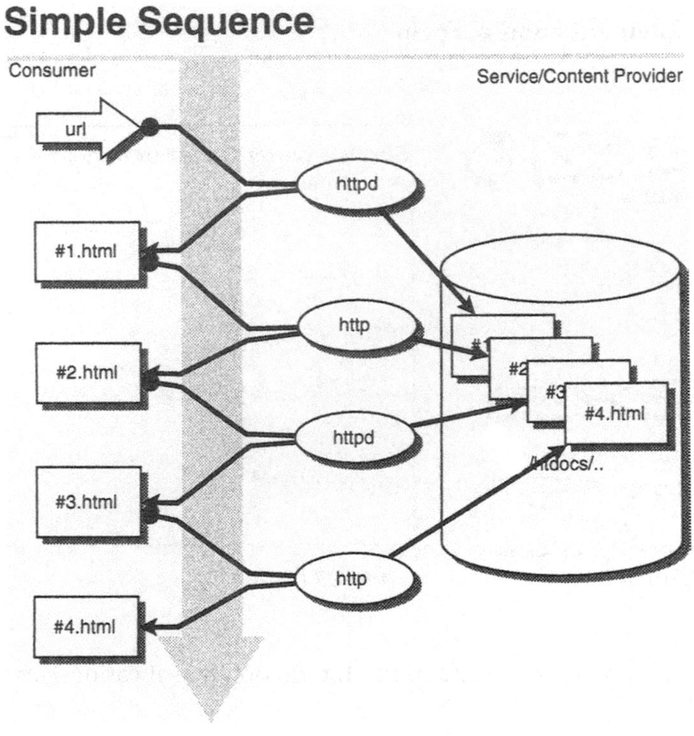

Simple Sequence

Consumer   Service/Content Provider

url

httpd

#1.html

http

#2.html

#2

#3

#4.html

httpd

/htdocs/..

#3.html

http

#4.html

Fig. 2.: An Example: A simple Sequence

A consumer knows about a URL, received via e-mail, informed guess or from a print medium. He or she enters it to his or her preferred web viewer and follows it. This URL represents the first state of the interaction process. Let us assume that the URL puts the consumer on some kind of guided tour. A reply informs the consumer about a state transition in his or her interaction flow with the information system. Between these two documents or states resides a transitional process and a crossing of organisational or functional borders.

More complex notations would be obtained if the tour crosses the borders of sites or if dynamic documents or a change of information systems i.e. from www to e-mail occurs.

4 InfoRadio-on-Demand, a Design Example

InfoRadio is a joint programme of the Ostdeutscher Rundfunk (ORB) and of the Sender Freies Berlin (SFB). It is a new 24 hours word programme for the region of Berlin and Brandenburg. The programme scheme offers news every 20 minutes. In between are placed features and indepth coverage of news.

The innovation of this transmitter is three fold. It is the first 24 hours word programme in germany. It is a joint project of two big stations which stem from the former different parts of germany.

But the main innovation lies in technology. The production of the programme is free of analog technologies. The audiofiles are stored in MPEG Layer 2 format [MC].

4.1 Interaction Specification

Figure 3 shows an overview of the information or module structure the website of InfoRadio offers. Most of it contains static documents which implies simple sequences as shown in figure 2.

The complex and interesting module is "Order a take" as shown in figure 4. It contains dynamic documents. Only the httpd process delivers static documents. It contains a switch in information systems and some off-line media types or consumer side processes.

Again I try to "illustrate" the interaction specification form.

First the consumer follows a link represented by the URL which causes the deliverance of the take-order-form. This happens immediatelly. This form offers some links to other modules like info-, archive or help services. If the consumer chooses to fill out the order form and submits it he or she will receive a web based acknowledge message that contains all entered parameters. Due to the time and date parameters entered, a longer phase of waiting might start now. Imagine that the consumer visited the programme page before and he knows about a feature to take place the other day. No matter how long it lasts the web is not the right medium to proceed with. In any way the respond time of such an order service will be longer than interaction with an undistributed interactive in formation system with static media elements. It should be evident to the consumer that he now has to wait for some time. The acknowledge message contains a hint to this situation.

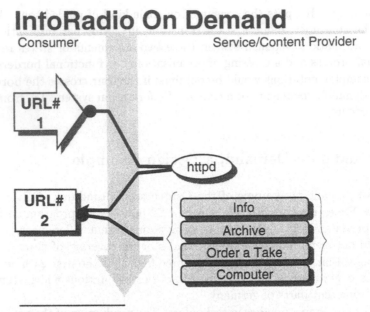

InfoRadio On Demand

Consumer   Service/Content Provider

URL#1: http://webforce.prz.tu-berlin.de/InfoRadio
URL#2: http://webforce.prz.tu-berlin.de/InfoRadio/index.html

Fig. 3.: An Application: InfoRadio-on-Demand

A scheduler controls the beginning of all pending processes like sampling, notification and cleanup. The call of the sampling process is generated immediately after receiving the order. It is registered using the standard unix command crontab.

The notification is triggered by the termination of the sampling process. Mainly it is the deliverance of a precompiled e-mail with an html part.

The cleanup process is started some hours after the generation of the audio file. This is a service quality the consumer might select due to its expectations when he or she might be able to pick up the result.

The latter process is not always a part that the consumer is confronted with. The consumer goes ahead with reading the notification e-mail. If the e-mail reader of the consumer is configured to detect html attachments he or she is able to proceed in webstyle. The browser displays the html part of the e-mail. It contains a link to the recorded audiofile. Note: it does not contain the audio data itself! This is due to the choosen billing solution which is invoked by a GET-Re quest which is issued by clicking on an audio icon within the notification e-mail.

Following the link doesn't directly delivers the audio file. In our case we considered the realisation of a DigiCash store [DC1] for accounting purposes. After accepting an ecash payment request the selling process delivers the audiofile. Finally the consumer might save it.

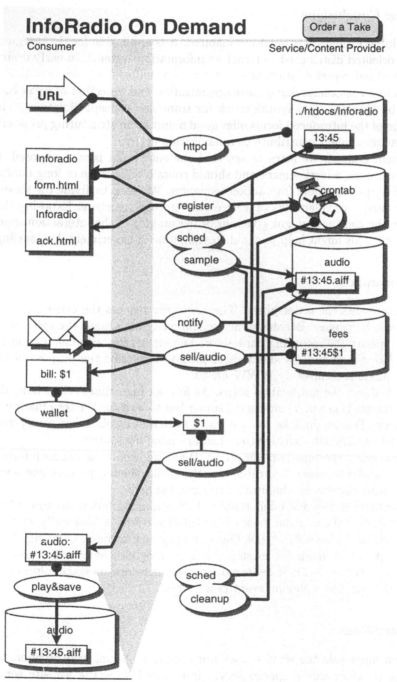

InfoRadio On Demand

Order a Take

Consumer   Service/Content Provider

URL

../htdocs/Inforadio

13:45

httpd

Inforadio form.html

register

crontab

Inforadio ack.html

sched

sample

audio

#13:45.aiff

notify

fees

sell/audio

#13:45$1

bill: $1

wallet

$1

sell/audio

audio: #13:45.aiff

sched

play&save

cleanup

audio #13:45.aiff

URL: http://webforce.prz.tu-berlin.de/InfoRadio/audioform.htm

Fig. 4.: InfoRadio-on-Demand: Order a Take

4.2 Some Conclusions

The introduced formalism is petri net inspired. It is applicable for the design of document oriented distributed in teractive information systems. In early design phases the visual representation helps to create a uniform anticipation among developers and customers. Some basic optimization and detection of weak concepts can be obtained by a syntax check for transition concept violations. The final version of the introduced forms offer good naming and structuring proposals and at least they might contribute to a navigation system.

As system designer we learn or see that the entrypoint is very exposed. It might appear in an advertisement and should contain no strange or long names. We should try to keep short Interaction sequences. We learn to divide the service in subtasks and receive an idea of a necessary storage structure. Exposing this diagram to the consumer might give him or her an idea of the interaction space of the service. This might help to avoid wasting time in experimental netsurfing.

4.3 Appearance

Figure 5 represents the order phase. The consumer reaches the order form via the InfoRadio homepage. Besides some general navigation items the form offers handles to specify the recording parameters and elementary communication information like e-mail address and a short memo to describe the purpose of the take. This phase is completely WWW based.

Figure 6 shows the notification steps. At first an immediate echo about the order parameters is given. Then the consumer has to wait for the termination of the recording. This might take some days. A switch of media takes place, from an interactive multimedia archive to a message handling system.

Figure 7 shows the consumption phase. What we need is an access information for the audiofile, some control about the audio playing process and some kind of an authorisation mechanism to retrieve the audio.

The webbrowser displays a deliverable which contains a link to an audiofile in the central store of the take database of the InfoRadio site. Additionally we see a manually activated gain control tool. Our micropayment scenario with DigiCashs ecash store [DC3] demands the existence of a running electronic wallet process. After payment the audio file is delivered. A visual netscape message informs the consumer that an audio playing event takes place.

4.4 Conclusions

On the consumer side the service does not require a special web browser. On the service provider side a special server is required. It is the website server of SiliconGraph ics. The communication between browser and server is based besides the ordinary http protocol on the common gateway interface [CGI].

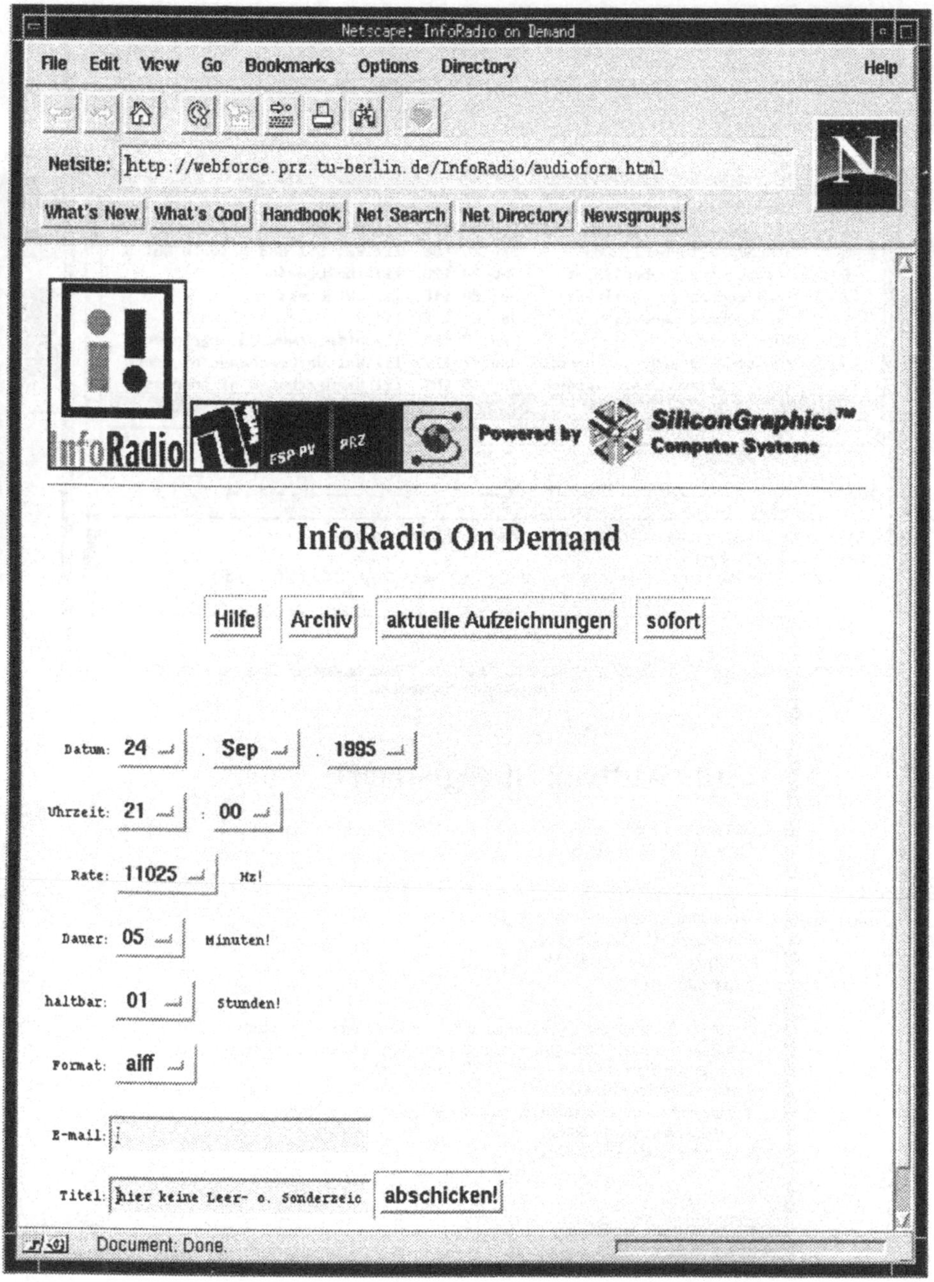

Fig. 5.: InfoRadio-on-Demand: Order Phase

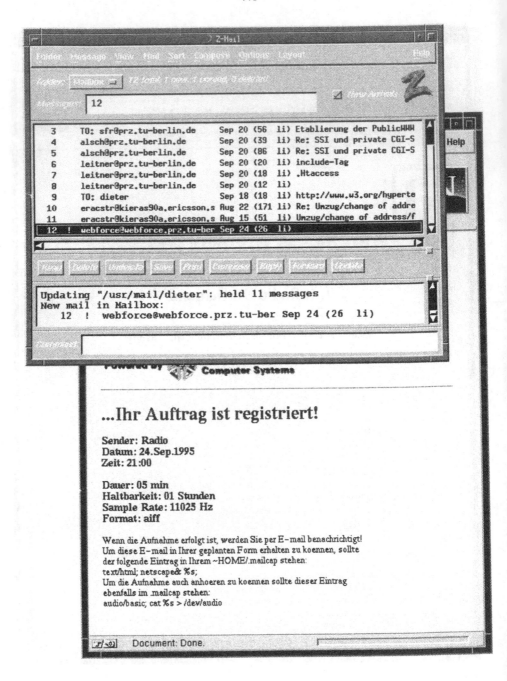

Fig. 6.: InfoRadio-on-Demand: Notification Phase

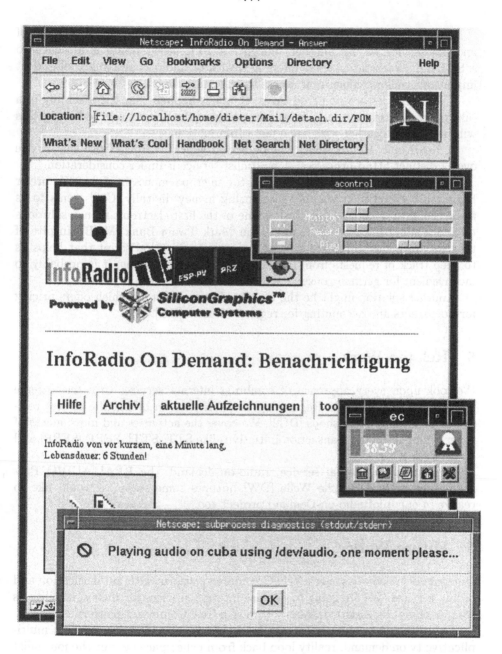

Fig. 7.: InfoRadio-on-Demand: Consumption Phase

Though the mpeg format mentioned earlier seems to be the right basis of an audioservice we use another concept. A PLL based Radio is attached to a SGI/Indy workstation. SGI offers a wealth of audio converting tools. Most important it allows concurrent access to the audio device.

The mpeg files are prepared takes. It might happen that the assembly of a take order yields into a leak. In a later phase of the project selected mpeg files will be offered together with some meta information.

A RealAudio Module [RA] will be added which will distribute the service over 2 distinct httpd processes. A multicast service is under consideration.

There is still no definitive solution for micropayments in sight. We prefer DigiCash because their way of representing money digitally [C92] seems to us to be the most adequate. DigiCash is one of the first electronic money solutions to find a suporting bank company - the Mark Twain Bank [MTB]. Inspite of that we are going to replace it with a simple registration script that helps us to keep track of requests from professionals i.e. radiostations. It is probably to inconvenient for german consumers to run a bank account in the US.

Another solution might be the use of a Hyper-G Server which offers pricing for documents and accounting for registered users [HG].

5 Related Work

We look upon every approach of combinig internet services to a telecomerce platform as related work. Regard ing our activities on billing the closest relationship exists to ecash shops [DC2]. We cover the activities and move ments of other billing or secure transaction initiatives like STT [STT], SEPP [SEPP] and CyberCash [CC].

Regarding the special service, radio-on-demand, the REAL-AUDIO Programming of the Deutsche Welle [DW] outlines some steps we would like to realize in our InfoRadio-on-Demand project too.

6 Future Work

Our goal is to define a generic Tele Commerce platform with authentication and billing services. We are going to analyse internet services for their suitability as components for a logistic infrastructure of a Tele Commerce platform.

Future plans of the project are to design value added services like multiplicative tv on demand, reality loop back from cyberspace i.e. put the journalist right into the internet. Pay per view, digital abos for multi media and Digi Cash shops.

References

[C92] Chaum, D.: Achieving Electronic Privacy. (invited) **Scientific American** August (1992) 96–101

[SM95] Thomas Schmid, Reiner Metzger et al.: Die taz im Internet **taz** (12.5.1995)
1–3 TUB-PRZ-W-1185 http://www.prz.tu-berlin.de/docs/taz/www/12.Mai/

[CGI] http://www.w3.org/pub/WWW/CGI/

[CC] http://www.cybercash.com/

[DTB] http://www.deteberkom.de/projekte/texte/history.html

[DW] http://www.dmc.net/dw/dw.html

[DC1] http://www.digicash.com/

[DC2] http://www.digicash.com/shops/alpha.html

[DC3] http://www.digicash.com/ecash/ecas-home.html

[DC4] http://www.digicash.com/ecash/trial.html

[IR] http://webforce.prz.tu-berlin.de/inforadio/impress.htm

[MTB] http://www.marktwainbank.com

[MC] Werner Oomen, Frans de Bont, and L. M. Van de Kerkhof: Variable Bit-Rate Coding for MPEG-1 Audio, Layers I and II **AES Preprints AES 98th Convention**, Palais des Congres, Paris, France, 1995 february 25D28, #3938 http://www.cudenver.edu:80/aes/preprints/paris.html#order

[RA] http://www.realaudio.com

[SEPP] http://www.mastercard.com/Sepp/sepptoc.htm

[STT] http://www.visa.com/visa-stt/index.html

[WP] http://www.prz.tu-berlin.de/docs/html/www/kurzinfo.html

[RoD] http://www.prz.tu-berlin.de/docs/internal/TUB-PRZ-W-1200.ps

[HG] Wolfgang Dalitz, Gernot Heyer: **Hyper-G**, Das Internet-Informationssystem der 2. Generation dpunkt-Verlag für digitale Technologien, Heidelberg (1995) ISBN: 3-920993-14-4. http://elib.zib-berlin.de/math.publ.books.hyper-g

Design of an Immersive Teleconferencing Application

G. Y. Georgiannakis, P. E. Trahanias, C. N. Nikolaou and S. C. Orphanoudakis

Institute of Computer Science, FORTH
and
Department of Computer Science, University of Crete

Abstract. This paper concerns the design of a system supporting tele-conferencing applications. This system aims at creating an immersive environment by compositing a synthetic background with the reconstructed images of remote participants. It also presents natural scenes by employing viewer tracking and rendering images from the vantage point of the viewer. Processing requirements are met by exploiting existing networks of workstations by means of a *quality of service* based resource management scheme. This approach offers advantages with respect to the application itself (teleconferencing) and resource requirements. By restricting the transmitted images to the participants only, the required bandwidth becomes much smaller and video quality can be achieved. The employed resource management scheme limits computational resources to general purpose workstations. On the other hand, a synthetic background that matches the real meeting room can be easily designed, giving the impression of a *virtual meeting room* as an extension of the real one. In this way, remote conference sessions that resemble real life meetings can be held.

Keywords: teleconferencing applications, immersive environment, virtual meeting room, viewer tracking, active vision, adaptive systems, QoS based resource management

1 Introduction

In the last few years, an outburst has taken place in research concerning *multimedia systems*. Multimedia systems offer the possibility to combine text, computer graphics, video and audio, as well as other forms of information in computer displays. This research has been extented to *teleconferencing* applications to support remote conferencing with systems that feature the above capabilities. Such systems offer substantial money and time savings, being an interesting substitute to actual conferences between remotely located parties.

Teleconferencing is a broad term applicable to a wide spectrum of communication sessions, where two or more parties at different locations may collaborate by exchanging and/or manipulating information. A particular term, namely *media space* [4], aims at supporting the inherently social and technical collaborative work by existing technology means. In such a setting, groups of people may work together, although they may be separated by long distances, by exploiting visual and acoustic environments that resemble actual meetings.

Unfortunately, the audio and video media that are used in teleconferencing convey only a limited subset of visual and auditory information when compared to actual face-to-face meetings. Therefore, media spaces can be currently regarded as an inferior substitute for actual meetings. In fact, in media space environments the perceived information is partial when compared to the rich information grasped in real life meetings.

In this paper we are primarily concerned with a teleconferencing application, where audio and visual communication between persons at different locations is immersive. In other words, the whole setting creates a virtual environment where people involved may meet and discuss as if they were face-to-face. Such an environment exploits vision and stereo techniques, so that participating partners have the illusion of being next to the other without the need of special virtual reality equipment. This application exploits available computational resources within an organization, so that image processing techniques can isolate participating persons while rendering and compositing may incorporate participants in artificially created backgrounds. Such an environment is particularly useful in meetings where body language, gestures and location of partners are essential.

The rest of this text is structured as follows. In the next section we review teleconference applications that aim at creating a virtual representation of the actual meeting place and participants. Then we present the major issues that should be addressed by teleconferencing applications. The remainder of the paper is dedicated to the Immersive Teleconferencing Application (ITA). Initially, the major components of ITA and their interconnection are presented. Then, resource management issues are discussed and concluding remarks are made.

2   Teleconference Applications

Recently there has been an increasing interest in *media spaces* as a means to support synchronous collaboration. These systems allow simultaneous, two-way transmission of auditory and visual information and, thus, simulate the every day media that people use to collaborate. The term *media space* actually indicates the analogy between these artificial environments to the actual environments, where collaborating people communicate every day.

There are two different approaches to create such systems. The first approach is a computer centered approach, where collaboration is realized by means of shared window systems, and applications where images of collaborating partners are presented in a small window on the computer displays.

The second approach creates shared workspaces based on audio and video communication. Such systems handle information that is external to the computers, such as voices and images of people. They aim at providing a sense of "telepresence" by presenting live images of collaborating persons as well as their facial and gesture expressions, together with their speech. A brief presentation of three typical such systems follows.

In *Video Window* [7], conferencing parties are displayed on large screens (with aspect ratio that corresponds to HDTV), while audio is transferred through 4 different channels in order to admit spatial localization of speaking partners. The large screens provide life size images, which together with multisource sound enable multiple persons to communicate simultaneously, thus creating an increased sense of shared space between participants.

The *MAJIC* system [17] attempts to look like a round table meeting by using curved displays where life size images are projected. This system can be used for face-to-face meetings between two or three attendants; its strong point is that participants can observe facial expressions and direction of gaze. Images are captured by video cameras and directly projected at half mirror screens which, however, fail to provide high quality images. Nevertheless, the system captures the attendants' emotions through eye contact.

A different approach is taken in ClearBoard [11] where face-to-face communication is obtained through a shared drawing surface. In this system each participant sits in front of a semi-transparent surface where images as well as drawings of other participants are presented by means of rear projection. The same screen is used by each participant for the creation of his own drawings. This system aims at studying dynamics of human interaction and collaboration rather than exploiting processing power to achieve realistic results.

In [8] a discussion and comparison of the properties that capture perception and interaction in every day media as well as media spaces is presented. According to this work, images and sound may be combined to achieve awareness of vision, hearing, motion and localization of partners in a collaborative environment. In the following section the special issues that have to be addressed in order to achieve a media space that resembles the physical meeting environment are discussed.

3   Media Space Issues

In teleconferencing systems, the partners that communicate by means of live visual and audio information may be located in sites that are far apart. Audio and visual data must conform to two different constraints in order to be meaningful. Audio and video consist of a sequence of samples and frames, respectively, that must be presented continuously in time, otherwise their consistency and meaning are lost. Furthermore, timing relationships must hold between audio samples and video frames so that speech is in correspondence with appropriate lip movements. The traffic of "continuous media" (audio and video) is time-constrained by end-to-end delay and jitter parameters.

The above parameters impose time requirements [16] on the communication media as well as the applications and hardware that manipulate continuous media.

Data transmission poses important requirements on the interconnection network. Audio and especially video data demand high throughput, up to 100 Mbits/second. In addition, transfer rates must satisfy real-time constraints imposed by the stream like behavior of continuous image and audio data.

Human factors is another important aspect in capturing audio and visual information from one site as well as in its presentation in other participating sites. For example, life size stereo images and stereo sound capture important parameters such as human gestures, the location of speaking partners and point of attention, which enable collaborating partners to feel as in a face-to-face meeting.

Image processing and graphics techniques can enhance the quality of image data that are presented at each site. Such techniques, especially in the case of image sequences, are inherently complex and usually require specialized hardware and many processors for their implementation. On the other hand, they can spare network resources by avoiding transmission of the "background" scene, and can be used for *immersing* partners in any desired scene as discussed later.

A complete teleconferencing system consists of the interconnection network, high performance workstations as well as image and audio acquisition and reproduction devices. These components must be integrated in a manner that assures time requirements as well as quality criteria of continuous media. These parameters can be guaranteed by appropriate dynamic resource management on an intercomponent rather than intracomponent basis. In other words, the objective of resource management is the integrated system's performance rather than efficient resource management in each of the components that comprise the system.

4   The Immersive Teleconferencing Application

We are interested in a teleconferencing application that enables people at remotely located sites to collaborate in a virtual, yet as natural as possible environment. The virtual environment at each site is perceived as an extension of the real space and the remote participants are immersed in it (hence the term *immersive*). The purpose of this system is to facilitate face-to-face meetings in a most natural way. Existing technologies provide a basis for builting such a system, where high performance can be accomplished by appropriate usage of available computational and network resources.

This application is similar to the applications reviewed, in the sense that conference participants are projected on a full-wall display rather than a computer screen. It is innovative in two different aspects: (a) the composition of real images (participants) with synthetic backgrounds, and (b) the exploitation of available computational resources for the processing tasks via a *quality of service* (QoS) management scheme. Image rates in the range of 20-25 frames per second in conjunction with viewer tracking and synthetic backgrounds create an illusion of a *virtual meeting* area. This area, being an extension of a real meeting room, creates a natural environment which can be used for a variety of purposes, such as distributed negotiation, remote consultation, communication for the physically disabled, tele-learning, and of course conferencing and collaboration. Stereo images and sound enable participants at one site to locate participants within the virtual environment representing the other site. Moreover, 3D full body images of the participants are presented, with respect to the viewer's position. These features are necessary for conferencing environments where body language and facial expressions are essential for communication.

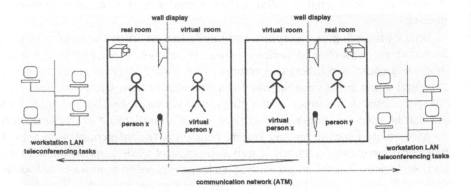

Fig. 1. System Architecture

The whole system, as presented in Fig. 1, is made up of a number of image and audio acquisition and reproduction devices. These devices are controlled by workstations whose typical function is to serve the everyday computational needs of the organization where the whole environment is set. The same workstations are used for the image and sound processing needs of the conferencing application; rendering and compositing may be performed by specialized hardware that is part of high performance graphics workstations.

4.1 Environment

We can view the whole teleconferencing system from two different vantage points: (a) as an aggregation of cooperating components, i.e. a systems point of view, and (b) system operation and coordination, i.e. an operational point of view. The whole system diagram and operation is illustrated in Fig. 2. The dashed rectangles represent software components that perform specific ITA tasks, while the continuous lines correspond to information flow. Each of the illustrated components is discussed in detail later.

A. System. The basic system consists of two sites communicating over ATM networks. A special room in each site is dedicated for ITA conferences. This room is equipped with audio and visual data acquisition and reproduction devices. Two stereo configured cameras, mounted on an active head, are responsible for stereo image capturing. The active head aims at tracking the participants and

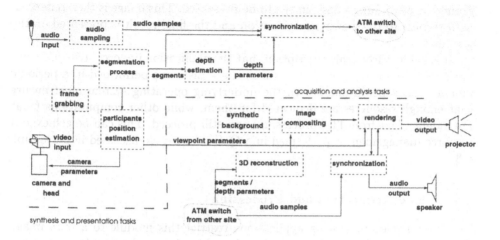

Fig. 2. Block diagram/datapath and corresponding processing

is controlled by the computers at that site. A couple of microphones are used for stereo sound sampling. One of the room's walls is replaced by wall-sized display, where the images of the other site are presented. Images received by the other conferencing site are rendered and composited and the result of this task is presented by two high-luminosity video beamers configured for rear-projection. Audio reproduction is performed by a pair of high fidelity loudspeakers, so that stereo sound is achieved. Input and output to audio and video reproduction and acquisition devices, respectively, is manipulated by appropriate off-the-shelf converters. The existing workstation network at each site is responsible for controlling all devices and for the ITA processing tasks.

B. Operation. System operation is the coordination of three different activities, namely data acquisition and processing, data transmission and delivery and finally, reproduction and presentation. Communication between the conferencing sites is established via ATM networks, which supply the high aggregate bandwidth required. Audio signals are transformed to digital form and transmitted to the other site as soon as they are captured. Image data, on the other hand, are locally processed so as to segregate the participants from their background. This is accomplished by image segmentation and feature extraction performed by computers at the site where these images are acquired. In this manner only a small fraction of the acquired images is necessary for the reconstruction process. Therefore, the image data that are transmitted are significantly less than the actual data acquired, thus sparing network resources.

At the remote site, viewer tracking enables the system to create an appropriate viewing specification to render image data. Received audio data can be directly played back without any need for special processing. On the other hand, received image data require significant processing. Initially, 3D reconstruction of the subjects is performed and this result is composed with a synthetic background so as to form a basic image to be presented. This image is then rendered, with respect to the viewing specification and the final result is presented on the wall display.

It is evident from this description that the application imposes stringent computing requirements at each site. Since these tasks are performed in a periodic manner (on a per frame basis), the underlying operating system must ensure that enough resources are dedicated for them, while other computations (that are independent from ITA processing) can still proceed. This can be achieved if resource management is performed in a QoS manner, as discussed in paragraph 4.8.

4.2 Video Acquisition and Processing

Traditional teleconferencing applications restrict this module to a pure image data capture facility, perhaps combined with a data reduction (compression) capability. In the application under study, however, this is upgraded to an *active* image acquisition system with additional *image analysis* capabilities. Image analysis capabilities are also needed at the other end of the system, that is the *Presentation Module*; more specifically, this module should be able to track the position of the viewer in 3D space and, particularly, the position of the viewer's eyes. This is used in the rendering procedure in order to render (present) the scene that "should be seen" by the viewer.

4.3 Viewer Tracking

The primary concern is that no special sensors need to be attached or worn by participants. To achieve this goal, image analysis techniques are employed to locate the positions of the participants' eyes. An initialization phase is first entered where the eyes are detected using appropriate masks [2] and color information. This step uses information from the step of *subject segmentation*, in order to restrict the search space; *subject tracking* also facilitates the task of viewer tracking since it provides the position of the subject across frames. It should be noted that limited accuracy at this step can be tolerated since slight deviations of the eye positions are not detectable in the rendered result.

An issue raised here concerns the situation of multiple viewers, which dictates the existence of more than one viewing positions. We overcome this in two ways: (a) an arbitration is used that gives priority to a certain participant externally (e.g. through an operator), and (b) an averaging scheme is used that calculates the rendering position as the mean of the positions of all participants.

4.4 Subject Segmentation

Traditionally, this task is skipped by employing a special recording studio (e.g. blue room) and chroma-keying technique. However, this restricts the applicability of the system since it is confined to very controlled environments. To alleviate for that, image analysis techniques are employed to segregate the images of the participants from the images of the meeting room. Towards this goal, texture segmentation techniques [20] provide an initial estimate as of the location of the subject. The algorithm employed here is a clustering one that utilizes a list of texture features [1]. The features are ordered in this list according to their significance in the segmentation; in this way, the computation of features is terminated according to the processing time allocated for this task, without a significant decrease in performance. Subsequently, using simple motion detection techniques [21], motion segmentation is performed and the subjects are tracked by means of a Kalman filter whose state vector describes positional features.

Using the stereo configuration, depth estimation follows the segmentation task, only for the image points that have been characterized as subjects (participants). This is based on fairly standard stereo vision techniques (disparity computation). An alternative here is to compute *ordinal* depth; although, our first studies in this direction show promising results [15], computational requirements still prohibit the employment of this technique.

The segmentation results provide feedback to the image acquisition process in order to modify the camera position and/or zoom accordingly. In other words, knowledge of the participants' position in the scene permits the camera to move accordingly and keep all participants in the center of the scene; An active vision head is used for this purpose that implements four degrees of freedom (pan, tilt, independent vergence for each camera) along with active control of zoom, focus and iris.

4.5 Rendering and Compositing

Image rendering is a computationally intensive task that may be performed by means of specialized hardware due to the latter's wide availability. A homogeneous array of processors (renderers) transforms its primitives to a full size image of the part of the graphics database it is responsible for. An image composition network, which is implemented in hardware too, composites the partial images into a single image that corresponds to a single frame in the conferencing application.

The projected background may be different at each site and may consist of still or continuous images. In the latter case the background images may be retrieved by a continuous media storage server [18].

4.6 Audio Sampling and Playback

Audio is sampled using two or more microphones in order to achieve stereo sound and is reproduced in a respective number of speakers. There is no need to perform any audio processing (although custom built codecs provide such operations). Thus, the most important aspect of audio is the transmission from one site to another and synchronization with the corresponding images. An ATM connection can guarantee audio sample delivery at a rate of 1.4 Mbps (which corresponds to CD quality audio) [12]. End-to-end delays may be in the range of 80 milliseconds (or about 20 milliseconds for distributed music rehearsals) [9].

4.7 Communication

Even if the processing modules reviewed in the previous paragraphs manage to operate in a manner that satisfies the continuous media timing constraints for the teleconferencing operation, the whole system is unable to operate in a continuous manner unless the interconnection network between the various sites can satisfy end-to-end timing constraints.

Actually, continuous operation of the system requires that images are transferred at a rate of 20-25 frames per second, with each frame having an approximate size of 3 megabytes. This would require a bandwidth of about 80 Mbps in a typical application; however, this is not the case with ITA, because only the participants' part of each image is transmitted. CD quality audio requires a bandwidth of 1.4 Mbps. In order to achieve lip synchronization the skew between audio samples and corresponding images is no more than 80 ms. The above requirements can only be satisfied if the interconnection network is ATM based [3, 16].

ATM networks can guarantee end-to-end delivery constraints and can support high aggregate bandwidths. The conferencing application can specify the required QoS parameters such as bandwidth and transfer delays. Appropriate layers of the communication network may decide whether these requirements can be met and can therefore grant the appropriate network resources.

So far we have considered communication between the two (or more) sites in the teleconferencing environment. Nevertheless, communication and synchronization between computers in one site is equally important. The reason is that various different processors work together so that audio and image processing tasks are performed in time. These processors may compute partial results which have to be transmitted either to presentation devices or other processors.

4.8 Resource Management

As we have already mentioned, the Immersive Teleconferencing Application poses great computational and communication requirements. In addition, the need for frame rates in the range of 20-25 frames per second implies that computations described in previous paragraphs must be performed in a periodic manner within strict time limits (approximately 35 ms).

Therefore, the system operation resembles that of a periodic real-time system. In such systems, application processing requirements, together with deadlines, are usually known *a priori*. Every process is dedicated to special processors and timely execution of tasks is achieved by assigning more resources than actually needed. Therefore, a reasonable fraction of resources is wasted, only to guarantee that processing is performed within the specified time intervals.

Hopefully, this is not the case with ITA. Of course, timely execution can provide high quality conferencing sessions, but the most important aspect of the system is that communication between remotely located partners can be established and maintained with affordable auditory and visual quality. Moreover, it is impossible to draw exact figures, rather rough estimates, for the processing requirements of ITA computations because they depend on the actual scenes manipulated and presented.

In typical workstation networks the resources are underutilized most of the time [10] and only momentarily do their demand and consumption reach peak values. In this manner, ITA attempts to exploit resource availability in order to achieve appropriate conferencing sessions. However, during high system loads, a set of necessary tasks that achieve basic acceptable teleconferencing sessions (in terms of audio and visual quality) must be executed. Complementary procedures and tasks may be used in order to achieve high performance and quality sessions, if resource availability permits their execution. This is a *quality of service* based behavior rather than a best effort system, since system operation is characterized by the data to be processed [1] as well as transient changes in system resource demands. Operating system support for continuous media applications is a subject of current research and a number of different mechanisms [5, 6, 13], that aim at supporting traditional processes too, have been proposed.

Each basic system component (as presented in Fig. 2) is structured as a set of communicating processes with timing and quality requirements expressed in an IDL language [19]. In section 4.4 we pointed out that a variety of methods may be used in order to achieve subject segmentation of varying quality without significant performance decrease. Therefore, the IDL description contains alternative process chains that provide different quality results with respect to time and resource availability. An *imprecise computation* [14] model exploits different process schedules. Moreover, image analysis tasks are inherently parallel, therefore the IDL description contains different granularity parallel processes that exploit varying numbers of available processors. As illustrated in Fig. 2, various process components of the application can be performed in parallel. All ITA operations must be accomplished on a per frame basis, since continuity of visual and audio data is necessary in order for them to convey meaningful information. Units of work may contain mandatory and optional operations, whose execution depends on availability of resources. An example is subject segmentation features, which are sorted in an ordered list according to their significance. The first elements of the list are mandatory, providing essential segmentation information, while the rest of the elements are optional and are used to achieve better segmentation parameters and revise the results of the former. We can view a unit of work as a conferencing session spanning various consecutive frames. Audio and visual information in a unit of work is considered as plain information to be processed by actors/agents that correspond to the actual operations (by means of image processing tasks for example) performed by ITA in order to successively terminate the corresponding units of work. Units of work and corresponding operations contain descriptions of the requested resources as well as their timing

---

[1] For example, when conferencing participants are very active in gestures – an example of a situation where consecutive images need more time to be processed

parameters (such as deadlines, release and computation times).

Since the system is decomposed to a large number of cooperating processes, IPC performance is of major impact in overall system performance, which must obey timeliness and quality constraints. Synchronous and asynchronous IPC have been addressed in [9].

In order to exploit available resources, such as processors or memory, the system must maintain resource state information via some *resource monitor*. The information of this monitor is periodically updated and the *resource management module* decides the assignment of processes to processors. In this manner, a dual scheme of scheduling is exhibited, in the form of local and global scheduling. In other words, the resource management module decides on which processors may accept ITA processes so that their processing requirements are met. Every processor contains a local scheduling mechanism that decides on the way the ITA processes are executed in it. The above are shown in Fig. 3. ITA tasks and their quality requirements are submitted to the resource management module of some processor. If the resource allocation and monitoring unit determines that there are enough available resources for it, then the task is submitted to the ITA scheduler, and the corresponding resources are considered *as used*. Otherwise, the task is submitted to the resource management modules of other processors.

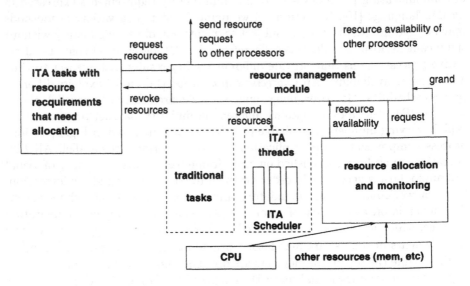

Fig. 3. Resource Management Architecture

ITA tasks at some processor are scheduled by a special ITA scheduler, which tries to accomplish their timing requirements. This scheduler is running in supervisor mode with high priority and passes control to computation threads that actually perform the ITA processing. Threads communicate via messages containing timing as well as data information. Corresponding models are available in the literature [5, 6].

During system initialization the experienced workload is monitored and the ITA resource management modules can decide whether the available resources can satisfy ITA requirements. During this phase an initial assignment of ITA processes to corresponding processors is performed. This assignment changes dynamically during system operation, corresponding to availability or lack of requested resources.

Whenever a unit of work is executed its requirements are dynamically modified according to the experienced resource consumption and actual execution time. In this manner, units of work perform sampling on their actual behavior and their parameters are continuously updated. Periodic updates of the resource allocation measures are necessary for the global scheduler to produce efficient schedules. On the other hand, due to the dynamic behavior of the system, these values become stale at very small time intervals. Yet, they provide a useful approximation of actual system load, on which scheduling decisions are based.

Resource allocation for the ITA is based on units of work. The importance of these units of work depends on their laxity. Thus, a unit of work is assigned the requested resources as soon as it arrives, or whenever it becomes critical. These resources are revoked by the resource manager, once the unit of work is finished, or another more important unit of work arrives at the system and there are not enough available resources for both of them.

Scheduling tasks outside the scope of ITA arriving at some processor depend upon the importance of these tasks and availability of resources. ITA units of work arriving at the system are inserted in appropriate waiting queues with respect to their resource requirements and laxity parameters. The response time to these units of works as well as user processes depends on their level of importance.

Processes that control devices (such as the active head or the microphones) do not impose important computational requirements and can be statically assigned to any of the existing workstations. Of course, their timely behavior is satisfied by the corresponding local scheduler.

5 Concluding Remarks

Teleconferencing applications are receiving increased attention lately due to the inherent advantages of remote conferencing. Therefore, a great deal of research effort is devoted to the design and development of systems that support efficient ways of communication. In this paper we have presented our approach towards the design of an *immersive* teleconferencing system. The innovations of this system are the employment of QoS resource management techniques in task allocation and the compositing of real image data with a synthetic background. The latter creates the illusion of a virtual room, being an extension of the real room. Therefore, participants "perceive" a meeting area where both the local and remote members are present.

The design of this system has been based on available components, where possible and on solutions that utilize the computer power of an existing installation. The extra hardware components of such a system are the ones needed for audio and video acquisition and presentation. The network requirements have been kept to a minimum by transmitting the images of the participants only, instead of the whole scene. On the other side, this has increased the image processing demands, by adding a segmentation and depth estimation step. Viewer tracking enables the presentation of "natural" scenes according to the viewer's position. To achieve real-time performance, efficient resource management techniques have been employed that exploit unused resources, without the need of special hardware and/or software components.

References

1. L.W. Abele. Feature Selection by Space Invariant Comparison with Applications to the Segmentation of Textured Pictures. In *5th Intl. Conf. Pattern Recogn.*, Miami Beach, Florida, December 1980, pp. 535-539.
2. A.L. Yuille, P.W. Hallinan, and D.S. Cohen. Feature Extraction From Faces Using Deformable Templates. *Int. J. Computer Vision*, Vol. 8, No. 2, 1992, pp. 99-111.
3. M. Batubara and A. J. McGregor. "An Introduction to B-ISDN and ATM". Technical report, Robotics and Digital Technology - Monash Univ., September 1993.
4. S. A. Bly and S. R. Harrison. "Media Spaces: Bringing People Together in an Video, Audio and Computing Environment". *Communications of the ACM*, Vol. 36, No. 1, January 1993, pp. 30-47.
5. Tatjana M. Burkow. "Operating System Support for Distributed Multimedia Applications; A Survey of Current Research". Technical report, Univ. of Cambridge Computer Laboratory, Jun 1994.
6. G. Coulson and G. S. Blair. Microkernel Support for Continuous Media in Distributed Systems. In *Computer Networks and ISDN Systems*, 1994.
7. Robert S. Fish, Robert E. Kraut, and Barbara L. Chalfonte. The VideoWindow System in Informal Communications. In *CSCW 1990 Proc.*, pages 1-11.
8. William W. Gaver. The Affordances of Media Spaces for Collaboration. In *CSCW 1992 Proceedings*, pp. 17-24.
9. Ramesh Govindan. *Operating System Mechanisms for Continuous Media*. PhD thesis, Computer Science Div., Univ. of California, Berkeley, Jul 1992.
10. Eoin Andrew Hyden. *Operating System Support for Quality of Service*. PhD thesis, Wolfson College, University of Cambridge, February 1994.
11. H. Ishii, M. Kobayashi, and J. Grudin. Integration of Inter-Personal Space and Shared Workspace: ClearBoard Design and Experiments. In *CSCW 1992 Proceedings*, pages 33-42.
12. James Lane. ATM Knits Voice, Data on any Net. *IEEE Spectrum*, Vol. 31, No. 2, February 1994, pp. 42-46.
13. Ian M. Leslie, D. McAulley, and Sape J. Mullender. "Pegasus - Operating System Support for Distributed Multimedia Systems". In *Proceedings of the Summer Usenix Conference, Boston MA*, June 1994.
14. C. Liu, J. Lin, W. Shih, A. Yu, J. Chung, and Z. Wei. Algorithms for Scheduling Imprecise Computations. *IEEE Computer*, Vol. 24, No. 5, May 1991, pp. 58-68.
15. M. Lourakis. "Ordinal Instead of Metric Depth: An Alternative". Master's thesis, University Of Crete, Computer Science Department, 1995.

16. Klara Nahrstedt and Ralf Steinmentz. Resource Management in Networked Multimedia Systems. *IEEE Computer*, Vol. 28, No. 5, May 1995, pp. 52-63.

17. K. Okada, F. Maeda, Y. Ichikawaa, and Y. Matsushita. Multiparty Videoconferencing at Virtual Social Distance: MAJIC Design. In *CSCW 1994 Proceedings*, pp. 385-393.

18. P. Venkat Rangan and Harrick M. Vin. Designing File Systems for Digital Audio and Video. In *Proceedings of 13th ACM Symposium on Operating Systems Principles*, ACMSIGOPS, Oct 1991, pp. 81-94.

19. B. Schiemann and M. Rosenberger. IDL for Load Balancing. Technical report, LYDIA/WP.4/T.4.1/D1, May 1995.

20. T.R. Reed and J.M. Hans du Buf. A Review of Recent Texture Segmentation and Feature Extraction Techniques. *CVGIP: Image Understanding*, Vol. 57, No. 3, May 1993, pp. 359-372.

21. W.B. Thompson and T.C. Pong. Detecting Moving Objects. *International Journal of Computer Vision*, Vol. 4, 1990, pp. 39-57.

The Secure Conferencing User Agent
A Tool to Provide Secure Conferencing with MBONE
Multimedia Conferencing Applications

Elfriede Hinsch, Anne Jaegemann, Ian C. Roper, Lan Wang

Abstract: This report briefly describes the Secure Conferencing User Agent (SCUA), which provides secure conferencing with privacy and authentication. The SCUA was implemented using the MICE multimedia conferencing applications with built–in encryption and the security infrastructure developed in the Password Project. Both MICE and PASSWORD were projects of the European Union. The paper describes the first prototype of the SCUA which was developed by GMD in the MICE project and the planned enhancements of it.

Content

1 The MICE Project

MICE ('Multimedia Integrated Conferencing for European Researchers') [1] was an Esprit Project of the European Union with the objective of providing for European scientists means and ways for multimedia conferencing.

The project started as a one year project in December 1992 and was subsequently extended until September 95. The security work was started July 94.

Partners of the project were: University College of London UCL (UK), project leader, GMD Darmstadt (Germany), INRIA (France), Telenor (Norway), Oslo University (Norway), Rechenzentrum der Universitaet Stuttgart (Germany), Swedish Institute for Computer Science (Sweden), and Universite Libre de Bruxelles (Belgium).

2 Motivation

One characteristic of the present MICE technology is its openness. Once someone has started a conference anyone who gets to know of the used addresses and port numbers can participate. Since the conference tools make use of the Internet Mbone broadcast facilities, there is no support by the system to prevent other (unauthorized) users from taking part in a conference.

Some applications may require that a conference be restricted to a determinable closed user–group. Users outside such a user–group must not be able to take part. Examples are (tele–)seminars where only those who have paid the fee for it can participate or (tele–)meetings which are restricted to the members of a project. Such applications need some kind of access control to prevent unauthorized users from taking part in the conference. Other applications may require in addition, that the information exchanged among the partners be kept confidential.

3 The Conferencing Technology

The basic philosophy for MICE multimedia conferencing was to make good use of available equipment and tools and to require as little as possible in addition to general purpose workstations and data networks. Participating in MICE conferences is possible from either a single workstation or a conference room. A workstation is usually found on an individual's desktop. For the purpose of MICE, it has to be equipped with video camera, microphone, loudspeaker, and appropriate conferencing software.

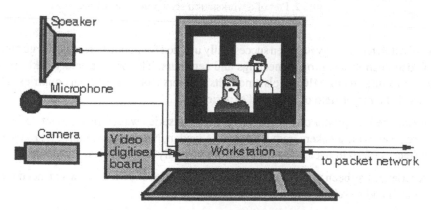

Fig. 1. Multimedia Workstation performing video coding and decoding in software

The infrastructure for the data transport is based on packet switched networks with Internet protocols and on the Mbone as a virtual network [2], which allows applications to work in a multicast mode (one–to–many connections) without the need for any central service. Among the software tools used in MICE are the following: SD is a tool for creating, announcing and joining a conference [5], VAT is the conference tool used for audio [3], WB is a whiteboard which substitutes for a regular whiteboard as well as a slide projector [4], IVS [6,7] or VIC [8] are used for the user video interface in workstations. An example of a part of a workstation screen in a conference is shown in figure 2.

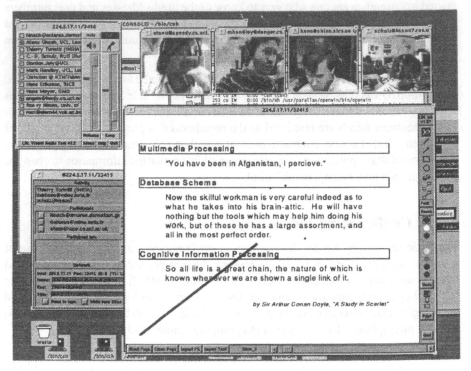

Fig. 2. Part of a workstation screen in a conference

The MICE technology has been successfully utilized for about 3 years in a large number of demonstrations, project meetings and seminars. The project held weekly project tele–meetings using MICE tools among its partners from 6 European countries. These provided a major field of trials and experiences.

During the last quarter of 1993, a MICE seminar series was started. About 25 lectures were given with speakers from USA, UK, Sweden, Norway, Germany and France and audiences of 10 to over 50 attendants from virtually all countries.

Experience has been very positive overall, but has also shown areas which need further research and development:

- the tools IVS, VAT, and WB were generally judged by the participants as having good functionality, in particular VAT. Yet a certain amount of familiarity with their use does greatly improve both comprehension and the flow of conferences.

- the network often causes problems. Audio and video quality depend very much on the network load and the network behavior related to loss, delay, and jitter. Improved tools will be needed for monitoring network performance. MICE started to bring in other networks (ATM, ISDN).

- audio is the most important component of multimedia conferencing. Beside network problems, there still exist local problems with audio (microphones, plugs, cables, background noises, echo feedback). To properly set up and use the peripherals, some audio–visual experience is extremely useful. Attention will be given to improved audio tools copying with network peculiarities and adjusting audio levels.

4 The Security Technology [17,18]

4.0 Security

Secure multimedia conferencing is needed in open telecooperation when confidentiality and privacy are an issue of multi–party communication and when it is desired to authentically identify parties.

For the continuation of MICE in 1994, GMD has taken charge of the security work package; contributing partners were INRIA and UCL. The following description gives the requirements of MICE technology with respect to authentication and confidentiality, presents an overview of the used security functions and defines how these functions could be applied to enhance the MICE services.

4.1 Requirements

The OSI Reference Model has been extended by a security architecture [9,10], which defines the following functions:

- *Authentication* is needed to confirm the identities of the communicating conference partners. For some application areas this is a highly important requirement. Examples are business applications where the conference participants want to be sure that the audio, video, and other data are produced and consumed by exactly the persons they think produced and consumed them.

- *Access Control* should prevent unauthorized use of resources. This is important for conferencing to prevent unallowed people from participating in a conference. In a centralized conferencing approach this can be achieved by the central controller. In the decentralized approach described here access control is achieved by means of authentification and encryption. It is important for applications where conference conveners want to be sure that only admitted people (e.g. no competitors, no publicity) or people who have paid their entrance fee for example for a seminar get knowledge of the content of a conference.

- *Data Confidentiality* covers two aspects: data protection and traffic flow confidentiality. Data which have to be protected are: exchanged and stored data to prepare a conference, shared workspace data, voice data, video data, conference results exchanged and stored. This confidentiality is achieved by means of encryption. The traffic flow confidentiality keeps the following information confidential: participants, location, date, time and duration of a conference, newcomers, leaving partners, activities of the participants (who is active, who is quiet, who is writing) and other activities with objects such as databases etc.

- *Data Integrity* depends on the underlying network and the protocol in use. It is a problem in the conference environment discussed here (Internet, Mbone) as one has to deal with loss of data (e.g. packet loss).

- *Non–Repudiation* provides proof of origin and delivery of data. This is relevant for example for the conference invitation (proof of origin: sent out by whom and when; proof of delivery: delivered to whom and when). Other relevant data may be modifications, commitments, conclusions and resolutions.

The MICE tools should be enhanced by these security functions as far as the technology at hand allows extensions at a reasonable effort. Though the transport technology presents some problems (e.g. traffic flow confidentiality...), we feel that it will be possible to offer secure conferencing in an acceptable manner.

One possibility to fulfill these requirements is to add security functions to the MICE technology, to encrypt the information broadcast by Mbone and to keep the encryption key confidential among authorized participants.

Encryption allows both access control and confidentiality. In case of centralized conference services with point–to–point connections to the clients, it would be sufficient to restrict the conference access by an authenticity control function. Encrypting the transmitted data is only required for confidential conferences.

In case of decentralized conference services and multicasting over Mbone, if a conference shall be restricted to a specified set of participants, the broadcast information will have to be encrypted, since Mbone does not offer any access control facilities.

Most MICE tools have already provisions for the support of encryption –such as VAT, WB, VIC, and IVS.

4.2 Security Functions Used

4.2.1 Overview

Symmetric cryptography is used for encrypting large data volumes. In order to achieve authenticity and to guarantee confidentiality of datastreams, they will be encrypted by means of a so called session key. This key may be valid for one or more sessions, depending on the particular situation, and it may differ depending on the type of data.

The session key to be used to encrypt and decrypt the audio, Shared Workspace, and video datastreams must be distributed to all conference participants. The key has to be distributed confidentially so that unauthorized users cannot get it.

Several methods may be used to distribute small amounts of confidential information. Common to most of them is the application of a Personal Security Environment (PSE). The PSE comprises the management of an asymmetric key pair which represents the kernel of all security functions. This key pair consists of a public key and a private key. The public key is normally certified by a trusted third party – the certification authority – in order to confirm the correct identity of the key owner. The private key must be kept secret by the owner. Any user who wants to take part in confidential conferences needs a PSE.

Everyone needs a key pair of his/her own and a certificate for the public key. For this purpose there have to be certification authorities and software in every workstation to generate an asymmetric key pair and to communicate with the corresponding certification authority. This procedure can be performed application independent and has to be done before starting the conference. It has been decided to use the formats and procedures of the European PASSWORD project [11,12,13], because these are widely available. Software for this purpose exists for example at the MICE partners INRIA, UCL and GMD (e.g. the SecuDE [14,15] software package of GMD).

Available security packages, like SecuDE or others, allow to generate an asymmetric key pair for the user to do encryption and decryption, to support the certification of the public key, and to generate and to read PEM (Privacy Enhanced Mail [16]) letters. The PASSWORD project has set up a European infrastructure for certification. It suggests to use PEM for key distribution.

4.2.2 Description of the Used Security Package [14,15,19]

SecuDE is a portable general–purpose security toolkit for Unix and MS–DOS systems.

SecuDE is a security toolkit which incorporates well known and established symmetric and public–key cryptography. It offers a library of security functions and a well documented C API which allows you to incorporate security into multimedia conferencing applications and others with the following features:

- Basic cryptographic functions like RSA, DSA, DES, various hash functions, DSS and Diffie–Hellman key agreement,

- Security functions for origin authentication, data integrity, non–repudation of origin, and data confidentially purposes on the basis of digital signatures and symmetric and asymmetric encryption,

- X.509 key certification functions, handling of certification pathes, cross–certification, certificate revocation,

- Public Key Cryptography Standards (PKCS),

- Utilities to sign, verify, encrypt and decrypt files,

- Utilities and library functions for the operation of certification authorities (CA) and interaction between certifying CAs and certified users,

- Utilities and library functions for PEM processing according to RFC 1421 – 1424 (the PEM functions are well tailored so that implementation of non–RFC 1421 PEM functions, like MIME–PEM, should be easy)

- Secure access to public X.500 Directories for the storage and retrieval of certificates, cross–certificates and revocation lists (integrated secured DUA using strong authentication and signed DAP operations),

- Integrity–protected and confidentiality–protected storage of all security relevant information of a user (secret keys, verification keys, certificates etc.) in a so called

Personal Security Environment (PSE). A PSE typically contains the user's private and public key (the latter wrapped in an X.509 certificate), the public root key which the user trusts, the user's distinguished name, the user's login name, and the forward certification path to the user's root key. In addition, the PSE allows to securely store other's public keys after their validation (allowing henceforth to trust them like the root key without verifying them again), and cerficate revocation lists (CRLs).

SecuDE provides two diferent PSE realizations: A SmartCard enviroment, and a DES–encrypted Unix or MS–DOS directory. Both are only through the usage of PINs (Personal Identification Numbers). Smartcards require a particular Smartcard enviroment to be purchased where RSA and DES cryptography is done in the Smartcard reader (infomation available on request).

SecuDE Privacy Enhanced Mail: An Internet Privacy Enhanced Mail imlementation (PEM RFC 1421 – 1424) is part of SecuDE. It provides a PEM filter which transforms any input text file into a PEM formatted output file and vice versa, and which should be capable of being easily integrated into Mail–UAs or CA tools.

SecuDE–PEM realizes all formats and procedures defined in the Internet Specifications RFC 1421 – 1424 except that it only supports asymmetric key management. It is possible to securely cache other's certificates and CRLs as this is part of the general SecuDE functionality.

SecuDE–PEM supports the certification and CRL procedures defined in RFC 1424 and is integrated into the SecuDE CA functionality. As an additional functionality which goes beyond RFC 1421 –1424, SecuDE–PEM may be configured with an integrated X.500 DUA which allows, for instance, automatic retrieval of certificates and CRLs during the PEM de–enhancement process.

There are several internal and external projects in GMD which use SecuDE. For example digital signatures based on the SecuDE security technology are used routinely by the GMD workflow management system DISCO [20], in particular in the workflow application "request for vacation" which has currently about 180 users. So both personal security environments (PSEs) and digital signatures have been tried and tested internally and are available for multimedia conferencing.

5 The Secure Conference User Agent (SCUA)

The preparation of a conference where people physically meet at the same place is normally done by electronic mail or letter mail, for example by distributing an agenda. The solution implemented follows this well–known procedure though other means of distributing conference information can be thought of as www, directory services and others.

There are different possibilities to use mail. For the initial implementation we decided to use UNIX mail and PEM. Later implementations may operate on other platforms or use other formats, such as MIME.

The core of the SCUA is a mailtool which allows:

- to exchange encrypted messages (Privacy Enhanced Mail, using the SECUDE program package) and

- to put conference related information in a message and open a conference directly from a message.

To send out a PEM the user has to have a PSE. That means the user has a RSA key pair which is certificated. The certification authority in our case is GMD. So the sender of a PEM is strongly authentificated and the body of the e-mail is electronically signed. The body of the mail is DES encrypted and the DES key is encrypted with the public key(s) of the sender and receiver(s).

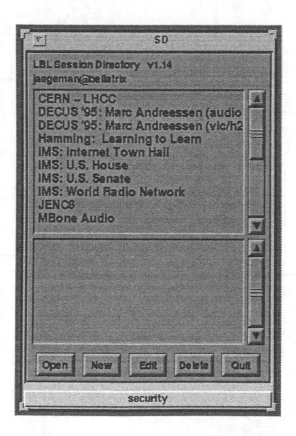

Fig. 3. Integrated User Interface of SD and SCUA

The SCUA provides a user interface (written in TCL/TK) which allows users to create and distribute conference information such as keys and the agenda, receive conference information and open a conference. As SD is the conference announcement tool for the open conferences, the new interface was designed as an integrated user interface of SD and SCUA (see fig. 3). To create or receive information related to a secure conference one would push the security button and the mailtool will be opened (see fig. 4).

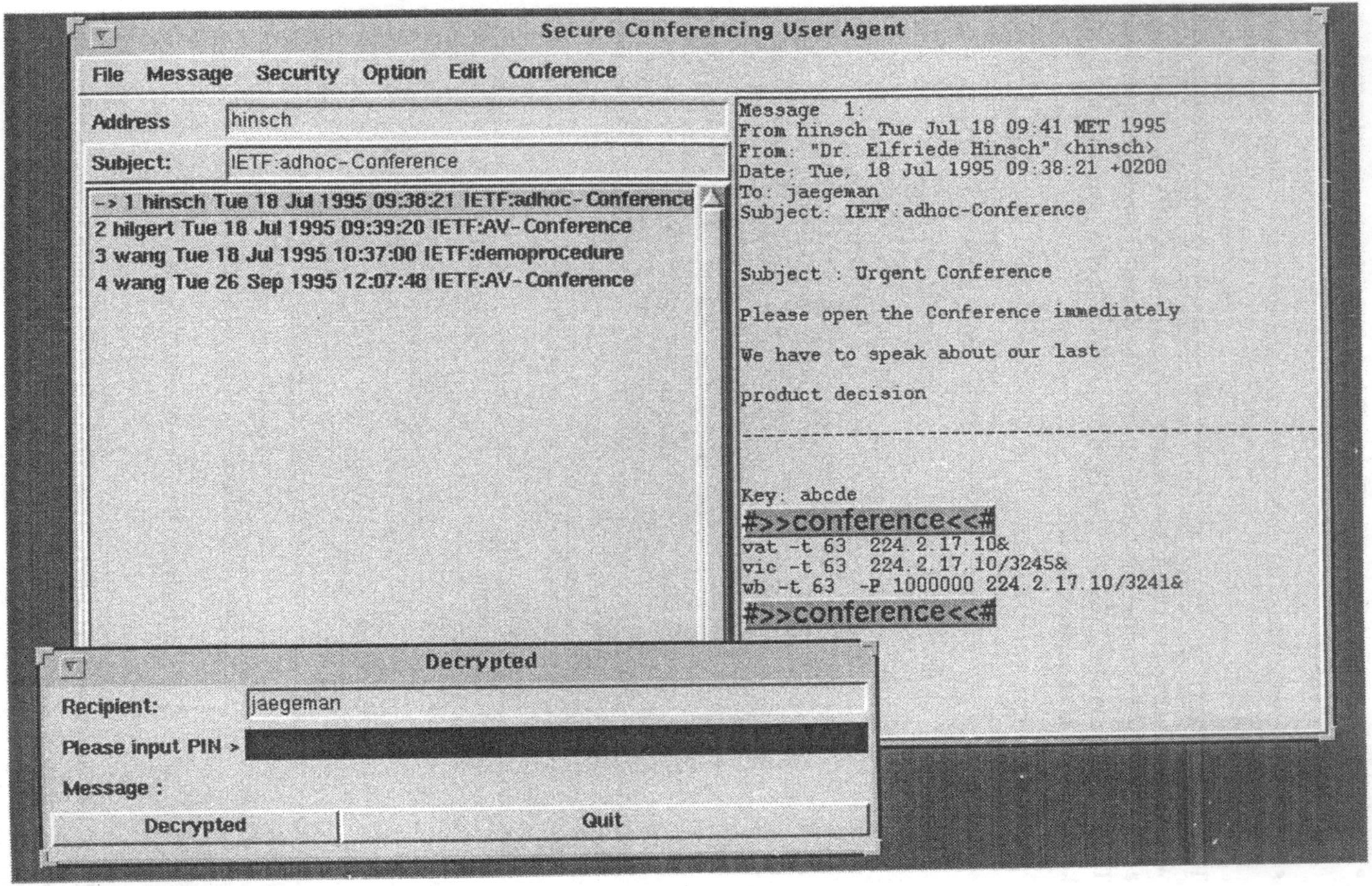

Fig. 4. Secure Conferencing User Agent

Within the resulting window, one has the functionality of a normal mailtool enhanced by the following functionalities:

- encrypting and decrypting messages. To do this the Security button in figure 4 has to be pushed.

- information on the used tools (e.g. video, audio and WB) is put between special bars (fig. 4). When one pushes one of the bars, the conference is opened directly from the mail. The control strings within the bars can be defined in a window which opens when one pushes the option button.

- conference related messages can be distinguished from other messages by the subject.

Till now the conference related information is given in a human readable form. So a user who has no SCUA but can decrypt the message is also able to start the conference manually by cutting and pasting the information in a command window.

6 Description of a Secure Conference

A conference has three phases preparing, running and evaluating. The solution presented here covers the first two phases.

Preparing a conference:

The SCUA tool is used to prepare a conference invitation with the agenda and the information about the tools required for the conference (including all their relevant parameters and the encryption key). This is encrypted and sent out.

A received encrypted conference invitation is decrypted and the conference is started by clicking on the special bars in the mail.

Running the conference:

Depending on the tools they can be either started with a session key as parameter for encryption or they can be started without encryption and then the key can be introduced via the user interface. The first method is more convenient for the user, but it is a security risk the process parameters can be queried from everyone who logs in the machine. The second one is more secure but the burden is on the user. The current version of VAT allows only to introduce the key manually.

7 Experience and Further Work

Secure conferencing was demonstrated on the IETF conference July 95 in Stockholm with the other sites at RUS Stuttgart, UCL London, GMD Darmstadt, FTZ Darmstadt (connected over ATM). The SCUA tool gave no problems. The quality of audio, video and WB was determined by the network, but in no way reduced by encryption.

The SCUA is used within GMD for announcing, creating and starting conferences in the VIRTME project (Virtual Meeting Room project, with the aim to allow cooperation between locally distributed meeting rooms). Though the SCUA is operable and in use, it is still being further developed. In the moment the user interface and the functionality are enhanced based on the experiences made, so for example more help is implemented for the user to create a conference.

The provision of PSEs presented no problem. We used the software implementation of PSEs. The smartcard solution may be integrated later.

We used the available encryption (DES) of the tools IVS, VAT and WB. We looked into their usability but did not investigate these tools themselves with respect to their security. Though it is possible to permit users to bring in other tools with other encryption methods, we would prefer to have an application independent software package which provided several encryption modes for the tools without interfering with them.

Experiences:

- The usability and the distribution of the conference mail was well accepted by users, especially the feature to start a conference from within the mail.

Further plans are:

- to go to other mail format (MIME), when available in the SecuDE security package.

- to adopt a more formal format for the conference related information. The format of SD could be a possible solution.

- to improve the usability, (e. g. more help for creating a conference and provision of a conference reminder)

- to go to other platforms such as Apple Macintosh.

Currently we are working with the built–in encryption in the tools IVS,VIC, WB and VAT. We would prefer to have an application independant encryption. So we started to provide a security package which en/decrypts the data exchanged between the applications without going in applications.

References

[1.]   P. T. Kirstein, M. J. Handley, M. A. Sasse: Piloting of Multimedia Integrated Communications for European Researchers (MICE), *Proc.INET 1993.*

[2.]   Casner: Frequently Asked Questions (FAQ) on the Multicast Backbone (MBONE), available by anonymous ftp from venera.isi.edu in the mbone/faq.txt, May 6th93.

[3.]   V. Jacobson: 'VAT' manual pages, Lawrence Berkeley Laboratory (LBL), February 17th 93, available by anonymous ftp from ee.lbl.gov.

[4.]   V. Jacobson: 'WB' README file, Lawrence Berkeley Laboratory (LBL), August 12th 93, available by anonymous ftp from ee.lbl.gov.

[5.] V. Jacobson: 'SD' README file, Lawrence Berkeley Laboratory (LBL), March 30th 93, available by anonymous ftp from ee.lbl.gov.

[6.] C. Huitema, T. Turletti: Packetization of H.261 video streams, INTERNET–DRAFT, December 5, 1993.

[7.] T. Turletti: H.261 Software Codec for Videoconferencing Over the Internet, *Research report No 1834*, INRIA, January 1993.

[8.] S. McCanne, V. Jacobson: 'VIC' maual pages, Lawrence Berkeley Laboratory (LBL), November, 1994, available by anonymous ftp from ee.lbl.gov. Encryption was included by Ian Wakeman (UCL)

[9.] ISO/IEC DIS 10745: Information technology – Open Systems Interconnection – Upper layers security model.

[10.] ISO/IEC DIS 10181–4: Information technology – Open Systems Interconnection – Security frameworks in Open Systems.

[11.] P. Kirstein, P. Williams: Piloting Authentication and Security Services within OSI Applications for RTD Information, *Computer Networks and ISDN Systems 25*, 1992 pp. 483 – 489.

[12.] W. Schneider, PASSWORD: Ein EG–Projekt zur pilotmäßigen Erprobung von Authentisierungsdiensten, Kommunikation und Sicherheit, *Teletrust Deutschland e.V., 1992.*

[13.] PASSWORD Reports, available by anonymous ftp from cs.ucl.ac.uk.

[14.] W. Schneider (Hrsg.): SecuDE Overview, Version 4.1, *Arbeitspapiere der GMD 775,* Sept. 1993

[15.] SecuDE Documentation, available by anonymous ftp from darmstadt.gmd.de: W. Schneider (Hrsg.): SecuDE, Vol.1 Principles of Security Operations, Vol.2 Security Commands, Functions and Interfaces, Vol.3 Security Application's Guide

[16.] US Internet RFC 1113 – 1115

[17.] K. Bahr, E. Hinsch, G. Schulze: Incorporating Security Functions in Multimedia Conferencing Applications in the Context of the MICE Project, second international workshop, IWACA '94, Heidelberg, Germany, September 26–28, 1994; *proceedings/Steinmetz, Ralf [Hrsg],* ISBN 3–540–58494–3

[18.] E. Hinsch, G. Schulze: Security Requirements and Proposed Facilities, Draft Version 4.0, June 1995 (Deliverable of WP6 of the MICE Project)

[19.] S. Kolletzki: GMD Security Technology – SecuDE Overview availabe in WWW: http://www.darmstadt.gmd.de/TKT/security.

[20.] K. Guenther: The DISCO Project available in WWW: http://www.darmstadt.gmd.de/TKT/projects.html

Personal Mobility for Multimedia Services in the Internet

Henning Schulzrinne

GMD Fokus*

Abstract: Personal mobility is one of the goals of Universal Personal Telecommunications (UPT) being specified for future deployment. Most current efforts focus on telephony, with SS7 signaling. However, many of the same goals can be accomplished for multimedia services, by using existing Internet protocols. We describe a multimedia call/conference setup protocol that provides personal videophone addresses, independent of the workstation a called party might be using at the time. The system is set up to use the existing Internet email address as a videophone address. Location and call handling information is kept at the subscriber's home site for improved access and privacy.

1 Introduction

The use of multimedia has progressed from stand-alone applications, to point-to-point, mostly local applications such as video-on-demand or LAN-based video conferencing. Across the wide-area, low-bandwidth circuit-switched teleconferencing (such as those using the H.320 standard) are spreading, as well as simple multimedia file delivery in the World-Wide Web context. H.320 conferences use the call control facilities available for either ISDN or plain old telephony (POTS). H.320 conferences use multipoint control units (MCUs) for multiparticipant conferences and tend to scale badly with increasing numbers of conference participants.

IP multicast has been used experimentally in the Internet for both interactive conferencing and audio/video distribution [1, 2] for groups up to several hundred participants. For the MBONE, conferences and seminars are typically announced worldwide or regionally through a multicast session directory. While IP multicast scales nicely to large groups, a multicast session directory is not suitable for thousands of concurrent phone calls or small-group conferences.

Recently, a number of companies have introduced applications and speech compression algorithms that allow personal computers to conduct voice conversations across the Internet even from modem-connected personal computers. These calls are point-to-point, audio only and assume that the called party resides at a known IP address. Generally, all Internet-based conferencing tools lack an easy-to-use mechanism to call up other users or invite them to a conference. That functionality is the subject of this paper.

We also intend to show that much of the control functionality envisioned for "intelligent networks" [3] can be supplied by simple extensions of existing Internet services,

---

* This work was supported in part by the ACTS project Multicube (AC 422) and the Berkom project MMTng.

running on workstations and personal computers. We describe a multimedia call control agent that offers flexible support for mobility and call processing. We use this to argue how computer-oriented intelligent networks should be structured for maximum flexibility and competitive service provision.

2 Multimedia Signaling and Mobility

Two kinds of mobility can be distinguished: *terminal mobility* and *personal mobility*. Terminal mobility allows to move a terminal (or end system in Internet parlance), i.e., a telephone, workstation, laptop, PDA, etc., from one location to another, while maintaining communication. (Further distinctions can be made as to whether, say, on-going TCP connections or phone calls are kept up across moves, with or without data movement.) While terminal mobility is typically associated with wireless access, wired mobility, i.e., the ability to plug in a terminal at different locations, is also of interest.

Mobile IP efforts [4] provide the ability to move during a call without losing packet-level connectivity. Also, IP multicast [5] can be used to ensure continuous packet-level connectivity in a multimedia conference as long as the end system can listen and transmit in two cells simultaneously, so that it can join the multicast group in the new cell while still receiving data packets from the old cell.

"Personal mobility is the ability of end users to originate and receive calls and access subscribed telecommunication services on any terminal in any location, and the ability of the network to identify end users as they move. Personal mobility is based on the use of a unique personal identity (i.e., 'personal number')." [6, p. 44]. The issue of naming will be discussed in detail in Section 2.1.

Terminal and personal mobility are two aspects of the "intelligent network" envisioned by telecommunication network operators (PNOs). Some current services such as 800-numbers (free phone) and call forwarding are viewed as first-generation intelligent network services. Recently, the moniker Universal Personal Telecommunication (UPT) has been used to describe the ability to enable communication with a person at any time, at any place, and in any form [6, 7].

The work described here provides a form of personal mobility. The call mechanism assigns each subscriber a permanent address naming a "home base" that manages call handling and forwarding to the terminal the callee is currently using. That terminal may be wired or wireless. While the "home base" should be continuously reachable, the terminal may not be.

Currently, most residential PCs acessing the Internet via modem are only connected to the Internet a few minutes or hours a day, making it difficult to use the PC as a communication terminal for private use. In the longer term, continuously connected systems are desirable, with low-power standby PCs and continuous network connectivity. Continuous connectivity is particularly easy if access is provided by a shared medium like CATV, as lower-layer call setup can be avoided. For IP-over-ISDN, the router at the Internet service provider will automatically set up an ISDN call when the first signaling packet arrives.

2.1 Naming for Personal Mobility

The most visible manifestation of personal mobility is the change from a telephone number as an identifier of a jack in the wall and a terminal to a personal number identifying a person. Thus, a person would maintain the same number even when moving or when switching from a wireline telephone to a mobile. The same telephone number can sometimes be maintained when moving within the area served by the same exchange. "700" and "800" telephone numbers in the US already have that property, although they are typically linked to a single wireline terminal for extended periods of time. However, it seems likely that numbers will remain national, so that a move across borders will require adopting a new identifier. Also, while "800" numbers have recently been made portable across network providers, "700" numbers currently remain provider-specific.

Even if freed from its role as a terminal and location identifier, a telephone number remains a number, with all the disadvantages for human interaction:

- hard to memorize, even more so if any "predictable" components like area codes are removed;
- not guessable from a person's name, residence or professional affiliation. (This "feature" currently provides the only protection against nuisance calls - security through obscurity.);
- lack of redundancy leads to misdialed calls;
- area codes and other parts of the phone number are subject to wholesale changes;
- for analog lines, different communication modes for the same person have different numbers (fax and phone, say), however, for ISDN, a service type can be specified;
- assignment in an environment with competitive local service is difficult;
- the number to be dialed depends on the call origin, e.g., the area code or country code must not be dialed for numbers within that area code or country.

On the other hand, the Internet has had a fairly usable naming mechanism for many years, in the form of the domain name system [8, p. 650ff]. Here, individual Internet hosts are designated by a hierarchical domain name, e.g., `ursa.fokus.gmd.de`. For electronic mail, RFC 821 specifies the familiar @ notation, with the form "name@host" or "name@domain". For private users without their own domain name, the email address currently contains the name of the service provider, e.g., `smith@aol.com`. Some professional organizations offer mail forwarders, so that one can maintain a single address, say, `j.doe@ieee.org`, despite changing employers or residence. Currently little used, there is also the possibility of geographical names, e.g.,

`j.smith@provider.amherst.ma.us.`

Initially, email addresses designated the Internet-attached host responsible for electronic mail and the user name on that host, leading to such email addresses as `bub9193@vax135.ho.att.com`. Many domains offer more friendly naming. First, various combinations of first and last name can be used, which are then mapped locally to a user account (login) name. Secondly, only the domain needs to be named, rather than the actual host responsible for receiving mail. The translation of domain names to the host name handling mail for a particular domain is carried out by the domain name system (DNS). So-called MX records map a domain name to a preference-ordered list of mail exchanger hosts. For example, the domain name sun.com maps to the hosts mercury.sun.com as the preferred mail host and venus.sun.com as a secondary one, should the first one be unreachable or busy. Equal-weight hosts can be specified for load sharing purposes. Compared to telephone numbers, "modern" email addresses can be easily remembered or even guessed. For example, knowing that somebody works at AT&T, it is sufficient to simple send e-mail to somebody@att.com. A list of candidate names and email addresses is returned should the name be ambiguous. Also, email addresses allow functional rather than personal designations, such as info@fokus.gmd.de. Even in computer-supported communication, the ability to memorize and pronounce addresses has proven to be important, as the virtual demise of the structured, but unwieldy X.400 addresses has shown. Unlike telephone numbers, the same email address can be used from anywhere in the Internet and it contains sufficient redundancy to likely fail outright rather than reach the wrong destination.

Email-style addresses have some drawbacks, in particular their larger size (compared to telephone numbers) and their limitation in character sets to letters, digits and hyphens. The use of Unicode may make it possible for those with accented names to be represented appropriately. However, this would further exacerbate the input problem, in that a much larger keyboard is already needed than for numbers. This is a particular problem for mobile devices, but for messaging and other uses, some form of alphabetic input will have to be provided in any event. (In the U.S., at least, there have been efforts from the beginning of dial telephony to use names instead of numbers. American telephones have letters printed next to each digit; corporations often advertise spelled-out names (1-800-CALL-ATT) rather than numbers. Indeed, early on, the numbers of exchanges used to be based on their names.) For private use, it remains to be seen whether there is demand for provider-independent, "neutral", but by necessity geographically-based mail exchangers. It would also have to deal with the issue of name duplication within larger geographic locales. More realistically, some set of directory services might be used to map from common names and other attributes to a provider-specific name. Unfortunately, deployment and maintenance of Internet white pages (X.500 and otherwise) has not been a great success. It appears unlikely that a single directory hierarchy can be created, so that competing address services need to be searched.

2.2 Locating the Called Party

Implementing personal mobility requires locating the called party, more precisely, the workstation or other terminal that the callee currently has access to. Full personal mobility also calls for the ability to locate the appropriate network or type of communication device. In the system described here, scripts set up by the user make that choice.

The method of locating a called party is independent of the call setup protocol and can be designed according to local performance and privacy requirements. Typically, the called party can only answer a multimedia call when logged into the console of a workstation, limiting the amount of information that needs to be tracked.

As will be described later, our call setup protocol features one or more per-domain servers handling calls by querying a local location service for the current whereabouts of the called party. The interaction of the server handling incoming calls and the location server is a local matter, and can range from integrating the location server with the call server to a full CORBA-based location daemon operating in the local area network. Location servers can be either centralized, with the attendant increased failure probability and load concentration problems, or distributed. Location servers can use active badges [9], or more traditional Unix services such as rwho, rusers or finger. (Unfortunately, rusers and rwho use data link layer broadcasts and are thus usually disabled.)

User location can be *on-demand, polled* or *event-driven* plus a combination of these. In on-demand user location, the location server only tries to determine the user's location when a request arrives. In a polled system, the location server maintains a user location database. Finally, in an event-driven system, users logging in and out send location updates to one or more location servers. On-demand user location is advantageous if calls are less frequent than user login changes or moves. They are also necessary if a user is logged onto several different workstations at the same time, and the workstation where the user has been most recently is to be located.

An effective method of demand-driven user location multicasts a search request when a call arrives. Login names are hashed into one of a range of multicast addresses. Each host subscribes only to the multicast group to which the user logged in the console belongs, thus significantly reducing its processing load for location requests. This method requires a daemon which, on every host, interacts with the login process or periodically checks the utmp file and responds to multicast queries.

In many cases, the number of workstations a user is likely to frequent within her domain is rather small. Thus, without any additional support on workstations, login location information can be guessed at by having the finger protocol randomly probe hosts based on past experience, noting the last login-from terminal.

3 The MUCS Protocol

In this section, we describe the basic mechanism used for establishing and changing multimedia calls and changing their parameters. The MUCS (multimedia conferencing system) protocol allows great flexibility in the location of decision making. Because of the advantages spelled out in Section 2.1 and because it is already widely available from network directory services to business cards and advertisements, the protocol uses the standard electronic mail address for reaching potential multimedia call participants. However, it is possible to use a different address, using the same format. We will generically refer to the name@host-style address for multimedia conversations as the *videophone address*.

The protocol follows the standard Internet client-server model, with the caller acting as client. Like many other Internet protocols including SMTP [10] (electronic mail), NNTP [11] (network news), HTTP [12] (WWW), ftp and telnet, the MUCS protocol consists of requests and replies written as ASCII text lines. The requests begin with a one-line command, as described below. The replies start with the protocol identifier and version, followed by a numeric status code and an optional reason phrase. Status codes have three digits, with the first digit indicating an information response (1), success (2), redirection (3), a client error (4) or a server error (5). A client does not have to understand a particular code, but can simply use the first digit to detect success or failure. Request and reply may be followed by a sequence of type-value headers, terminated by a blank line. The request and reply formats, as well as other protocol details, are modeled on the Hypertext Transfer Protocol (HTTP) [12]. Currently, protocol requests are not pipelined [13], as each caller is likely to generate only one request.

Naturally, the basic protocol could be implemented in a binary encoding, such as ASN.1, but request rates are expected to be low enough that the advantages of easy generation and parsing by programs such as Tcl [14] and humans outweigh efficiency costs.

3.1 Call Setup

Two-party calls and invitations to multicast conferences proceed in the same manner. During a multicast conference, additional conferees can be invited by any participant with the same mechanism. The call proceeds in two stages. First, the caller's client locates a MUCS server for the called party, and then sends the call request. A flow chart for locating a MUCS server is shown in Fig. 1. The sequence of lookups is designed to work even when only a few systems implement the MUCS protocol and makes maximum use of the email infrastructure for obtaining current location information. DNS address (A) records map a host name to one or more Internet addresses, while mail-exchange (MX) records [15], as mentioned, map a domain name to the host name of its mail exchange host. Rather than using MX records and thus forcing MUCS servers to be co-located with mail exchangers, a new service (SRV) resource record [16] can be used, once it is implemented more widely. However, using the mail host as a MUCS server has practical advantages. Due to the importance of electronic mail, it is likely to be well cared for and reliable. It is also often the only host that resides outside a corporate firewall.

If no server can be found or the hosts do not accept MUCS connections, the client attempts to map the videophone address to a more current one with the verify (VRFY) SMTP command or to expand a group alias to a list of addresses with the EXPN command.

If no working MUCS server can be located, a MIME mail message of type application/mucs is sent and the call attempt ends. Since mail delivery can be slow, taking from minutes to hours, there is no success/failure indication to the caller in this case. If the call request contains a multicast address, the callee simply joins that group whenever she reads the mail message, assuming the life time of the conference (see below) has not expired. For unicast calls, the recipient of the mail message in turn initiates a MUCS call.

If a working MUCS server has been found, a simple protocol exchange

- offers hints on the subject and urgency of the call;
- determines the type of media to be used during the call;
- establishes common media encodings;
- provides encryption keys for media.

The MUCS protocol currently uses TCP to a MUCS-specific well-known port to reliably exchange requests and replies. Handshake delays can be reduced by transactional TCP [17].

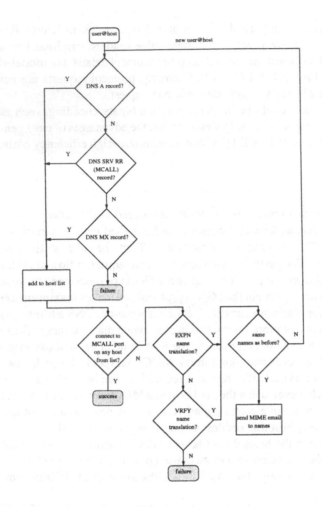

Fig. 1. Mapping a videophone address to a MUCS server

It could be argued that the call setup protocol should contact callees via IP multicast. However, this implies the need for a reliable multicast protocol, an effort probably not worthwhile given the typically low number of targets. It also has a bootstrapping problem, in that the called parties (and only those) have to subscribe to a common multicast group.

A sample call request in shown in Fig. 2. The first line indicates the desired action action, the name part of the videophone address, and the protocol version. This request line is followed by a number of header items indicating, for example, the caller name (From), user agent software (User-Agent) and call priority (Priority). The Call-Id, formatted like e-mail message identifiers, is used to identify a particular call for later changes (Section 3.2). The To field indicates that this particular call has been forwarded from an original group destination to several individual names. It has been referred to this host (in proxy mode, see below) by ceres.fokus.gmd.de.

Media are listed as Required or Accept headers. Each such header represents one media, with alternatives within each media listed in decreasing order of preference. The caller wishes to communicate only if the callee supports one of the media encodings listed in each Required headers and would also like to use the media listed in Accept headers, but leaves that up to the callee. If the callee does not support at least one of the media listed in a Required header, it returns "None available" and the call fails.

Media descriptions uses the MIME grammar. The SDP [18] format could have been used instead, but appears more cumbersome and breaks with Internet header conventions. Each media entry lists the type (audio, video, application, ...), the encoding and a list of parameter/value pairs, including the port number, the transport protocol, the RTP payload type [19], any floor control properties and the bit rate to be reserved.

In the example, the caller is only interested in a call if the callee can communicate in one of the three audio formats listed, with PCMU (μ-law PCM), one channel, 16000 Hz sampling rate, preferred. The callee must also support either video at 128 or 250 kb/s, or, if all else fails, a shared whiteboard application. A shared editor is also a possibility, if the callee wishes to use it.

If the callee wishes to use a media, it returns Accept headers and lists all acceptable encodings, in the same order as given. (Listing all acceptable encodings rather than just the preferred one is necessary to allow the caller to contact called parties in turn and successively narrow the range of possible encodings. We do not support negotiation about the order of preference within media, as we guess that such a feature would be rarely used or implemented due to the complicate semantics. It would also require adding some indication of strength of preference and a voting mechanism.)

Media are identified for error reporting or for media format changes (see Section 3.2) by a random 32-bit nonce expressed in hexadecimal.

The protocol only implements a one-round negotiation for media types. If more complicated negotiations, including voting, with several participants are required, a more sophisticated protocol such as the agreement protocol [20] must be used. However, it seems likely that most applications will support a range of encodings, with large common subsets, so that elaborate negotiations may not be necessary. Applications are free to switch encodings during the call to any one of those accepted, for example to adapt to changing network congestion conditions or quality requirements [21]. We assume that applications can receive different media types concurrently and that the media type sent does not have to equal the media type received. This is generally true for today's MBONE applications, with the exception of different audio sampling rates, but may not be true for hardware devices.

If the callee has moved permanently, e.g., after leaving a company, the server returns status code 301, "Moved permanently", and provides a list of possible new locations, if known, as Location headers. The calling application will likely indicate a failure and possibly allow updating of a local phone directory. If the user has left without leaving a forwarding address, code 410 "Gone" can be returned. If the callee is at a different host, but only temporarily, status code 302, "Moved temporarily", is returned instead. This is one of the mechanisms for providing personal mobility.

The callee (or her authorized software agent) can also indicate that she is temporarily unable or unwilling to take the call:

Request timeout: the called party could not be reached;

Busy: too many other calls or otherwise occupied;

Forbidden the caller is not allowed to reach the callee or the callee doesn't exist;

Identification required: A From header is required;

Authentication required: The request must be authenticated (see Section 3.5).

Optionally, the server can indicate a more opportune time for calling with the Retry-After header or can suggest a substitute with the Location header. For example, a response indicating two possible locations may look like this:

```
MUCS/1.0 302 Callee has moved temporarily
Location: jones@salt.lab3.company.com
Location: jones@pepper.lab3.company.com
```

```
CALL hgs@lupus.fokus.gmd.de 1.0
User-Agent: coco/1.3
From: Christian Zahl <cz@cs.tu-berlin.de>
To: Henning Schulzrinne <schulzrinne@fokus.gmd.de>
Call-Id: 9510021900.AA07734@lion.cs.tu-berlin.de
Referer: ceres.fokus.gmd.de
Expires: Mon, 02 Oct 1995 18:44:11 GMT
Required: fc99cb08 audio/pcmu; port=3456; transport=RTP;
   rate=16000; channels=1; pt=97; net=224.2.0.1; ttl=128,
   audio/gsm; port=3456; transport=RTP; rate=8000; channels=1,
   audio/lpc; port=3456; transport=RTP; rate=8000; channels=1
Required: 83ae5290 video/h261;port=4134;transport=RTP;rate=128,
   video/nv;port=4136;transport=RTP;rate=250,
   application/x-wb;port=1236
Accept: 56af7e9c application/editor;port=3500
Phone: +1 413 555 1212
Email: Christian Zahl <cz@cs.tu-berlin.de>
Location: Technical University Berlin; tz=MET;
   loc=52 32 00 N 13 25 00 E
Priority: urgent
Reach: first
Key: C7 48 90 F4 27 7B A1 CF
Subject: New MUCS error codes
```

Fig. 2. Sample MUCS Request

At any time, either caller or callee can terminate the call attempt by closing the TCP connection. No explicit indication of ringing is provided. Note that the TCP connection is only open while ringing the callee, not during the actual call. A caller may also close the connection if it is trying to reach a user at several different locations simultaneously and gets the first positive answer.

A server can operate in two modes. In *proxy mode* (Fig. 3), the server tries to locate the called party locally, and only forwards the final result of its attempts to the client. For the local users, the proxy server acts like a caller and thus needs to implement both server and client operations, including loop detection on the client side. Proxy mode is appropriate for fire-walled companies, or when the location of users should not be revealed. In this mode, a tree of connections can be established, which must be torn down if any of the root links is severed. Proxy mode differs from the usual email message forwarding in that the original connection from caller to proxy remains open while the proxy contacts other hosts. This greatly simplifies error reporting and is rather more appropriate for an interactive medium. Proxy mode is similar to the resolution strategy employed by the X.500 or DNS directories.

In *redirect mode* (Fig. 4), each call server only provides further clues as to the location by issuing redirects. The client can then decide which, if any, of the locations to contact. The client is also responsible for detecting forwarding loops. The redirect mode is similar in philosophy to the whois++ [22] directory traversal mode. The two modes can be freely mixed within a call.

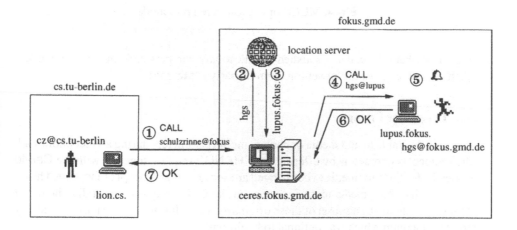

Fig. 3. MUCS operation in proxy mode

Note that, after locating a MUCS server, the protocol makes no distinction between mail server hosts and regular hosts.

Server-side group addresses such as `info@fokus.gmd.de` can be resolved either as *first* or *all*, specified by the Reach header. The *first* mode terminates the call attempts as soon as the first one from the group answers, while *all* contacts all possible candidates and invites them to participate. A reach of type first is appropriate for applications like

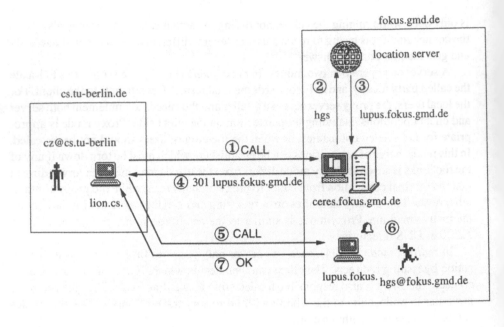

Fig. 4. MUCS operation in redirect mode

help lines where the caller is satisfied to talk to any one person from a group, while a reach of type all is useful for setting up multiparty conferences.

3.2 Parameter Changes

It is often desirable to add media or change media parameters during a videophone call. The protocol supports this by offering the CHANGE request, together with the Call-Id header. Definitions for media to be changed are sent as either Accept or Required headers, using the 32-bit media identifier nonce in the CALL request. Generally, the list of media types should be a subset of those originally listed. It is not a good idea to suddenly require a medium which was optional to begin with.

The media change request can be used to implement a simple centralized media negotiation facility. In the first round, the call initiator contacts each party, gathering the subset of media acceptable to all, the most important conferees, the majority or some other policy. The initiator then distributes this subset of media to all callees that have accepted the call through change requests. Since different media encodings may imply invoking different media agents, it is preferable for the initial round of negotiations to extend the protocol a bit. The caller would leave the TCP connection open after the CALL request, gather all media encoding preferences from the participants and then issue a round of CHANGE requests with the final set of encodings. Only then, after the caller has closed the connection, does the called conference controller start media agents based on the final list of encodings. (This delayed-start approach does not help when media changes occur due to late joins.)

Conference control applications have to use discretion to avoid conflicting CHANGE requests being issued by different parties, but there is insufficient practical experience to recommend particular mechanisms to restrict change requests.

If a server operates in proxy mode, it should cache active call identifiers and their respective user location in stable storage to avoid having to locate the user again. However, should it "forget" a particular call, for example, after a reboot, it can always treat a change request like a newly arriving call and locate the user. Change requests for group addresses with a Reach of "first" have to be rejected, since the proxy does not remember who is fielding that call. To avoid that problem, the server returns the mapping of group address to the party that actually "picked up the phone" through a Location header, which is then used by the caller to issue CHANGE requests. If a host has an active user, but no record of the call, it treats it like a newly arriving call.

3.3 Conference Membership Information

Membership in a conference is best described through media participation, with the conference membership as the union of the membership sets for each individual medium. Note that unless there is a "required" medium, it is quite possible that two members of such a conference have no common communication medium. Thus, network outages or members turning off particular media agents can change the conference membership. Also, we do not require that all conference members are invited by MUCS; others may join based on information from, say, a directory service (see Section 6).

When the conference initiator invites participants, complete membership information is not available, and thus cannot be distributed. For multicast media distribution, it appears best to distribute membership information periodically via multicast, using RTCP [19] for real-time media. Maintaining membership information for conferences run over a web of unicast connections or per-site point-to-multipoint connections, say, in ATM or ST-II, is cumbersome without a central conference registry or a distinguished conference initiator. Both of these are undesirable, as they make it difficult to continue conferences after the initiator has left or the central registry is no longer reachable.

Another approach to maintaining a membership list has been explored by the Sticky conference control protocol [23], where transitive closure of reachability is passed around. This approach is also usable here. If the initiator has contacted the initial set of members, it can then issue a change request to all members, containing To fields for all. If the called parties are contacted sequentially, each party can in turn call all the other parties listed, using the same Call-Id.

Because of these complications and since ST-II is rarely used in the Internet context, we currently only support two-party point-to-point and multicast calls.

3.4 Terminating a Call

There is no explicit call termination mechanism within MUCS. If a participant wants to leave a particular media, it uses per-media mechanisms to signal that to the other group members. For RTP, an RTCP Bye packet is sent. For unicast, the sender will receive a port unreachable ICMP message if it continues to send after the other side has closed the socket. All RTP based applications also implement a time-out mechanism that curtails sending to a particular host if that host has not been heard from recently, either via a data or RTCP (control) message. At the network layer, IP multicast requires no additional mechanisms, since data distribution to a particular host will cease automatically when the last group member leaves the multicast group.

The call server on the host where the conferencing applications are actually run (i.e., the final destination of the call request), maintains as a file in /tmp/Call-Id a description of the call state. This file will be automatically removed when the system is rebooted and can be used to restart media agents.

3.5 Security

For security, all exchanges can be sent as PGP encapsulated messages, either authenticated or encrypted. Encryption is useful if the identity of the caller or the subject of the call should only be revealed to the callee and not to any of the MUCS proxy servers. Only the request line has to remain unencrypted. PGP keys are also email addresses, so that the re-use of these addresses by MUCS yields another benefit.

Other security mechanisms like the Secure Socket Layer (SSL) [24] or IP-level authentication or encryption could be used. If the CALL request is encrypted, in can also be used to transfer a media session key (the Key header in Fig. 2).

3.6 Interaction with Other Signaling Protocols

The MUCS protocol has to interact with a number of other "signaling" protocols in the Internet. Audio and video applications may use RTP [19] and its associated signaling protocol, RTCP. Each participant periodically multicasts an RTCP packet containing information about itself, such as the user name, real name, physical location, email address, and the like (SDES information), about the amount of data it has sent and reception reports indicating the quality of service for other hosts. The RTCP messages also serve as a connectivity indicator, particularly when hosts send media data only sporadically, as audio might be during a conference. Some of the SDES information can be distributed via the MUCS protocol, avoiding duplicate transmission of the same information with different media. However, given MUCS's use of point-to-point TCP connections, RTCP is a better match for multicast conferences.

The MUCS protocol does not reserve network resources. It is expected that individual applications, when opening network sockets, will also issue resource reservation requests, usually through the resource reservation protocol (RSVP) [25]. For most audio encodings, the necessary information for bandwidth reservation is implied by the media type, for video and other sources, the media description contains the desired bandwidth. The separation of concerns, with MUCS handling invitation and cross-media setup and RSVP responsible for resource reservation, has the advantage that either could be exchanged for a different protocol or omitted. However, the separation into two protocols does introduce an additional failure mode, in that a called party could accept a call, but the resource reservation might fail. A called party could delay accepting a call until the resource reservation succeeds, possibly tailoring its **Accept** responses accordingly. This has not been implemented. We also anticipate that, if Internet videophone service is to be useful, call failures due to busy or no answer are going to be much more common than those due to lack of network resources, just as in POTS.

RSVP, in turn, communicates with the reservation and signaling protocols of the underlying protocol stack, in particular ATM Q.2931 or SPANS signaling. This interaction is a subject of on-going research and beyond the scope of this paper.

4 Implementation

Large parts of the MUCS architecture have been implemented on a Unix platform. The components and their interaction are indicated in Figure 5. The figure shows only the direct interaction between a caller and a conference daemon, without mail host or forwarding.

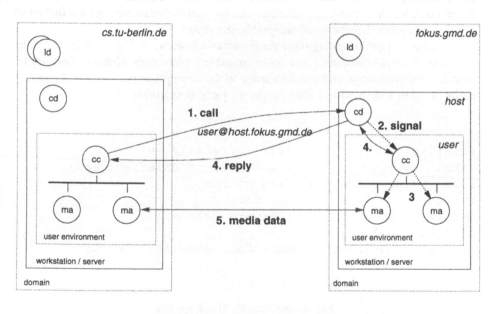

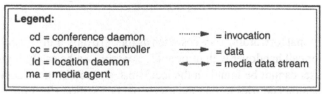

Fig. 5. MUCS Components

The conference daemon (call server) process is started by inetd when a call arrives. The conference controller (call client), called coco, is responsible for originating and answering calls. It is started either by the user or by conference daemon when a call arrives. The conference daemon maps the name part of the videophone address to a local user name, using the same database employed by the mail transfer agent (MTA). If a call arrives, a user-specified Tcl script is executed in a safe environment, allowing automatic forwarding of calls, similar in spirit to the ideas presented in [26] for interfacing with a traditional telephone or the scripts used for forwarding and filtering electronic mail. If the script has not disposed of the call by forwarding or rejecting it, the conference daemon tries to determine if the called party is logged on the local console. If so, a pop-up window appears asking whether to accept, forward or reject the call. If not, the location daemon is queried for the current location and the call forwarded to that host. If the user is not logged in anywhere, the call is rejected with an appropriate status code. If active badges [9] are in use, the call might be forwarded to a console located in the office visited by the badge owner. (This has not been implemented yet.)

Based on the media listed first in the Accept or Required headers, the conference controller maps the media and parameters to a media agent and starts it. If CHANGE requests come in, the conference controller uses the local multicast message bus described in [27] to communicate the set of acceptable encodings.

A sample script illustrating some simple actions is shown in Fig. 6. In the example, calls after 6 pm are forwarded to a home "number", while calls whose subject header contains the name of project, are forwarded to the appropriate person. The From: * action invokes a script named after the calling party, if available.

```
Priority: urgent        {ring firebells.au}
From:   my_boss         {ring hail_to_chief.au; ask}
From:   @insurance.com  {reject busy}
From:   *               {$From}
Subject: TOMQAT         {forward deffner}
if {$hour > 18} {
   forward hgs@home -reason "Gone home for the day"
}
```

Fig. 6. Sample Call Handling File

Additional forwarding services, such as forward only if the intended receiver accepts the call, or call handover with prior audio contact, can be easily implemented.

If a user cannot be found on the local host, the conference daemon contacts the location daemon and tries to find the user's likely location (Section 2.2) and returns that location to the conference controller (redirect mode). The conference controller can be configured require manual confirmation for redirections within the same domain or only if outside the called domain. If the conference daemon cannot find such a location (say, the user has left for the day), the daemon logs the call and rejects it.

5 Performance Issues

Call volume differs dramatically in different settings, spanning the gamut between private residences attached to an Internet service provider, a research corporation with mostly internal calls to a telephone-sales outfit. A typical local office sees three 3-minute calls in the busy hour per line [28, p. 141], that is, 3 BHCA (busy hour call attempts). A large PBX for 10,000 stations is designed for about 100,000 busy hour calls, i.e., BHCA of 10. Typical dimensioning of outside lines for offices assumes about one outside call per hour and station. Also, ITU recommendation Q.543 lists a BHCA range from 1.2 to 6.8. Thus, even a mail server responsible for handling MUCS needs for several thousand staff members would see a load far less than a moderate-usage web server. A local network serving 200 employees would see a location request at most once every two seconds during the busy hour, which seems manageable even if broadcast were to be used.

Signaling delays are also bounded by telephony expectations. Q.543 (Table 13) specifies, for example, that the delay from end of dialing to start of ringing should have a mean value less than 650 ms, while Q.709 specifies a maximum delay of 1170 ms. This delay limits the number of forwarding operations which can be performed. Delays can be minimized by having the client cache the last successful location within the same domain for a particular user and thus, in many cases, avoid the redirect through the mail server. If the called is not at that location, the call server on that workstation will redirect as before. If for some reason only the mail exchange host has user location capabilities, the workstation server simply forwards any calls for users not logged on its console to the mail exchange host. The forwarding request also has the caller invalidate its cache. Besides reducing forwarding delays, location caching also reduces the call handling load seen by the mail exchange host.

6 Related Work

A number of conference control protocols have been described and implemented. Here, we only consider those that do not require a conference server. The Conference Control Channel Protocol (CCCP) [29] allows communication between different components of a conference, either located on a single host or distributed. It assumes that conference members have been notified or invited by other means, one of which may well be MUCS.

The Connection Control Protocol (CCP) [30], partially implemented in the mmcc conference controller, supports invitations and negotiation. The protocol is far more complex than MUCS, with numerous states and its own multicast reliability mechanism. Unlike MUCS, it is active during the whole conference. CCP does not support the notion of forwarding, does not interact with SMTP and implements no call handling features. MUCS is also an attempt to show that the functionality actually used for small-group communications can be implemented in a very simple manner.

On the MBONE, seminars, space shuttle launches and other events are announced using the session directory sd developed at Lawrence Berkeley Laboratory. It offers a single, non-hierarchical "TV guide" to upcoming events and also allocates multicast addresses. sd supports viewer-initiated conferences, with notification of events usually provided through mailing lists or newsgroups. sd is part of the light-weight session model [31], where participants communicate principally via IP multicast and maintain "soft" (i.e., fragile and periodically refreshed) state. The MUCS protocol currently operates under that model for the interaction of individual media, but can be used in other environments.

Integration of conferencing and the World-Wide Web has also been pursued. In the Virtual Places approach [32], a subscriber could be met via multiple media at different places (that is, pages) within the web. A very much simplified version can be offered by having a MUCS link in one's home page which simply returns the current videophone address as a URL of method 'mucs'.

7 Conclusion and Future Work

The MUCS protocol allows to establish multimedia conversations across the Internet, offering personal mobility without changes to the existing Internet infrastructure. Together with sufficient bandwidth and resource reservation, it provides another missing component on the way to the multimedia Internet. Users can be reached even if only their own workstation supports the protocol, rather than the site's mail server or dedicated MUCS server. Lifelong personal and trans-national videophone addresses can be offered by any number of service providers, without need for coordination. The call setup protocol can be used with a number of different resource reservation protocols; it works best, however, if the network supports IP multicast and receiver-based resource reservation. The services can be deployed without any changes to the network itself, unlike the substantial, coordinated switch upgrades envisioned for offering UPT services. Since call handling information is only kept on the user's premises, privacy is enhanced and programmed, rather than table-driven call handling can be readily offered. The forwarding service can be offered by competing service providers that are distinct from the bit carriers, making it easy to use several different providers depending on time-of-day, caller, and the like. The MUCS protocol also needs a multicast address allocation service [33].

The re-use of the existing electronic mail address also allows to benefit from the existing infrastructure for email addresses, from address books to mailing lists, PGP keys and aliases.

Interoperation of this MUCS protocol with plain old telephony (POTS), mobile telephony and ISDN remains to be investigated. Telephone numbers in ITU E.123 notation can be used as user names. Together with existing proposals for the integration of email and fax [34] and access to paging services [35,36], a complete program-controlled communication environment could then be offered.

For personal mobility, the subscriber must have the possibility of securely changing the forwarding characteristics. This can be done remotely with a WWW browser, or an email messaging interface, amongst others.

Despite its limitations when invoking complex functions, the basic telephone set has a human-"computer" interface that even the most techno-illiterate can handle. We are investigating the advantages of attaching a simple telephone set to a workstation, so that a user can accept an Internet phone call in the accustomed manner, by picking up the receiver. Since echo cancellation for speaker phone operation remains difficult and acoustic privacy is often desirable, a phone receiver remains also an attractive audio I/O device.

With the advent of high-speed IP connectivity provided by ISDN or cable TV, Internet telephony may offer advanced services far sooner (and possibly cheaper) than traditional telephone operators.

8 Acknowledgements

Discussions about PBX and central office sizing with the GMD telecommunications office and M. R. Lundberg were very helpful. Mark Handley provided valuable comments. The system was implemented by Frank Oertel and Christian Zahl, TU Berlin.

References

1. H. Schulzrinne, "Internet services: from electronic mail to real-time multimedia," in *Proc. of KIVS (Kommunikation in Verteilten Systemen)* (K. Franke, U. Hübner, and W. Kalfa, eds.), Informatik aktuell, (Chemnitz, Germany), pp. 21–34, Gesellschaft für Informatik, Springer Verlag, Feb. 1995.

2. H. Eriksson, "MBONE: The multicast backbone," *Communications ACM*, vol. 37, pp. 54–60, Aug. 1994.

3. J. Tränk, "Signalling and the IN," *Telecommunications (International Edition)*, vol. 29, pp. 88–89, July 1995.

4. C. E. Perkins and P. Bhagwat, "A mobile networking system based on the internet protocol," *IEEE Personal Communications*, vol. 1, pp. 32–41, First Quarter 1994.

5. S. E. Deering and D. R. Cheriton, "Multicast routing in datagram internetworks and extended LANs," *ACM Transactions on Computer Systems*, vol. 8, pp. 85–110, May 1990.

6. R. Pandya, "Emerging mobile and personal communication systems," *IEEE Communications Magazine*, vol. 33, pp. 44–52, June 1995.

7. European Telecommunications Standards Institute, "Universal personal telecommunication (upt): Phase 1 – service description," tech. rep., European Telecommunications Standards Institute, Sophia Antipolis, France, June 1995.

8. D. C. Lynch and M. T. Rose, *Internet system handbook*. Reading, Massachusetts: Addison-Wesley, 1993.

9. A. Hopper, "Communication at the desktop," *Computer Networks and ISDN Systems*, vol. 10, pp. 1253–1265, July 1994.

10. D. Crocker, "Standard for the format of ARPA internet text messages," STD 11, RFC 822, Internet Engineering Task Force, Aug. 1982.

11. B. Kantor and P. Lapsley, "Network news transfer protocol: A proposed standard for the stream-based transmission of news," RFC 977, Internet Engineering Task Force, Feb. 1986.

12. T. Berners-Lee, R. Fielding, and H. Frystyk, "Hypertext transfer protocol – http/1.0," Internet Draft, Internet Engineering Task Force, Aug. 1995. Work in progress.

13. N. Freed and A. Cargille, "SMTP service extension for command pipelining," RFC 1854, Internet Engineering Task Force, Oct. 1995.

14. J. K. Ousterhout, *Tcl and the Tk Toolkit*. Reading, Massachusetts: Addison-Wesley, 1994.

15. C. Partridge, "Mail routing and the domain system," STD 14, RFC 974, Internet Engineering Task Force, Jan. 1986.

16. A. Gulbrandsen and P. Vixie, "A DNS RR for specifying the location of services," Internet Draft, Internet Engineering Task Force, Oct. 1995. Work in progress.

17. R. Braden, "T/TCP – TCP extensions for transactions functional specification," RFC 1644, Internet Engineering Task Force, July 1994.

18. M. Handley and V. Jacobson, "SDP: Session description protocol," Internet Draft, Internet Engineering Task Force, Aug. 1995. Work in progress.

19. H. Schulzrinne, S. Casner, R. Frederick, and V. Jacobson, "RTP: A transport protocol for real-time applications," internet draft (work-in-progress) *draft-ietf-avt-rtp-*.txt*, IETF, Nov. 1995.

20. S. Shenker, A. Weinrib, and E. Schooler, "Managing shared ephemeral teleconferencing state: Policy and mechanism," Internet Draft, Internet Engineering Task Force, July 1995. Work in progress.

21. I. Busse, B. Deffner, and H. Schulzrinne, "Dynamic QoS control of multimedia applications based on RTP," in *First International Workshop on High Speed Networks and Open Distributed Platforms*, (St. Petersburg, Russia), June 1995.

22. P. Faltstrom, R. Schoultz, and C. Weider, "How to interact with a Whois++ mesh," Internet Draft, Internet Engineering Task Force, Mar. 1995. Work in progress.

23. C. Elliott, "A 'sticky' conference control protocol," *Internetworking: Research and Experience*, vol. 5, pp. 97–119, 1994.

24. K. Hickman and T. Elgamal, "The SSL protocol," Internet Draft, Internet Engineering Task Force, June 1995. Work in progress.

25. L. Zhang, S. Deering, D. Estrin, S. Shenker, and D. Zappala, "RSVP: a new resource ReSerVation protocol," *IEEE Network*, vol. 7, pp. 8–18, Sept. 1993.

26. S. A. Uhler, "PhoneStation, moving the telephone into the virtual desktop," in *Proc. of Usenix Winter Conference*, (San Diego, California), pp. 131–140, Jan. 1993.

27. H. Schulzrinne, "Dynamic configuration of conferencing applications using pattern-matching multicast," in *Proc. International Workshop on Network and Operating System Support for for Digital Audio and Video (NOSSDAV)*, Lecture Notes in Computer Science (LNCS), (Durham, New Hampshire), pp. 231–242, Springer, Apr. 1995.

28. B. E. Briley, *Introduction to Telephone Switching*. London: Addison-Wesley, 1983.

29. M. Handley, I. Wakeman, and J. Crowcroft, "The conference control protocol (CCCP): a scalable base for building conference control applications," in *SIGCOMM Symposium on Communications Architectures and Protocols*, (Cambridge, Massachusetts), pp. 275–287, Sept. 1995.

30. E. M. Schooler, "The connection control protocol: Specification (version 1.1)," technical report, USC/Information Sciences Institute, Marina del Ray, California, Jan. 1992.

31. V. Jacobson, S. McCanne, and S. Floyd, "A conferencing architecture for light-weight sessions," Nov. 1993. MICE seminar series (transparencies).

32. E. Shapiro, "Virtual places – a foundation for human interaction," in *Proc. of the Second World Wide Web Conference'94*, (Chicago, Illinois), Oct. 1994.

33. S. Pejhan, A. Eleftheriadis, and D. Anastassiou, "Distributed multicast address management in the global internet," *IEEE Journal on Selected Areas in Communications*, vol. 13, pp. 1445–1456, Oct. 1995.

34. C. Malamud and M. Rose, "Principles of operation for the TPC.INT subdomain: Remote printing – technical procedures," RFC 1528, Internet Engineering Task Force, Oct. 1993.

35. M. Rose, "Principles of operation for the TPC.INT subdomain: Radio paging – technical procedures," RFC 1703, Internet Engineering Task Force, Oct. 1994.

36. A. Gwinn, "Simple network paging protocol - version 2," RFC 1645, Internet Engineering Task Force, July 1994.

A Security Architecture for Tenet Scheme 2

Rolf Oppliger
Amit Gupta
Mark Moran
Riccardo Bettati

Abstract. The bandwith requirements of interactive multimedia applications are exhaustive, causing network congestion to be a major problem. One way to deal with this problem is to use a resource reservation scheme, such as e.g. Tenet Scheme 2. This paper proposes a security architecture for Tenet Scheme 2. The basic ideas are to use Internet layer security protocols, such as the IP Security Protocol (IPSP) and Internet Key Management Protocol (IKMP), to establish authentic communication channels between RCAP daemons, to handle client authentication and authorization locally, and to use a proxy-based mechanism to distribute access rights for target sets and channels. The security architecture uses as its building blocks a collision-resistant one-way hash function and a digital signature system.

1 Introduction

To cover the future needs of business and residential customers in the information age, interactive multimedia applications are envisaged or being developed and installed. But the bandwith requirements of interactive multimedia applications are exhaustive, causing network congestion to be a major problem. One way to deal with this problem is to use a resource reservation and billing scheme that allows particular users to obtain preferential access to network resources, under the control of an admission control mechanism. Permission to make a reservation will depend both upon the availability of the requested resources along the path of the data, and upon satisfaction of policy rules. Several resource reservation schemes and corresponding protocols have been proposed so far. Examples are the resource reservation setup protocol (RSVP) [1] and the Internet stream protocol version 2 (ST-II), as well as the Tenet realtime protocols.

However, the use of a resource reservation scheme requires security to be considered with care. A cryptographic message origin authentication mechanism has been added to the specification of RSVP [2], and this paper proposes a security architecture for Tenet Scheme 2. The basic ideas are

- to use Internet layer security protocols, such as the IP Security Protocol (IPSP) and Internet Key Management Protocol (IKMP), to establish authentic communication channels between RCAP daemons,
- to handle client authentication and authorization locally, and
- to use a proxy-based mechanism to distribute access rights for target sets and channels.

The security architecture uses as its building blocks a collision-resistant one-way hash function and a digital signature system. The rest of this paper proceeds as follows: The Tenet Scheme is briefly introduced in section two. The terminology that is used to subsequently describe the security architecture for Tenet Scheme 2 is introduced in section three. The evolving protocol standards that can be used to provide Internet layer security are overviewed in section four, and the security architecture for Tenet Scheme 2 is described and fully discussed in section five. Conclusions are finally drawn in section six.

2 Tenet Scheme

The Tenet Group at the University of California and the International Computer Science Institute (ICSI) in Berkeley has been working since 1988 to provide practical solutions to the problem of realtime communications [3]. The initial goal of the work was to devise and specify a set of algorithms that, when implemented in a network, would enable the network to offer a realtime communication service to its clients. Such a set of algorithms was called a realtime communication scheme, or Scheme for brevity. Meanwhile, Tenet Scheme 1 has been embodied in a suite of realtime protocols, namely the Tenet Suite 1[1].

In the Tenet realtime protocol suite, the task of channel setup is performed by the Real Time Channel Administration Protocol (RCAP). RCAP is a control protocol that takes client requests containing traffic descriptions and performance requirements and sets up realtime channels accordingly. The data transfers are done by the Realtime Internet Protocol (RTIP) which schedules datagrams according to the resource reservations made by RCAP. At the transport layer, the Tenet Suite consists of two protocols, namely

- the Realtime Message Transport Protocol (RMTP), which is intended for message-based realtime transport between endpoints, and
- the Continuous Media Transport Protocol (CMTP), which offers a stream-based interface and a time-driven mechanisms for applications, such as audio and video transmission.

The protocol that controls data transfers, primarily reacting to the detection of error conditions, is called the Realtime Control Message Protocol (RTCMP). RTCMP performs functions similar to those of ICMP in the Internet protocol suite.

The Tenet Group is currently working on Scheme 2. The main focus of this work is to extend the basic realtime communication service provided by Tenet Suite 1 in two respects [4, 5, 6]:

- to provide abstractions and techniques for efficient multi-party realtime communication;
- to make the client-service interface more flexible.

---

[1] Further information on Tenet Suite 1 can be obtained in the World Wide Web by following the URL http://tenet.berkeley.edu/tenet-software.html.

In Tenet Scheme 2, the key networking abstraction is the target set, which is similar to the host group in IP multicast [7, 8]. Receivers join a target set depending on their interest in a certain transmission, and channels are established from data sources to the members of a target set accordingly. Join and leave primitives support dynamic membership in target sets, as well as the associated change in multicast channels.

From the security point of view, the fact that RCAP uses TCP/IP connections to exchange messages between clients and RCAP daemons must be considered with care. The use of the TCP/IP protocols does neither allow RCAP daemons to authenticate client requests, nor to protect the authenticity and integrity of messages in exchange. As a matter of fact, the TCP/IP protocol suite have been known to be vulnerable and exposed to various attacks, and it is only due to the emerging use of the Internet for commercial purposes that TCP/IP and Internet security have recently become an issue [9].

3 Terminology

A principal refers to a human user or system entity that is registered in and authenticatable to a system. Authentication refers to the process of verifying the claimed identity of a principal, authorization to the process of determining the (access) rights of this principal, and access control to the process of enforcing these access rights. With regard to Tenet Scheme 2, users, clients, and RCAP daemons are considered as principals, and access must be controlled with regard to target sets and channels.

The following notation is used in this paper to refer to users, clients, RCAP daemons, target sets, and channels:

- U_i is used to refer to user $i (i \geq 1)$.
- Every user U_i may have several clients running on his behalf, and C_{ij} is used to refer to client j of user $U_i (i, j \geq 1)$.
- D_i is used to refer to RCAP daemon $i (i \geq 1)$.
- TS_i is used to refer to target set $i (i \geq 1)$.
- Every target set TS_i may have several channels associated with it, and Ch_{ij} is used to refer to channel j of target set $TS_i (i, j \geq 1)$.

A protocol specifies the format and relative timing of messages exchanged between communicating parties. A cryptographic protocol is a protocol that uses cryptographic techniques, meaning that all or parts of the messages are encrypted on the sender' side, and decrypted on the receiver' side. Both the Internet layer security protocols and the protocols that are used for client authentication, authorization, and access rights distribution represent cryptographic protocols. The reader of this paper is thus assumed to be familiar with both cryptography, and the use of cryptographic protocols in computer networks and distributed systems [10, 11]. The following notation is used to describe cryptographic protocols:

- K is used to denote a secret key, and the term $\{m\}K$ is used to refer to a message m that is encrypted with K. The same key is used for decryption, so $\{\{m\}K\}K$ equals m. If K is used to compute a message authentication code (MAC), then the term $\langle m \rangle K$ is used to refer to a MAC computed for message m and key K. An efficient way to compute and verify a MAC is to use a collision-resistant one-way hash function, such as MD4 [12], MD5 [13] or the Secure Hash Standard (SHS) [14], and to key it with a secret key as described e.g. in [15, 16].
- (k, k^{-1}) is used to denote a public key pair, with k referring to the public key, and k^{-1} referring to the corresponding private key. The term $\{m\}k$ is used to refer to a message m that is encrypted with a public key k. The message can be decrypted only with the corresponding private key k^{-1}, so $\{\{m\}k\}k^{-1}$ equals m. In a digital signature system, such as RSA [17], ElGamal [18], or the Digital Signature Standard (DSS) [19], the user's private key is used to digitally sign messages, and the corresponding public key is used to verify the signatures. In this case, the term $\{m\}k^{-1}$ is used to refer to a digital signature giving message recovery, and the term $\langle m \rangle k^{-1}$ is used to refer to a digital signature with appendix [20]. In the latter case, $\langle m \rangle k^{-1}$ abbreviates $(m, \{h(m)\}k^{-1})$, with h being a collision-resistant one-way hash function. The signature can be verified only with the public key k.

In either case, key subscripts may be used to indicate principals, target sets, or channels.

4 Internet Layer Security Protocols

With regard to the Internet' security concerns, both the Internet Research Task Force (IRTF) and the the Internet Engineering Task Force (IETF) have launched corresponding activities. The IRTF Privacy and Security Research Group (PSRG) is adapting the OSI security architecture for the Internet, and the IETF has chartered an Internet Protocol Security Protocol (IPSEC) Working Group (WG) to standardize an Internet layer security protocol. As a matter of fact, the IETF IPSEC WG seeks to standardize both an IP Security Protocol (IPSP) and an Internet Key Management Protocol (IKMP).

4.1 IPSP

The idea of having a standardized network layer security protocol is not new, and several protocols had been proposed even before the IPSEC WG started to meet:

- The Security Protocol 3 (SP3) was proposed by the National Security Agency (NSA) and the National Institute of Science and Technology (NIST) as part of the Secure Data Network System (SDNS).

- The Network Layer Security Protocol (NLSP) was proposed by the International Organization for Standardization (ISO) to secure the Connectionless Network Protocol (CLNP) [21].
- The Integrated NLSP (I-NLSP) was proposed to provide security services for both IP and CLNP.
- SwIPe was yet another network layer security protocol proposal [22].

In spite of their different names and specifications, all of these protocols have one thing in common: they all use IP encapsulation as their enabling technique. IP encapsulation allows IP datagrams to be encrypted and enclosed in outer IP headers. Based on these outer IP headers, the datagrams are then routed through an internet. At a peer systems, the outer IP headers are stripped off, and the IP datagrams are decrypted and forwarded to their final destinations.

The current version of IPSP uses IP encapsulation as its enabling technique, too. In particular, the IPSP suggests the use of two security mechanisms that may be used together or separately:

- The Authentication Header (AH) provides data origin authentication services for IPSP datagrams. In essence, the sender of a datagram computes a MAC over the constant parts of the datagram, and sends the result as AH together with the datagram to the receiver. The receiver extracts the AH, recalculates the MAC, and verifies, whether the value matches the AH that he has originally received from the sender.
- The Encapsulating Security Payload (ESP) uses IP encapsulation to provide confidentiality services for IPSP datagrams.

The IETF IPSEC WG has proposed keyed MD5 [13] as a default algorithm for the AH mechanism, and the Data Encryption Standard (DES) in Cipher Block Chaining (CBC) mode [23, 24] for the ESP mechanism. However, export, import and use of encryption may be regulated in some countries, and other algorithms and modes may be used instead.

4.2 IKMP

With regard to a possible IKMP standard, several proposals have been submitted to the IETF IPSEC WG for further consideration:

- The Modular Key Management Protocol (MKMP) uses long-term master keys to derive short-term session keys that provide perfect forward secrecy [25].
- The Simple Key-Management for Internet Protocols (SKIP) uses implicitly shared long-term Diffie-Hellman keys to derive keys on a per-session or per-datagram basis [26].
- The Photuris[2] Key Management Protocol combines a Diffie-Hellman key exchange with a subsequent exchange of RSA signatures.

---

[2] "Photuris" is the latin name for the firefly, and "Firefly" is in turn the name for a classified key exchange protocol designed by the NSA for the STU-III secure telephone.

Quite recently, the Internet Drafts related to the IPSP have been approved by the Internet Engineering Steering Group (IESG) as Proposed Standards for the Internet in RFC 1825 to 1829. With regard to the IKMP, the focus of the IETF IPSEC WG is on the Photuris proposal. As a matter of fact, the MKMP proposal has been gathered up in favor of an enhanced version of the Photuris proposal named Photuris Plus or SKEME (Secure Key Exchange Mechanism) [27].

5 Security Architecture

It has already been mentioned previously that the basic ideas of the security architecture for Tenet Scheme 2 are to use Internet layer security protocols to establish authentic communication channels between RCAP daemons, to handle client authentication and authorization locally, and to use a proxy-based mechanism to distribute access rights for target sets and channels. Having overviewed the Internet layer security protocols that can be used to establish authentic channels between RCAP daemons in section four, this section addresses the remaining questions, namely how to authenticate and authorize clients locally, and how to distribute access rights for target sets and channels to other clients. The assumptions are as follows:

- Every RCAP daemon D_i holds a long-term public key pair $(k_{D_i}, k_{D_i}^{-1})$ that can be used in a digital signature system. Note that the public key pair may (but need not) be the same as the public key pair that is used for any Internet layer key management protocol. Also note that key revocation is considered as a problem that is not necessarily related to Tenet Scheme 2, and thus not discussed in this paper.
- Every user U_i (and thus every client C_{ij} that acts on U_i's behalf) is associated with a particular RCAP daemon D_k, and this RCAP daemon is referred to as U_i's (and C_{ij}'s) home RCAP daemon.
- Every RCAP daemon D_i has a list of users who are authorized to have D_i create target sets. The acronym UAL (User Authorization List) is used to refer to this list.

With regard to the last two assumptions it should be made explicit that the notion of a home RCAP daemon has been introduced to avoid the necessity of having and maintaining a global naming scheme. In this case, a RCAP daemon must only know its local users. However, the security architecture as described in this section does not suffer any fundamental change, if home RCAP daemons are clustered or made obsolete by introducing a global naming scheme.

5.1 Authentication

If user U_i has client C_{ij} contact his home RCAP daemon D_k, C_{ij} and D_k must authenticate each other. In principle, C_{ij} has to show that he's acting on U_i's behalf, and D_k has to show that he's U_i's (and thus C_{ij}'s) home RCAP daemon. There are several authentication protocols available today that can be used for this task. An overview is given in [28]. The protocols require either a secret to be shared between U_i and D_k, or the use of public key cryptography:

- With regard to the first possibility, the secret shared between U_i and D_k may be a personal identification number (PIN) or a password. In this case, a single sign-on mechanism can be used to authenticate a user based on a secret that is comparably weak, and provide him with a cryptographically strong session key.
- With regard to the second possibility, both U_i and D_k must have a public key pair, of which they keep the private key secret and make the public key available to the others. Note that D_k already fulfills these requirements, as $k_{D_k}^{-1}$ is D_k's private key and k_{D_k} is assumed to be publicly available. Consequently, the problem is only relevant for U_i. One possibility to solve the problem is to equip U_i with a personal token that stores $k_{U_i}^{-1}$ on his behalf. However, this solution requires the use of special hardware devices, such as chipcards or PCMCIA cards, and the cost of this solution may be prohibitive. A more realistic approach is either to locally store $k_{U_i}^{-1}$ encrypted with a password-derived key encryption key, or to have D_k store $k_{U_i}^{-1}$, and to use a password-based mechanism to control access to this key.

Note that some operating systems offer a possibility that, in principle, would allow RCAP daemons to authenticate users without having to store additional authentication information. For example, if D_k had read access to the password file of a UNIX system, the entries of this file could be used to authenticate users and clients. Taking advantage of this possibility would simplify authentication considerably. However, it is only fair to mention that it would also expose the users' passwords to malicious software attacks from the RCAP daemon. One way to deal with this problem is to have the RCAP daemon authenticate to a client, before the client requests and delivers the user's password.

Having discussed the various approaches for authentication, it is assumed that a corresponding protocol is used, and that this protocol provides C_{ij} and D_k with a strong session key K_{ik}. This key can then be used for the lifetime of a session to authenticate the origin of messages, and to establish authentic communication channels between clients and RCAP daemons accordingly.

5.2 Authorization and Access Control

To create a target set TS_l on U_i's behalf, C_{ij} has to randomly select a public key pair (k_l, k_l^{-1}), and request D_k to create TS_l by using the following protocol:

$$1 : C_{ij} \longrightarrow D_k : \text{Target\_Set\_Create\_Request}(\langle TS_l, k_l \rangle K_{ik})$$
$$2 : D_k \longrightarrow C_{ij} : \text{Target\_Set\_Create\_Confirmation}(\langle TS_l, k_l \rangle k_{D_k}^{-1})$$

In step 1, C_{ij} sends a target set create request message to D_k. The message includes TS_l and k_l, as well as a MAC to protect message origin authenticity. C_{ij}

uses K_{ik} to compute the MAC, and D_k uses the same key to verify the MAC. If the MAC is valid, D_k assumes the request to be authentic. If U_i is enumerated in D_k's UAL, D_k creates the target set, and returns a target set create confirmation message to C_{ij} in step 2. Note that the message in this case represents a digital signature with appendix for TS_l and k_l, generated with D_k's private key $k_{D_k}^{-1}$. D_j and C_{ik} both store the message for backup purposes. Finally, C_{ik} announces C_{ij}, D_k, and $\langle TS_l, k_l \rangle k_{D_k}^{-1}$ in public.

If a client C_{xy} is to perform a specific operation on TS_l, such as join or leave, or create a channel on TS_l, he must be authorized accordingly. In principle, he must be granted a proxy that provides him with the corresponding (access) rights by C_{ij}. Therefore, C_{xy} randomly selects a public key pair (k, k^{-1}), and uses the following protocol to request a proxy:

$$1 : C_{xy} \longrightarrow C_{ij} \ : \ \text{Target\_Set\_Proxy\_Request}(TS_l, \{R, C_{xy}, k\}k_l)$$
$$2 : C_{ij} \longrightarrow C_{xy} \ : \ \text{Target\_Set\_Proxy\_Confirmation}(TS_l, \langle R', C_{xy}, k \rangle k_l^{-1})$$

In step 1, C_{xy} sends a target set proxy request message to C_{ij}. The message includes TS_l, an encoded set R of requested access rights, C_{xy}, and the public key k. R, C_{xy}, and k are encrypted with k_l which is the public key of the target set TS_l. After having received the message, C_{ij} decrypts the encrypted part with k_l^{-1}, and decides whether he wants to grant access rights to C_{xy}. If he does, he selects a corresponding set R' of access rights, and returns a target set proxy confirmation message to C_{xy} in step 2. The message includes TS_l, R', C_{xy}, and k, with the last three components being digitally signed with k_l^{-1}.

Note that, in general, C_{xy} and C_{ij} needn't be associated with the same RCAP daemon. If U_x and C_{xy} are associated with D_z, and U_i and C_{ij} with D_k, then the target set proxy request and confirmation messages must pass along a path between D_z and D_k, and this path may include several RCAP daemons. The messages that are exchanged between RCAP daemons are assumed to be protected by using the IPSP AH mechanism. Provided that an IPSP connection can be established between D_z and D_k the protocol to request a target set proxy is as follows:

$$1 : C_{xy} \longrightarrow D_z \ : \ \text{Target\_Set\_Proxy\_Request}(\langle TS_l, \{R, C_{xy}, k\}k_l \rangle K_{xz})$$
$$2 : D_z \longrightarrow D_k \ : \ \text{Target\_Set\_Proxy\_Request}([[TS_l, \{R, C_{xy}, k\}k_l]])$$
$$3 : D_k \longrightarrow C_{ij} \ : \ \text{Target\_Set\_Proxy\_Request}(\langle TS_l, \{R, C_{xy}, k\}k_l \rangle K_{ik})$$
$$4 : C_{ij} \longrightarrow D_k \ : \ \text{Target\_Set\_Proxy\_Confirmation}(\langle TS_l, \langle R', C_{xy}, k \rangle k_l^{-1} \rangle K_{ik})$$
$$5 : D_k \longrightarrow D_z \ : \ \text{Target\_Set\_Proxy\_Confirmation}([[TS_l, \langle R', C_{xy}, k \rangle k_l^{-1}]])$$
$$6 : D_z \longrightarrow C_{xy} \ : \ \text{Target\_Set\_Proxy\_Confirmation}(\langle TS_l, \langle R', C_{xy}, k \rangle k_l^{-1} \rangle K_{xz})$$

The target set proxy request message is passed from C_{xy} to D_z in step 1, from D_z to D_k in step 2, and from D_k to C_{ij} in step 3. In return, the target set proxy confirmation message is passed from C_{ij} to D_k in step 4, from D_k to D_z in step 5, and from D_z back to C_{xy} in step 6. The authenticity of the messages that are exchanged between clients and RCAP daemons are protected by MACs, and the authenticity of the messages that are exchanged between RCAP daemons are protected by the IPSP AH mechanism. The latter protection mechanism is indicated by using double square brackets in steps 2 and 5.

If C_{xy} wants to use the proxy that he has been granted by C_{ij}, he contacts D_k with the following challenge response protocol:

$1 : C_{xy} \longrightarrow D_k \quad : \text{Target\_Set\_Access\_Request}(TS_l, C_{xy}, \langle R', C_{xy}, k \rangle k_l^{-1})$
$2 : D_k \longrightarrow C_{xy} \quad : \text{Target\_Set\_Access\_Request\_Challenge}(N)$
$3 : C_{xy} \longrightarrow D_k \quad : \text{Target\_Set\_Access\_Request\_Response}(\{N\}k^{-1})$

Note that the protocol is given in its short form, without going through all intermediate RCAP daemons between C_{xy} and D_k. In step 1, C_{xy} provides D_k with TS_l, C_{xy}, and the digitally signed part of the target set proxy that he has received from C_{ij} for TS_l. D_k can compare the client information in the request with the client information in C_{ij}'s confirmation. If they match, D_k assumes the access request to be valid. He challenges C_{xy} with a fresh nonce N in step 2, and C_{xy} is to answer with a digital signature for N in step 3. Note that C_{xy} can generate the correct response only if he holds the private key k^{-1} that corresponds to k. If C_{xy} is able to correctly respond with $\{N\}k^{-1}$, D_k assumes that the proxy has indeed been issued for C_{xy}.

In Tenet Scheme 2, a target set may have several channels associated with it, and the right to create a channel on a target set must be granted by the owner of the target set. Consequently, if C_{ij} is the owner of target set TS_l, C_{xy} has to be granted a proxy to create a channel Ch_{lk} on TS_l by C_{ij}. If C_{ij} provides C_{xy} with such a proxy, C_{xy} can use it to have D_k set up Ch_{lk}. In this case, D_k registers C_{xy} with the public key k' as owner of the channel. If another client C_{vw} wants to access channel Ch_{lk}, he has be provided with a proxy by C_{xy}. In this case, C_{xy} uses k'^{-1} to issue and digitally sign proxies for Ch_{lk}. The protocol to request a proxy for a channel is similar to the protocol to request a proxy for a target set. C_{vw} randomly selects a public key pair (k'', k''^{-1}), and uses the following protocol:

$1 : C_{vw} \longrightarrow C_{xy} \quad : \text{Channel\_Proxy\_Request}(Ch_{lk}, \{R, C_{vw}, k''\}k')$
$2 : C_{xy} \longrightarrow C_{vw} \quad : \text{Channel\_Proxy\_Confirmation}(Ch_{lk}, \langle R', C_{vw}, k'' \rangle k'^{-1})$

Again, the connection between C_{vw} and C_{xy} may lead through intermediate RCAP daemons, and to keep the description simple, the protocol is given in its short form. In step 1, C_{vw} sends a channel proxy request message to C_{xy}. The message includes Ch_{lk} and $\{R, C_{vw}, k''\}k'$. Note that only the legitimate owner of the Ch_{lk} holds the private key k'^{-1}, and can decrypt the second part of the message accordingly. In step 2, C_{xy} returns a channel proxy confirmation message to C_{vw}. The message includes Ch_{lk}, as well as R', C_{vw}, and k'', digitally signed with k'^{-1}. C_{vw} can use the channel proxy by using the following challenge response protocol:

$1 : C_{vw} \longrightarrow D_k \quad : \text{Channel\_Access\_Request}(Ch_{lk}, C_{vw}, \langle R', C_{vw}, k \rangle k'^{-1})$
$2 : D_k \longrightarrow C_{vw} \quad : \text{Channel\_Access\_Request\_Challenge}(N)$
$3 : C_{vw} \longrightarrow D_k \quad : \text{Channel\_Access\_Request\_Response}(\{N\}k''^{-1})$

This protocol is analogous to the protocol that is used to use target set proxies. In step 1, C_{vw} sends a channel access request message to D_k. The message includes Ch_{lk} and C_{vw}, as well as the channel proxy $\langle R', C_{vw}, k \rangle k'^{-1}$. D_k knows the public key k', and can verify the digital signature that is appended to the message accordingly. In step 2, D_k challenges C_{vw} with a nonce N, and in step 3, C_{vw} responds with $\{N\}k''^{-1}$, which is a digital signature for that nonce.

The proxy-based authorization mechanism proposed in this paper is similar to the restricted proxies described in [29]. Both mechanisms use a certificate that carries a public key, and a corresponding private key that links the proxy to its legitimate owner. The main difference between the two mechanisms is related to the way in which the private key is selected and distributed. Whereas in the mechanism described in this paper, the client that requests a proxy selects a public key pair and has the public key digitally signed by the proxy grantor, it is the grantor that selects a public key pair and provides the client with both the certificate and the corresponding private key in [29]. It is assumed that the mechanism described in this paper is advantageous in situations that can't assume secret channels to be available between clients, as well as in situations in which non-repudiation services must be provided, too. Note that if the proxy grantor selects the client's private key, there is, in general, no possibility to provide non-repudiation services. On the other hand, it is assumed that in situations that require a distribution of many proxies to various clients, the mechanism proposed in [29] has scalability advantages. It is, in general, more convenient for a client to be provided with the proxies he needs, instead of having to interactively request them. Nevertheless, it should be noted that both mechanisms need further investigation. In fact, the mechanisms are not mutually exclusive, and both mechanisms could be used in Tenet Scheme 2. For example, one possibility would be to use the mechanism proposed in [29] to distribute bearer proxies that can be used by anyone, and to use the mechanism described in this paper to distribute delegate proxies that can be used only by the clients they name.

6 Conclusions

The bandwith requirements of interactive multimedia applications are exhaustive, causing network congestion to be a major problem. One way to deal with this problem is to use a resource reservation scheme, such as e.g. Tenet Scheme 2. This paper has proposed a security architecture for Tenet Scheme 2. The basic ideas are to use Internet layer security protocols, such as the IP Security Protocol (IPSP) and Internet Key Management Protocol (IKMP), to establish authentic communication channels between RCAP daemons, to handle client authentication and authorization locally, and to use a proxy-based mechanism to distribute access rights for target sets and channels. Note that none of these ideas is directly coupled to the internals of Tenet Scheme 2. It is thus assumed that the security architecture proposed in this paper is applicable to other resource reservation schemes, too. Also note that the security architecture uses as its building blocks a collision-resistant one-way hash function and a digital signature system. Neither of them is subject to U.S. export controls. It is thus assumed that an implementation of the security architecture proposed in this paper would be exportable from the United States.

Acknowledgments

We would like to thank Domenico Ferrari for his encouragement and support through the design of the security architecture proposed in this paper.

References

1. R. Braden, L. Zhang, D. Estrin, S. Herzog, and S. Jamin. Resource ReServation Protocol (RSVP) — Version 1 Functional Specification. Internet Draft, November 1995. work in pogress.
2. F. Baker. RSVP Cryptographic Authentication. Internet Draft, November 1995. work in pogress.
3. D. Ferrari, A. Banerjea, and H. Zhang. Network support for multimedia – A discussion of the Tenet Approach. *Computer Networks and ISDN Systems*, 26:1267 – 1280, 1994.
4. A. Gupta and M. Moran. Channel Groups — A Unifying Abstraction for Specifying Inter-stream Relationships. TR-93-015, International Computer Science Institute (ICSI), Berkeley, CA, March 1993.
5. A. Gupta, W. Howe, M. Moran, and Q. Nguyen. Scalable resource reservation for multi-party real-time communication. TR-94-050, International Computer Science Institute (ICSI), Berkeley, CA, October 1994.
6. A. Gupta and D. Ferrari. Resource partitioning for multi-party real-time communication. TR-94-061, International Computer Science Institute (ICSI), Berkeley, CA, November 1994.
7. S. Deering and D.R. Cheriton. Multicast Routing in Datagram Internetworks and Extended LANs. *ACM Transactions on Computer Systems*, 8(2):85 – 110, 1990.
8. S. Deering. *Multicast Routing in a Datagram Internetwork*. PhD thesis, Stanford University, December 1991.
9. R. Braden, D. Clark, S. Crocker, and C. Huitema. Report of IAB Workshop on Security in the Internet Architecture, February 8-10, 1994. Request for Comments 1636, June 1994.
10. B. Schneier. *Applied Cryptography: Protocols, Algorithms, and Source Code in C*. John Wiley & Sons, Inc., New York, NY, 1994.
11. D. Stinson. *Cryptography Theory and Practice*. CRC Press, Boca Raton, FL, 1995.
12. R.L. Rivest. The MD4 Message-Digest Algorithm. Request for Comments 1320, April 1992.
13. R.L. Rivest and S. Dusse. The MD5 Message-Digest Algorithm. Request for Comments 1321, April 1992.
14. NIST. Secure Hash Standard (SHS). FIPS PUB 180, Gaithersburg, MD, May 1993.
15. L. Gong. Using One-Way Functions for Authentication. *ACM Computer Communication Review*, 19(5):8 – 11, 1989.
16. G. Tsudik. Message Authentication with One-Way Hash Functions. *ACM Computer Communication Review*, 22(5):29 – 38, 1992.

17. R.L. Rivest, A. Shamir, and L. Adleman. A Method for Obtaining Digital Signatures and Public-Key Cryptosystems. *Communications of the ACM*, 21(2):120 – 126, 1978.

18. T. ElGamal. A Public Key Cryptosystem and a Signature Scheme Based on Discrete Logarithm. *IEEE Transactions on Information Theory*, IT-31(4):469 – 472, July 1985.

19. NIST. Digital Signature Standard (DSS). FIPS PUB 186, Gaithersburg, MD, May 1994.

20. ISO/IEC. Information Processing Systems — Open Systems Interconnection Reference Model — Part 2: Security Architecture. ISO/IEC 7498-2, 1989.

21. ISO/IEC. Information technology — Telecommunications and information exchange between systems — Network Layer Security Protocol. ISO/IEC 11577, 1993.

22. J. Ioannidis and M. Blaze. The Architecture and Implementation of Network-Layer Security Under Unix. In *Proceedings of the USENIX UNIX Security IV Symposium*, pages 29 – 39, Berkeley, CA, October 1993. USENIX Association.

23. NIST. Data Encryption Standard. FIPS PUB 46, Gaithersburg, MD, January 1977. Originally issued by National Bureau of Standards (NBS).

24. NIST. DES Modes of Operation. FIPS PUB 81, Gaithersburg, MD, December 1980. Originally issued by National Bureau of Standards (NBS).

25. P.C. Cheng, J.A. Garay, A. Herzberg, and H. Krawczyk. Design and Implementation of Modular Key Management Protocol and IP Secure Tunnel on AIX. In *Proceedings of the USENIX UNIX Security V Symposium*, Berkeley, CA, June 1995. USENIX Association.

26. A. Aziz, M. Patterson, and G Baehr. Simple Key-Management for Internet Protocols (SKIP). In *Proceedings of the Internet Society International Networking Conference*, June 1995.

27. H. Krawczyk. SKEME: A Versatile Secure Key Exchange Mechanism for Internet. In *Proceedings of the Internet Society Symposium on Network and Distributed System Security*, February 1996.

28. A. Liebl. Authentication in Distributed Systems: A Bibliography. *ACM Operating Systems Review*, 27(1):31 – 41, 1993.

29. B.C. Neuman. Proxy-Based Authorization and Accounting for Distributed Systems. In *Proceedings of the 11th International Conference on Distributed Computing Systems*, pages 283 – 291, May 1993.

Features of
the ACCOPI Multimedia Transport Service*

Laurent Mathy

University of Liège

Abstract. In this paper, we present early considerations on the design of a multimedia transport service. The proposed design provides not only support for Quality of Service (QoS) and group communications, but also has the property to treat multimedia communications "as a whole". This differs from most of the current transport services which transfer multimedia data as several independent monomedia.

1 Introduction

During the last few years, we have been witnessing tremendous changes in the communication environment. Those changes are not only due to the availability of higher data rates in the communication networks but also to the appearance of new application types such as the client/server paradigm or multimedia applications.

After a brief review of the changes encountered in the network services and in the application requirements caused by the introduction of multimedia, we will focus on the issues related to the design of a transport service that fills at best the gap between the high-speed networks and the distributed multimedia applications.

1.1 The Technology Push

For some years, many researches have been done to drastically improve the communication networks. The most obvious of those improvements is certainly the gain in the achievable data rates. Bandwidth in the range of hundreds of megabits to several gigabits per second is now a reality (e.g. FDDI, B-ISDN).

But performance improvement has not been the only one. We have also seen a clear trend to the design of networks providing performance guarantees [ATM93][FBZ92][FeV90][Top90][ZDE93]. Although there exist different types of guarantees (e.g. statistical or deterministic) and even though not all the networks provide them, performance guarantees provide support for realtime communications on a wide-area basis.

* This work was partially supported by the Commission of the European Communities under the RACE M1005 project ACCOPI: "Access Control and Copyright Protection for Images".

Besides performance improvement and guarantees, another feature that is becoming ubiquitous in the communication networks is multicasting [ATM93] [Top90][DEF94], that is the conveying of a same data to several destinations in one sending. Multicasting obviously allows a better utilization of network resources (bandwidth, buffer space and processing time in routers) than when sending out a separate copy of the data to each destination. It is, of course, the favourite transmission mode for distributing data within the networks.

The key point with most of those features is that they are now leaving the local (LAN)/ metropolitan area (MAN) environment where they have been available for quite a long time to reach the wide area (WAN) environment. This is pushing for the introduction in the WAN environment of applications that were formely only possible in the local environment.

1.2 The Application Pull

Multimedia is Breaking Through. As we are entering the "telecommunication century", multimedia is emerging as a powerful communication tool. Indeed, it allows to communicate by jointly using different information types (i.e. different media) such as video, audio, text, still images, and so on. Each of these different media having its own characteristics, also has its own requirements. Those requirements may greatly differ from one medium to another. For instance, some media are said to be continuous (e.g. video, audio) while others are said to be discrete (e.g. text, still images). Other characteristics, such as the required bandwidth or delay also differ from one medium to another.

In the past, to deal with that heterogeneity in the media, several independent specialized networks were developed to transport the different specific information type. Among those specialized networks, we find:

1. The Public Switched Telephone Networks (PSTN) designed for classical two-way voice conversation.
2. The Community Antenna TeleVision networks (CATV) designed for the distribution of television signals. Most of these networks do not allow any interactivity.
3. The Packet Switched Data Networks (PSDN) designed to transport computer data in the public domain. Such networks may be based, for instance, on the X.25 protocol suite.
4. The Local Area Networks (LAN) designed to transport computer data at high speed and low cost in the private domain. Ethernet or token ring are examples of LANs.

A straightforward and apparently appealing way to achieve multimedia communications, is to transport each specific medium on its specialized network type.

However, such a solution suffers from several major flaws, among which we find:

1. The use of several networks multiplies the costs of network equipments, network maintainance, network operation, and so on.
2. The proliferation of customer devices. This not only increases customers' costs but also the number of addresses through which a customer is reached.
3. Although a multimedia message has to be interpreted as a whole, its components (the different media) are independently transfered of one another on different networks. Any control to be exercised on the multimedia communication has thus to be done by the customers.
4. Different media cannot share resources, which enduces very poor resource usage.
5. Each specialized network has been built to meet the requirements of a given medium, thus offering inflexible performance.

Fortunately, due to the advances in digital network technology, computers' processing power and digitalization techniques, it is now possible to build a single network able to transport the different information types at the same time. This single network is said to integrate the services (i.e. the different information types). Such a network not only solves the problems discussed above for the previous solution, but also offers a better adaptation to changing media requirements (due to changes in coding/ compression schemes).

Model of Multimedia Communications in an Integrated Network. As already mentioned in the previous section, each medium of a multimedia communication imposes its own requirements, which will be expressed in terms of Quality of Service (QoS) parameters, on the underlying network. It is easy to show that those requirements may differ from one medium to another. As an example, let us compare audio and text.

While humans can cope with noise in audio information, it is much more difficult for us to accept too long or too variable delays in the delivery of that audio information. Therefore, audio allows some error rates, but has stringent delay and delay jitter requirements. Moreover, the coding/ compression schemes will impose some transmission rates as well.

On the other hand, what is important for text is the correctness of the message. Whether the transfer of the whole text takes more or less time or the different pieces of the text are not received at regular intervals is not very important. Therefore, text will require full reliability (i.e. no error) while having rather loose performance requirements.

Moreover, the same medium does not always impose the same requirements on the communication network. Indeed, audio can be Hi-Fi quality as well as telephone quality. In the same way, video can be black-and-white, colour or HDTV quality. Some coding schemes, called hierarchical coding schemes [Ste94, Ste94b], provide for a "layered" medium, each level adding some quality to the previous one. We thus see that there is not only an heterogeneity in requirements from one medium to another, but that the heterogeneity can also exist "within" a given medium.

In order to cope with that heterogeneity, a multimedia communication is modelled as an association composed of several conversations [ISO 9161], each conversation being "shaped" to given requirements. Figure 1 shows a single association used for teleconference scenario.

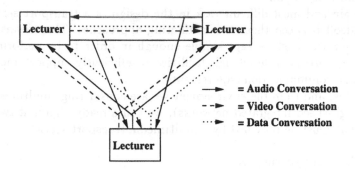

Fig. 1. Model of Multimedia Communications.

The model described in this section is a commonly accepted one [ISO 9161].

In the sequel, we will discuss features that should or should not be exhibited by a transport service in order to support at best multimedia applications while exploiting the capabilities offered by the underlying high-speed communication networks. As we will now discuss service issues, we will not use the terms "association" and "conversation", which are protocol oriented terms, any longer. Instead, we will respectively use the terms "call" and "connection".

2 General characteristics of a Multimedia Transport Service

The role of the transport layer is manyfold:

1. To provide the application (or at least the multimedia platform or teleservice layer) with a suitable data communication scheme.
2. To bring up to the transport service interface the facilities available in the communication network (e.g. multicast facility, QoS support facility).
3. To release the applications from any concern about the underlying communication networks while maximally exploiting the capabilities of those networks. The transport service interface thus provides the applications with a unified interface which is independent from the communication networks.

From the application developers' point of view, the more facilities provided by the transport service, the better. Indeed, what has already been done by the transport service need not be done again by the applications, which simplifies greatly the development of those applications. This argues in favor of "heavy-weight" transport services offering lots of facilities.

However, we must keep in mind that the transport layer is, from a performance point of view, an important part of any protocol stack, which argues in favor of "lightweight" transport services offering minimal facilities in order to be as performant as possible.

The main and most difficult task in the design of a transport service is to find a tradeoff between those two conflicting approaches. This means that the transport service must be kept simple enough in order to be performant, but that it must also provide enough facilities to efficiently support most of the applications' communication requirements.

From this, and from the environment we are considering (multimedia applications/ high-speed integrated networks), we can already highlight two general features that must be provided by a multimedia transport service:

1. some kind of QoS support.
2. some kind of group communications.

The reason why those two features should be found in a multimedia transport service is rather obvious, since they are most of the time provided by the underlying networks and required by the multimedia applications. In the following sections, we will discuss "how far" those features should be integrated in a transport service.

There is also a constraint to be kept in mind while designing a multimedia transport service. This constraint is that the group communication facitilies should be such that, when a communication is needed between only two service users, the "added" burden is small enough so that the use of separate peer-to-peer communication facilities is not justified. In other words, the group communication facilities should be the only communication provided facilities.

3 Quality of Service Support

3.1 Various Types of QoS Semantics

QoS support in the transport layer is the answer to performance requirements in the application layer.

Although the QoS concept has been introduced in the OSI Reference Model, the OSI transport service offered by TP4 provides what is called best-effort QoS. This is called best-effort because nothing happens if performance, corresponding to the QoS values selected by the transport service users, is not achieved by the service provider. Therefore, there is here no strong relation between the QoS "support" offered by the transport service and performance it actually achieves. The QoS values specified by the transport service users are thus appearing as nothing but a wish. This best-effort semantics (or even no-effort at all) is a common characteristic of the transport services offered by transport protocols that were mainly designed for file transfers (e.g. TCP) which only require reliability as we have already seen. It is clear that such a semantics is not suited to multimedia communications at all.

On the other side of the "QoS support spectrum", we find the concept of guaranteed QoS which, when used with a deterministic (also called hard) semantics, ensures that the required performance is going to be achieved throughout the communication lifetime. This is obviously the strongest QoS support semantics that could ever be dreamt of. However, achieving this semantics in the transport layer requires that this semantics be already supported in both the underlying networks and the Operating Systems (OS) supporting the applications. Unfortunately, even though several networks and OS have been designed to exhibit performance guarantee characteristics (such networks and OS are often qualified "real-time"), their usage is not currently generalized and may never be.

A good candidate for the QoS support in a multimedia transport service is therefore the enhanced QoS [DBL94] defined in the OSI95 peer-to-peer transport service [DBL92]. In the OSI95 Connection-oriented Transport Service a QoS parameter is seen as a structure of three values, respectively called "compulsory", "threshold" and "maximal quality". Each value has its own well-defined meaning and is the result of a contract between the service users and the service provider.

The main idea behind the introduction of the enhanced QoS is that the service provider is committed to some well-defined duties, known by each side. For instance, if the service provider cannot completely execute a service facility without violating the requested performance, it will either notify the user or abort the service facility.

The main advantage of the enhanced QoS is that they may be equivalent to guaranteed QoS when resource reservation mechanisms are available but can also work without such mechanisms (while, in such a case, guaranteed QoS are not applicable). For details about the enhanced QoS, see [DBL92][DBL94][Bag95].

3.2 QoS Support for Group Communications

In [MaB94], it has been shown how the enhanced QoS semantics and negotiation can be extended to the case of multicast connections (i.e. $(1 \rightarrow N)$ connections).

An interesting result from [MaB94] is that, in the multicast case, QoS parameters are characterized as:

1. Connection-wide QoS parameters, whose scope is the whole multicast connection (and thus affect the sender and all the receivers). The throughput is a typical connection-wide QoS parameter.
2. Receiver-selected QoS parameters, whose scope is limited to one receiver. For such a QoS parameter, a different value may be selected between the sender and each receiver. The transit delay and the delay jitter are examples of receiver-selected QoS parameters.

3.3 QoS Re-negotiation

Besides QoS negotiation which always takes place at connection establishment time, another interesting feature concerning QoS is QoS re-negotiation. QoS re-negotiation allows service users to change their QoS requirements while exchanging data (i.e. during the connection lifetime). It therefore allows a connection to be adapted to changing application requirements, which adds to the flexibility of the transport service. QoS re-negotiation will be discussed in Sect.4.6 within the context of multicast connections.

4 Group Communication Support

From the point of view of the transport service, a group communication is a communication involving two or more service users. There are basically two ways to identify a group of service users. It can either be identified by a set of individual addresses or by a group address. While the former solution is rather simple since it requires no special functionality for group management, it imposes to deal with lists of addresses in both the transport service and the transport protocol. On the other hand, the latter solution requires special group management functionalities but simplifies the treatement of addresses.

Considering group management, we can observe that:

1. A group will most of the time be created outside any instance of communication.
2. A group will most of the time have a rather static evolution, which means that the composition of a group will not often change from one communication to another.
3. Changes in a group at the transport level will most of the time occur as a consequence of changes in a corresponding group at the application level. This means that a complete view of group management across the whole protocol stack could simplify the management of the different groups at each level.

Those observations are thus leading us to rely on the management stack of the network architecture rather than on the communication stack for the management of group addresses. We therefore believe that a multimedia transport service does not need to support group management functionnalities. Instead, the multimedia transport service will see the group of users as either a group address (managed by the management) or a set of individual addresses (since we cannot ensure that the management will provide for group management).

4.1 Topology supported by the ACCOPI Multimedia Transport Service

Due to its inherent heterogeneity (see Sect.1.2), it is clear that, in general, a multimedia communication is rather complex.

At the transport service level, the question that has to be answered is to know what types of topologies (in terms of transport connections) have to be supported.

The simplest form of group communication is the one where there is one sender and several receivers. The topology of such a group communication is said to be of the $1 \rightarrow N$ type. A multimedia transport service must provide this communication scheme in the connection-oriented mode since it represents the basic communication scheme for media distribution. Such $(1 \rightarrow N)$ simplex connections are also called multicast connections or multicast streams. Several transport services have already been designed to provide this type of communications [DCS92][ISO SC6/WG4 806]. A protocol such as XTP [XTP95] can also offer this type of service.

Other types of group connections, such as $(1 \rightarrow N)$ duplex connections, $(N \rightarrow N)$ connections or $(N \rightarrow 1)$ connections, could also be considered at the transport service but we are against them. This is firstly because it has been shown [Hen94][MLB94] that any topology can be achieve using only multicast connections.

Secondly, our work on QoS in group communications [MaB94] showed that it is really difficult to deal with QoS parameters on connections other than multicast connections.

Finally, embodying complex connections in the transport service may complicate the design of the corresponding transport protocol and hence jeopardize performance of the transport layer.

In Sect.1.2, it has been shown that a multimedia communication is made up of different media having each their own performance requirements. At the transport level, each of these media (or even each part of a given medium) will often be transferred on a multicast connection taylored to the adequate performance. However, with most of current transport services [DCS92][ISO SC6/WG4 806] [XTP95], the multicast connections are independent of each other, which does not preserve, at the transport layer, the relations that exist between the media at the application layer.

As the transport layer is the last one that is directly concerned with the pure transfer of data, it could be interesting to express relations between multicast connections transporting media making up a single multimedia communication. Such relations could be expressed as QoS dependencies. For instance, suppose that near-synchronisation has to be preserved between a video stream and an audio stream at the transport service boundary. If the transport multicast connections transporting those two streams are independent, the transport service user establishing those multicast connections will have to first establish one of them with a given transit delay and a given delay jitter and then try to establish the second one with the same delay and jitter characteristics. The problem here is that the desired value for the QoS parameters on the second connection may only be achieved after several unsuccessful establishment attempts, which increases the time elapsed before the multimedia communication can actually begin. Moreover, during the establishment of the second connection, the first one being already established is possibly consuming network resources whereas no data is exchanged on it yet. Those shortcomings could be avoided if the transport service users had a means to ask the transport service provider to simultaneously establish two multicast connections and thus to negotiate them such that they reach the same selected transit delay and delay jitter. In the same way, it could also express that if the transport service provider fails to establish any of the multicast connections then there is no point in to establishing (or retaining) the other one. Therefore, our goal is to:

1. Design a transport service that allows its users to group several multicast connections together in what we will name a call.
2. Allow those users to express QoS dependencies between the multicast connections of a call.
3. Allows the users to express conditions on the existence of a call in terms of multicast connections.

Such a transport service is very appealing and well suited to the needs of multimedia applications.

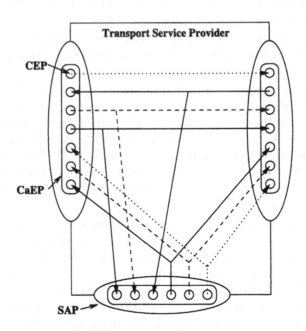

Fig. 2. Complex Transport Call.

This approach using calls made up of multicast connections has already been used in [Hen94]. However, the transport service described in [Hen94] can provide for very complex topologies which allow for a direct support, at the transport layer, of complex multimedia communications as presented in Sect.1.2. This means that any transport service user involved in a given call can be, simultaneously, both sender and receiver. Figure 2 illustrates a call that can be provided by [Hen94].

Although the topologies provided by [Hen94] match closely the application needs, they however make the call rather difficult to control and manage since the call is decentralised and thus the mechanisms to be implemented in the protocol will be rather complex.

Moreover, if we consider the QoS dependencies, it is clear that their interest resides mainly in the possibility to control connections emerging from a same source. Indeed, most of the time, what is important is to play coherently the multimedia data from a given sender rather than "correlating" the multimedia data transmitted by different sources.

Therefore, restricting the transport service to provide only centralised topologies, that is calls on which there are only one sender and several receivers, appears to be a good simplifying compromise. Moreover, such centralised calls are sufficient to fully support multimedia distribution. Figure 3 illustrates a centralised call as provided by the ACCOPI multimedia transport service. Among the simplifications brought by those centralised topologies, we find:

1. As there is only one sender, it is natural that this sender controls the call and the associated connections, that is only the sender can establish and release the call and the connections.
2. The receivers can only join or leave the call and the connections.
3. The monitoring and the management of the QoS parameters are simplified.

Therefore, complex distributed control functions may be avoided in centralised calls.

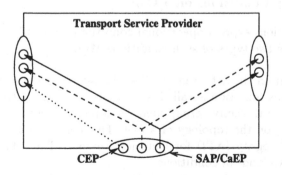

Fig. 3. Centralised Transport Call.

4.2 Identification of a Call and its Connections

Global Identification. A globally unique identifier must be available in order to allow potential receivers to identify a call that has already been established.

This identifier is called the *Callid* and is used by a receiver joining the call (see Sect.4.4). Since the calls considered here are centralised, the uniqueness of the *Callid* can easily be achieved.

A global connection identifier, called *Cid*, unique in the scope of a call and identifying a given connection of that call, is also needed during the join operation (see Sect.4.5).

Local Identification. Call and connection endpoints will also be required to allow service users to associate data service primitives with the appropriate connection of the call. There are two possible ways to provide those local identifications:

1. We use call endpoints (CaEP) and connection endpoints (CEP) within service access point (SAP) to respectively identify the different calls and their connections (see Fig.2). This is the more general approach but this introduces the new concept of CaEP in addition to the concepts of SAP and CEP in the OSI RM.
2. We restrict the use of a given SAP to only one call, which allow us to locally identify the call by the SAP and then the connections by CEPs (see Fig.3) . This introduces no new endpoint concept into the OSI RM but the price to pay is a restriction on the use of a SAP.

As those two solutions are being considered by the ISO members, we leave this issue open. However, in the sequel, we will use the term CaEP to refer to an endpoint of a call.

4.3 Integrity Conditions on a Call

Integrity conditions express operational conditions on a call.

There exists two types of such conditions[MLB94]:

1. A condition on the active group (i.e. the set of participants in the call) of the call. This condition is called Active Group Integrity (AGI) and specifies conditions on the active group membership of the call.
2. A condition on the topology of a call. This condition is called Association Topology Integrity (ATI) for historical reasons. The ATI is actually composed of two kinds of conditions:
   (a) Conditions on the existence of each multicast connection of the call, expressed in terms of multicast connection active group integrity (MC-AGI).
   (b) Conditions on the call as a whole in terms of existing multicast connections (i.e. the connections for which the MC-AGI is verified).

The ATI condition is considered to be verified if the conditions on the call as a whole are verified.

Including integrity conditions into a multimedia transport service relieves the transport service users from at least a part of the burden of monitoring those conditions.

Although there is no a priori restriction on the complexity of the integrity conditions, we however believe that only a few condition types have to be supported by a transport service. The selected ones being, of course, both useful and simple to verify. Such restrictions are introduced to prevent the incorporation of too complex mechanisms into the transport layer, which would prevent the achievement of high performance.

Among the more useful conditions we propose to support the following ones:

1. Quorum: the minimum number of required elements for the condition to be considered as satisfied. In the case of an AGI (resp. MC-AGI) condition, the elements are the participants of the call (resp. the multicast connection), whereas in the case of an ATI condition, the elements are the multicast connections.
2. Key elements: the set of required elements for the condition to be considered as verified. In the case of an AGI (resp. MC-AGI) condition, the elements are the participants of the call (resp. the multicast connection), whereas in the case of an ATI condition, the elements are the multicast connections.
3. The logical AND of the two previous cases.

These three types of conditions seem to cover most of the needs of multimedia applications. Moreover, it is rather simple for the transport service provider to count the number of participants on a call or a multicast connection and to verify the presence of some given participants.

Integrity conditions are used to express the operational conditions of a call. In other words, no data transfer can occur unless all integrity conditions are fulfilled.

There are two possible ways to prevent data transfers on a call. We can either release the call (hard integrity conditions) or suspend any data transfer (soft integrity conditions)[MLB94]. Although the soft integrity conditions appear to be well suited to the data consistency and other problems at the application level, we do not believe that this integrity condition semantics is useful at the transport level. Indeed, after an integrity condition has been falsified, having it satisfied again can take a possibly infinite time. From the network point of view, suspending data transfers can then be considered as wasting resources (e.g. reserved link bandwidth, buffers in routers). Therefore, it will often be chosen to release network resources when the data transfers are suspended at the application level.

Since, when needed, the soft semantics is supported at the application level anyway, we do not see any interest in providing it at the transport level where there is a close relationship between the topology and the active group of a transport call and the underlying network capabilities. To the argument that releasing both the transport call and the network resources could prevent an application association to resume, we can reply that even if nothing is released during the data transfer standstill, it could never be guaranteed that additional network resources would be available in order to have the integrity conditions satisfied again. We therefore choose to only provide hard integrity conditions in the transport layer.

4.4 Facilities Defined at the Transport Call Level

Transport Call Establishment. As we are considering centralised calls, it seems rather natural to restrict the use of the call establishment functionality to the sender (i.e. the central service user of the call). In other words, we do not allow a call to be created by a receiver. This is mainly because, most of the time, the service user issuing a multimedia message has a total control on that message and hence on the multimedia communication.

The sender uses either a group address or a set of individual addresses to identify the set of potential receivers. It also specifies the AGI condition of the call. As a result of the successful establishment of a call, the corresponding *Callid* is created.

At this point, the following question can be raised: "What is the minimal topology of a call?". Although nothing would theoritically prevent to consider "empty calls", that is calls comprising no multicast connections, such a concept does not appear to be relevant to the transport layer and also complicates the management of the call. Therefore, we impose that a call be composed of at least one multicast connection. In the same idea, we also impose that, to be considered as a call participant, a service user be a participant in at least one of the multicast connections composing the call. This is simply because a call is established in order to exchange data. Therefore, the establishment of a call will trigger the establishment of at least one multicast connection.

This also imposes that the sender specifies the MC-AGI of the multicast connections being established and whether these connections are key ones. Any quorum on the ATI condition must also be specified.

At the end of the call establishment phase, each participant of the call is attached to a CaEP identifying locally that call.

Transport Call Release. The transport call release facility is used to terminate a call. The release of a call can occur at any time and is abrupt (i.e. data may be lost). It is destructive, which means that the result of the release is that the call, and the associated multicast connections, do not exists any longer.

Only the sender and the transport service provider can invoke that facility.

Transport Call Join. The transport call join facility is used to allow a transport service user to participate in an already established call. The transport service user issues a join request service primitive specifying the *Callid* of the call (which is globally unique).

This service facility is equivalent to a transport multicast connection join (see Sect.4.5) on each established multicast connection of the call.

This service facility can be invoked at any time by any transport service user.

Transport Call Leave. This service facility is used to withdraw a participant from a call. This facility is equivalent to a transport multicast connection Leave (see Sect.4.5) on each multicast connection for which the service user is a participant.

4.5 Facilities Defined at the Transport Multicast Connection Level

Transport Multicast Connection Establishment. This facility is used by the sender of a call to add a new multicast connection to an already established call. At the establishment time of a multicast connection, the sender specifies a MC-AGI on the connection and whether the connection is a key one. The sender also specifies the QoS dependancies of that new connection with the already existing ones (see Sect.4.6).

Since the sender is already attached to a CaEP identifying the call, it does not need to use either the group address, the set of individual addresses, or the *Callid*. Indeed, the transport service provider knows already what are the peer CaEPs of the one on which it receives the connection establishment request primitive. As a consequence, only participants of the call will be involved in the establishment of a new connection (i.e. no external service users will be involved).

The sender also proposes QoS parameters to be applied on the connection. Among the QoS parameters, those for which a QoS dependency exists, are not negotiated (or more exactly are negotiated on a "take it or leave it" basis) and the others are negotiated between the three parties involved in the connection establishment phase: the sender, the service provider and the set of call participants. It has been shown [MaB94] that incompatibilities may occur between the service users involved in the QoS negotiation process. Those incompatibilities are due to the impossibility to reach a consensus on the value of a connection-wide QoS parameters. Therefore, the task of the service provider will be to select among the participants of the call a subset of receivers having compatible QoS requirements. Such a subset has to be selected in such a way that the MC-AGI specified by the sender for the connection being established be verified. The selection of the subset of receivers may be based on the optimisation of a given cost fonction.

As a result of the successful establishment of the multicast connection, a *Cid* is assigned to it and data transfer may occur.

Transport Multicast Connection Release. The transport multicast connection release can only be invoked be the sender or the service provider. It is abrupt and destructive. This facility can be invoked at any time.

Transport Multicast Connection Join. The transport multicast connection join facility is used to allow a transport service user to participate in an already established connection. If the transport service user is already a participant of the call, it simply issues a join request service primitive specifying the *Cid* of the connection on the corresponding CaEP. However, if the transport service user is not a participant of the call yet, it will have to also specify the *Callid* in order to identify the corresponding call.

A QoS negotiation phase will also take place during the join phase. However, the following restrictions will apply to that QoS negotiation:

1. The connection-wide QoS parameters are negotiated on a "take it or leave it basis", which means that the joining service user cannot introduce incompatibility among the participants of the connection.
2. The joining service user will be allowed to select values for the receiver-selected QoS parameters but in the range that was suggested by the sender at the establishment of the connection. However, if the connection the service user is joining is linked to other connections of the call by the QoS dependency functionality (see Sect.4.6) and if the service user is already a participant on at least one of those linked connections, then the value of that receiver-selected parameter has to be negotiated on a "take it or leave it basis". This is simply to avoid that the join facility invoked for a connection induces modifications on other connections.

This service facility can be invoked at any time (provided that the connection exists) and by any transport service user (since the primarily goal of a transport service is to achieve data transfer, security issues are not relevant to it).

Transport Multicast Connection Leave. That service facility is used to withdraw a participant from the connection. This facility is abrupt (data may be lost) and can be invoked at any time by either the concerned participant or the service provider.

If that facility is used to withdraw a service user from the last connection on which it was a participant, it also results in the withdrawing of the service user from the call.

4.6 Properties of Transport Multicast Connections

Reliability. Since there are several simultaneous receivers on a multicast connection, one can define several degrees of reliability [MLB94]:

1. k-reliability (k ranging from zero to the total MC-active group size, but fixed) means that each Transport Service Data Unit (TSDU) is received by at least k participants of the multicast connection.
2. all-reliability means that all the participants of the multicast connection receive each TSDU.

As the multicast connections of a call will be used to transport the different parts of a multimedia communication, the degree of reliability required on each of these multicast connections will depend on the type of medium.

For multicast connections transporting continuous media (e.g. video and audio) the degree of reliability may be set to 0-reliable. This is because, due to the stringent transit delay and delay jitter requirements of such media, no retransmission of lost or corrupted TSDUs can be afforded. Moreover, as continuous media are information redundant, such lost or corrupted TSDUs cause no problem if the error rates stay within some well known ranges (depending on the coding/compression scheme) for each receiver. Moreover, better error rates can always be achieved thanks to Forward Error Correction (FEC) methods.

On the other hand, a multimedia message may also include discrete media such as text, still images, pure data (files), and so on. Most of those media exhibit the characteristics that they make sense to a receiver only if that receiver gets the data "error free". Therefore, the degree of reliability for multicast connections transporting discrete media will be set to all-reliable.

From this, we see that, among the range of degree of reliabilty, a multimedia transport service must support the following ones: 0-reliability and all-reliability. This excludes any "non-zero-k-reliability" that have no direct interest for the multimedia communications considered here and that also introduce some kind of imbalance between the receivers, which is something not desired at the transport level.

Ordering.

Local Ordering. A common characteristic of the media of a multimedia communication is that they require in-sequence delivery of the TSDUs at the transport service boundary. This is not only true for the discrete media where the all-reliability imposes in-sequence delivery, but this is also true for the continuous media whose data units exhibit a temporal relationship that has to be preserved in order for the message to make sense. Therefore, the TSDUs of a given multicast connection must be delivered to the receivers in the same relative order the sender submitted them. Such a characteristic is called local ordering.

More Complex Forms of Ordering. Other forms of ordering have also been defined [ISO 9161]. These are the partial ordering, the causal ordering and the total ordering. Those ordering policies involve all the multicast connections of a call and hence together relate all the TSDUs submitted by the sender.

Even though some applications may require such ordering characteristics, the typical multimedia applications we are considering (tele-conferences, multimedia distribution, CSCW applications) do not require them. Moreover, the applications requiring complex ordering are often of the $(N \rightarrow N)$ type and will hence need proper ordering mechanisms above our transport service since the transport service users see no order between the TSDUs from different senders (i.e. here different calls). Finally, some delayed TSDUs on certain connections could, for ordering reasons, prevent the delivery of TSDUs on other connections, which could reduce the performance observed on the whole call. Therefore, providing those ordering characteristics at the transport layer appears as non relevant and redundant.

Quality of Service.

Definition of the QoS Parameters. In order to allow the sender to tailor a multicast connection to the media it conveys, the following QoS parameters have to be specified:

1. throughput, which is a connection-wide parameter
2. transit delay, which is a receiver-selected parameter
3. delay jitter, which is a receiver-selected parameter
4. error rates, which is a receiver-selected parameter
5. reliability, which is a connection-wide parameter

See [DBL92][DBL94] for detailed definitions of those parameters.

QoS Dependencies. We have already discussed (Sect.4.1) the interest of having some QoS dependencies between certain multicast connections of a call. Many relations between the QoS parameters of the multicast connections can express such dependancies. Allowing all those different relations would complicate the QoS negotiation and the design of the transport protocol. That is why we limit the relations between the multicast connections as follows:

1. A dependency relation will be expressed by the equality of the selected values for a QoS parameter from one connection to another.
2. There is at most one dependency relation per parameter, that is, all the dependent connections exhibit the same selected values for the corresponding QoS parameter.

For a teleconference, the sender may express a dependency between the transit delay of audio and video connections in order to keep the two streams in near-synchronisation (even if the selected values are the same, the instantaneous values may be different). As no dependency has been expressed on the throughput parameters, the throughput on each of those connections may be different. Moreover, a third connection, with no dependency at all, may be established with its own independent values for the QoS parameters (for instance, for the transfer of text). We therefore see that our restricted QoS dependencies are still well suited to typical cases and can thus be considered as sufficient.

QoS Negotiation. QoS negotiation is a challenging issue in QoS support. Although it allows for a good flexibility during connection establishment, several existing transport services do not provide it but are rather based on the "take it or leave it principle". This is undoubtedly due to the complexity of the QoS negotiation process which involves all the actors (i.e. service users and provider) of communications [Bag95]. We are however convinced that the gain in flexibility brought by QoS negotiation is something important in supporting multimedia applications and is therefore worth being provided by a multimedia transport service.

QoS parameters are negotiated during establishment of the multicast connections. See [MaB94] for details about the QoS negotiation on a multicast connection.

QoS Re-negotiation. Due to the complexity of QoS support in group communication, the QoS re-negotiation should be available on a "per parameter" basis, which means that a re-negotiation may only affect one QoS parameter of a connection whereas the value of the other parameters are left unchanged.

Obviously, the re-negotiation of a connection-wide QoS parameter can only be initiated by the sender, whereas a receiver can initiate the re-negotiation of its receiver-selected parameters. Either allowing the sender to initiate the re-negotiation of a receiver-selected parameter (which would concern all the receivers) or not requires further study, as race conditions could appear with a receiver initiated re-negotiation for the same parameter.

If a re-negotiation occurs for a QoS parameter involved in a QoS dependancy relation, this re-negotiation will affect all the linked connections so that, at the end of the re-negotiation, the QoS dependancy is preserved (the equality of the selected QoS values for that parameter on each linked connection is preserved).

We saw in Sect.4.5, that the sender specifies the QoS dependencies at the establishment of the connections. It appears interesting that the sender could destroy such QoS dependencies at any time, or in other words that the sender could remove a connection from a QoS dependency relation. This means that during the following re-negotiation of the concerned parameter on the "unlinked" connection, that parameter is re-negotiated "alone" (there is no impact on other connections). Allowing the sender to link a connection to others at a time other than the establishment of that connection requires further study, as race conditions could appear between the creation of that link and a possible re-negotiation of the concerned parameter.

5 Conclusion

In this paper, we have proposed an overview of the ACCOPI multimedia transport service providing the multimedia applications with a suitable communication scheme while allowing the achievement of high performance communications. The main features of that multimedia transport service is QoS and group communications support.

The provided communication scheme is based on the concept of call, which allows a transport service user, namely the sender, to group and possibly relate together several multicast connections. This allows to transfer, at the transport layer, multimedia information as a whole and not as independent monomedia information as it is mostly the case with existing transport services.

There is an obvious analogy between the call/ multicast connection structure in this transport service and the VP/ multicast VC structure in ATM. This analogy could be exploited when this multimedia transport service is used over an ATM network.

Moreover, as the multicast connections of a call can only be related to one another by the selected values for QoS parameters and the ATI condition, those multicast connections appears as independant during the data transfer phase, which cannot jeopardize at all the achievable performance on this type of connection.

Finally, the facilities provided by that multimedia transport service have been studied and chosen so that the multimedia transport service be as simple as possible while being well suited to the transport of multimedia information.

References

[ATM93] ATM Forum: ATM User-Network Interface Specification, Version 3.0, September 1993.

[Bag95] Y. Baguette: Towards a Unified View of Usual Quality of Service Negotiation Schemes, Internal Report, University of Liège, 1995.

[DBL92] A. Danthine, Y. Baguette, G. Leduc, L. Léonard: The OSI 95 Connection-mode Transport Service - The Enhanced QoS, *High Performance Networking, IV* , IFIP Transactions C-14, A. Danthine, O. Spaniol, eds., Elsevier (North-Holland), pp 235-252.

[DBL94] A. Danthine, O. Bonaventure, G. Leduc: The QoS Enhancements in OSI95, *The OSI95 Transport Service with Multimedia Support*, A. Danthine, ed., Springer-Verlag, pp 124-149.

[DCS92] C. Diot, P. Cocquet, D. Stunault: Specification of ETS, the Enhanced Transport Service, Research Report RR 907-I-, Institut IMAG, Grenoble, May 1992.

[DEF94] S. Deering, D. Estrin, D. Farinacci, V. Jacobson, C-G. Liu, L. Wei: An Architecture for Wide-Area Multicast Routing, *Proc. SIGCOMM '94*, London, Augustus 31- September 2, 1994, Computer Communication Review, Vol. 24, no. 4, October 1994.

[FBZ92] D. Ferrari, A. Banerjea, H. Zhang: Network Support for Multimedia - A Discussion of the Tenet Approach, Technical Report TR-92-072, International Computer Science Institute, Berkeley, November 1992.

[FeV90] D. Ferrari, D. Verma: A Scheme for Real-Time Channel Establishment in Wide-Area Networks, *IEEE Journal on Selected Areas in Communications*, April 1990, Vol.8, No.3, pp 368-379.

[Hen94] L. Henckel: Multipeer Transport Services for Multimedia Applications, *Participant's Proc. 5th IFIP Conference on High Performance Networking*, Grenoble, June 27-July 1, 1994, S. Fdida, ed., pp 165-183.

[HSF93] D. Hoffman, M. Speer, G. Fernando: Network Support for Dynamically Scaled Multimedia Data Streams, *Proc. 4th International Workshop on Network and Operating Systems Support for Digital Audio and Video*, Lancaster, November 3-5, 1993, pp 251-262.

[ISO 9161] ISO/IEC JTC1: Second Draft on Multipeer Taxonomy, ISO/IEC JTC1/SC6 N9161, October 18, 1994.

[ISO SC6/WG4 806] USA National Body contribution: Proposed Draft Text for a High Speed Transport Service (HSTS) Definition, ISO/IEC JTC1/SC6/WG4/N806, 19 Dec. 1992.

[MaB94]   L. Mathy, O. Bonaventure: QoS Negotiation for Multicast Communications, International COST 237 Workshop on Multimedia Transport and Teleservices, Vienna, November 13-15, 1994, *Lecture Notes in Computer Science no. 882*, D. Hutchison et al., eds., Springer-Verlag, pp 199-218.

[MLB94]   L. Mathy, G. Leduc, O. Bonaventure, A. Danthine: A Group Communication Framework, *3rd International Broadband Islands Conference*, Hamburg, June 7-9, 1994, O. Spaniol et al., eds., Elsevier Science Publishers (North-Holland), 1994, pp 167-178.

[Ste94]   R. Steinmetz: Data Compression in Multimedia Computing- Principles and Techniques, *Multimedia Systems*, Springer-Verlag, 1994, Vol. 1, pp 166-172.

[Ste94b] R. Steinmetz: Data Compression in Multimedia Computing- Standards and Systems, *Multimedia Systems*, Springer-Verlag, 1994, Vol. 1, pp 187-204.

[Top90]   C. Topolcic: Experimental Internet STream Protocol, Version 2 (ST-II), Internet RFC 1190, 1990.

[XTP95]   XTP Forum: Xpress Transport Protocol Specification - Revision 4.0, XTP 95-20, March 1, 1995.

[ZDE93]   L. Zhang, S. Deering, D. Estrin, S. Shenker, D. Zappala: RSVP: A New Resource ReSerVation Protocol, *IEEE Network*, September 1993, Vol.7, No.5, pp 8-18.

Video Communication and Media Scaling System "Xnetvideo": Design and Implementation

Robert Hess, Tino Hutschenreuther, Alexander Schill

Dresden University of Technology

Abstract: Today's networks are characterized by heterogeneous environments. Various transmission techniques coexist and offer different bandwidths at different costs. For example, it is possible to transmit 155 Mbps and more with the Asynchronous Transfer Mode (ATM). As opposed to that, most LANs are based on Ethernet links, which allow only a 10 Mbps transfer rate. The major problem of multimedia communication systems is the lack of resource reservation protocols such as RSVP in current practical environments. Scaling of media streams is a current possibility and trade-off to meet the needs of the end user, to prevent the waste of bandwidth and to react onto phases of low available bandwidth.

This paper presents the approach and architecture of the video communication system "Xnetvideo", which is scaleable in terms of SNR (signal to noise ratio)-scaling, image size and frame rate. The description of this architecture, and the discussion of implementation issues and performance results are the major topics of this contribution. As a networking basis, we assume a heterogeneous environment, where shared media are included, so that no reservation possibilities are available in this case; in practice, both ATM and Ethernet are used in our lab.

Keywords: scaling, scaleable media-streams, multimedia, video conferencing, client/server

1. Introduction

There is currently great interest in the problem of transmitting digital audio and video in real time across local area networks. Different networks have different characteristics like the actual traffic and load, bandwidth, etc. For the transmission of digital audio and video, a high bandwidth is required. ATM offers high bandwidth at low latency, but ATM has not been introduced so far on a broad basis yet. Most LANs use Ethernet with the relatively low bandwidth of 10 Mbps.

Another problem is the continuity of the media stream. It is created continuously but has to be transmitted in packet switching networks. This leads to buffering at sender and receiver side so that additional delays are added. Low latency means that for a video stream in real-time a latency of 250 ms must not be exceeded. Furthermore it is necessary to synchronize several streams to guarantee for instance lip synchrony.

These considerations shall be detailed further (see also /STN95/): An audio stream in CD quality requires a bandwidth of 689 Kbps while a video stream at PAL standard needs 253 Mbps for its transmission. This can't be realized over Ethernet. Therefore, several compression techniques like MPEG and JPEG have been developed to compress the data and allow their transmission over conventional networks. Both procedures use the cutting of high frequent picture information, because human beings can hardly notice these frequencies. Another possibility to reduce the volume of data is to separate the brightness information from the color information and code the color information with a lower priority because color differences cannot be observed so precisely.

MPEG is a standard for the coding of image sequences. In addition to the above mentioned techniques, MPEG uses similarities between subsequent images to reduce the amount of data. The algorithm takes blocks in the size of 8 x 8 pixels and looks for similar picture fragments in the subsequent picture. After finding a similarity only the position in the previous picture and the location change of the picture fragment are described. The MPEG algorithm is very powerful and reduces the amount of data considerably, depending on which standard is used.

In spite of these algorithms there are several problems with the transmission of digital audio and video. The basis of the Ethernet is the CSMA/CD procedure. For the transmission of a data packet, one has to wait for an idle carrier. There is no guaranteed time for getting access to the carrier. The results are different queuing delays in the end systems. This leads to a variable overall delay of several data units. If the delay is too high, the data unit becomes invalid. This leads to gaps in the playout of the media stream and can become unacceptable for the user. Furthermore, as mentioned above, the required bandwidth can be higher than the maximum bandwidth of the carrier.

There are two approaches to fulfill these requirements:

- The first approach is the reservation of network resources and resources of the end system to guarantee the required resources. Reservation based protocols are for instance ST-II and RSVP /DHH94, ZDE93/. The difference between these protocols is the reservation order. ST-II is a sender based and RSVP is a receiver based algorithm. But these protocols can only realize these requirements if they can map the requirements to an underlying base system. Ethernet doesn't support reservations.

- The second approach is the scaling of the media stream in order to adapt it to the available resources of the network. There are several scaling techniques useful in these terms. Scaling can be done with and without loss. Loss sensitive procedures are the temporal and quality scaling. With spatial scaling the full information can be obtained.

Two ways of scaling are possible: transparent scaling and non transparent scaling. Transparent scaling includes actual knowledge of the network resources in order to influence the media stream. This approach is more difficult to implement than non transparent scaling, because on Ethernet the available network resources may often vary. With non transparent scaling the user has the opportunity of adapting the media stream to his needs and to the network resources interactively.

In order to allow video and audio transmission in all these environments we developed an architecture where the user can handle situations with low bandwidth and cases where he doesn't need high quality images. Our conceptual base is the scaling of media streams in order to run the application also in a low bandwidth environment.

In section 2 we discuss related work on quality of service issues. Section 3 introduces the general approach and some system specific concepts. Several scaling techniques are also discussed in more detail. After having described the architectural model and implementation in section 4 we will detail and explain our experiences with Xnetvideo and show some selected measurement results in section 5. Section 6 concludes with an outlook to future work in terms of networks, multimedia communication and QoS architectures.

2. Related Work

Substantial work has been done on multimedia transport systems, specification and mapping of QoS and reservation of the required resources. Two sample approaches are CINEMA /BDF94/ and HeiTS /DHH94/, which define abstractions for QoS and offer an implementation on top of a special transport system. An own approach with a similar flavor is described in /SMH95/. A survey of several other approaches is found in /VKB95/.

CINEMA is a configurable integrated multimedia architecture /BDF94/. It is conceived as a development and runtime support platform for distributed applications. It is also designed to support QoS handling at the application and transport level. This also includes QoS-mapping between these levels. In CINEMA, a multimedia application is divided into components such as ports, links, clocks and sessions. Data units are produced at output ports of a component and are processed at input ports. Timing of an application is controlled by clocks. Components are integrated via links in order to connect output and input ports.

The other approach mentioned above has been developed at the IBM European Networking Center in Heidelberg and is known as "The Heidelberg High Speed Transport System" (HeiTS) /DHH94/. Its aim is the creation of a distributed multimedia platform for interconnected workstations. It also discusses possibilities of spatial and temporal scaling techniques. Furthermore it is embedded in an ATM environment, where reservations can be made.

At our institute a framework for the transmission of multimedia streams has been developed /SMH95/. It defines abstractions for transport-level QoS parameters and provides a channel library for an efficient and easy assistance on set up and handling of network connections. This approach provides an abstract class „channel", which can be detailed by several QoS parameters to configure and simplify the access of applications to the transport system.

These approaches are difficult to compare. The CINEMA architecture was developed for the support of multimedia applications and offers comprehensive assistance in programming and runtime management of multimedia applications. It is a programming environment and a powerful tool for description of multimedia applications.

HeiTS is more a platform than a programming environment. It uses adapted transport and network protocols and is based on a resource reservation algorithm. The functionality is directed to assist multimedia applications concerning network transmission issues.

The QoS-architecture and the channel library of our institute address another field of the communication behavior. The aim is to assist applications for accessing the transport system. With this approach applications don't have to deal with the QoS configuration of the transport protocol and handling of the socket interface.

Furthermore there are other video conferencing and communication systems like JVTOS /HAF94/, MMC /ADH93/ and the video tools nv and vat of MBONE /MAB94/. Most of them use the multicast algorithm for the transmission to distribute the video to several receivers. It is more difficult to scale in multicast settings because of the multiparty communication with potentially heterogeneous receivers. There are also approaches for multicasting conferences /DEL93/ /KAN93/, but we address the propagation of scaling techniques in this approach and therefore we demonstrate it using a point-to-point video communication.

To summarize, all these architectures address different fields of the communication behavior. Nevertheless, they have in common that media scaling is only addressed in a limited way, for example by extensions of the HeiTS approach. Our contribution detailed below is to introduce a systematic scaling architecture and implementation for further supporting multimedia applications also over conventional networks.

3. General Approach and System Environment

We took a point-to-point video conference as a sample for our approach. So it was possible to apply the scaling techniques at the source and not at intermediate hosts and to put the attention on the scaling techniques and not on the multicast algorithm.
Our approach includes the scaling of media streams in a user specific manner. Scaling is particularly applicable to video streams. It is much more difficult to scale audio

streams and hardly possible without a loss in quality. It is a good approach to scale at the source of the media stream in order to decrease the amount of data already before transmission. Scaling is linked with loss in quality if data units are dropped or loss sensitive procedures are applied. Time sensitive data streams like audio and video streams are well suited for scaling techniques, which use redundancies between subsequent data units.

There are different mechanisms for scaling available:

- Spatial scaling starts from the idea that images have two dimensions. It is created based on the dropping of some picture lines in the uncompressed material. Spatial scaling works only on image data of complete pictures. If the picture sequences are compressed, they have to be decoded for this algorithm. This leads to a delay before the transmission of the data units. The quality of the pictures, which can be expressed in resolution, sharpness and picture rate, is preserved.

- Temporal scaling stands for the influence on the rate of the data units. This kind of scaling works with the dropping of whole data units like pictures or scan values. Another approach is to influence the frame or audio grabbing process. So it is possible to estimate a new meantime between two grabs and consequently influence the rate of the data units without dropping. Dropping of several frames leads to irregular time gabs between pictures that can be observed by the user.

- SNR (signal to noise ratio) scaling is used for the level of quantisation in the information. The more the information is quantisized, the larger the disturbances are observable. After an SNR scaling the original information can't be restored completely.

There are further scaling techniques, like spectral scaling of the color space and hybrid scaling techniques. These types are not used so often, because they need extensive hardware assistance or are not applicable in real-time.

The implementation of our scaling techniques is based on the multimedia system architecture MME (Multimedia Environment) of Digital UNIX (OSF/1) (see fig. 1). It allows the transmission of audio and video data based on different connections. Only the picture of the communication partner is presented to minimize the communication links required. The implementation is based on the client/server principle; upon request, the server delivers image data to the client that are received and further processed there. TCP is applied to guarantee the order of the data units and a safe transmission. Also some conditions for synchronization are fulfilled.

Client Application

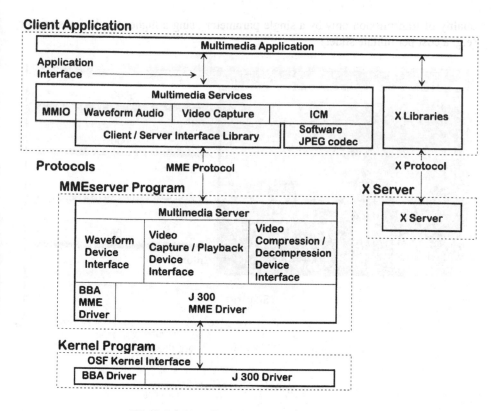

Fig. 1: Multimedia system architecture of OSF/1

The MME system is divided into three levels of abstraction. The functionality of the hardware can be used via a user interface. The user utilizes functions of the MME library within the application. It isn't possible to access the hardware and their parameters directly. The user interface offers functions in four categories: first the input and output of multimedia items on the basis of AVI- files is supported (MMIO). Secondly, waveform audio is enabled; this category offers the functionality for audio input and output. With these functions, one can handle the dedicated audio hardware. Thirdly, video capture is a part of the architecture; the functions of this category can be used for recording and playing of video sequences. The last category is ICM. This is the interface to the video compressor/ decompressor. Videos are finally displayed at the client site based on the X windows system.

4. Architecture and Implementation

In the course of our research on scaling of media streams, a QoS aware prototype for video and audio transmission via networks was developed at our institute (also based on ideas of /ADH93, CCN94, SMH95/). The application called Xnetvideo includes source scaling of Motion-JPEG-quality, frame rate and picture size. In addition, a possibility to scale the absolute bandwidth used by the application is given.

By now the user has to control the parameters via a graphical interface (see figure 2), but the long term aim is to provide mapping functions that allow users to control quality of transmission only by a single parameter using a higher level of abstraction (e.g. a cost per minute slider).

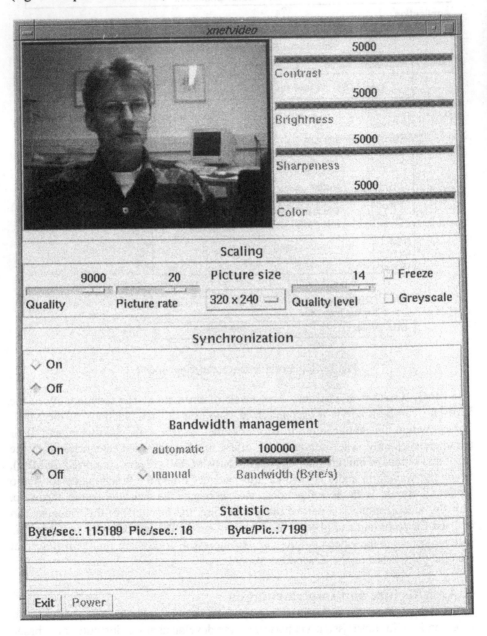

Fig. 2: Graphical user interface of the scaleable video communication system

The implementation follows the above mentioned client server approach. On both sides we find a sending (server) and a receiving (client) component (see figure 3). So a duplex connection as a base for videoconferencing and similar applications is realized.

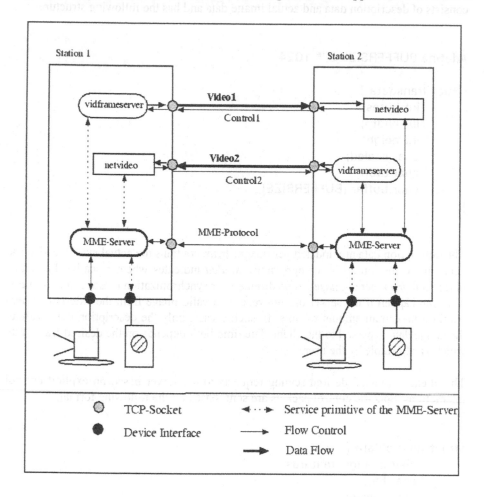

Fig. 3: Video communication system architecture

As illustrated above, the user controls via the client application both the local decoding component and the remote video server, which in turn controls the local coding component. So both channels can be operated separately with different QoS-parameters.

The network communication is based on classical IP over ATM or over Ethernet. The client and the user components on one machine are independent processes. The access to the codec component is serialized via another server process. The system has been implemented under Digital UNIX (OSF/1) on DEC Alpha AXP 700 workstations using J300 framegrabber & motion JPEG boards. The workstations are interconnected via Ethernet and via an 155 Mbps ATM network based on DEC Gigaswitch ATM. The actual transfer of video data is based on packet communication. Each packet consists of description data and actual image data and has the following structure:

```
#define BUFFERSIZE 9 * 1024

struct transdata {
        int bytes;
        int width;
        int height;
        char scaled;
        char drop;
        char buffer [BUFFERSIZE];
};
```

The description data are updated per image; *bytes* contains the actual size (the size can vary due to motion JPEG compression), *scaled* indicates whether scaling has taken place, and *drop* marks images to be dropped for synchronization reasons, for example. This can happen if the server did not receive a valid image from the external camera within a maximum amount of time. In such a case, only the description data without the image data is passed to the client. The time limit depends on the desired frame rate which is adjustable by the user.

The client can signal desired scaling requests to the server based on explicit control interactions. Specific control packets are sent, based on the following format:

```
struct controldata {
        char change_features;
        char bw;
        char freeze;
        short int contrast;
        short int brightness;
        short int sharpening;
        short int saturation;
        short int new_width;
        short int new_height;
        short int new_framerate;
        short int quality;
};
```

If *change_features* is set, the client has signaled an explicit request. In this case, the subsequent components are evaluated by the server (*contrast, brightness, sharpening,* and *saturation*). Based on these values, the video channel is configured by the server. An explicit scaling request is indicated by the components *new_width* and *new_height* (spatial scaling), *new_framerate* (temporal scaling), and *quality* (SNR scaling).

Scaling itself is implemented by a special function at the server site with the following signature:

```
int scale (int type, int width, int height, float rate, int quality);
```

It is parameterized by the requested type of scaling (*temporal, spatial,* or *SNR*), the picture dimensions, the frame rate, and the desired quality level. The scaling requests are mapped onto low-level system routines. Performance results are reported in the next section.

In summary, a facility to transmit audio and video with a very fine grained bandwidth control is enabled, for example to establish videoconferences of adaptable quality between participants in heterogeneous networks. Right now efforts to port the system to Windows NT are underway. This would allow integration of further application fields in our generic distributed multimedia system environment.

5. Performance and Experiences

Scaling attempts to achieve a reduction of the data stream while permitting only limited loss of information. These operations apply only on user demand. This can happen if the video stream hasn't the required quality because of low available bandwidth or the user doesn't want to spend so much money for the transmission. The user has the chance of reducing the overall quality, which is a hybrid approach, or use special scaling techniques, which he can apply according to his desire.

Below we will show some diagrams where the differences and effects of the several scaling mechanisms are to be seen. The major factor concerning reduction of the image data size results from coding in motion JPEG. It is possible to achieve a reduction of the data size to 10 % without loss of quality. Further reduction based on scaling is possible as outlined below.

Spatial scaling
The application allows six different dimensions for the picture size. In figure 4 the significant reduction of image data can be seen. There is an almost linear dependence on the picture size, if no other scaling techniques are applied.

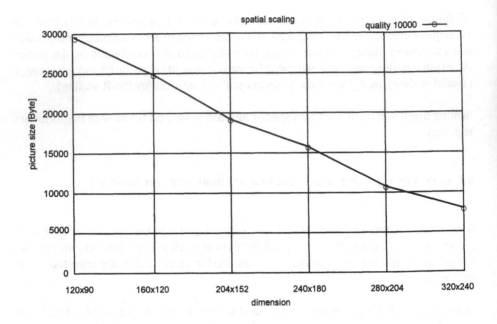

Fig. 4: Image data with the influence of spatial scaling

Temporal scaling

Temporal scaling has a similar influence on the data stream like spatial scaling. According to the constant picture size, a reduction of the frame rate causes a linear course in the diagram (see figure 5).

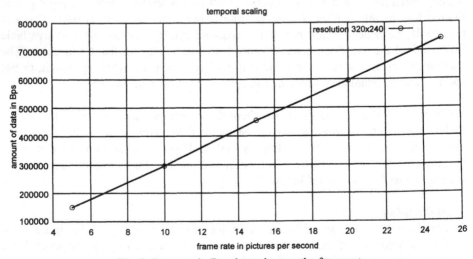

Fig 5: Data rate in Bps dependent on the frame rate

SNR scaling

SNR scaling is the major feature of the JPEG compression algorithm. The algorithm can be configured, according to the desired quality of the created image. The quality of an image is the most deciding factor for information loss. Figure 6 shows the dependency between the data size and the quality of the image. If the quality is near the lower border, the contents of the image can't be recognized any more. A reduction of quality of more than a half leads to highly adverse effects in the image. A further reduction of quality does not achieve a further remarkable reduction of data (as shown in figure 6). So it can be concluded that SNR scaling is only useful in certain boundaries.

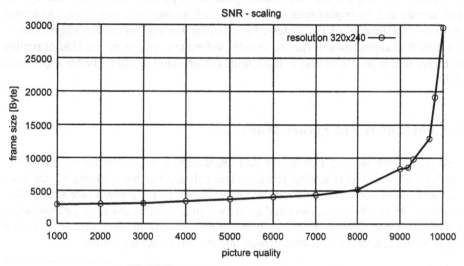

Fig. 6: Data size dependent on image quality

Experiences:

The prototype implementation has been completed, and the system is in practical use for our research efforts. Parts of the multimedia functionality have been implemented within separate projects. Experiences with the prototype are as follows:

- *General approach:* The performance results encouraged us to use scaling techniques on a broader basis in order to adjust bandwidth requirements according to the available network characteristics. Especially in heterogeneous network environments, the approach appears to be rather useful. In particular, our related mobile computing research group also exploits the results for transferring image data via GSM networks, for example.

- *Architecture:* The developed client/server architecture has proven suitable as a basis for managing distributed multimedia scenarios (cf. also /SCH95/).The architecture enabled the use of client/server industry standards at the implementation level. Advanced distributed object-oriented solutions could further enhance transparency and manageability according to our experiences (cf. also /OMG93, NWM93/).

- *Genericity:* Our implementation mainly addresses scaling of video streams. However, the basic architecture is independent of the specific implementation solution. This enables reusability and a general applicability of the approach for further practical investigation and measurements in the field of QoS research. For example, other compression and scaling techniques have already been integrated within our mobile computing project work.

Altogether, our experiences are mainly positive, especially concerning the system architecture and the implementation. However, additional work is necessary to further increase functionality of the system, for example towards automatic adaptations to bandwidth changes, towards the use of user preferences concerning the kind of scaling to be applied or how to extend to multipoint conferencing to offer a better application field.

6. Conclusions and Future Work

This paper presented an architecture and implementation for distributed multimedia applications with media scaling features. The solution has been illustrated based on the example of video transmission. We have shown that a client/server architecture based on off-the-shelf equipment and industry standard communication mechanisms is a feasible basis. Moreover, it has been illustrated that generic support for such applications in terms of QoS management and media scaling is possible.

The current implementation is under further evaluation and is also in practical use. Current implementation work is focusing on improving the internal structure, and on the integration of further codecs and framegrabber hardware. Moreover a port to Windows NT is ongoing, and the results are also transferred into our mobile computing group as discussed above.

Concerning the more distant future, we plan to evaluate our mechanisms based on other multimedia applications, especially in the medical application field /SKZ95/ and in the educational field /WOH95, SCH94/. Enhanced user control features and the use of automated, contents based transmission control will play an important role in these areas.

Acknowledgments
We would like to thank Digital Equipment Corporation for the generous support of our work. Moreover, we would like to thank all colleagues and students who contributed to the implementation of the presented approach.

References

/ADH93/ Altenhofen, M., Dittrich, J., Hammerschmidt, R., Käppner, T., Kruschel, C., Kückes, A., Steinig, T.: The BERKOM Multimedia Collaboration Service; ACM Conf. on Multimedia, 1993

/BEB94/ Beitz, A., Bearman, M.: An ODP Trading Service for DCE; 1st IEEE Int. Workshop on Services in Distributed and Networked Environments (SDNE), Prag, Juni 1994, pp. 42-49

/BDF94/ Barth, I., Dermler, G., Fiederer, W.: Levels of Quality in CINEMA, Technical Report, University of Stuttgart, Institute of Parallel and Distributed High Performance Systems

/CCN94/ Campbell, A., Coulson, G., Hutchison, D.: A Quality of Service Architecture; Computer Communication Review, Vol. 1, No. 2, April 1994, pp. 6-27

/DCE94/ Distributed Computing Environment - An Overview; Open Software Foundation, 1994

/DEL93/ Delgrossi et al: ACM Multimedia 93 : proceedings First ACM International Conference on Multimedia, Anaheim, California, August 1 - 6, 1993

/DHH94/ Delgrossi, L., Herrtwich, R.G., Hoffmann, F.: An Implementation of ST-II for the Heidelberg Transport System; Internetworking: Research and Experience, Vol. 5, 1994, pp. 43-69

/GON94/ Goscinski, A., Ni, Y.: Trader Cooperation to Enable Object Sharing Among Users of Homogeneous Distributed Systems; Computer Communications, Vol. 17, 1994, pp. 218-229

/HAF94/ Hafid, A.: On JVTOS QoS experiments; GMD-Studien Gesellschaft für Mathematik und Datenverarbeitung, Bonn ; 236; 1994

/KAN93/ Kanakia et al: Communications architectures, protocols and applications : SIGCOMM '93; conference proceedings ; September 13 - 17, 1993, San Francisco, California, USA / ACM SIGCOMM

/KRE95/ Kretschmar, J.: Untersuchung zur Skalierbarkeit von Medienströmen; Diplomarbeit, TU Dresden, 1995

/MAB94/ Macedonia, M. R., Brutzman, D.P.: Mbone Provides Audio and Video Across the Internet; April 1994

/MII94/ Mittasch, Ch., Irmscher, K.: On the Way to Competitive Market of Services in Heterogeneous Networks - IFIP World Computer Congress, Hamburg 1994 - IFIP Transactions - Applications and Impacts, Volume II, Brunnstein, Raubold (ed.), pp. 57-62

/MML94/ Merz, M., Müller, K., Lamersdorf, W.: Service Trading and Mediation in Distributed Computing Systems; 14th IEEE Int. Conf. on Distributed Computing Systems, Poznan, Juni 1994, pp. 450-457

/NAS95/ Nahrstedt, K., Steinmetz, R.: Resource Management in Networked Multimedia Systems; IEEE Computer, Vol. 28, No. 5, May 1995, pp. 52-63

/NWM93/ Nicol, J.R., Wilkes, C.T., Manola, F.A.: Object-Orientation in Heterogeneous Distributed Computing Systems; IEEE Computer, Vol. 26, No. 6, 1993, pp. 57-67

/ODP92/ ISO/IEC JTC1/SC21/WG7: A Structural Specification of the ODP Trader with Federating Included, 1992

/OMG93/ Object Management Group: The Common Object Request Broker: Architecture and Specification; OMG, 1993

/SCH94/ Schank, R.: Active Learning Through Multimedia; IEEE MultiMedia, Vol. 1, No. 1, Spring 1994, pp. 69-78

/SCH95/ Schill, A.: Cooperative Office Systems: Concepts and Enabling Technology; Prentice Hall, 1995

/SCK95/ Schill, A., Kümmel, S.: Leistungsanalyse und Vergleich von RPC-Systemen für heterogene Workstation-Netze, PIK - Praxis der Informationsverarbeitung und Kommunikation, 1995

/SKZ95/ Simon, R., Krieger, D., Znati, T., Lofink, R., Sclabassi, R.: Multimedia MedNet: A Medical Collaboration and Consultation System; IEEE Computer, Vol. 28, No. 5, May 1995, pp. 65-73

/SMH95/ Schill, A., Hutschenreuther, T., Wildenhain, F.: A Quality of Service Abstraction Tool for Advanced Distributed Applications; IFIP Inf. Conf. on Open Distributed Processing, Brisbane, Australia, 1995

/STN95/ Steinmetz, R., Nahrstedt, K.: Multimedia Computing, Communications and Applications; Prentice-Hall, Englewood Cliffs, NJ, 1995

/THO93/ Thomas, G.: Design, Implementation and Evaluation of an Adaptive User Interface; Knowledge-Based Systems, Vol. 6, No. 4, Dec. 1993, pp. 230-238

/VKB95/ Vogel, A., Kerherve, B., Bochmann, G., Gecsei, J.: Distributed Multimedia and QoS: A Survey; IEEE Multimedia, Vol. 2, No. 2, 1995, pp. 10-19

/WOH95/ Wolf, B., Hall, W.: Multimedia Pedagogues: Interactive Systems for Teaching and Learning; IEEE Computer, Vol. 28, No. 5, May 1995, pp. 74-80

/ZDE93/ Zhang, L., Deering, S., Estrin, D., Shenker, S., Zappala, D.: RSVP: A New Resource Reservation Protocol; IEEE Network, Sept. 1993, pp. 8-18

Scheduling Mechanisms Reducing Contention Situations in Multimedia Systems

Jörg Werner, TU Chemnitz-Zwickau
Lars C. Wolf, IBM European Networking Center

Abstract: Multimedia applications have time dependancies and require appropriate resource management and scheduling mechanisms. Additionally, such applications have typically large resource requirements, hence, methods to reduce these requirements are desirable. Contention situations occur when the execution of processes overlaps in time. This leads to additional management efforts like context switches and to the increasing demand for resources like memory space. In this paper we present alternative scheduling methods suitable for real-time processes in multimedia systems. These methods serialize the execution of processes in order to reduce the occurence of overlaps. On the basis of measurements the described scheduling mechanisms are evaluated concerning their effectiveness and the required expenses.

1 Introduction

Multimedia applications are time critical and have typically large resource requirements. To process the data packets of a continuous-media stream, resources such as buffer space are necessary. A simple approach for the assignment of that resource is the fixed, non-shared assignment of buffer space to a stream. This way, the buffer space is always available at the arrival of a data packet. However, the buffer space is unused after the processing of a packet has been finished until the next packet arrives. If a different assignment (which allows sharing) is applied, the total buffer space amount needed for all streams is much smaller, hence, potentially more streams can be served [Williamson95].

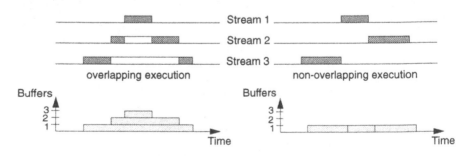

Fig. 1. Resource Utilization.

This buffer space can be shared among streams only if the processing of these streams does not overlap, e.g., due to preemption. This is illustrated in Figure 1, the left side shows the resource requirements if overlapping occurs and the right side presents the case where resources can be shared since no overlapping happens.

In addition to the possibility to apply space sharing strategies, further improvements can be gained if the processing of streams does not overlap. For instance, preemption involves context switch costs, and the execution time for several system mechanisms for synchronization and coordination, e.g., semaphores, is larger due to the management effort if several processes execute them concurrently.

In this paper, scheduling mechanisms are presented and evaluated which reduce the amount of overlapped processing and hence the number of contention situations. A rate-monotonic scheduler is used as the basis for the given mechanisms [Liu73, Wolf96].

The scheduling mechanisms must meet several requirements with respect to correctness and efficiency, i.e., they must:

1. guarantee that no deadlines are missed,
2. avoid overlapped processing whenever possible,
3. use as few resources (CPU time, memory) as possible for scheduling decisions,
4. allow continuous-media processing with as large as possible CPU utilization.

The correctness (1) is the most important item, efficiency aspects are only second. An optimality criterion is given by (2). The scheduling mechanism should not consume all the resource savings itself (3) and it should not reduce the CPU utilization for continuous-media processing (4), compared with the original rate-monotonic scheduler.

2 System Model

Before the examined mechanisms can be described, it is necessary to present the model underlying the design of the mechanisms.

Currently we restrict ourselves to the uniprocessor case. Whether the scheduling methods can be applied successfully to multiprocessors is subject to further investigations.

Each process is periodic and its deadlines are equal to the ends of the periods. When a new period begins, a process is, in principle, ready to run, i.e., its arrival times are known. However, in order to avoid overlappings the scheduler can later change the actual arrival times of a process, so that they do not necessarily coincide with the beginning of the periods (as with the rate-monotonic scheduler). This introduces variability into the start time of the processing of the data packets (jitter), bound by the length of the period. But also for preemptive rate-monotonic scheduling, there exists no guarantee *when* a process executes within a period. It is only guaranteed that processing is finished before the deadline, hence, the worst-case jitter does not deteriorate.

Each process is working with its distinct priority according to the rate-monotonic scheme: the higher the rate of a process, the higher is its priority. The execution time per period given for a process is a worst-case value and includes context-switch overhead so this can be ignored later. All real-time processes are independent and are not influenced by non-real-time processes.

A process never yields the processor voluntarily. This means that a process need not suspend itself to wait for data, e.g., from the filesystem or the network. For the file system, such waiting times, and hence the suspension, can be avoided if a specifically designed continuous-media filesystem such as *Shark* is used [Drake94, Haskin93]. When reading data from a network, such blocking avoidance is not generally possible.

For the time being, only processes that send but not receive, for instance processes inside a video server, can fulfill the requirements given above. They never need to block and have a known behaviour with respect to arrival times. Therefore, the scheduling mechanisms described in the next section are restricted to that class of processes.

Section 4 briefly discusses a method which is able to avoid the blocking of processes when receiving data from the network, but, on the other hand, introduces variable arrival times. Approaches to schedule such processes are presented there, too.

3 Scheduling Methods for Processes with Known Arrival Times

3.1 Non-Preemptive Scheduling

The simplest approach to completely avoid contention situations among processes is to use non-preemptive scheduling, where each process runs without interruptions until its execution for that period has finished. To find out whether a specific process set is schedulable, an appropriate schedulability test must be applied, here, the non-preemptive rate-monotonic method [Nagarajan92].

This scheduling mechanism is optimal with respect to the avoidance of contention situations since at no time more than one process is executing. There are no scheduling efforts during run time because the rate-monotonic scheme assigns priorities in a static manner.

The drawback of this approach is that the possible CPU utilization is potentially lower than using the preemptive rate-monotonic scheduling algorithm. This occurs if a process has a long execution time compared with the periods of other processes. Then even for relatively low CPU utilizations, deadline violations might happen. Such a set of processes would be rejected by the schedulability test since it is not schedulable.

The applicability of this approach depends therefore on the usage scenario. For instance, if the scheduler is used for a video server (which has a processing time of a few milliseconds per period and a much longer period), in most cases non-preemptive execution is possible without deadline violations even for CPU utilizations achievable with preemptive rate-monotonic scheduling.

3.2 Non-Preemptive Scheduling of Processes with Equal Rates

The previous section showed that (for specific sets of processes) non-preemptive scheduling can lead to low CPU utilization. However, a modified method can allow for CPU utilizations equal to those achievable with the preemptive rate-monotonic algorithm. The modification is that the execution of a process is non-preemptive with respect to processes with the same rate, however, processes with higher rates may preempt its execution, i.e., processes are grouped into sets of processes with equal rates and preemption can only occur among processes which belong to different sets.

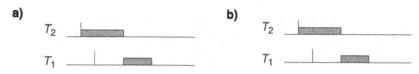

Fig. 2. Possible Execution Sequences of Processes with Equal Rates.

This scheme allows the same maximum CPU utilization as the preemptive rate-monotonic scheduling as explained by the following example. T_1 and T_2 are preemptable processes. In the left side of Figure 2, T_1 has a higher priority than T_2, thus, T_1 preempts process T_2. If the priority order is reverse, i.e., the priority of T_2 is higher than that of T_1, no preemption occurs (right side of Figure 2), and the serialization is achieved without any non-preemptability.

The rate-monotonic scheduling algorithm assigns a unique priority to each process. For processes with equal rates the priority order among them is arbitrary [Liu73]. Therefore, it is permitted to execute T_2 non-preemptively with respect to T_1 independent of the assigned priorities. Since this scheme is still within the conditions of the preemptive rate-monotonic scheduling algorithm, the maximum CPU utilization is the same for both schemes.

Due to the non-preemptive scheduling of processes with equal rates, the execution of such processes never overlaps. Preemptions can now only be caused by processes with a higher rate (and therefore a higher priority). This means that for a process set with n distinct rates at most $n-1$ preemptions may occur.

The applicability of this scheme depends on the usage scenario, yet, it can be justified as follows. While the processing of continuous-media data is done in principle with different rates, the number of that rates is usually limited. For instance, within video-on-demand applications the data packet transmission is performed with a certain packet rate chosen from a normally small set of rates, hence, the processing of several streams is performed with the same rate. Scaling of streams in regard to their rates will also be possible with a small set of rates only.

A drawback of this method is that it is not optimal with respect to contention avoidance. For a process set with several distinct rates it will generate a schedule that contains overlaps. However, using a different algorithm it might be possible to find a non-overlapping schedule. Further, the algorithm works only well for process sets with a limited number of different rates.

3.3 Modification of Arrival Times

Now a method is presented which offers the same CPU utilization as the preemptive rate-monotonic scheme and avoids overlapped processing whenever possible, i.e., it is optimal with regard to this criterion. The principle approach is to modify all arrival times of the processes individually, hence, processes do not always become ready at the begin of a new period. For instance, process T_1 in Figure 3, which has a higher priority than T_2, does not become ready at t_1 since it would preempt T_2. Instead, the arrival time of T_1 is set to t_2 when T_2 has finished its work, therefore, no preemption can occur.

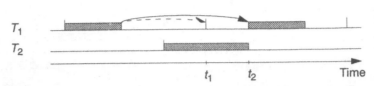

Fig. 3. Modification of Arrival Times.

To apply that technique it must be checked that the delay of T_1 is permitted. It is only allowed to execute a low-prioritized process T_i without preemptions if no higher priority process misses its deadline within that period. Processes with a lower priority than T_i need not to be considered since it has no influence on them whether higher priority processes are executed with or without preemptions. The total CPU requirement is equal in both cases.

This scheme does not change the possible CPU utilization compared with preemptive rate-monotonic scheduling. It uses the laxity of the processes, i.e., the time until the deadline is reached, to inhibit overlapped execution.

The arrival times can be determined either by a static precalculation or dynamically during run time. Both approaches will be discussed in the following subsections.

Modification of Arrival Times – Static Precalculation

The length of the time interval for which the precalculation must be done depends on the periods of the processes. To avoid overlapped processing, it is necessary to examine the current phasing of the periods of all processes at each time instance. It is sufficient to consider an interval with a length given by the lowest common multiple of the period lengths of the processes since it contains all possible period phasings. After the first interval of that length has passed, all further intervals are only replicas of the first one. Hence, the precalculation of the schedule must be done for the length of that interval only. The schedule can be applied repeatedly after each such interval has finished (Figure 4).

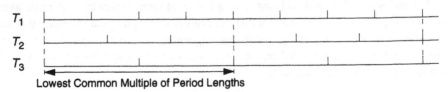

Lowest Common Multiple of Period Lengths

Fig. 4. Schedule Repetition Interval.

To create the schedule, the processes must be arranged for that interval so that each process finishes before its deadline and in summary as few as possible overlaps occur. This way, for each process in each period a time is determined when the process should become ready. These arrival times can be stored in a table. During run time, after the execution of a process has finished for a certain period, the next ready time can be retrieved from the table. If the table is exhausted, it can be applied again, whereas the stored arrival times must be adapted to the current time.

The schedule is determined by simulating the execution of the processes. It must be decided whether the execution of process T_i can continue at time t if the period of a process with a higher priority begins at this moment. To this end, it must be checked whether all processes with a higher priority than T_i meet their deadlines even if T_i is executed non-preemptively. This is done by arranging all processes in a non-preemptive manner, storing the times at which the execution of a process begins in the table, until either the schedule has been completed or a deadline violation occurs. In the latter case, the last part of the schedule must be dropped. The deadline violation must have its reason in the non-preemptive execution of a lower priority process because the process set is schedulable under the preemptive rate-monotonic scheme. The process T_j with the lowest priority among the processes responsible for the deadline violation is determined and it is temporarily marked and handled as preemptable. The simulation continues from the start of the process T_j in the considered period (Figure 5). After all higher priority processes have finished their execution, T_j is marked as non-preemptable again and continues to work. Note that during other periods this process may execute without any preemptions. Moreover, it might be necessary to perform multiple of the described backtracking steps until all higher priority processes can be executed before their deadlines.

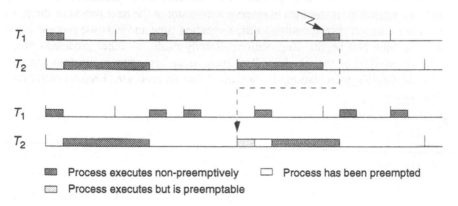

Fig. 5. **Backtracking During Simulation due to Deadline Violation.**

The run-time overhead of this method is low since it consists only of the retrieval of the next ready time from the table. The complex part of the scheme is the calculation of the scheduling table which must be performed when the process set changes, i.e., each time a process is created or deleted or when the parameters of a process change, e.g., due to stream scaling. The overhead for the precalculation depends on the process set but can be time and space consuming if the lowest common multiple is large.

Modification of Arrival Times – Dynamic Determination

As an alternative to the static precalculation, the arrival time for each process in each period can be determined dynamically during run time. Again, overlappings can be avoided by considering the execution times of other processes. This dynamic approach promises flexibility. Changes in the process set such as created or deleted processes and changed process parameters are taken into account immediately. Additionally, no memory space to store arrival times is necessary because that information is generated only when it is needed.

However, a major drawback is the run-time overhead which must be paid for each process in each period, hence it must be as small as possible. If, for instance, the execution time of a process per period is in the order of a few milliseconds, an overhead in a similar order is absolutely unacceptable. Therefore, the algorithm must be simple, even if its scheduling decisions are not optimal in the sense that potentially avoidable overlapping situations occur.

The schedule is created in the following way. At the end of its processing for a period each process calls the scheduler to calculate the next ready time for this process. The scheduler needs information about the behavior of the other processes during the next period of the considered process. This information is generated and managed inside the scheduler. It attempts to reserve a time slot in the next period of the process which has a length corresponding to the execution time and puts the process to sleep until that time slot begins. Reservations already made for other processes must be taken into account by the scheduler. This reservation procedure is illustrated in Figure 6. To simplify the presentation, it is assumed that all processes become ready for the first time.

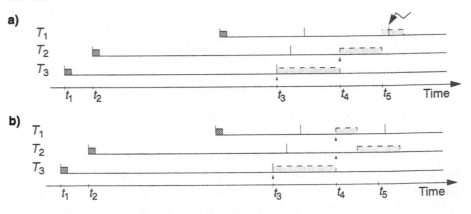

Fig. 6. Time Slot Reservation.

In the upper part, at time t_1 the first process T_3 becomes ready. To reduce conflicts with possibly running processes, no stream processing is performed during the first period, but only the scheduler is called to reserve a time slot for the next period. Since no reservations have been made so far, T_3 is scheduled for the time slot beginning with its next period at t_3. At time t_2 the second process T_2 becomes ready and calls the scheduler. Since a reservation has been set for T_3, the ready time for T_2 is set to t_4 so that the execution of T_3 is not preempted by T_2. If the same procedure is applied to process T_1, it will not be schedulable without deadline violation.

This shows the difficulties which occur at the time slot reservation for a high-priority process. Due to longer periods (compared with high-priority processes) the processes with low priorities such as T_3 perform their reservation early and find enough unreserved time slots. For processes with a high priority this is exactly the opposite. For example, in the above scenario the next time slot available to process T_1 begins at t_5 which is too late to finish before the deadline. Even if T_1 could be processed just in time, this would mean that priorities are not taken into consideration because T_2 would be executed before T_1.

For this reason, a reservation is not fixed in time (lower part of Figure 6). Since T_1 has a higher priority than T_2, the scheduler reserves a time slot for T_1 at t_4 and moves the reservation for T_2 accordingly. In order to reduce the overhead, the arrival time of T_2 is not adapted. This is not necessary because at time t_4 process T_1 is dispatched due to its higher priority. But it is required to move the reservation for T_2 to indicate that T_2 will be processed within that interval.

If the scheduler detects that a process cannot finish its processing in time (either a process which tries to reserve a time slot or a process for which the reservation has just been moved) then the process which is the reason for that violation must be executed preemptably. To this end, its reservation is removed which results in new reservations within this interval for other, higher priority processes. Since the process will wake up at the originally scheduled time, overlaps may occur.

4 Scheduling Methods for Processes with Varying Arrival Times

Section 3 presented mechanisms to reduce the amount of overlapped processing which can be used successfully for certain types of applications such as video servers. In such a scenario a process must never wait for data to transmit and, therefore, never yields the processor voluntarily. However, this is not true for receiver processes.

For example, a receiver process in a video conference must wait until a packet has been received from the network before further processing can be done. The wait time might vary between periods due to jitter introduced by the network (if the used network provides no tight jitter guarantee). If the process would start at the begin of the period and then block to wait for a data packet, overlapping would be introduced if another process would execute meanwhile. However, prohibiting other processes from execution during that wait time leads to unused processor cycles and reduces the CPU utilization contradicting the goals of the algorithms. This problem can be solved if wait times are eliminated.

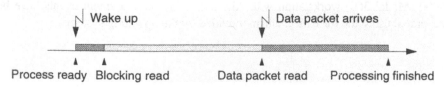

Fig. 7. Wait Times During Processing Period.

Figure 7 illustrates that two events are necessary before a receiver process can run to completion in a period: the process must wake up and the data packet to be processed must have been received. If the process is not awoken before both events occurred as shown in Figure 8, the process can read the packet immediately. This way, it does not have to wait, and the execution can be performed without interruptions.

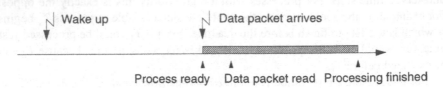

Fig. 8. Elimination of Wait Times.

If that approach to eliminate the wait times is used, no information is available when a receiver process will actually wake up. Receiving processes are now of a more sporadic nature than sending processes which are mostly strictly periodic and have known arrival times. Therefore, the scheduling algorithms must be examined whether they are able to schedule processes with varying arrival times.

The exact arrival time of a receiver process is not known because it depends on the receipt of the data packet. Thus, the algorithms which modify the arrival times (static and dynamic version) can not be used. They are based on the idea that a process indeed starts its execution at the scheduled time. Hence, only the non-preemptive methods can be applied successfully.

5 Evaluation

The purpose of the scheduling mechanisms examined in the previous sections is the reduction of contention situations among real-time processes. Therefore, the following evaluation should clarify to which extend the algorithms are able to fulfill this goal. Since specific mechanisms are needed to avoid overlapped execution, the additional costs, i.e., the amount of resources needed for these mechanisms, must be evaluated as well. The additional costs for the non-preemptive algorithms consists of the functions to inhibit preemptions. For the algorithms which modify the arrival times, the scheduling itself leads to overhead: for the static version the table must be calculated resulting in processing time and memory space requirements, in the case of the dynamic version the next arrival time must be determined. Only the static precalculation of arrival times needs significant memory space to store the scheduling table.

The processing time measurements have been performed on a IBM RISC System/ 6000 (Model 360) workstation with AIX 3.2.4. The measurement events have been generated using the trace mechanism provided by the operating system.

Tab. 1. Process Sets.

	Number of Processes	Process Parameters			CPU Utilization
		Rate	Period	Processing Time/Period	
Process Set 1	6	$5\ s^{-1}$	200 ms	7 ms	67.5 %
	6	$10\ s^{-1}$	100 ms	4 ms	
	5	$15\ s^{-1}$	66.5 ms*	3 ms	
Process Set 2	20	$5\ s^{-1}$	200 ms	7 ms	70 %
Process Set 3	1	$5\ s^{-1}$	200 ms	60 ms	77.2 %
	1	$11.1\ s^{-1}$	90 ms	20 ms	
	1	$25\ s^{-1}$	40 ms	10 ms	

* rounded to keep the lowest common multiple reasonably small

Scenarios

The developed algorithms are only partially usable for scenarios with varying arrival times, but can be used for applications with known arrival times, for instance, a video server. Therefore, the measurement setup resembles such an application; the test processes execute with timely characteristics found in a video server.

To perform a worst-case evaluation of the implementation of the algorithms, the process sets have been chosen in such a way that the overall CPU utilization is large, i.e., close to the maximum permitted by the preemptive rate-monotonic algorithm. The process sets are given in Table 1.

In *process set 1* for each of the three different rates approximately the same number of processes exists resembling a video server supporting three different retrieval rates, e.g., for heterogeneous clients.

The *process set 2* contains only processes with the same rate. As explained before, such a scenario can be considered as typical for video server which might support only one standard rate. This scenario is directed to the examination of the non-preemptive scheduling of processes with equal rates which should be able to schedule the process set without overlaps.

The purpose of the last scenario, *process set 3*, is to examine the scheduling algorithms if a process set is not schedulable without overlaps. Here, the non-preemptive mechanism cannot be used. This can easily be seen looking at the process parameters which have not been taken from a video server: the long processing time of the first process (60 ms) inhibits the third process from meeting its deadline at the end of its period (40 ms). In this scenario the performance of the remaining algorithms is of major interest.

Results – Reduction of Overlapped Execution

The following figures show the ability of the algorithms to reduce the number of overlaps occurring during the execution of the process sets. The bars symbolize the normalized measurement interval. Each section of a bar specifies (in average) the portion of the measurement interval where n processes were executing concurrently. n is given for each section. For comparison purposes, the degree of concurrency when using the preemptive rate-monotonic scheduling algorithm is shown, too. Note that the shaded part corresponds to the CPU utilization of the process set in question.

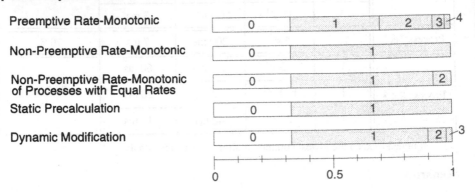

Fig. 9. Reduction of Overlapped Execution for Process Set 1.

Figure 9 illustrates that a large amount of concurrent execution can be observed if the preemptive rate-monotonic scheduling algorithm is used. As expected, the non-preemptive algorithm avoids overlapped execution completely. The algorithm which schedules processes with equal rates without preemptions can reduce the number of overlaps significantly.

The static precalculation is an optimal mechanism. Since the process set is schedulable non-preemptively, this method should also find a schedule without any preemptions, and it is indeed able to do so.

It has been expected that the results for the dynamic modification of the arrival times are comparable to the results gained by the static precalculation (both take a similar approach). However, the number of overlaps using the dynamic scheme is higher; up to three processes are executing concurrently. The reason is that the implementation, in order to reduce the overhead, does not adapt the wake-up times accordingly if time slot reservations are moved. Thus, several processes may wakeup simultaneously. In principle, the execution of the processes should nevertheless be serialized due to their distinct priorities. However, since the number of real-time priorities in AIX 3 is limited, the (logical) process priorities must be mapped to the smaller number of available real-time priorities. Now several processes can have the same priority. Processes with the same real-time priority are scheduled using the round-robin scheme with a maximum but not guaranteed time slice of 10 ms [Britton93], so that a process might be dispatched even if another has not yet finished its execution.

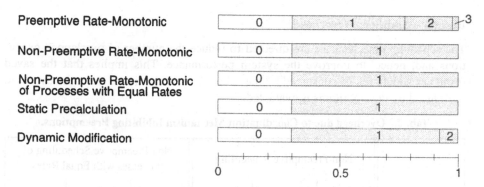

Fig. 10. Reduction of Overlapped Execution for Process Set 2.

The results for process set 2 are better for all scheduling algorithms (Figure 10). The preemptive rate-monotonic scheduling scheme leads also for this process set to a considerable number of overlaps. As expected, both non-preemptive methods are able to schedule the process set without any preemptions and the static precalculation performs equal to them. The dynamic modification scheme achieves a better result than for process set 1, however, its result is still worse than any of the other three methods.

Process set 3 is not schedulable with the non-preemptive rate-monotonic algorithm, hence, Figure 11 presents the results for the other schemes only.

Using the preemptive rate-monotonic scheduler, two processes are executing concurrently for a large portion of the measurement interval. The result for the non-preemptive scheduling of processes with equal rates is similar. The reason is that no two processes have the same rate, so the method is basically identical to the preemptive scheme. That the behavior is slightly better is simply by accident.

The static precalculation approach is able to reduce the number of overlaps significantly. This case demonstrates clearly the difference to the non-preemptive scheduling. While the non-preemptive scheduler rejects the process set, the static precalculation can serialize the execution of the processes in an optimal manner. Whenever possible it allows the non-preemptive execution otherwise preemptions are permitted.

Once again, the result gained by the dynamic modification method is not acceptable.

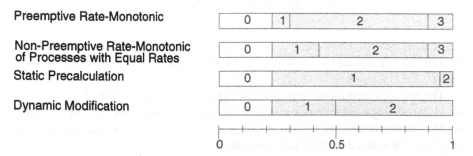

Fig. 11. Reduction of Overlapped Execution for Process Set 3.

Results – Additional Overhead

The scheduling mechanisms are directed to reduce the number of overlapped executions and, hence, to improve the system performance. This implies that the saved resources should not be consumed by the scheduling mechanisms. Here, the overhead introduced by the algorithms is evaluated.

Tab. 2. Overhead due to Coordination Mechanism Inhibiting Preemptions.

	Non-Preemptive Scheduling			Non-Preemptive Scheduling of Processes with Equal Rates		
	Minimum	Maximum	Average	Minimum	Maximum	Average
Process Set 1	2 μs	26 μs	8 μs	2 μs	15 μs	8 μs
Process Set 2	2 μs	22 μs	10 μs	2 μs	15 μs	9 μs
Process Set 3	–*	–*	–*	2 μs	3 μs	2 μs

* not schedulable

Table 2 shows the costs (processing time) generated by the non-preemptive scheduling schemes. For them, coordination mechanisms are required which ensures that the processes execute without preemptions. The overhead for the non-preemptive scheduling mechanism is larger than that for the non-preemptive scheme among processes with equal rates. The reason is that the number of processes to be coordinated is larger for the first scheme since the second must consider smaller subsets only. In both cases the overhead must be paid for each process in each period.

The static precalculation algorithm leads to processing time and storage space overhead, i.e., to calculate and to store the scheduling table. Both depend on the process set what can also be seen in Table 3 showing the costs for the three considered process sets. For a process set $\{T_1, ..., T_n\}$ the required space M (in bytes) to store the scheduling table can easily be computed since each process entry consumes 12 bytes and each stored arrival time needs 8 bytes in the current implementation:

$$M = \sum_{i=1}^{n} \left(12 + \frac{\text{lowest common multiple}}{T_i} \times 8 \right)$$

For a short period, while calculating a new scheduling table, more space is needed because the old schedule is valid and must be kept until the new table has been computed.

The required time for the schedule calculation presented in Table 3 has been measured under a significant real-time processing load, i.e., while the system was executing the respective process set. The run-time overhead when retrieving the next ready time from the scheduling table is neglectable.

Table 3 also showes the overhead for the algorithm which modifies the arrival times dynamically. It must be noted that these computation times are necessary for each process in each period.

Tab. 3. Scheduling Overhead.

	Static Precalculation					Dynamic Modification		
	Lowest Common Multiple	Storage Space	Processing Time			Processing Time		
			Min.	Max.	Ave.	Min.	Max.	Ave.
Process Set 1	26.6 s	35356 bytes	148 µs	29840 µs	6734 µs	2 µs	22 µs	5 µs
Process Set 2	0.2 s	400 bytes	147 µs	923 µs	498 µs	2 µs	23 µs	7 µs
Process Set 3	1.8 s	628 bytes	142 µs	724 µs	365 µs	2 µs	22 µs	4 µs

6 Related Work

Real-time scheduling mechanisms which consider the usage of resources have been studied by several research groups.

[Zhao87] presents a method with the two goals that each process meets its deadlines and that each process has exclusive access to resources which must be specified accordingly. No a priori information about process arrival times are required by this method. The scheduling is done each time when a process arrives. The algorithm creates a tree of possible schedules and performs a heuristic search on that tree to determine whether a new arriving process can be scheduled without violating the guarantees given to already existing processes, i.e., that processing can complete before the deadlines and that all exclusive resources required are available exclusively.

The method described in [Xu90] guarantees not only processing before deadlines and exclusive access to resources but also considers precedence relations among parts of different processes. Since the algorithm is aimed to be used for the pre-runtime calculation of the schedule, the process set must be completely known in advance. Each process consists of a set of segments with known arrival times, execution durations and deadlines. Precedence and exclusion rules can be specified between pairs of segments. The precedence rules allow to specify that the processing of one segment must be finished before the execution of the other segment may start. Exclusion rules can be used to get exclusive access to a resource during a segment. The unit considered for scheduling is not a process but a segment. Again, the schedule is generated with the help of a search tree.

Another scheduling algorithm which guarantees execution before deadlines and exclusive access to resources was developed as part of YARTOS [Jeffay90]. Here, resources are shared software objects which can be accessed by only one process at a time. Processes are characterized by an execution time and a deadline, the former is partitioned into phases. By definition, a process accesses at most one resource during each phase. The unit considered for scheduling is a phase. A process can only be preempted by a higher priority process if the higher priority process does not require a resource which is accessed by the currently running process during this processing phase; priority inheritance is used to avoid priority inversions.

In addition to guaranteeing that the processing finishes before the deadline, it is a common characteristic of these three methods that they can ensure that a process can exclusively access specific resources without explicit coordination mechanisms such as semaphores. To be able to provide these guarantees, the last two methods need the information for each process when which resources are required and for how long. The first method assumes that exclusive resources are needed during the whole execution time. Then a given process set, i.e., the set of processes and their resource usage specifications, is only schedulable and hence accepted if all processes can finish their execution before their deadlines and if all specified resources can be accessed exclusively.

Even though these mechanisms ensure that a process can access a resource exclusively, it might nevertheless be preempted by other processes which do not require access to this resource at that time. Hence, conflicts, with respect to the definition used in this paper, can still occur. These methods can avoid overlapping execution only for the special case when the resource *processor* is specified as a resource for which exclusive access is required.

Scheduling mechanisms, such as the methods described in this work, which have been designed to reduce overlapped execution can provide for better efficiency and universality. For instance, it cannot be assumed that resource access characteristics in terms of when and how long resources will be used are usually known. This would require the provision of that information by the operating system which is not the case, e.g., in the used AIX operating system. Further, the methods examined within this work (except the pure non-preemptive mechanism) can accept process sets even if they cannot be executed without overlaps. This increases the processing time spent due to operating system overhead and requires explicit coordination of the processes, however, the advantage is that a larger number of process sets can be scheduled.

7 Summary

A large amount of resources is needed for the processing of continuous-media data. This can be reduced if the execution of processes working on such data does not overlap. To achieve this, several scheduling algorithms have been developed and evaluated by measurements.

Non-preemptive scheduling avoids overlapped processing a priori. The measurements show that only a small additional overhead is required for it. However, it restricts the schedulable process sets to a relatively large extend. Thus, its usability depends strongly on the application scenario. If it is used for process sets where it can be guaranteed that all processes will hold their deadlines even for large CPU utilizations, then this scheme leads to good results.

The same degree of overlap avoidance has been reached by the static precalculation algorithm. Further, this method can always schedule process sets which are schedulable under the preemptive rate-monotonic scheduling scheme, i.e., it leads to equal CPU utilizations. At least for the measurements performed, the overhead to calculate and to store the scheduling table was acceptable. Hence, this scheme offers a good overall performance.

The results of the other two mechanisms are less promising. The number of concurrently active processes is less than using the original preemptive scheduling, however, not satisfactory, especially for the dynamic scheme. The overhead introduced by each method is relatively low. While both schemes can schedule the same process sets as the preemptive scheduler, only the non-preemptive scheduling of processes with equal rates seems to be usable. If the typical process set of an application contains several processes with equal rates, this scheme may be applied successfully.

References

[Britton93] B. Britton: AIX 3.2 Multiuser System Tuning and the New Performance Tuning PTFs, *AIXPRESS*, January 1993, pp. 9-13.

[Drake94] S. Drake, IBM Almaden, private correspondence, May 1994.

[Haskin93] R. L. Haskin: The Shark Continuous-Media File Server, Proceedings of COMPCON '93.

[Jeffay90] K. Jeffay: Scheduling Sporadic Tasks with Shared Resources in Hard-Real-Time Systems, TR 90-039, University of North Carolina at Chapel Hill, Department of Computer Science, November 1990.

[Liu73] C. L. Liu, J. W. Layland: Scheduling Algorithms for Multiprogramming in a Hard-Real-Time Environment, *Journal of the ACM*, Vol. 20, No. 1, January 1973, pp. 46-61.

[Nagarajan92] R. Nagarajan, C. Vogt: Guaranteed-Performance Transport of Multimedia Traffic over the Token Ring, TR 43.9201, IBM European Networking Center Heidelberg, Germany, 1992.

[Williamson95] J. Williamson, L. C. Wolf: Reducing Buffer Space Requirements for Multimedia Data Streams: Analysing the effects of staggering streams and preemption in buffer pools, TR 43.9504, IBM European Networking Center, Heidelberg, Germany, 1995.

[Wolf96] L. C. Wolf, W. Burke, C. Vogt: Evaluation of a CPU Scheduling Mechanism for Multimedia Systems, to appear in *Software – Practice and Experience*, 1996.

[Xu90] J. Xu, D. L. Parnas: Scheduling Processes with Release Times, Deadlines, Precedence, and Exclusion Relations, *IEEE Transactions on Software Engineering*, Vol. 16, No. 3, March 1990, pp. 360-369.

[Zhao87] W. Zhao, K. Ramamritham, J. A. Stankovic: Scheduling Tasks Under Time and Resource Constraints, *IEEE Transactions on Computers*, Vol. 36, No. 8, August 1987, pp. 949-960.

QoS Filters: Addressing the Heterogeneity Gap

Nicholas Yeadon, Andreas Mauthe, Francisco García[†] and David Hutchison

Computing Department, Lancaster University

[†]Telecoms Management Department, Hewlett-Packard Laboratories

Abstract: Disparities in current computer technologies exist between networks, end-systems and user applications. Problems resulting from this *heterogeneity gap* are at their most acute in distributed multipeer environments. This paper addresses Quality of Service (QoS) disparities in heterogeneous multipeer internetworking and proposes the use of *filters* to bridge this aspect of the heterogeneity gap. These filter mechanisms must be sufficient adaptive to handle dynamic changes in both end-system and network capabilities. This paper discusses various filter mechanisms implemented at Lancaster University and the software developed to evaluate the feasibility of these mechanisms within a dynamic QoS controlled architecture.

1. Introduction

It has become evident from surveying the literature and from our own experimentation that the problem of resolving heterogeneity in modern multipeer communications is not a trivial one. While adaptive QoS control mechanisms have been proposed by some researchers, little implementation of such mechanisms exists. The motivation for the work reported in this paper was to implement a dynamic QoS control led architecture capable of optimising the variety of requirements evident amongst a large group of simultaneous receivers. In this way, the true potential of distributed multimedia systems can begin to be realised. We also noted that, while a great deal of research work is currently addressing multicast problems and separate work is investigating multimedia data transfer problems, little work has been done in the conjunction of these areas.

Previous work at Lancaster, in the area of QoS support for distributed multimedia applications, has concentrated on resource management strategies for an extended Chorus micro-kernel [Robin94] and a Quality of Service Architecture (QoS-A) [Campbell94] which proposes a framework to specify and satisfy the required performance properties of multimedia applications over ATM networks. This work is however focused on supporting peer-to-peer communications. Presently, we are motivated by the need to support group communications [Mauthe94] within an environment which consists of PCs, workstations and specialised multimedia enhanced devices connected by ATM, ethernet, mobile, and proprietary high-speed networks [Yeadon96b]. This environment is suitable for investigating QoS support mechanisms for multipeer services in truly heterogeneous systems within a local environment.

The work reported in this paper deals with the concept of filter mechanisms which operate within dissemination-based multimedia multicast streams. The filter methods and mechanisms developed and engineered at Lancaster University were initially engendered by the work of Pasquale [Pasquale92,93]. Implementations of a distributed continuous media filtering system are under way to investigate and evolve the filter concept fully.

The paper is structured in 6 sections. The next section outlines the primarily motivation for this work following that, section 3 discusses the media compression standards used and how filtering can exploit certain characteristics of these schemes. Section 4 described the filter mechanisms in detail, section 5 reports on our experiments using these filter mechanisms and section 6 gives the future directions and conclusions.

2. QoS Challenges

As a result of information technology expanding into new sociological and geographical areas, there now exists a vast assortment of end-system and communication architectures, not to mention the multitude of application software. In trying to interconnect these systems, the problems of establishing a true open environment emerge. While the proliferation of the Internet Protocol (IP) has gone some way to solve the interconnection problems for data transfer, the issues relating to the transfer of real-time continuous media are still not fully resolved. This problem is particularly acute in distributed group applications where many disparate receivers require to exchange continuous media data with each other despite capability and architectural differences.

2.1 Heterogeneity

The range of multimedia applications and user requirements is highly diverse. For example, multimedia conferencing may require only low resolution video but high quality sound. Industrial and medical applications, involving for example the output from highly specialised monitoring devices such as microscopes and X-ray machines, will require very high image resolution. Generally, the perception of video and audio quality is user-dependent and hence users may express different requirements for playout qualities. This will be encompassed in the specification of distinct QoS requirements by the users.

Considering end-system hardware, heterogeneity is present in: CPUs, I/O devices, storage capabilities, compression support (dedicated boards / software), internal inter-connect architecture, communication protocol support, network interfaces, etc. These issues place limits on the end-system's capabilities to process, consume and generate multimedia data.

End-systems are likely to be connected to different networks which not only have different bandwidth capabilities but also varying access delay characteristics. For example: medium access control mechanism, maximum and minimum data unit size, service types, packet loss rates, propagation delays, congestion, etc. In the last couple of years we have seen the proliferation of wireless networks and also that users of such networks would like multimedia capabilities. For wireless communications, not only do we need to bridge across the low bandwidth capabilities of the links, but more importantly we need to deal with problems caused by the poor error resilience capabilities of such links.

2.2 Resource Utilisation

As well as the heterogeneity problem there exists the ever present problem of limited resources. This is inherent in continuous media distributed applications, as such services have a high demand for network bandwidth allocation, storage capacities and processor time.

Typically, the transfer of continuous media, even compressed continuous media, requires a significant percentage of the overall bandwidth available in current networks, even for a single peer-to-peer transfer. Any method or mechanism that can reduce this bandwidth requirement must be investigated. Pasquale [Pasquale93] proposed the use of filters primarily for this purpose; we see this as an important issue but secondary to the problems of heterogeneity.

The rationale for using filters to reduce bandwidth required is that it is unnecessary to transmit data to receivers that either cannot use it or do not wish to use it. For example, sending stereo audio to a receiver with a single speaker is wasteful . If fully and correctly implemented, filters cut out the unwanted data at the earliest opportunity, hence achieving optimum bandwidth utilisation.

Limited resources in end-systems result in buffer overflows, lateness in processing data and inability to process data. This manifests itself to the user as unacceptable playout delays, lost images, lost audio segments, reduced frame rates and playback speeds and also poor user interaction.

If the processing of continuous media in a multipeer session can be distributed among a number of nodes and some processing completed before it reaches an overloaded client, this reduces the demands on that client. Pasquale proposes the use of filter mechanisms within the network, i.e. on switches and gateways, to perform part of this processing; we also see such operations potentially outside the functionality of switches and thus propose specialised servers to perform the more complex filtering actions.

2.3 Dynamic Quality of Service

Solving the heterogeneity problem involves providing for individualist QoS, while achieving resource optimisation implies accurate QoS levels; to realise both of these in a continually changing environment, as most systems are, requires the ability to dynamically adapt and alter QoS levels.

The most important factor to consider when implementing a dynamic QoS mechanism is the *cost*, in terms of resources required and of processing to change the current QoS levels. To perform a complete end-to-end re-negotiation within a multiparty connection may take up to three signalling messages per receiver [Mathy94] and may involve resynchronising, i.e. initialising, and altering parameters of codec hardware. Therefore, the cost of end-to-end adaptation [Yeadon94] or scaling [Delgrossi93] determines the frequency at which re-negotiation may take place and how dynamic the QoS monitoring and control system is.

Where a feedback system is used for QoS control there is also the possibility of the control system becoming unstable and oscillation arising. This may occur if too short a period or the wrong algorithm is used for adjustment of the data flow [Delgrossi93].

While a connection wide co-ordinator, or *session manager*, may be required for instantiation of filter mechanisms, once in operation their effect is the localisation of dynamic QoS control. That is, fine adjustments to a client's received data rate can be made which only require interaction between a receiver and its closest filter agent.

Localisation of control offers a number of advantages over end-to-end control. The propagation delay between client and flow control process may be much smaller, thus allowing more accurate and reactive feedback control. The signalling messages between client and control nodes traverse fewer hops and are therefore less significant to existing end-to-end bandwidth. Moreover, they have less chance of suffering the effects of a congested network (even if the signalling data is prioritised it may still be delayed in a congested non-reservation based network).

By precluding the source from the majority of QoS level adjustments the (potentially costly) process of changing encoding and compression parameters can be avoided. There is also the possibility that control of the source's output characteristics is privileged and it is not possible to adjust the rate, etc., such as in an MBONE style broadcast; filtering can still be performed locally in such a case.

3. Encoded Video and Audio

As with text file interchange formats and compression schemes, many digital video and audio compression schemes exist. Hence, not only do we have a heterogeneity problem to solve with respect to end-systems and networks, but also with respect to digital video and audio compression schemes. Our belief is that *openness* is the key to interoperability amongst heterogeneous systems and for this reason one needs to adopt internationally agreed compression standards. The benefit in doing so is that only a finite set of these standards need be considered for communication with the vast majority of the community. Also, any further developments are kept compliant with older technology allowing for gradual evolution of existing systems to current trends, while at all times being capable of sustaining an operational environment. The international compression standards considered here are JPEG [JPEG93], MPEG 1 [MPEG-1,93], MPEG 2 [MPEG-2,94] and H.261 [H.261,93].

These standards not only define the compression techniques employed, but because they have been developed in the light of supporting existing and future storage and transmission systems, they also define the generated bit stream syntax, semantics, and sub-sets of suitable bit rates to support specific application domains. This knowledge can assist the consolidation of a multimedia QoS-A. In this section we provide a brief summary of the major differences and commonality in the characteristics of these compression standards. This will help us explain and demonstrate the complexity of our developed filter mechanisms.

The different standards have been brought about to address different application areas: JPEG is intended for still image compression, H.261 has been developed to support video telephony, MPEG 1 video and its associated audio compression standard was developed for storage media devices which can provide a continuous transfer rate of approximately 1.5 Mbit/s, i.e. CDs, and the MPEG 2 standard is intended for broadcasting and telecommunications. MPEG2 also provides a scalable syntax, which allows lower quality decoders (e.g. MPEG 1 decoders) to reconstruct useful video from pieces of the entire bit stream. The JPEG compression scheme is also used in a format called Motion-JPEG for the compression of moving pictures where each picture is encoded independently.

All these encoding standards employ the *baseline sequential* process, defined for lossy encoding within the JPEG standard, for the coding of independent pictures. These pictures are employed within H.261, MPEG 1 and 2 as prediction reference points for the encoding of other pictures which exploit temporal redundancy. The encoding steps performed by a typical baseline sequential encoder are illustrated in Figure 1.

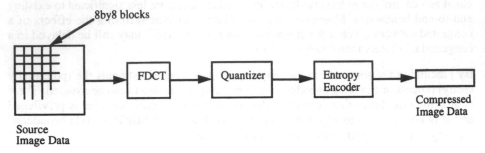

Fig. 1: Processing steps for a lossy mode encoder.

The H.261 standard defines two types of frames: *intraframe* coded pictures which are encoded independently from any other pictures; and *interframe* pictures which are encoded with reference to previous pictures by exploiting temporal redundancy. MPEG primarily defines three types of frame: I-pictures which are the equivalent of intraframe pictures in H.261; P-pictures, equivalent to interframe pictures; and B-pictures which are bi-directionally predicted from I and P pictures. B-pictures demonstrate the highest degree of compression and are never used as reference points for further prediction.

The are a number of features which are common to the above compression standards which must considered if performing transcoding (see section 4.1) or other filter operations; All intra-coded frames are encoded using the same *discrete cosine transform* (DCT) algorithm based on blocks of 8x8 pixels. The similarities between JPEG and I-pictures in MPEG video are such that Motion-JPEG streams can be converted to I-picture video sequences suitable for MPEG decoders relatively easily.

After the forward DCT stage the DCT values are quantizes. The quantization process again is similar across the standards, both MPEG and JPEG allowing quantize matrices to be specified by the encoding algorithm. H.261 uses flat 8x8 matrices for this process and only a level of quantization can be specified.

The major differences between the standards is the schemes used for entropy encoding. While all the standards use the same form of variable length coding (VLC) called Huffman coding [Huffman52], the bit-streams produced by this process a different. This is primarily because the of the Huffman *trees* used for encoding and decoding: MPEG and H.261 use a 'left-handed' tree and JPEG employs a 'right-handed' tree. Entropy decoding is generally required for the more complex filter operations.

MPEG	JPEG	H.261
Picture Layer	Picture/Scan Layer	Picture Layer
Slice Layer	Restart Segment	Group-of-Blocks Layer
Macro Block Layer	Minimum Coded Unit	Macro Block Layer
Block Layer	Block Layer	Block Layer

Table 1: Hierarchical Representation of a Picture in MPEG, JPEG and H.261.

Across the standards, the generated bit-stream syntax is of course different. However, below the picture layer the structural composition is very similar as illustrated in Table 1. This makes the conversion process easier as, at least conceptually, direct comparisons can be made at the different layers.

MPEG 2, H.261 and JPEG all offer some form of scalable syntax, such as multi-resolution, temporal, signal-to-noise ratio or data partitioning. This scalable syntax could be used for interoperability between distinct encoding formats. For example, the MPEG 2 scalable syntax can be structured so that the base layer is encoded only using I-pictures similar to those employed by Motion-JPEG. The enhancement layer(s) may include B- and P-pictures for full MPEG 2 compatibility. Also, these substreams may be appropriately reformatted into a single stream for MPEG 1 compatibility.

4. Filter Mechanisms

Filter mechanisms at Lancaster are applied to codec-generated data. These mechanisms exploit and adapt the structural composition of this type of continuous media traffic to ensure that end-user, application, end-system, network capabilities and requirements are met.

The concept of filtering continuous media data is becoming an accepted approach to meeting distinct QoS capabilities and requirements for multicast communications. As is evident from research [Delgrossi93][Hehmann91][Hoffman93][Pasquale92,93] [Schulzrinne93][Braden95] into the filter concept, distinct approaches are taken according to the particular problem being looked at. These include: optimisation of bandwidth usage, adoption of filters for handling client heterogeneity, optimisation of resource allocation, optimisations in the retrieval process of stored media, etc.

4.1 Implemented Filters

The filter mechanisms currently implemented broadly fall into the 6 categories listed below. Some of these have been designed with wireless communications in mind. They include filters that produce large reductions in data rate, such as the frame dropping filter, and filters that can improve bit-streams error resilience, namely the slicing filter.

• **Codec filter.** A codec filter can be used to compress or decompress a bit-stream. It is more commonly used to perform transcoding between different compression standards. Depending on the compression scheme used, transcoding can often be performed without the need for full decompression and recompression.

• **Frame-dropping-filter.** This is a media-discarding filter used to reduce frame rates. The filter has knowledge of the frame types (e.g. Intra- or Inter- frame coding type) and drops frames according to importance. For example, the pecking order for dropping frames from an MPEG 1 video stream would be B-, P-, and finally I-pictures. The frame-dropping-filter is used to reduce the data rate of a stream in a sensible way by discarding a number of frames and transmitting the remaining frames at a slower rate. The filter may be used to ensure that a receiver gets frames at a rate suitable to its processing capabilities or because it can only decode one type of picture (e.g. I-pictures). This filter operation can also be employed to save network resources by discarding frames that are late or have been corrupted by loss of constituent packets [Ramanathan93].

• **Frequency-filter.** A frequency filter performs operations on semi-uncompressed data. That is, it operates in the frequency domain on the values of the DCT-coefficients. Semi-decompression/compression involves just entropy decoding/encoding. Filter mechanisms include low-pass filtering, colour reduction filtering and colour to monochrome filtering. Low-pass filtering is where the higher frequency DCT-coefficients are discarded on recoding, leaving only the DC DCT-coefficient and a number of low-frequency components. Colour reduction filtering performs the same operation as the low-pass filter but only operates on the chrominance information in the bit-stream. The colour-to-monochrome filter removes all colour information from a bit-stream. In MPEG this is done by replacing each chrominance block by an empty block. A colour to DC-colour filter performs the same operation as the colour to monochrome filter except that the DC DCT-coefficient is left untouched, giving coarse blocks of colour. Unlike the frame-dropping filter the frequency filter, and later on the re-quantization filter, reduces the required bandwidth without affecting frame rate. Of course this is at the cost of image quality.

• **Mixing-filter.** This filter is used to mix streams together or to multiplex audio and video where the encoding supports this kind of structure (e.g. MPEG). Mixing can be performed in a couple of ways, either on a frame basis or a slice basis. Frame based mixing simply interleaves two streams into the same stream. This requires a more complex demultiplexing or decompression process in the end-system. Slice-mixing filtering involves more processing by the mixer but can be decoded as a single stream. The slice-mixing merges two frames from different sources into the one larger frame by adding slices from each stream into the target stream, see Figure 2.

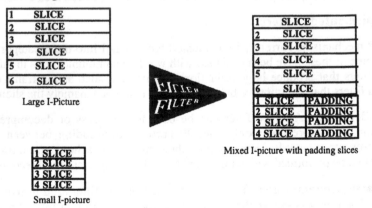

Fig. 2: Slice based mixing

The slice structure of the frames sometimes needs to be altered so that each row of macro-blocks is contained in one slice (see slicing filter below). Extra blank padding slices are needed if the two streams are of different window sizes; to make the resultant image rectangular. Mixing two streams in this way means that the receiving end-system needs only one decompression board or one decoding process. Also there is a reduction in transmission overhead as one and not two streams will be transferred.

• **Re-Quantization-filter.** The re-quantization filter, like the frequency filter, operates on the DCT-coefficients but also dequantizes the coefficients. The coefficients are then re-quantized using a larger quantizer step. As quantization is the most lossy process in the DCT based compression algorithms, requantization can produce some strange edge effects. However, the bit-rate reduction achieved by this filter can be quite substantial.

• **Slicing filter.** The slicing filter increases the number of slices in an MPEG stream, or restart segments in Motion-JPEG, per frame. Slices are identifiable from byte aligned slice headers. Slices are used to provide protection from errors occurring within a picture. The variable length decoder (entropy decoder) is realigned on each slice header. Therefore, if the bit-stream is corrupted and the decoder becomes misaligned with the variable length codes in the bit-stream, erroneous effects will not carried over past the end of the slice. The penalty for adding a slice header consists of a 32 bit byte aligned header code, followed by a 5 bit quantizer scale and a 1 bit extra information bit, i.e. 38 bits plus up to 7 padding bits to make the start code byte-aligned.

5. Experiences with Filtering

In this section we describe some of the main software components which have been developed to allow us to experiment with the filter mechanisms described above. We also report on our experiences with filtering and provide some performance results. These components represent several modules of a much wider QoS Architecture (QoS-A) being developed for multimedia communications. However, the emphasis in this paper is to report on our experiences with filtering and not on the other QoS related issues. For further details, the overall architecture is described in [García96].

While our intention is to develop and experiment with filter mechanisms for both video and audio that conform to the encoding and compression standards described above, at present the filter mechanisms described have only been applied to MPEG 1 and M-JPEG video streams. Currently we do not have any capabilities to decode and play MPEG 2 video streams.

5.1 Experimental Software

To evaluate the filtering mechanisms outlined above and to experiment with other research issues such as filter propagation and dynamic QoS control, we have developed some experimental software based around the Berkeley software video player [Rowe92]. The main components which make up this software are depicted in Figure 3.

The *file daemon* module listens on a well known port for new MPEG 1 video clip requests. When a request is received and verified it invokes an *MPEG 1 video agent* which packetizes and transmits the video data in compliance with our continuous media transport protocol (CMP) [Coulson91][García93]. The protocol provides two communication threads, one for handling control and signalling data and the other to deal with the continuous media data. For the experiments outlined in this paper, the protocol runs above UDP and employs 4.3 BSD Unix sockets to create the two required communication threads. The MPEG 1 video data stream is encapsulated as illustrated in Figure 4 whereby logical data unit boundaries are preserved to simplify both filtering and the process of new clients joining an ongoing session at a particular point in a dissemination tree (see Section 5.2 below). Essentially sequence header data, group of pictures (GOP) data and each individual picture type (I, P and B-pictures), as defined in the MPEG 1 video syntax [MPEG-1,93], are packetized independently and uniquely identified.

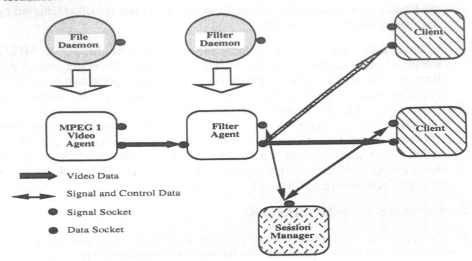

Fig. 3: Experimental Software.

Data transfer, for these experiments, is rate regulated above UDP by a token bucket variant [Partridge93]. While a feedback loop could be set up for a client which monitors the delivered QoS and dynamically changes the transfer data rate to reflect underlying network and end-system conditions, this functionality is achieved in the constructed dissemination tree by appropriately invoking a filter operation at a specific node. This step ensures that other clients connected to the same dissemination tree are not limited by a single client's poor capabilities to consume and process data or because of various network path limitations (i.e. congestion, low speed link, etc.) en route to a particular client.

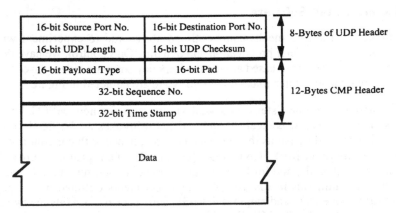

Fig. 4: CMP Packetization above UDP.

Each *client* corresponds to a Berkeley video player which has been adapted to run with two sockets as required by the CMP protocol. One communication thread is used for control and signalling data while the other is used for receiving the MPEG 1 video stream. The CMP protocol monitors the received QoS and can deliver updates of this to the identified *session manager*.

The *filter daemon*, like the file daemon, awaits for initial filter requests when a multipeer session is established and invokes a *filter agent* to perform the required functionality. The agents interpret the CMP protocol and employ it for data transfer but unlike the other software modules they use three sockets: one for control and signalling, one for continuous media data input, and the other for continuous media data output. These agents may be initially invoked without performing any filtering. Instead they can be used to emulate multicasting whereby data delivered at the input socket is duplicated and sent out to multiple destinations via the output socket. Each destination is given a unique sub-stream identifier. The destination need not be a client, but may be another filter agent. Filter agents are self-monitoring with respect to QoS and can deliver updates to identified session managers. Subsequent filter invocation or modification requests may be delivered to the control and signalling socket. These requests may act on all the data sub-streams generated by the agent or on specifically identified sub-streams only.

Using these filter agents we can transparently configure and build our own dissemination trees above our existing networks. There are two reasons why we have chosen to do this. First, we can develop our own session management and filter control and signalling protocols without interfering with existing services and protocols on the networks. Second, as any host machine connected to the network can potentially run a filter daemon we can easily study filter propagation issues as each host on the network can pretend to be a router or gateway. The various components give us flexibility to build complex dissemination trees and if necessary to experiment and develop new QoS based routing protocols [Ferrari90][Zhang93].

5.2 Adding Clients to the Dissemination Tree

As filter agents are appended to the dissemination tree, the MPEG 1 sequence header and current GOP header information packets are propagated to them. These are retained by the filter agent. On request by the session manager to add a new client (or new filter agent), at that particular point in the dissemination tree, they are the first packets to be forwarded to the new client. Continuous media data transfer to the new client continues as soon as the next logical I-picture packet has been processed by the filter agent. The sequence header and current GOP header information is required to initialise the decoding process at the new client.

5.3 Filter Complexity

In Figure 5 the points at which operations can be performed on the compressed bit-stream are illustrated. Region A is the uncompressed raw data where operations can be performed relatively simply, e.g. resizing/stretching, but the amount of data that has to be processed is very large due to its uncompressed nature. In region B the data is the same size as the raw data, but if the bit-stream is being decompressed in order to accomplish a particular operation and then recompressed (e.g. quantization factor adjustment), performing operations at this point avoids completing the computationally intensive functions of Forward-DCT and Inverse-DCT transforms. At point C the many zeros produced by the FDCT have been removed and the data is considerably smaller; operations that are feasible at this point include: colour to monochrome conversions, data partitioning, frequency filtering and simple codec-conversions. Operations on the fully compressed data, in region D, are standard-specific and relatively simple, such as intelligent frame discarding or frame rate adjustment.

It is apparent that by careful encoding and intelligent use of the various compression standards, transcoding need not involve a total decompression of one stream and recompression into another format. For example, the codec filter can perform Motion-JPEG to I-picture video suitable for MPEG video decoders by simple entropy decoding/encoding and stream syntax conversion. Operations on semi-uncompressed Motion-JPEG data have been the work of [Smith94], where streams can be faded to black or mixed with other Motion-JPEG streams.

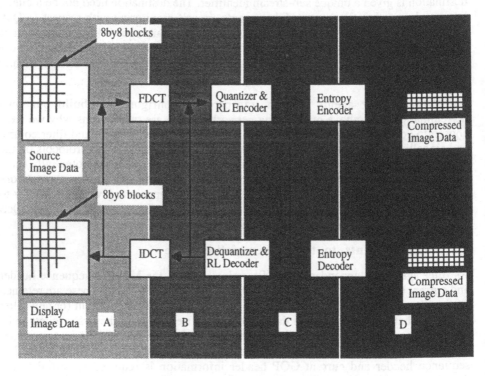

Fig. 5.: Levels of compression

Figure 5 shows that a filter function can be *optimised* by performing the operation at the correct stage in the compression/decompression algorithm.

5.4 Filter Location

A key issue in the engineering of any filter model is the topological placement of the filter operation. In the path between a source and a recipient, a filter operation can be performed either within the network fabric or at the network edge (i.e. end-systems and gateways). The placement algorithm should obviously instantiate the operation at the optimum location. The criteria for determining this location depend on the factors discussed below:

• **PDU Encapsulation** - The amount of information a particular node knows about a stream, and hence its ability to execute a filtering function, is reliant on the way the data is encapsulated within the protocol data unit (PDU). Separate video frames, for example, could be encapsulated within separate PDUs, and so a gateway or router could perform a frame dropping function by dropping PDUs. This may either be as a result of an explicit instruction or because corruption within the PDU is detected.

• **Switch Capability** - If a gateway or router is to carry out various filtering operations this must be done without adversely affecting the other traffic through the switch. This is dependent on the switch's processing power and current loading. Implementing filtering within switches, except for connection based scaling, will require reprogramming of the switch. It is unlikely, at least at the present time, that these operations will be introduced to wide area or service switches. Such operations are more likely to be introduced into the local domain where control and responsibility for switches is local. Here, it is plausible that switches could be reconfigured and reprogrammed to incorporate filter operations.

• **End-system Capability** - End-systems in certain cases are the optimum place for filters. The term end-systems includes, as well as sources and receivers, high level gateways as these are also at the network edge. Certain sources or low end receivers may not have the necessary capabilities to execute a particular operation, that is, to execute it within the imposed time constraints. The operation may therefore be performed at a less optimal location on the network.

• **Available Bandwidth** - If the manipulation of a stream involves a major change in the bit rate, such as compression or decompression, then to utilise the network resources to best effect the operation must be executed where the stream will not cause adverse network loading. That is, an operation that produces a larger bit-stream should be executed as close to the receiver as possible and conversely an operation that reduces the size of the bit-stream should be located as close to the source as possible.

• **Time Constraints** - As real-time data is being manipulated, the time constraints imposed on generation, transmission and playout of a particular sequence must be considered before any kind of operation is performed on the bit-stream. This is because no matter how powerful a filtering engine may be, time will always be consumed! This affects both the transmission delay experienced and the jitter. A trade-off has to be reached between the benefits of filtering, network performance and time constraints.

• **Propagation** - In a dynamic heterogeneous network the optimum location for a particular filter operation may change over time, hence a filter must have the ability to move or *propagate* to a more suitable node. Propagation may occur when a client joins or leaves a current session, or if a node or link becomes heavily loaded and some processing must be off-loaded to neighbouring nodes. Care must be taken to ensure that a network is not too dynamic, i.e. filter control messages propagating wildly around the network causing oscillations in QoS levels. For this reason filter propagation may only occur either a set intervals or as a final action if other QoS control mechanisms fail.

The decision of where best to perform filtering is still a matter of debate. Some filter models only perform filtering at the end-system [Delgrossi93][Pasquale93], whereas other models are network-based [Zhang93]. Putting filters into switches does have advantages; it is the most logical place, but this may be detrimental to the overall performance of the switch. End-system filtering is easier to implement and causes least disruption to existing services but does not realise the full potential of filtering operations.

5.5 Performance Results

In this section we present and discuss the current results from our filtering work. The primary characteristics to consider are the effect on throughput that a particular type of filter may have and also the delay incurred by performing the filter operation. Table 2 shows the effect of a number of different filters on a sample stream. The sample stream was a fully intra-coded MPEG (I-pictures only) sequence. The stream was transmitted at 15 frames per second, producing a average data-rate of 30Kbytes/sec between three machines: a file server machine, a filter agent machine and a client machine. The results shown are generated by a 100MHz 586 PC, running the Linux OS, acting as the filter agent.

Filter Type	Average Processing Time per frame (mean/ s.d. μsec)	Post-filter throughput (mean/ s.d. bytes/sec)
Col->Mono	13353 / 2529	21479 / 5644
Col->DC-colour	13436 / 2549	22687 / 5862
Lowpass CO=1	10516 / 1425	8226 / 640
Lowpass CO=2	11142 / 1587	10734 / 1459
Lowpass CO=4	11903 / 1702	16482 / 2532
Lowpass CO=8	12786 / 2115	21067 / 4449
Lowpass CO=16	14085 / 2632	26825 / 6429
Lowpass CO=32	15089 / 3085	31244 / 8395
Requant Q+=8	14639 / 2871	16654 / 3270
Requant Q+=16	13867 / 2590	12554 / 1960
Col->Mono + Lowpass CO=4	11323 / 1617	12701 / 2232
Col->Mono + Requant Q+=8	14238 / 2755	12042 / 2655
Lowpass CO=4 + Requant Q+=8	14135 / 2262	13512 / 2433

Average Pre-Filter Throughput: 33002, standard dev.: 8960bytes/sec

Table 2: Filter Characteristics

The processing time column includes the time for a frame to be Huffman decoded, any further processing/filtering, and the time to Huffman encode the frame. The filters shown, in table order, are colour to monochrome, colour to DC-colour, low pass with different cut-off (CO) frequencies, requantizer with different quantizer increments (Q), and the results from combining selected filters.

The salient point from Table 2 is that all filter operations can be performed in a reasonable amount of time on what is a relatively low capability machine. Further experiments will involve more Pentium machines and Sparc workstations. All the filters produce a lower data-rate to varying degrees.

The colour to monochrome filter reduces the bit stream by approximately 25-30%. The colour to DC-colour takes slightly longer to process and produces a reduction not quite as good, yet the user perceived quality is improved, over the colour to monochrome filter, as some colour still exists.

The characteristics of the low pass filter are better presented as shown in, Figure 6. The effect of the filter depends on how much high frequency component exists within an image. The Forward-DCT and quantization procedures are intended to leave much of the block, in particular the higher frequency components, as zero. Hence where the cut-off frequency is higher less information is discarded and the reduction in data-rate is less. The lower curve in Figure 6 shows that most of the information is held in the lower frequency coefficients. The time to process each frame also reflects this; as more DCT-coefficients are thrown away, i.e. the cut-off frequency decreases, the time to Huffman re-encode each DCT-block, and hence each frame, becomes smaller.

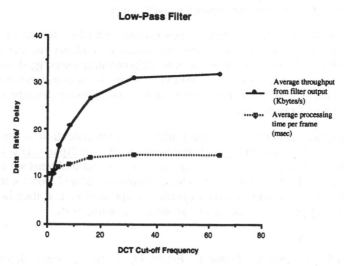

Fig. 6: Delay and post-filter throughput characteristics of the low pass filter.

The requantization filter involves more processing and for this reason takes longer than the other filter mechanisms. As each DCT-value is requantized the values become smaller (some are rounded to zero) and so Huffman re-encoding becomes a faster process. Requantizing produces a large reduction in data-rate, while maintaining a reasonable image quality, but at the expense of incurred delay.

Interesting results are observed when filters are combined. Filter combination produces yet larger reductions in data-rate without increasing the processing time required. This is achieved by performing the processing intensive functions of Huffman decoding and encoding once only. With this method all the processing is performed on the semi-decompressed data.

6. Future Directions and Conclusions

Our research to date has produced some interesting open issues. While the relationship between filter mechanisms and network characteristics, based on delay and throughput, are understood, relating user level QoS demands to the underlying QoS control and filter mechanisms requires extensive study. The 'when and where' of filter instantiation and propagation also requires further investigation. The software outlined in this paper provides us with a simple tool to look into these issues. We also intend to integrate any developed mechanisms into existing services and protocols, and to attempt to inform the current work in the development of the Next Generation IP and its suite of protocols [IETF95]. Another important issue for future research includes the routing implications of using filters and filter servers.

We now intend to exploit these results and the experience gained in developing such mechanisms to bridge across wireless communications [Yeadon96a]. For wireless communications we need to consider both the low bandwidth capability of the links and more importantly the poor error resilience capabilities of such links.

Work is also continuing towards the other end of the bandwidth spectrum where filter mechanisms are being applied to ATM based architectures [Yeadon94] to support integration into our existing network infrastructure.

The software we have developed to experiment with filters has also proved a valuable tool in the teaching of compression techniques to students and colleagues. A world wide web site (http://www.comp.lancs.ac.uk/computing/users/njy/demo.html) has been set up containing post-filtered MPEG 1 clips to demonstrate our current filter mechanisms. The source code of the experimental software described in section 5.1 is also available from this site.

QoS support for audio and video multipeer communication is distinguished from common QoS provision through the number of participants and their distinctive, individual QoS requirements. To overcome the inherent problems we employ filters, on data streams which can tolerate data loss, to provide tailored QoS for individual clients. We have already found that such operations are feasible and they help us bridge the heterogeneity gap evident in today's networked environments.

References

[**Braden95**] Braden, R., Zhang, L., Estrin, D, Herzog, S. and S. Jamin, "Resource ReSerVation Protocol (RSVP) - Version 1 Functional Specification" Internet Draft available via anonymous ftp from nic.nordu.net/internet-drafts/draft-ietf-rsvp-spec-07.ps, July 1995.

[**Campbell94**] Campbell, A., Coulson G., and D. Hutchison, "A Quality of Service Architecture", ACM Computer Communications Review, Vol. 24, No 2, April 1994, pp. 6-27.

[**Coulson91**] D. Coulson, F. Garcia, D. Hutchison, D. Shepherd, "Protocol Support for Distributed Multimedia Applications", Proceedings of 2nd International Workshop on Network and Operating Systems Support for Digital Audio and Video, Heidelberg, Germany, November 1991.

[Delgrossi93] Delgrossi, L., C. Halstrick, D. Hehmann, R. Herrtwich, O. Krone, J. Sandvoss and C. Vogt. . "Media Scaling for Audiovisual Communication with the Heidelberg Transport System.", Proceedings of ACM Multimedia 93, Ananheim, California, 1993, pp. 99-104.

[Ferrari90] D. Ferrari and D. Verma, "A Scheme for Real-Time Channel Establishment in Wide-Area Networks", IEEE Journal on Selected Areas in Communications, 8 (3), April 1990, pp. 368-379.

[Garcí a93] F. García, "A Continuous Media Transport and Orchestration Service" Ph.D. Thesis, Department of Computing, Lancaster University, Lancaster LA1 4YR, UK.

[García96] García, F., Mauthe, A., Yeadon., N. and D. Hutchison, "QoS Support for Distributed Multimedia Communications", to appear in proceedings of International Conference in Distributed Processing, Dresden, Germany, February 1996.

[H.261,93] H.261, "Video Codec for Audiovisual Services at px64 kbits", International Telecommunications Union Telecommunications Standardisation Sector, ITU-T Recommendation H.261, 03/93, 1993.

[Hehmann91] D. Hehmann et. al. "Implementing HeiTs: Architecture and Implementation Strategy of the Heidelberg High-Speed Transport System", Proceedings of 2nd International Workshop on Network and Operating Systems Support for Digital Audio and Video, Heidelberg, Germany, November 1991.

[Hoffman93] Hoffman, D., M. Speer and G. Fernando. "Network Support for Dynamically Scaled Multimedia Data Streams", Proceedings of 4th International Workshop on Network and Operating System Support for Digital Audio and Video, Lancaster University, Lancaster, UK. 1993, pp. 251-262.

[Huffman52] Huffman, D. A. "A Method for the Construction of Minimum-Redundancy Codes." Proceeding of IRE, Vol. 40, 1952, pp. 1098-1101.

[IETF95] Internet Engineering Task Force, Drafts, RFCs and standards available via anonymous ftp from nic.nordu.net.

[JPEG93] ISO IEC JTC 1; "Information Technology - Digital Compression and Coding of Continuous-Tone still Images", International Standard ISO/IEC IS 10918, 1993.

[Mathy94] Mathy, L. and O. Bonaventure, "QoS Negotiation for Multicast Communications", Proceedings of International COST 237 Workshop on Multimedia Transport and Teleservices, Vienna, Austria, November 1994.

[Mauthe94] Mauthe, A., Hutchison, D., Coulson, G., S. Namuye, "From Requirements to Services: Group Communication Support for Distributed Multimedia Systems", Proceedings of 2nd International Workshop on Advanced Teleservices and High-Speed Communication Architectures (IWACA'94), Heidelberg, Germany, September 26-28, 1994.

[MPEG-1,93] ISO IEC JTC 1; "Information Technology - Coding of Moving Pictures and Associated Audio for Digital Storage Media up to about 1.5Mbit/s", International Standard ISO/IEC IS 11172, 1993.

[MPEG-2,94] ISO IEC JTC 1; "Information Technology - Generic Coding of Moving Pictures and Associated Audio Information", Draft International Standard ISO/IEC DIS 13818, 1994.

[Partridge93] Partridge, C. "Gigabit Networking", Addison-Wesley Professional Computing Series, ISBN 0-201-56333-9, 1993.

[Pasquale92] Pasquale, J., G. Polyzos, E. Anderson and V. Kompella. "The Multimedia Multicast Channel", Proceedings of 3rd International Workshop on Network and Operating System Support for Digital Audio and Video (NOSSDAV 92), San Diego, California, 1992, pp. 185-196.

[Pasquale93] Pasquale, J., G. Polyzos, E. Anderson and V. Kompella. "Filter Propagation in Dissemination Trees: Trading Off Bandwidth and Processing in Continuous Media Networks", Proceedings of 4th International Workshop on Network and Operating System Support for Digital Audio and Video (NOSSDAV 93), Lancaster University, Lancaster, UK, 1993, pp. 269-278.

[Ramanathan93] Ramanathan, S., P. Venkat Rangan and H. Vin, "Frame-Induced Packet Discarding: An Efficient Strategy for Video Networking" Proceedings of 4th International Workshop on Network and Operating System Support for Digital Audio and Video, (NOSSDAV 93), Lancaster University, Lancaster, UK, 1993, pp. 175-186.

[Robin94] Robin, P., Campbell, A., Coulson, G., Blair, G., and M. Papathomas, "Implementing a QoS Controlled ATM Based Communication System in Chorus", 4th IFIP International Workshop on Protocols for High Speed Networks, Lancaster University, Lancaster LA1 4YR, March 1994.

[Rowe92] Rowe, L. and B. Smith, "A Continuous Media Player", Proceedings of 3rd International Workshop on Network and Operating System Support for Digital Audio and Video (NOSSDAV 92), San Diego, California, 1992, pp. 334-344

[Schulzrinne93] Schulzrinne, H. and S. Casner, Frederick, R., and V. Jacobson, "RTP: A Transport Protocol for Real-Time Applications", Internet-Draft, draft-ietf-avt-rtp-05.txt, July 1994.

[Smith94] Smith, B., "Fast Software Processing of Motion JPEG Video". Proceedings of 2nd ACM Multimedia, San Francisco, October 1994.

[Yeadon94] Yeadon, N., F. Garcia, A. Campbell and D. Hutchison, "QoS Adaptation and Flow Filtering in ATM Networks", Proceeding of the 2nd International Workshop on Advanced Teleservices and High-Speed Communication Architectures (IWACA '94) IBM-ENC, Heidelberg, Germany, 1994, pp. 191-202.

[Yeadon96a] Yeadon, N., Garcia, F., D. Shepherd and D. Hutchison, "Continuous Media Filters for Heterogeneous Internetworking", To be presented at SPIE Multimedia Computing and Networking, San Jose, CA, January 1996.

[Yeadon96b] Yeadon, N., Garcia, F., D. Hutchison and D. Shepherd, "Filters: QoS Support Mechanisms for Multipeer Communications", To appear in the IEEE Journal on Selected Areas in Communications forthcoming issue on Distributed Multimedia Systems and Technology.

Deterministic Admission Control Strategies in Video Servers with Variable Bit Rate Streams

Johannes Dengler[1], Christoph Bernhardt, Ernst Biersack
Institut Eurécom[2]

Abstract: Video servers are a key component in multimedia systems. Due to the real-time requirements and high resource demand of digital media, a video server must restrict the number of simultaneously serviced media streams. We consider the admission control problem in video servers for the retrieval of media data from secondary storage. Admission control decides whether or not a new request can be accepted without affecting the service given to the already admitted streams. Traditional retrieval methods, such as cyclic retrieval of variable size data segments or retrieval at the stream's mean bit rate, either cannot profit from smoothing media traffic over larger intervals or suffer from excessive buffer demand and latency. We introduce, for the first time, retrieval techniques for variable bit rate data that are non-buffer-conserving in nature and cover all traditional methods as special cases. For all the schemes, we carry out a comparative performance analysis and show how they allow to trade-off buffer requirement, disk I/O efficiency, and latency. All the schemes considered support the full set of VCR operations such as fast forward, pause, or fast reverse.

Keywords: Video Server, Admission Control, VBR

1 Introduction

Emerging high-speed networks allow the introduction of interactive distributed multimedia services, such as *video-on-demand* (VOD), *news-on-demand*, *tele-shopping*, and *distance learning*. A typical scenario consists of a **video server** connected to *clients* via a *communication network*. The video server stores digitized, compressed continuous media information on high-capacity secondary or tertiary storage [Rowe93]. The secondary storage devices are random accessible and provide short seek times compared to tertiary storage. An on-demand copy of the requested material is provided via the network to the client upon request.

While high bandwidth may become ubiquitous at modest cost, video servers are regarded as the critical components of future interactive multimedia systems. Their design differs significantly from that of traditional data storage and retrieval servers because real-time storage and retrieval techniques are required [Rang92],[Stei91]. Additionally, video servers must provide efficient mechanisms for storing, retrieving, indexing, and manipulating data in large quantities at high speeds [Rowe93]. A video

---

[1] Now with: McKinsey & Company, Inc., Taunusanlage 21, 60325 Frankfurt, Germany, email: JoDengler@aol.com.

[2] 2229 Route des Crêtes, 06904 Sophia-Antipolis — France, Phone: +33 93002611, FAX: +33 93002627, email: {bernhard,erbi}@eurecom.fr

server can only deliver a limited number of video streams simultaneously. Before admitting a new client, a video server must consequently use an admission control algorithm that is not needed in traditional servers for file storage.

We identify and formalize traditional schemes for the retrieval of *variable bit rate* video data from magnetic disks. Traditional methods, such as the cyclic retrieval of variable size data segments or the retrieval at the stream's mean bit rate, either cannot profit from smoothing media traffic over larger intervals, or they suffer from excessive buffer demand and latency. We derive novel techniques that are generally non-buffer-conserving in nature and cover traditional methods as special cases. When offering a deterministic service, the novel schemes can drastically decrease the buffer requirement and server latency in an interactive multimedia service by sacrificing some disk I/O efficacy, and vice versa. We state the admission control criteria for the investigated schemes and derive the buffer, latency, and efficiency trade-off. The trade-offs are first derived in theory and illustrated through by simulations using traces of variable bit rate videos.

2 Deterministic Retrieval Schemes in Video Servers

A video server must meet the requirements that stem from the continuous nature of audio and video and must guarantee the delivery of continuous media data in a timely fashion. Video information can be encoded to produce: (i) a **constant bit rate stream** (**CBR**) of variable quality, or (ii) a **variable bit rate stream** (**VBR**) of constant quality. CBR video has the advantage of being easy to deal with from both the network and the server perspective. VBR video corresponds more closely to the actual data format of compressed video, and is thus preferable from the application point of view. However, VBR requires more sophisticated resource reservation mechanisms in server and network to guarantee a good utilization of existing resources and a constant quality playback. We focus here on a VBR based video server. Our models are in fact generic enough to be able to accommodate CBR as a special case.

In the simplest case, continuous playback can be ensured by buffering the entire stream prior to initiating the playback [Gemm95]. Such a scheme, however, requires very large buffer space and may also yield a very large latency. Consequently, the problem of efficiently servicing a single stream becomes one of preventing buffer starvation while at the same time minimizing the buffer requirement and the start-up latency. In the most general sense, the buffer requirement in a video server at time t can be stated as the difference between the cumulative arrival function $a(t)$ of the video information read from secondary storage, and the cumulative consumption function $c(t)$ denoting the video information sent to clients.[3] The difference is often referred to as *backlog* function [Knig94]:

---

[3] The functions $a(t)$ and $c(t)$ can be alternatively stated in terms of frames or in terms of media data. If stated in terms of frames, the deterministic buffer requirement in terms of data is then determined by the relation between a number of frames and their respective maximum data size.

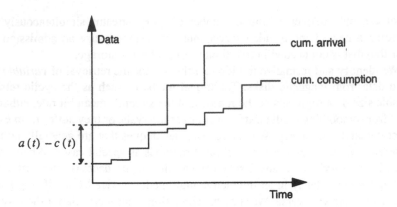

Fig. 1. Backlog function: cumulative arrival – cumulative consumption

We define a situation of **buffer starvation**[4] at time t as $a(t) - c(t) < 0$. If b_{total} denotes the total amount of available buffer in a video server, then $a(t) - c(t) > b_{total}$ will lead to **buffer overflow**.

In order to avoid buffer starvation or buffer overflow, almost all approaches to multi-stream continuous media retrieval that address these constraints have the following characteristics [Gemm95]:

1. Processing stream requests in cyclic rounds.
2. Arrival keeps up with consumption.

A video server that operates in rounds does generally avoid starvation by *reading ahead* an amount of data that lasts in terms of playback duration through the next round. If on a round-by-round basis the arrival of data never falls behind the consumption, the scheduling algorithm is referred to as **buffer-conserving.** Algorithms which proceed in rounds but are **non-buffer-conserving** are also conceivable but more complex [Gemm95]. Such an algorithm would allow the arrival to fall behind the consumption in one round, and then make it up later.

Offering VCR functions, such as fast forward and fast reverse, can have great impact on the bandwidth and buffer requirements. The VCR functions fast forward and fast reverse can either be implemented by playing back media at a rate higher than normal, or by continuing playback at the normal rate while skipping some data. Whereas the former approach yields significant increase in the data rate requirement [Dey94], data skipping may be complicated by the presence of inter-data dependencies introduced by compression schemes that reduce the temporal redundancies in a video stream, or may result in output of poor quality due to higher compression. The admission control schemes considered in this paper allow VCR functions under the condition that the data rate required to support these functions is *not higher* than the data rate for normal playback.

---

[4] The terms *buffer starvation* and *buffer underflow* are used interchangeably throughout this paper.

Choosing VBR as data model for a video server requires one to choose one of two models for storing data on the disks of a video server. There are two ways of mapping video data onto **data blocks (segments)** stored on the disk. Chang and Zakhor [Cha94a] have identified two techniques, referred to as **constant data length (CDL)** and **constant time length (CTL)**:

- CTL data placement is characterized as having *variable length data blocks* with *constant real-time playback duration* τ for stream s_i. During any one service round of duration τ, $\tau \cdot r_i$ frames[5] are retrieved from secondary storage, where r_i denotes the constant frame rate of stream s_i.

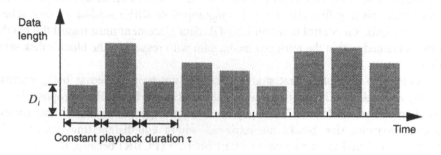

Fig. 2. Constant time length data placement

- For CDL, the size of all the data blocks is the same and the playback time of one data block can vary from data block to data block. Notice however, that the size of the data blocks is constant for all retrievals of data for stream s_i (all service rounds) but need not be the same for all streams. They may vary from stream to stream depending on the characteristics of the video.

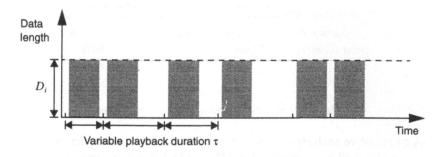

Fig. 3. Constant data length data placement

---

[5] We assume $\tau \cdot r_i$ to take integer values such that during each service round exactly $\tau \cdot r_i$ frames are read. If the assumption is dropped, the number of integral frames is given by $\lfloor \tau \cdot r_i \rfloor$.

Each of the two data placement strategies, CTL and CDL, has several advantages and disadvantages. Given the real-time requirements of continuous media and the periodic nature of video playback, CTL data placement appears to be the more natural strategy. It can easily be implemented because media quanta are always handled in terms of frames for which the time-scale is essential. A sequence of frames that must be sent to a client can therefore easily be mapped to disk I/O requests. Moreover, CTL data placement allows for disk scheduling algorithms that proceed in rounds of constant length in time, which can significantly reduce the seek overhead.

When using CDL data placement, the amount of data retrieved at a time does not vary. It can correspond in size to a disk block, allowing for efficient disk layout. Since CDL experiences the variation of variable bit rate video in the delays between consecutive retrievals it at first glance appears incompatible with round-based disk scheduling. An admission control criterion for CDL data placement must regard the playback time contained within the retrieved media data with respect to the block's disk service time.

These two data placement strategies should not be regarded as being exclusive. Chang and Zakhor [Chan94] as well as del Rosario and Fox [dR95] propose the combination of *both* CDL and CTL data placement strategies *at once* such that for every stream, constant size blocks are retrieved within equidistant time intervals. This method is referred to as **pseudo-constant bit rate (PCBR)** because it makes a VBR video stream appear as constant bit stream. While PCBR offers smooth disk and network traffic, it entails some major disadvantages: first, PCBR retrieval of course requires substantial buffer space because all burstiness of variable bit rate video is smoothed by *prefetching*. A large buffer may be needed to conceal the burstiness of the video. Second and related to the prefetching of media data, a large **start-up latency** can be introduced. Furthermore, if the client jumps to a different portion of the video, the prefetched data will become obsolete and the video server will be required to prefetch again.

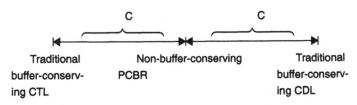

Fig. 4. Classification of storage and retrieval schemes

A comparative analysis of these various data placement strategies, which has been missing so far, will be carried out for CTL and PCBR in this paper. Throughout Section 4 we derive general non-buffer-conserving data retrieval schemes that cover CTL and PCBR as special cases, as indicated by figure 4. Specifically, we are able to show that between CTL and PCBR, respectively, there exists a continuum of non-buffer-conserving retrieval strategies that allows for a trade-off between disk I/O efficacy, latency, and buffer demand. A detailed analysis of CDL and its comparison with CTL and PCBR is omitted in this paper due space limitations.

3 Constraint Functions for Variable Bit Rate Video

3.1 Maximum Media Traffic

To provide deterministic QOS, the admission control criterion must employ *worst-case assumptions*, thus setting strict bounds to the number of streams to be admitted. The traffic model employed is necessarily deterministic in nature. We use frame size traces of MPEG-1 encoded video sequences[6] obtained at the University of Würzburg [Rose95] for the admission control schemes. A video trace consists of exact frame sizes expressed in bits or bytes, and the frames' arrival times [dR95]. If frames are assumed to arrive at a monotone rate, the video playback rate can be used interchangeably to express the arrival times. The so-called **empirical envelope** presented in [Knig95] provides the most accurate traffic constraint function for a given video trace. Consider the empirical envelope $\varepsilon(\tau)$ as a worst-case traffic model as follows. If $A_i[t, t+\tau]$ denotes an upper bound to the amount of data consumed by a stream s_i in the time interval $[t, t+\tau]$, an empirical envelope function is defined as:

$$\varepsilon_i(\tau) = \max_t A_i[t, t+\tau] \tag{1}$$

The function $\varepsilon_i(\tau)$ is defined for all $\tau, 0 \le \tau \le T_{total}$ where T_{total} defines the total playback duration of the video. Clearly, if $\tau = k \cdot r_i^{-1}$ for any integer k, τ takes the worst-case sum of k consecutive frames[7] within stream s_i. Therefore, if the value of τ corresponds to the playback time r_i^{-1} of a single frame of stream s_i, $\varepsilon_i(\tau)/\tau$ will correspond to the stream's peak bit rate,[8] and if τ corresponds to the playback time of the whole video, then $\varepsilon_i(\tau)/\tau$ will take the mean bit rate of stream s_i.

For any value of τ between the playback duration of one video frame and the video's duration, $\varepsilon_i(\tau)/\tau$ consequently takes values between the peak bit rate and the mean bit rate. We regard frames to be *consumed instantaneously* when they are scheduled to be sent off to the client, that is, between the deadlines of two consecutive frames no media data are consumed while at the point of the deadline, all data of the due frame are consumed at once. The empirical envelope $\varepsilon_i(\tau)$ will consequently take the form of a staircase function if we define:[9]

---

[6] The sequences are encoded with GOP-size 12 and pattern 'IBBPBBPBBPBB'. Each sequence contains 40,000 frames of size 384 × 288 picture elements with 24 bit color information. We simulate replay of the sequences at 30 frames per second.

[7] Without loss of generality we refer to the video information segments that are sent to the client as frames. However, several segments may make up one video image or may contain several images, depending on the chosen granularity, and may contain audio information as well.

[8] The peak bit rate is defined as the size of the largest frame divided by the playback duration of one frame.

$$
\varepsilon_i(\tau) = \begin{cases} 0 & \text{for } \tau = 0 \\ \max_t A\,[t, t + kr_i^{-1}] & \text{for } \tau \in \,(\,(k-1)\,r_i^{-1}, kr_i^{-1}\,]\,, k = 1, 2, \ldots \end{cases} \quad (2)
$$

For any scheduling discipline, using admission control tests with the empirical envelope results in the *highest resource utilization* achievable in a deterministic service with full VCR capabilities. By definition, the empirical envelope is an *optimal* traffic constraint function because no other traffic constraint function can for a given interval state a worst-case video traffic that is less than the value of the empirical envelope [Knig95].[10]

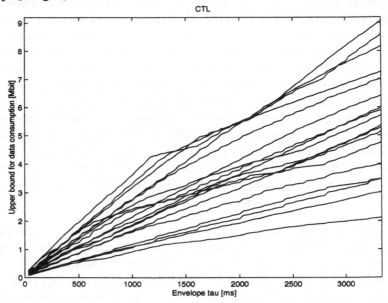

Fig. 5. Empirical envelopes as optimal traffic constraint functions.

We use empirical envelope functions $\varepsilon_i(\tau)$ that were obtained from the eighteen available video traces. Function values for $0 \le \tau \le 3333$ ms are shown in figure 5. It is reasonable to assume that the required video trace information is available in a video server since it can be very easily extracted from the frame size information contained within JPEG or MPEG frame headers. The computational complexity of traffic constraint functions, such as the empirical envelope, is also not very critical since we assume most on-demand multimedia services be rather read-only [Gemm95]. A traffic constraint function like the empirical envelope can therefore always be computed once *off-line*.

---

[9] Note that in [Knig95], values of $\varepsilon_i(\tau)$ for the intervals $(\,(k-1)\,r_i^{-1}, kr_i^{-1}\,]$, $k = 1, 2, \ldots$ are obtained by interpolation between $\varepsilon_i(\,(k-1)\,r_i^{-1})$ and $\varepsilon_i(kr_i^{-1})$.

[10] To see this, consider another traffic constraint function $\tilde{\varepsilon}$, with $\tilde{\varepsilon}(\tau) < \varepsilon(\tau)$ for $\tau \in [0, T_{total}]$. By definition (1), $\tilde{\varepsilon}(\tau)$ must then be the empirical envelope.

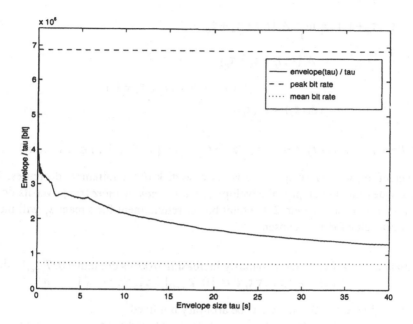

Fig. 6. Worst-case traffic $\varepsilon(\tau)$ in τ, divided by τ

For any value of τ between the playback duration of one video frame and the video's total playback time, $\varepsilon_i(\tau)/\tau$ consequently takes values between the peak bit rate (dashed line) and the mean bit rate (dotted line). Specifically, if τ equals the playback duration of one frame, $\varepsilon_i(\tau)/\tau$ will take the peak bit rate of the video, and if τ corresponds to the duration of the whole video, then $\varepsilon_i(\tau)/\tau$ will take the mean bit rate of the video stream. All values given for the MTV video trace.

Figure 6 underscores the significance of the interval τ with respect to the worst-case observed traffic bit rate $\varepsilon_i(\tau)/\tau$ in τ. When τ increases, the ratio, $\varepsilon_i(\tau)/\tau$ quickly decreases from the peak bit rate,[11] illustrated by the dashed line, and converges toward the mean bit rate that is indicated by the dotted line.

We now proof some useful properties of $\varepsilon_i(\tau)$:

Theorem 1. $\varepsilon_i(\tau_a) + \varepsilon_i(\tau_b) \geq \varepsilon_i(\tau_a + \tau_b) \quad \forall \tau_a, \tau_b > 0, i \in \{1, ..., n\}$ (3)

Proof.   Let $i \in \{1, ..., n\}$ and $\tau_a, \tau_b > 0$ be arbitrary but fixed.
From definition (3) holds $\varepsilon_i(\tau_a) = \max_t A_i[t, t + \tau_a]$ and
$\varepsilon_i(\tau_b) = \max A_i[t, t + \tau_b]$.
$\Rightarrow \exists \, t_a, t_b$ such that $\varepsilon_i(\tau_a) = A_i[t_a, t_a + \tau_a]$ and $\varepsilon_i(\tau_b) = A_i[t_b, t_b + \tau_b]$.
$\Rightarrow \varepsilon_i(\tau_a) \geq A_i[t_a, t_a + \tau_a] \quad \forall t \neq t_a$ and $\varepsilon_i(\tau_b) \geq A_i[t, t + \tau_b] \quad \forall t \neq t_b$
Therefore, we conclude that $\exists \, t_c$ such that:

---

[11] Note that this most likely resembles the size of the largest I-frame in the MPEG-1 video trace, divided by its playback duration.

$$\varepsilon_i(\tau_a + \tau_b) = \max_t A_i[t, t + \tau_a + \tau_b]$$

$$= A_i[\dot{t}_c, \dot{t}_c + \tau_a + \tau_b]$$

$$= A_i[\dot{t}_c, \dot{t}_c + \tau_a] + A_i[\dot{t}_c + \tau_a, \dot{t}_c + \tau_a + \tau_b]$$

$$\leq \varepsilon_i(\tau_a) + \varepsilon_i(\tau_b)$$

Corollary 1. $\quad \varepsilon_i(m_i\tau) \leq m_i\varepsilon_i(\tau) \quad \forall \tau > 0, \, m_i \in \{1, 2, ...\}, \, i \in \{1, ..., n\}$ (4)

Therefore, with growing τ_i the worst-case disk I/O requirement decreases. Theorem 2 states that the empirical envelope is *monotonously increasing* over its domain. Because of (9) and theorem 2, the total buffer requirement for stream s_i will increase if a larger value for τ_i is chosen:

Theorem 2. $\quad \varepsilon_i(\tau)$ is monotonously increasing over its domain $[0, T_{total}]$, that is,
$$\varepsilon_i(\tau) \geq \varepsilon_i(\tau') \quad \forall \tau, \tau' \in [0, T_{total}], \, \tau \geq \tau', \, i \in \{1, ..., n\} \quad (5)$$

Proof. Let $\tau, \tau' > 0$ with $\tau \geq \tau'$ be arbitrary but fixed.
From definition (3) holds $\varepsilon_i(\tau) = \max A_i[t, t + \tau]$ and $\varepsilon_i(\tau') = \max A_i[t, t + \tau']$.
$\Rightarrow \exists \, t_1, t_2$ such that $\varepsilon_i(\tau) = A_i[t_1, t_1 + \tau]$ and $\varepsilon_i(\tau') = A_i[t_2, t_2 + \tau']$

$$\Rightarrow \varepsilon_i(\tau) = A_i[t_1, t_1 + \tau]$$

$$\geq A_i[t_2, t_2 + \tau]$$

$$= A_i[t_2, t_2 + \tau'] + A_i[t_2 + \tau', t_2 + \tau]$$

$$\geq A_i[t_2, t_2 + \tau'] + 0$$

$$= \varepsilon_i(\tau')$$

Theorem 3. Consider the modified domain $M = \{0, r_i^{-1}, 2r_i^{-1}, ...\}$. Then $\varepsilon_i(\tau)$ is even strictly monotonously increasing over M, that is,
$$\varepsilon_i(\tau) > \varepsilon_i(\tau'), \quad \forall \tau, \tau' \in M, \, \tau > \tau', \, i \in \{1, ..., n\} \quad (6)$$

Proof. The proof is analogous to the proof of theorem 2. ∎

4 Constant Time Length Retrieval

4.1 Disk Model

Disk throughput is maximized when the seek times are minimized. We consider round-based retrieval techniques where each stream is served at-most once during each round. We use the **SCAN** algorithm where the head sweeps back and forth between the edge of the disk and its center serving the requests of one round. By ordering the requests according to the position of the data on the disk, SCAN minimizes the seek overhead.

Before we can formulate the exact admission control criterion for a single disk using the SCAN algorithm, we list all factors that need to be taken into account when computing the total time it takes to serve n streams during one round.

Let t_{track}, t_{seek} and t_{rot} express the **track-to-track seek time**, the **maximum seek time** and the **maximum rotational latency**, respectively, and let r_{disk} denote the **disk transfer rate**, and c_{cyl} the **capacity of a disk cylinder**. For the SCAN disk scheduling algorithm, in the worst case the maximum rotational latency of t_{rot} is introduced for each of the n streams. Furthermore, in the worst case a **full seek operation** across all cylinders is carried out during each round, which takes t_{seek}.

4.2 Constant Time Length Retrieval

After considering buffer-conserving CTL data placement we generalize CTL data placement and derive a novel data retrieval scheme for non-buffer-conserving CTL. The scheme contains both buffer-conserving CTL and PCBR as special cases. We finally summarize the fundamental trade-offs that exist between disk utilization, buffer demand, and start-up latencies.

Deterministic Admission Control

Consider the deterministic upper bound to the media traffic of a video in an interval τ given by the empirical envelope function $\varepsilon_i(\tau)$. Let D_i be the amount of data consumed by s_i during a disk round and let $\tilde{D}$ denote the sum of data that is consumed by all streams during a disk service round. Clearly, if τ corresponds to the duration of a disk service round, then $\varepsilon_i(\tau)$ will give an upper bound to the random variable D_i. An upper bound to the random variable $\tilde{D}$ can therefore be given by:

$$\tilde{D} \leq \sum_{i=1}^{n} \varepsilon_i(\tau) \tag{7}$$

Consequently, we obtain the **admission control criterion** that restricts the total disk I/O demand to satisfy the following condition:

$$\sum_{i=1}^{n} \frac{\varepsilon_i(\tau)}{r_{disk}} + \sum_{i=1}^{n} \left\lceil \frac{\varepsilon_i(\tau)}{c_{cyl}} \right\rceil \cdot t_{track} + n \cdot (t_{track} + t_{rot}) + t_{seek} \leq \tau \tag{8}$$

A lower bound for the total buffer requirement b_{total} is given by:

$$2 \sum_{i=1}^{n} \varepsilon_i(\tau) \leq b_{total} \tag{9}$$

However, this lower bound can be improved (reduced) because of the well-known worst-case characteristics of *subsequent data requests*. Consider two consecutive media data requests for stream s_i. Each one can in the worst case produce a read request for $\varepsilon_i(\tau)$ media data. Now assume that the requests refer to adjacent video quanta, that is, the video data of the second request is meant to be played back right after the data produced by the first request.[12] Two subsequent requests can then only total $\varepsilon_i(2\tau)$. According to corollary 1, this is always smaller than or equal to $2\varepsilon_i(\tau)$. The deterministic total buffer requirement hence decreases to:

$$\sum_{i=1}^{n} \varepsilon_i(2\tau) \leq b_{total} \tag{10}$$

4.3 Generalization of Constant Time Length Retrieval

Up to now, all papers on periodic retrieval schemes with deterministic service guarantees have assumed that

- the length of the **disk service round**, during which data for each stream are read exactly once from disk, and
- the length of the **CTL round,** for which we consider the worst case data consumption given by $\varepsilon_i(\tau)$ have the *same duration*. We are now going to distinguish the two and demonstrate the advantages of doing so.

The disk scheduling is still assumed to proceed in rounds of length τ. Additionally, we introduce a set $T = \{\tau_1, ..., \tau_n\}$ of **CTL rounds** depending on the video characteristics. The media data for stream s_i are retrieved from the disk such that during each τ_i, $\tau_i \geq \tau$, enough data to last for τ_i are retrieved. The CTL round duration τ_i must be a multiple m_i of the disk service round duration τ. The admission control criterion can now be extended to the use of $T = \{\tau_1, ..., \tau_n\}$ by the assumption that a request for media data of stream s_i is evenly distributed over $m_i = \tau_i/\tau$ disk service rounds. While over τ_i, the scheme is still buffer-conserving, i.e. the number of consumed frames equals the number of retrieved frames, in any disk service round within the CTL round, fewer frames may be read from the disk than be consumed by the client. The worst case data request during each disk service round, that is, an upper bound to $\tilde{D}$, is given by:

$$\sum_{i=1}^{n} \left\lceil \frac{\varepsilon_i(\tau_i)}{m_i} \right\rceil \tag{11}$$

Because of corollary 1, the worst-case data request is smaller than or equal to the corresponding sum of data requests for the case of $\tau_1, ..., \tau_n = \tau$ that was covered in the previous section:

---

[12] This can always be assumed if only the VCR functions play, pause and stop are considered.

Admission Control

Analogous to (8), we can now state the admission control criterion for restricted disk I/O:

$$\sum_{i=1}^{n} \left\lceil \frac{\varepsilon_i(\tau_i)}{m_i} \right\rceil r_{disk}^{-1} + \sum_{i=1}^{n} \left\lceil \left\lceil \frac{\varepsilon_i(\tau_i)}{m_i} \right\rceil c_{cyl}^{-1} \right\rceil \cdot t_{track} + n \cdot (t_{track} + t_{rot}) + t_{seek} \leq \tau \qquad (12)$$

The effect of the choice τ_i and τ on the number of clients that can be admitted to deterministic service is demonstrated in figure 7. The disk service round duration is varied between 33 ms and 3 s while the CTL parameter m_i takes integer values between 1 and 12. A CTL can therefore be up to 36 s long. Obviously, the smallest number of streams can be admitted if both parameters are chosen small.

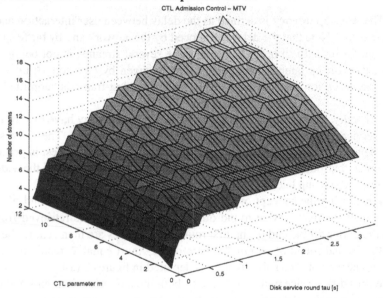

Fig. 7. Effect of service round and CTL parameter on the number of streams

In particular, there are two noteworthy effects of how the parameters τ and τ_i are chosen:

- The right edge of the graph indicates the curve for traditional, buffer-conserving CTL, i.e. $\tau = \tau_i$. The maximum number of admitted streams rises with a growing parameter τ for two reasons: first, as τ grows toward the duration of a video T_{total}, the amount of media data $\varepsilon_i(\tau)$ that must be retrieved in the worst case tends to get characterized by the mean bit rate instead of the peak bit rate.[13] The second reason for better disk I/O efficacy is given by a decrease in seek overhead when

---

[13] Recall that if τ takes the playback duration of one frame, then $\varepsilon_i(\tau)$ will equal the peak bit rate. For more detailed explanation, see section 3.3.1.

the media data are retrieved in larger segments.

- All other values depict admission control results for non-buffer-conserving CTL. Obviously, much larger numbers of simultaneous streams can be admitted. Notice that the service is still deterministic in nature, i.e. the server can guarantee the timely play-out of every frame of the video. Naturally, the greatest number of streams will be admitted if both τ_i and τ take large values.

Throughout the following section we assume τ to remain constant and evaluate the effect of τ_i with respect to the optimal start-up latency and the buffer requirements under deterministic conditions.

Start-up Latency and Buffer Requirements

The **start-up latency** is defined as the delay between user interaction and feedback by the server. Note that the delay introduced by the network and by buffering at the client site, for instance in order to synchronize several streams, is not being considered. Thus, the start-up latency of a video server is given by how long it takes the se.ver from the reception of a playback request until the first frame is submitted to the network.

Generally, a delay of τ is introduced because a client may have to wait for a whole disk service round duration before its request can be processed. The video server must then delay the play-out for another period $\hat{t}_i$ after the video request is processed so to guarantee that buffer starvation is avoided during the playback of the video. Consequently, the start-up latency is generally given by $\tau + \hat{t}_i$.

When using the concept of alternating buffers[14] with a CTL round of duration τ_i that equals the disk service round duration, $r_i \cdot \tau$ frames are retrieved from the disk into the buffer till the end of the first round. The frames are then sent to the client during the second round of length τ. Therefore, $\hat{t}_i$ must equal τ, resulting in an overall start-up latency of 2τ. This situation is depicted in figures 8 (a-b).

With a disk service round of τ, $\tau < \tau_i$, both the buffer requirements and the start-up latency can under deterministic conditions be reduced compared to a disk service round of τ_i. Every m_i subsequent disk service round of length τ, the video server reads sufficient media data to gain τ_i video playback for stream s_i. Yet the server does not have to delay playback for as long as τ_i because the data received from a number of disk service rounds before the expiration of τ_i may permit the server to play out frames under deterministic conditions. The server can so guarantee that buffer starvation is avoided even if playback is delayed for a shorter time than τ_i. This is demonstrated in figure 8 (c) where $\hat{t}_i$ is considerably smaller than τ_i.

Let random variable Z_i denote the number of frames contained within the media data D_i of stream s_i that are retrieved during a disk service round, and let observations of Z_i be denoted as $z_{i,l}$.

---

[14] The concept implies that one buffer gets refilled from storage while the other is emptied to the network.

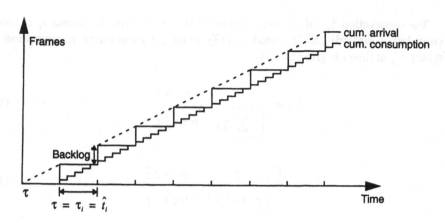

(a) Small disk service round τ and parameter $\tau_i = \tau$

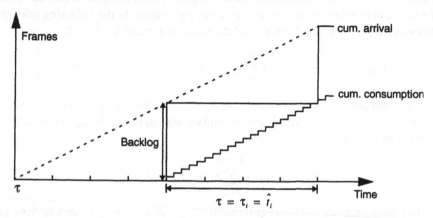

(b) Large disk service round τ and parameter $\tau_i = \tau$

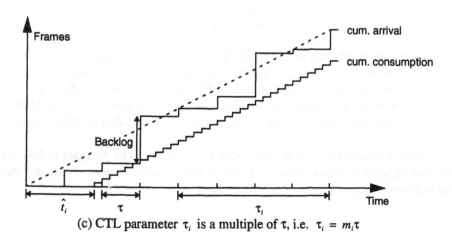

(c) CTL parameter τ_i is a multiple of τ, i.e. $\tau_i = m_i\tau$

Fig. 8. Traditional and generalized CTL data placement

The observation $\hat{z}_{i,t}$ of the total number of frames $\hat{Z}_t$ read for stream s_i at time t (**cumulative arrival**) can be stated as (13) while the **cumulative consumption** of frames $\hat{c}_{i,t}$ at time t is given by (14):

$$\hat{z}_{i,t} = \begin{cases} 0 & \text{for } t \leq \tau \\ \displaystyle\sum_{l=1}^{\lfloor t/\tau \rfloor} z_{i,l} & \text{for } t > \tau \end{cases} \tag{13}$$

$$\hat{c}_{i,t} = \begin{cases} 0 & \text{for } t \leq \hat{t}_i \\ \lfloor r_i(t - \hat{t}_i) \rfloor & \text{for } t > \hat{t}_i \end{cases} \tag{14}$$

Obviously, buffer starvation is avoided if the **backlog function**, that is the number of frames $\hat{z}_{i,t} - \hat{c}_{i,t}$ contained in the buffer, is greater than or equal to zero at all times. The problem of minimizing the start-up latency thus leads to the following rule for the **play-out delay** $\hat{t}_i$ (the total duration of the video is denoted by T_{total}):

$$\hat{t}_i = \min\left(t_i \in [\tau, T_{total}] \mid \sum_{l=1}^{\lfloor t/\tau \rfloor} z_{i,l} \geq \lfloor r_i \cdot (t - t_i) \rfloor, \forall t \in (t_i, T_{total}] \right) \tag{15}$$

The deterministic buffer requirement b_{total}^i for stream s_i is closely related to the worst case backlog. We first define the **maximum backlog** bl_{max}^i for stream s_i in terms of frames as

$$bl_{max}^i = \max_t \left(\sum_{l=1}^{\lceil t/\tau \rceil} z_{i,l} - \lfloor r_i(t - \hat{t}_i) \rfloor \right) \tag{16}$$

The **deterministic buffer requirement** b_{total}^i for stream s_i is then derived using the empirical envelope function as

$$\varepsilon_i\left(\frac{bl_{max}^i}{r_i} \right) \leq b_{total}^i \tag{17}$$

Notice that an arbitrary round-based disk scheduling algorithm may return video data for a stream at any time during a disk service round because concurrent requests are reordered to minimize the seek overhead. The worst case with regard to the start-up latency is thus given by assuming the *latest* possible arrival of media data while the worst case concerning the minimum buffer requires all media data to arrive as *early* as possible.

If VCR functionality, such as pause, stop and play, has to be provided to the client, the starting position within a video can also be very significant because playback starting at different frames produces different values for $\hat{z}_{i,t}$.

Theorem 4 states that throughout the playback of a stream, after each period of τ_i, there always remain the same number of frames in the buffer. This number is determined by the play-out delay $\hat{t}_i$. When using $\tau_i \equiv \tau$, for instance, the buffer is always half empty in terms of frames at the end of a round because the play-out delay equals the disk service round duration as shown in figures 8 (a–b).

It is therefore sufficient to calculate the play-out delay requirements for the first $\lfloor r_i \tau_i \rfloor$ frames as playback starting positions because all subsequent starting frames of the video can be viewed as phase-shifts from one of the first $\lfloor r_i \tau_i \rfloor$ frames, that is, they will periodically produce the same numbers for the deterministic start-up latency. To find the minimum play-out delay for a starting frame, one has to assume $\hat{t}_i = 0$ so to cause one or several conditions of buffer underflow $\hat{z}_{i,t} - \hat{c}_{i,t} < 0$. To prevent buffer starvation, the play-out must be delayed by at least the number of frames of the worst encountered buffer underflow, i.e. by $\min \{\hat{z}_{i,t} - \hat{c}_{i,t}\} \cdot r_i^{-1}$.[15]

The overall minimum play-out delay $\hat{t}_i$ is then determined by the smallest sufficient play-out delay of all observed starting frames. Again, both the minimum start-up latency $\tau + \hat{t}_i$ and the corresponding minimum buffer requirement can be computed once when the video is stored on the video server.

Theorem 4. Let $\tau_i > 0$ be arbitrary but fixed, $k, l \in \{1, 2, \dots\}$. Then follows
$$\hat{z}_{i,t} - \hat{c}_{i,t} \equiv \hat{z}_{i,t'} - \hat{c}_{i,t'} \qquad \forall t, t' : t = k\tau_i, \ t' = l\tau_i. \tag{18}$$

Proof. Let $k, l \in \{1, 2, \dots\}$, $t = k\tau_i$ and $t' = l\tau_i$ with $\tau_i > 0$ arbitrary but fixed. Because during τ_i the server is guaranteed to retrieve $r_i \tau_i$ frames, $\Rightarrow \hat{z}_{i,t} = r_i t$ and $\hat{z}_{i,t'} = r_i t'$.

From (14) then follows:

$$\hat{z}_{i,t} - \hat{c}_{i,t} = r_i t - \lfloor r_i (t - \hat{t}_i) \rfloor$$
$$= kr_i\tau_i - \lfloor kr_i\tau_i - r_i\hat{t}_i \rfloor$$
$$= kr_i\tau_i - kr_i\tau_i + \lfloor r_i\hat{t}_i \rfloor$$
$$= \lfloor r_i\hat{t}_i \rfloor$$

$$\hat{z}_{i,t'} - \hat{c}_{i,t'} = r_i t' - \lfloor r_i (t' - \hat{t}_i) \rfloor$$
$$= lr_i\tau_i - \lfloor lr_i\tau_i - r_i\hat{t}_i \rfloor$$
$$= lr_i\tau_i - lr_i\tau_i + \lfloor r_i\hat{t}_i \rfloor$$
$$= \lfloor r_i\hat{t}_i \rfloor$$
$$= \hat{z}_{i,t} - \hat{c}_{i,t}$$

---

[15] Similar methods for determining the start-up latency are stated in detail in [Chan94],[dR95].

In order to demonstrate the effect of the choice of τ_i, we have calculated minimum values of $\hat{t}_i$ and the associate buffer requirement for the MTV video trace independent of the starting frame.[16]

The values for $\hat{t}_i$ presented in table 1 allow for full VCR functionality because we consider the start-up latency of the worst case. The figures indicate that when using non-buffer-conserving CTL, one can reduce the start-up latency compared to buffer-conserving CTL by sacrificing disk I/O efficiency. For example, buffer-conserving CTL with a service round of 4 s entails a worst-case latency of 8 s whereas non-buffer-conserving CTL, for a disk service round of 1 s and a CTL round of 4 s, only requires a latency of 3.2 s.

τ [s]	τ_i [s]	Start-up latency		Buffer requirement for one stream		Number of admitted streams	
		Seconds	%	Bytes	%	Total	%
1	1	2.0	100%	676,724	100%	7	100%
1	2	2.6	132%	1,044,698	154%	8	114%
1	3	2.7	135%	1,182,035	175%	8	114%
1	4	3.2	160%	1,324,987	196%	9	129%
1	1,333	66.8	3,340%	12,362,938	1,826%	23	329%
1	1	2.0	100%	676,724	100%	7	100%
2	2	4.0	200%	1,324,987	195%	9	129%
3	3	6.0	300%	1,937,257	286%	9	129%
4	4	8.0	400%	2,339,260	346%	10	143%

Table 1. Start-up latency, buffer requirements, and admitted streams for CTL

For comparison, corresponding values in the lower half of the table are for the case that a *disk service round* equals the *CTL round*.

Values for "Start-up latency", correspond to $\hat{t}_i + \tau$. Column "Buffer requirement for one stream," states the corresponding minimum buffer requirement. The value for $\tau_i = \tau = 1$s , for instance, corresponds to $\varepsilon_i(2\tau)$. Row 5 contains the values for PCBR retrieval ($\tau_i = 1,333$ s) which is a special case of CTL data placement. All values are given for the MTV video trace.

If τ_i equals the duration of the whole video,[17] the proposed scheme effectively becomes the PCBR retrieval presented in [Chan94],[dR95]. Therefore, we provide a generalization for PCBR and CTL retrieval that covers the continuum between the two. We have also computed the deterministic buffer requirement.[18] The figures in

---

[16] For $\tau = 1$ s and $m_i = \{1, 2, 3, 4, 1.333 \times 10^3\}$.

[17] $\tau_i = 1.333 \times 10^3$ results in PCBR retrieval at the mean bit rate for a video of roughly twenty minutes (30 fps).

table 1 demonstrate that the buffer requirement grows *significantly slower* than m_i. For example, with a disk service round of 1 s and a CTL round of 1 s, the deterministic buffer requirement is 676,724 bytes. If we keep a disk service round of 1 s and increase the CTL round by a factor of 4 to 4 s, the buffer requirement will less than double from 676,724 bytes to 1,324,987 bytes. However, when choosing a disk service round equal to the CTL round, both of 4 s, the buffer requirement almost quadruples to 2,339,260. Hence, almost 1 Mbyte can be saved *per stream* if non-buffer-conserving CTL is employed.

This leads us to the following observations:

- When increasing the CTL round duration, one can admit more streams, i.e. improve the I/O efficiency at the expense of more buffer space and a higher start-up latency.
- When employing *non*-buffer-conserving CTL, the buffer demand and start-up latency are lower than for buffer-conserving CTL.
- The PCBR retrieval technique proposed in [Chan94],[dR95] is a *special case* of non-buffer-conserving CTL.

PCBR requires a start-up latency for the MTV video trace of well over *one minute*, and corresponding buffer allocation of close to *12 Mbyte per admitted stream*. Note that the play-out of the stream must be delayed for this long not only at the beginning of the playback but also after each pause. Similar results showing that PCBR is extremely demanding in terms of buffer space have been obtained by de Rosario and Fox [dR95] who have evaluated the buffer demand and start-up latency only for PCBR.

5 Conclusion

There are various papers that consider buffer-conserving CTL retrieval [Chan94]. However, we are the first to propose *non*-buffer-conserving CTL schemes where the CTL round length is *decoupled* from the disk round length. This permits to individually adapt the duration of the CTL round length *for each stream* to the buffer and start-up latency constraints at the client, while maintaining a common disk round length.

The separation of the disk service round from the CTL round, as done for the non-buffer-conserving retrieval, pays off. For non-buffer-conserving retrieval as compared to buffer-conserving retrieval we observe that

- a slightly smaller number of streams can be admitted
- the buffer requirements and start-up latencies decline drastically.

---

[18] The minimum amount of buffer space that guarantees that buffer overflow is avoided, given the play-out delay $\hat{t}_i$.

Furthermore, the PCBR scheme which performs the retrieval of media data at the stream's mean bit rate, is shown to be a special case of CTL retrieval. While PCBR achieves the most efficient disk I/O, it suffers the largest start-up latency and buffer demand.

Acknowledgment

The work described in this paper was supported by the Siemens Nixdorf AG, Munich.

6 References

[Chan94] E. Chang and A. Zakhor. "Admissions Control and Data Placement for VBR Video Servers." In *Submitted to Proceedings of the 1st International Conference on Image Processing*, Austin, Texas, November 1994.

[Dey94] J. K. Dey, J. D. Salehi, J. F. Kurose, and D. Towsley. "Providing VCR Capabilities in Large-Scale Video Servers." In *Proceedings of the 2nd ACM International Conference on Multimedia*, pages 25–32, October 1994.

[dR95] J. M. de Rosario and G. Fox. "Constant Bit Rate Network Transmission of Variable Bit Rate Continuous Media in Video-On-Demand Servers." Technical Report SCCS-677, Northeast Parallel Architectures Center, 111 College Place, Syracuse University, Syracuse, NY, July 31 1995.

[Gemm95] D. J. Gemmell, H. M. Vin, D. D. Kandlur, P. V. Rangan, and L. A. Rowe. "Multimedia Storage Servers: A Tutorial and Survey." *IEEE Computer*, 28(5):40–49, May 1995.

[Knig94] E. W. Knightly, R. F. Mines, and H. Zhang. "Deterministic Characterization and Network Utilizations for Several Distributed Real-time Applications." In *Proc. of IEEE WORDS'94*, Dana Point, CA, October 1994.

[Knig95] E. W. Knightly, D. E. Wrege, J. Liebeherr, and H. Zhang. "Fundamental Limits and Tradeoffs of Providing Deterministic Guarantees to VBR Video Traffic." In *Proceedings Joint International Conference on Measurement & Modeling of Computer Systems (Sigmetrics '95 / Performance '95)*, volume 23 of *Performance Evaluation Review*, pages 98–107, Ottawa, Canada, May 15-19 1995. Also available as technical report TR-94-067, International Computer Science Institute, Berkeley, CA.

[Rang92] P. V. Rangan, H. M. Vin, and S. Ramanathan. "Designing an On-Demand Multimedia Service." *IEEE Communications Magazine*, 30(7):56–65, July 1992.

[Rose95] O. Rose. "Statistical Properties of MPEG Video Traffic and Their Impact on Traffic Modelling in ATM Systems." Technical Report 101, Institute of Computer Science, University of Wuerzburg, University of Wuerzburg, February 1995.

[Rowe93] L. A. Rowe and R. R. Larson. "A Video-on-demand System." The University of California at Berkeley and International Computer Science Institute, 1993.

[Stei91] R. Steinmetz and R. G. Herrtwich. "Integrierte verteilte Multimedia-Systeme." *Informatik-Spektrum*, 14:249–260, 1991.

Appendix

A Disk Model Characteristics

Throughout the simulations a disk model with the characteristics of the "Micropolis 4110 AV" was used:

Micropolis 4110AV	
Maximum seek time t_{seek}	20.0ms
Track-to-track seek time t_{track}	1.5ms
Maximum rot.l latency t_{rot}	11.11ms
Disk cylinder capacity c_{cyl}	4×10^6 bits
Disk transfer rate r_{disk}	24×10^6 bps

Table 2. Characteristics of the Micropolis AV 4110 hard disk drive

A Control System for an Interactive Video on Demand Server Handling Variable Data Rates

Mathias Rautenberg, Helmut Rzehak
University of the Federal Armed Forces Munich
Department of Computer Science

Abstract: Providing an interactive Video on Demand (VoD) service to thousands of subscribers has been an area of active research. In this contribution we present the concept for a control system for an interactive VoD server. This control system is designed to anticipate upcoming periods of overload while giving statistical guarantees to the subscribers. This is achieved by enriching the data with additional control information and a special layout strategy on the disk. Therefore an overview about MPEG compression as far as meaningful to this work is given. At least mechanisms for the controlled reduction of the quality during overload situations are discussed. These mechanisms are intended to be fair and to minimize the damage to the subscribers.

Keywords: Video on demand server - Data request manager - Stream agent - Additional control information.

1 Introduction

New high speed networks based on ATM or DQDB and rapid advances in processor technology enable distributed multimedia applications. One of the most promising multimedia applications in the marketplace is VoD, which is intended to offer customers a service similar to that of a rental video shop. In this context interactive VoD means the subscriber is able to start, stop, pause and resume a requested stream. A good overview about architectural aspects of VoD servers is given by [1].

A VoD system consists of a server and several clients. The server is storing the digital videos in a compressed form. MPEG is the most widespread compression technique for this job. All the clients are connected to the server via a high speed network.

Initially a client specifies a request for the video stream it wants to see including the quality of service parameters such as frame rate, display size and resolution and sends a request to the server. If there are enough ressources for this subscription on the server it has to admit the subscriber. After that the server has to retrieve the requested data for this client – and for all the other clients too – in a way every client is able to playback the video stream continuously.

2 Related Work

In the past many investigastions concerning VoD servers took place. Lougher and Sheperd [5] focused on the layout of continuous media stored on disk arrays. They propose a round robin scheduling strategy for retrieving the data. Keeton and Katz [2] introduce layout strategies to store multiresolution video data on disk arrays. Ramakrishnan et al. [7] designed algorithms for admission control and scheduling based on different classes of tasks to integrate real-time tasks serving continuous media and non real-time traffic. A High Definition Television (HDTV) Storage Server is presented by Vin and Rangan [8]. They assume there will be disks in the future with a capacity of about 100 GBytes that are large enough to store several video streams. Strategies how to store multiple HDTV videos on disk and a quantitative study how to design a VoD server are presented. Furthermore a scheduling algorithm retrieving an amount of data proportionally to the playback rate of the stream is introduced.

However a compression technique like MPEG delivers variable bit rates. So an interactive VoD server has to provide variable amounts of data to the subscriber in each service round. Therefore we suggest a control system for an interactive VoD server based on the idea to serve the data requests of each subscriber individually in each service round. It is not a competition to scheduling algorithms giving statistical guarantees but an extension in the sense it recognizes upcoming overload situations of the server. Mechanisms are included for handling these overload situations in a fair manner minimizing the damage for the subscribers.

The rest of this paper is organized as follows. In section 3 we give a brief introduction to MPEG compression. The layout of MPEG data on disk is described in section 4. In section 5 a control system anticipating upcoming overload situations is developed and in section 6 mechanisms for handling these overload situations are discussed. Section 7 concludes the paper.

3 MPEG

The acronym *MPEG* (ISO/IEC IS 11172) stands for *Motion Picture Expert Group* and is the name of the ISO-committee which standardized that compression technique. MPEG is intended for the compression of digital video [4]. Basically an MPEG file is a sequence of pictures. There are three types of pictures:
- I: Intra coded pictures
- P: Predictive coded pictures
- B: Bidirectional predictive coded pictures

Intra coded means the picture contains all the information by itself necessary for decompression. Predictive coded pictures depend on the last picture of type I or P and result from motion compensated prediction. Bidirectional predictive coded pictures are obtained from the preceding I- or P-picture and the subsequent I- or P-picture using motion compensation and interpolation.

The two parameters M and N specify the sequence of I-, P- and B-pictures in an MPEG stream.

- M: The distance between I- or P-pictures.
- N: The distance between I-pictures.

Figure 1 shows the dependencies between the types of frames of a stream characterized by M=3 and N=9.

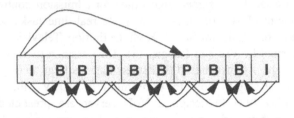

Figure 1 Dependencies between pictures

As we know from several investigations [3], [6] I-pictures are larger than P-pictures and those are larger than B-pictures. As a rule of thumb one can say the size of an I-picture is larger than the size of a B-picture by an order of magnitude.

There are a lot of reasons so that MPEG compression leads to variable bit rates. On the lowest level of compression MPEG uses pseudo entropy coding and entropy coded runlength symbols. Therefore the size of a picture depends among other things on its content. A simple content, e.g. the blue sky with a few white clouds, yields to a higher degree of compression than a meadow with thousands of flowers being in bloom.

The parameters M and N are also influencing the size of the compressed pictures. Imagine an MPEG encoder is compressing the same movie twice. First setting the parameters M=3 and N=9 and afterwards setting M=4 and N=12. No doubt the first output of the encoder is larger than the second.

Rate fluctuations are also caused by the differences in the contents of adjacent frames. This is because of the motion compensation. A car driving on a road e.g. leads to a high degree of compression because the background of the adjacent frames is identical and the car as the moving part in the picture is motion compensated, i.e. a few pieces of the picture are simply moved. On the other hand a flash light occurring in a video clip of a rock band e.g. is too different to use motion compensation. From this a lower degree of compression will be the consequence.

Very similar to the example described at last are changes between scenes in a movie. The whole content of the picture changes at once. This is the most troublesome reason for a fluctuating rate.

4 Storage of MPEG Video

In accordance with [8] we expect an increase in the capacity of disks to about 100 Gbytes. On such disks it will be possible to store a few MPEG compressed movies.

As stated above an MPEG encoder produces highly variable data rates. It is impossible to state the number of frames that are to be stored in one data block in advance. In other words one data block contains data for an unknown interval of time to be played back. The following question arises: "How shall the server determine the amount of data a subscriber needs in one service round to playback the video for a fixed interval of time?" The server has two ways to solve this problem.

First it can force a data block to contain data for a fixed a priori known interval of playback time by storing a fixed number of frames per block. This is not a good idea because it will be impossible to fill the data blocks completely. Remember video servers have to store and retrieve huge amounts of data. Less performance would be the consequence of wasting storage capacity because a lot of unused data would have to be transported across the system bus.

The second way to solve the problem is to store the data compactly and to determine the number of data blocks needed by each subscriber in every service round individually. Concerning this approach two main problems have to be solved. One is who tells the control system of a VoD server how many data blocks a stream needs to playback the video for a fixed interval of time. The other is that the time an intelligent control system may use to calculate the number of blocks used by each stream has to be very small compared to the time the server needs to retrieve the data.

One approach is to retrieve data blocks from disk and analyzing how many frames are contained within. This has to be done until as many frames are retrieved as necessary to playback the video at the client side for a given time. However analyzing the retrieved frames online is a time wasting job and therefore leads to an unacceptable performance.

But as far as we know no approach until now has taken advantage of enriching the data with control information which is stored on disk additionally. This additional control information in an MPEG stream is necessary for informing the control system about the demands of the streams during the next service round efficiently. This promises a good performance of the VoD server.

5 Modeling the Control System

After describing the problem of rate fluctuations caused by MPEG compression we present a concept for a control system of a VoD server handling these rate fluctuations individually. This concept is an optimistic approach in the sense the system gives no hard but only statistical guarantees for the service to the subscriber. The combination of handling rate fluctuations individually and giving statistical guarantees enables the system to service more subscribers then strategies retrieving constant amounts of data. By this way cheaper prices for the service are possible. This should compensate the short periods of reduced quality. Less quality is caused by accidental overlay of bursty MPEG scenes requested by some subscribers yielding an overload situation at the server side.

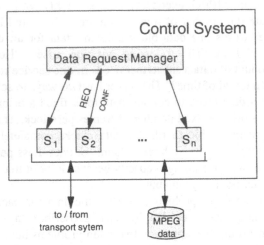

Figure 2 Architecture of the control system

If such situations occur occasionally some frames of the stream cannot be retrieved and have to be replaced e.g. by dummy frames at the client side. The control system has to decide which data not to retrieve in a manner that is fair and damages the streams minimally.

Now we will develop an algorithm for real-time retrieval of data in the way stated above henceforth called *I*ndividual *R*equest using *A*dditional *C*ontrol *I*nformation (*IRACI*). This algorithm is the core of the control system of an interactive VoD server. For the development of the IRACI algorithm the model introduced in [8] was adopted and adjusted to our necessities that it is particularly useful for.

As shown in Figure 2 the control system consists of n stream agents S_1, S_2, ..., S_n and the Data Request Manager (DRM). Each stream agent at the server is responsible for retrieving and sending the data to the subscriber at the client. Therefore every stream agent S_i requests the DRM for x_i frames needed in the next service round. The DRM collects the requests of all the streams for one service round and decides which data blocks are not to retrieve if an overload situation occurs occasionally.

To formulate the IRACI algorithm for the DRM precisely we have to give some definitions. In one service round every stream agent S_i with $i \in [1, n]$ has to retrieve x_i frames of different sizes. Since the data is stored in blocks of fixed size on the disk a varying number of frames is stored in each block (see Figure 3).

$B_i := \{bl_1, bl_2, ..., bl_{k_i}\}$ is the set of k_i blocks containing the x_i frames of stream S_i.

For each block we define the set of frames stored in that.

$bl_1 := \{f_1, f_2, ..., f_l\}$; $bl_2 := \{f_{l+1}, f_{l+2}, ..., f_m\}$; ... ; $bl_{k_i} := \{f_{v+1}, f_{v+2}, ..., f_{x_i}, f_{x_i+1}, ..., f_{x_i+pf_i}\}$; with $(l < m < v < x_i) \wedge (l, m, v \in IN)$. In bl_{k_i} the frames $f_{x_i+1}, ..., f_{x_i+pf_i}$ have to be prefetched that are used in the succeeding service round because usually the frames are stored across the border of data blocks. Note that a frame that is stored across two data blocks is always element

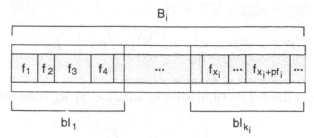

Figure 3 Storing MPEG frames

of the set corresponding to the second block per definition. The cardinalities of the sets $|bl_j|$ with $j \in [1, k_i]$ indicate the number of frames contained in that block and have to be stored as part of the additional information. Once per service round the number of prefetched frames has to be calculated for every stream. That is

$$pf_i = \sum_{j=1}^{k_i} |bl_j| - x_i. \qquad (1)$$

In the worst case $pf_i = |bl_{k_i}| + 1$ if the last data block has to be retrieved only for accessing one frame. Let us suppose fs_l ($l \in IN$) denotes the size of frame f_l and the constant BS is the size of a data block. Then the number of data blocks DB_i needed by stream S_i is given by

$$DB_i = \left\lceil (fs_1 + fs_2 + \dots + fs_{x_i - pf_i})/BS \right\rceil$$

$$= \left\lceil \sum_{l=1}^{x_i - pf_i} fs_l \Big/ BS \right\rceil. \qquad (2)$$

Assuming the streams are stored in contiguous files then the time for transferring the DB_i data blocks for one stream TB_i depends on the amount of data and the transfer rate of the disk R_{dr}.

$$TB_i = \frac{DB_i * BS}{R_{dr}} =$$

$$= \frac{1}{R_{dr}} * \left\lceil \sum_{l=1}^{x_i - pf_i} fs_l \Big/ BS \right\rceil * BS. \qquad (3)$$

But the time necessary to retrieve DB_i data blocks includes some overhead for switching from one stream to another. That is estimated by the sum of the maximum seek time of the disk head l_{seek}^{max} and the maximum rotational time l_{rot}^{max} of the disk. The time needed to retrieve all the blocks for one service round for a stream S_i is calculated adding the time needed for switching between streams and the time for transferring the blocks themselves.

$$TR_i = l_{seek}^{max} + l_{rot}^{max} + TB_i =$$

$$= l_{seek}^{max} + l_{rot}^{max} + \frac{1}{R_{dr}} * \left\lceil \sum_{l=1}^{x_i - pf_i} fs_l \Big/ BS \right\rceil * BS. \tag{4}$$

Since the control system has to serve the streams S_1, S_2, ..., S_n the time spent to retrieve the data denoted by TR is given by equation (5). R_{dr} is the data transfer rate of the disk.

$$TR = n * (l_{seek}^{max} + l_{rot}^{max}) + \sum_{i=1}^{n} TB_i =$$

$$= n * (l_{seek}^{max} + l_{rot}^{max}) + \tag{5}$$

$$+ \sum_{i=1}^{n} \frac{1}{R_{dr}} * \left\lceil \sum_{l=1}^{x_i - pf_i} fs_l \Big/ BS \right\rceil * BS.$$

Note that not necessarily all the clients consume their data at the same playback rate R_{pl}^i which is given in the unit frames per second. This is to attribute to different frame rates or different resolutions of pictures. The condition for satisfying n subscribers simultaneously is retrieving the data for all the subscribers in one service round takes less or equal time then the most demanding stream needs for playback its data. That is

$$n * (l_{seek}^{max} + l_{rot}^{max}) +$$

$$+ \sum_{i=1}^{n} \frac{1}{R_{dr}} * \left\lceil \sum_{l=1}^{x_i - pf_i} fs_l \Big/ BS \right\rceil * BS$$

$$\leq \min_{i \in [1,n]} \left(\frac{x_i}{R_{pl}^i} \right). \tag{6}$$

Because the VoD server is intended to be interactive the duration of a service round has to be in a range that is tolerable for the subscriber i.e. not exceeding one second. It is the job of the DRM to calculate the number of data blocks containing the frames requested by the clients for the next service round. More precisely DB_i formulated in equation (2) has to be calculated. Remember the number of frames $|bl_j|$ with $j \in$ IN in a data block is among others part of the additional information. Now the DRM has to search for the smallest k_i so that the following condition is fulfilled.

$$\sum_{j=1}^{k_i} |bl_j| \geq x_i - pf_i \tag{7}$$

For every stream S_i with $i \in [1, n]$ we get with the help of the additional information the simplification:

$$\left\lceil \sum_{l=1}^{x_i - pf_i} fs_l \Big/ BS \right\rceil = k_i \tag{8}$$

(8) together with (6) results in:

$$n * (1_{seek}^{max} + 1_{rot}^{max}) + \sum_{i=1}^{n} \frac{k_i * BS}{R_{dr}}$$

$$\leq \min_{i \in [1,n]} \left(\frac{x_i}{R_{pl}^i} \right).$$

(9)

Having conducted inequation (9) there is a condition for proofing an upcoming overload situation in the following service round for the VoD server. Next we focus on strategies to reduce the load in such situations.

6 Handling Overload Situations

The aspects that have to be kept in mind at the same time are fairness and minimal damage to the subscribers. The basic idea to reduce the load is: the server does not transfer some of the requested data blocks.

The alleviation of the load is done by the DRM in two steps. First the number of data blocks that are not to transfer has to be determined. Consequently the number of blocks not to transfer from disk denoted by DN is the quotient of the time leading to the violation of (9) and the time necessary for transferring one block as given by (10).

$$DN = \left\lceil \frac{n * (1_{seek}^{max} + 1_{rot}^{max})}{\frac{BS}{R_{dr}}} + \frac{\sum_{i=1}^{n} \frac{k_i * BS}{R_{dr}} - \min_{i \in [1,n]} \left(\frac{x_i}{R_{pl}^i} \right)}{\frac{BS}{R_{dr}}} \right\rceil$$

(10)

Having calculated DN the DRM has to choose the blocks not to retrieve carefully to supply the subscribers with reduced quality. For this purpose the DRM has to know how important the content of a data block i.e. the frames is for the quality of the stream. This question is specifically to the compression technique and will be answered for MPEG.

As stated above MPEG defines three types of frames. These are of different importance to the stream. This is because of the dependencies between the frames. Simplified one can say frames of type I are more important for the stream then frames of type P and those are more important then B-frames. In [9] the dependencies between the frames and the effects of missing frames of different types are discussed in detail.

For our concept we suggest a layout strategy for the MPEG coded streams arranging the frames of a group of pictures according to their importance for the quality of the stream. This means the I-frames are stored at first followed by the P-frames and the frames of type B.

This layout has the advantage that the most important data blocks for a stream can be read at first because the number of blocks containing frames of different types is minimized. If the DRM decides to reduce the quality of this stream only blocks of less importance can be picked out to be not transferred. Obviously the stream agent retrieving the data blocks has to arrange the frames in a way the client expects them to come before passing them to the transport system. To do this efficiently by a few pointer operations without searching or copying the data the additional information has to contain the starting addresses of the frames in each block. Note that preparing the data with additional information in the suggested manner is a time wasting job but this can be done offline separately.

As stated above $B_i := \{bl_1, bl_2, ..., bl_{k_i}\}$ is the set of k_i blocks containing the x_i frames requested by stream S_i. From this we define the set B containing the frames requested by all the streams:

$$B := B_1 \cup B_2 \cup ... \cup B_n = \bigcup_{i=1}^{n} B_i .$$

Let F be the set of all the frames f and T the set comprising all the types of frames i.e. $T = \{I, P, B\}$. We define the function g relating to every frame $f \in F$ its type $t \in T$:

$$g: F \to T \text{ and } g(f) = t.$$

Using the function g we define the sets $M_1, M_2, ..., M_7$.

M_1, M_2, M_3 are the sets of data blocks containing frames of type B, P and I respectively. Ideally blocks include only one type of frames.

$M_1 = \{ b \in B \mid \forall f \in b: g(f) = B \}$

$M_2 = \{ b \in B \mid \forall f \in b: g(f) = P \}$

$M_3 = \{ b \in B \mid \forall f \in b: g(f) = I \}$

M_4, M_5, M_6 are the sets of data blocks comprising frames of two types only. Since the data is stored compactly it is possible two types of frames are lying in one block.

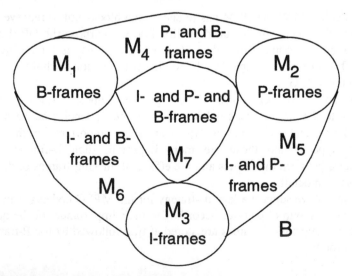

Figure 4 Dividing B into equivalence classes

$M_4 = \{ b \in B \mid (\forall f \in b\colon g(f) = B \vee g(f) = P) \wedge (\exists f_1, f_2 \in b\colon g(f_1) = B \wedge g(f_2) = P) \}$
$M_5 = \{ b \in B \mid (\forall f \in b\colon g(f) = I \vee g(f) = P) \wedge (\exists f_1, f_2 \in b\colon g(f_1) = I \wedge g(f_2) = P) \}$
$M_6 = \{ b \in B \mid (\forall f \in b\colon g(f) = I \vee g(f) = B) \wedge (\exists f_1, f_2 \in b\colon g(f_1) = I \wedge g(f_2) = B) \}$
M_7 is the set of data blocks consisting of all the three types of frames. Data blocks that are elements of M_7 almost result from changing scenes.
$M_7 = \{ b \in B \mid \exists f_1, f_2, f_3 \in b\colon g(f_1) = I \wedge g(f_2) = P \wedge g(f_3) = B \}$
As shown in Figure 4 B can be divided into the seven disjunct sets $M_1, M_2, ..., M_7$.
The sets $M_1, M_2, ..., M_7$ are to be interpreted as equivalence classes of data blocks having the same importance for the quality of the stream. Between these equivalence classes there can be defined an order of importance denoted by < based on the order of importance of the types of frames which is $B <_f P <_f I$. For the sets $M_1, M_2, ..., M_7$

$$M_1 < M_4 < M_2 < M_6 < M_7 < M_5 < M_3$$

is valid.

Now the algorithm of the DRM responsible for handling overload situations is able to assess the damage it causes by not confirming requested data. The open question is which of the blocks requested should be not confirmed to reach the aim of fairness and minimized damage to all the streams. For this purpose different strategies have to be discussed.

The most likely strategy is to punish all the streams in the average in the same way. This is accomplished by always choosing the stream that was least of all reduced. At the first glance this seems to be a good strategy. But the disadvantage is there can be determined a data block of a stream S_i belonging to the set M_k while another stream S_j is still served with data blocks from the set M_l and $M_l < M_k$ is valid with i, j $\in$ [1,n] and l, k $\in$ [1,7].

Another strategy is punishing the initiator of the trouble. That is lower the number of confirmed data blocks of the stream deviating from the negotiated quality of service parameters during the phase of connection admission mostly. Quality of service parameter for a VoD server interesting in this context are among others average and variance of the amount of data to retrieve by the server for a subscriber. Since data bursts requested in a service round are probably caused by frequently changing scenes in e.g. an action movie following this strategy leads to the same problem then the strategy of punishing all the streams in the same way.

The two discussed strategies have the goal of being particularly fair. Both of them suffer of missing the goal of minimizing the damage to the subscribers.

A third strategy following this goal consequently is to select the data blocks not to retrieve always from the set M_l with the lowest priority. The drawback of this strategy is being extremely unfair. Imagine two movies have to be retrieved. One is presenting a countryside recorded by slowly swiveling the camera and the other one is an action movie with a lot of changing scenes. Since the movie showing the countryside probably will request blocks of lower priority then the action movie does more of its data blocks will be not retrieved. Thus the quality of the countryside movie is reduced because of an overload situation probably caused by the action movie.

As we have seen fairness and minimal damage to the subscribers are conflicting goals. So we have to make a trade of by merging the strategies discussed above. We suppose a strategy reducing the quality the more the burstier the streams are. This can be accomplished by setting for every stream a number of blocks not to retrieve depending on the quality of service parameters negotiated during connection admission control. For this purpose we define a vector $V = (\ v_1,\ v_2,\ ...,\ v_n\ )$ storing these numbers. Subscribers with high requirements will have to go without more data blocks then those streams with less requirements. Every time it was decided to not retrieve a data block the component of the concerned stream stored in a vector $W = (\ w_1,\ w_2,\ ...,\ w_n\ )$ is decremented by one. For selecting the block not to retrieve the set of blocks with the lowest priority has to be determined. From this set any block is selected if it is allowed by vector W i.e. the corresponding component w_i with $i \in [1,n]$ is not equal to zero. If all the components of W are already equal to zero ($w_1 = 0 \land w_2 = 0 \land ... \land w_n = 0$) the vector has to be initialized again by the assignment $W = V$.

7 Concluding Remarks

We have presented the concept of a control system for an interactive VoD server. Basically this control system consists of n stream agents and the DRM. Since MPEG compression leads to streams of variable bit rate the stream agents request the DRM for permission to retrieve the data from disk in every service round. The DRM checks if an overload situation will occur using the IRACI algorithm by evaluating the requests and confirms individually the data blocks that are to retrieve to the clients. The IRACI algorithm and the algorithm choosing the blocks not to retrieve have to be implemented very efficiently to achieve a good performance of the system. Currently implementation is underway. Future work will consider the extension of the control system to support MPEG-2 coded streams.

References

[1] Gemmell, J.D., Vin, H.M., Kandlur, D.D., Rangan, P.V., Rowe, L.A.: Multimedia storage servers: a tutorial, *IEEE Computer*, no. 5, 1995, pp. 40-49.
[2] Keeton, K., Katz, R.H.: Evaluating video layout startegies for a high-performance storage server, *Multimedia Systems*, no. 3, Springer Verlag, 1995, pp. 43-52.
[3] Lam, S.L., Chow, S., Yau, D.K.Y., An algorithm for lossless smoothing of MPEG video, *Technical Report TR-94-04*, Dept of Computer Sciences, University of Texas, Austin, 1994.
[4] Le Gall, D.: A video compression standard for multimedia applications, *Communications of the ACM*, vol. 34, , no. 4, 1991, pp. 46-58.
[5] Lougher, P., Sheperd, D.: The design and implementation of a continuous media storage server, *Proccedings of the 3rd International Workshop on Network and Operating System Support for Digital Audio and Video*, San Diego, 1992, pp. 69-80.

[6] Patel, K., Smith, B.C., Rowe, L.A.: Performance of a software MPEG video encoder, *Proceedings of the First ACM International Conference on Multimedia*, Anaheim, CA, 1993, pp. 75-82.

[7] Ramakrishnan, K.K. et al.: Operating system support for a video-on-demand file service, *Multimedia Systems*, no. 3, Springer Verlag, 1995, pp. 53-65.

[8] Vin, M., Rangan, P.V.: Designing a multiuser HDTV storage server, *IEEE Journal on Selected Areas in Communications*, vol. 11, no. 1, 1993, pp. 153-164.

[9] Wittig, H., Winckler, J., Sandvoss, J.: Network layer scaling: congestion control in multimedia communication with heterogenous networks and receivers, *Proceedings of the COST 237 Workshop on Multimedia Transport and Teleservices*, Springer-Verlag, 1994, pp. 274-293.

A Synchronization Scheme for Stored Multimedia Streams

Werner Geyer[1], Christoph Bernhardt, Ernst Biersack
Institut Eurécom[2]

Abstract: Multimedia streams such as audio and video impose tight temporal constraints due to their continuous nature. Often, different multimedia streams must be played out in a synchronized way. We present a scheme to ensure the continuous and synchronous playout of *stored* multimedia streams. We propose a protocol for the synchronized playback and we compute the buffer required to achieve both, the continuity within a single substream and the synchronization between related substreams. The scheme is very general because it only makes a single assumption, namely that the jitter is bounded.

1 Introduction

1.1 Motivation

Advances in communication technology lead to new applications in the domain of multimedia. Emerging high-speed, fiber-optic networks make it feasible to provide multimedia services such as Video On-Demand, Tele-Shopping or Distance Learning. These applications typically integrate different types of media such as audio, video, text or images. Customers of such a service retrieve the digitally stored media from a **video server** [Ber95] for playback.

1.2 Multimedia Synchronization

Multimedia refers to the integration of different types of data streams including both **continuous media** streams (audio and video) and **discrete media** streams (text, data, images). Between the information units of these streams a certain temporal relationship exists. Multimedia systems must maintain this relationship when storing, transmitting and presenting the data. Commonly, the process of maintaining the temporal order of one or several media streams is called **multimedia synchronization** [Eff93].

Continuous media are characterized by a well-defined temporal relationship between subsequent data units. Information is only conveyed when media quanta are presented continuously in time. As for video/audio the temporal relationship is dictated by the sampling rate. The problem of maintaining continuity within a single stream is referred to as **intra-stream** synchronization. Moreover, there exist temporal

---

[1] Now with: Praktische Informatik IV, University of Mannheim, 68131 Mannheim, Germany, geyer@pi4.informatik.uni-mannheim.de

[2] 2229 Route des Crêtes, 06904 Sophia-Antipolis — France, Phone: +33 93002611, FAX: +33 93002627, email: {bernhard,erbi}@eurecom.fr

relationships between media-units of related streams, for instance, an audio and video stream. The preservation of these temporal constraints is called **inter-stream** synchronization. To solve the problem of stream synchronization we have to regard both issues which are tightly coupled.

One can distinguish between **life synchronization** for life media streams and **synthetic synchronization** for stored media streams [Ste93a]. In the former case, the capturing and playback must be performed almost at the same time, while in the latter case, samples are recorded, stored and played back at a later point of time. For life synchronization, e.g. in teleconferencing, the tolerable end-to-end delay is in the order of a few hundred milliseconds only. Synthetic synchronization of recorded media stream is easier to achieve than life synchronization: higher end-to-end delays are tolerable, and the fact that sources can be influenced proves to be very advantageous as will be shown later. It is, for instance, possible to adjust playback speed or to schedule the start-up times of streams as needed. However, as resources are limited, it is desirable for both kinds of synchronization to keep the buffers required as small as possible. [Koe94]

1.3 Related Work

Escobar et al. [Esc94] and Rothermel et al. [Rot95b] propose a scheme that requires globally synchronized clocks. Their synchronization mechanism relies on time stamps to determine the different kind of delays each stream experiences, using time stamps. At the receiver different delays are equalized to the maximum delay by buffering. Rothermel enhances this basic mechanism with a *buffer level control* and a *master-slave* concept.

Rangan et al. [Ran93] present a synchronization technique based on feedback. Synchronization is done at the senders side, assuming that the receiver stations send back the number of the currently displayed media-unit. Asynchrony can be discovered by the use of so-called relative time stamps (RTS). Synchrony is restored by deleting or duplicating media-units. Trigger packets are exchanged periodically so to calculate the relative time deviation between sender and receiver. Agarval et al. [Aga94] adopt the idea of Rangan and enhance the scheme by dropping the assumption of bounded jitter.

Our synchronization scheme is inspired by the work of Santoso [San93] intra-stream synchronization and the work of Ishibashi et al. [Ish95] on intra-stream synchronization and inter-stream synchronization. Ishibashi proposes a time-stamp-based synchronization and applies a concept based on delay estimations to perform synchronization in case of unknown delay. Once intra-stream synchronization is established, inter-stream synchronization can be maintained with a certain probability. Corrective actions are taken by skipping/pausing. The scheme assumes no clock drift.

1.4 Context of the Synchronization Problem

The synchronization problem addressed in this paper is motivated by our work on scalable video servers. We have designed and implemented a video server, called **server array**, consisting of n **server nodes** . A video is distributed over all server nodes using a technique called **sub-frame striping:** Each video frame is partitioned into n equal size parts, called **sub-frames**, that are stored on the n different servers. If $F_i = \{c_{i,1}, ..., c_{i,n}\}$ denotes the set of sub-frames for frame f_i, then: $\bigcup_{j=1...n} c_{i,j} = f_i$

The server array with the synchronization mechanisms presented in this paper has been fully implemented as a prototype [Ber95].

During playback, each server node is continuously transmitting its (sub-frames) to the client. The transfer is scheduled so, that all striping blocks that are part of the same frame are completely received by the client at the deadline of the corresponding frame. The client reassembles the frame by combining the sub-frames from all server nodes. An example for $n=3$ with each server sending with a rate of r frames per second is depicted in figure 1.

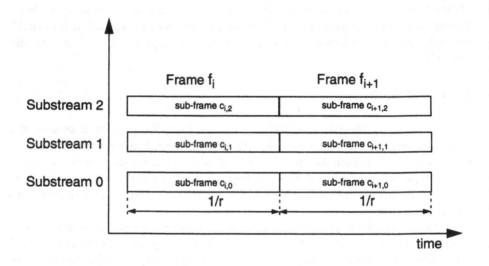

Fig. 1. Temporal Relationship for Sub-Frame Striping.

2 Synchronization Protocol

2.1 Overview

We propose a synchronization scheme for *stored media* that achieves both, suitable intra- and inter-stream synchronization. The scheme is *receiver-based* and does not assume global clocks. To initiate the playback of a stream in a synchronized manner we introduce a **start-up protocol.** Our protocol has been mainly influenced by the ideas of Ishibashi [Ish95] with respect to intra- and inter-stream synchronization. Based on Santoso's work [San93] we derive buffer requirements and playout deadlines to assure inter- and intra-stream synchronization. For *re*-synchronization, we adopt scheme similar to the one described by Koehler and Rothermel [Koe94], [Rot95c].

We derive our synchronization scheme by step-wise refinement: We first develop a solution for the case of zero jitter and then relax this assumption requiring bounded jitter only. We present two models:

Model 1 covers the problem of *different but fixed delays* on the network connections for each substream. We propose a synchronization protocol that compensates for these delays by computing well-defined starting times for each server. The protocol allows to initiate the synchronized playback of a media stream that is composed of several substreams.

Model 2 takes into account the **jitter** experienced by media-units travelling from the source to the destination. Jitter is assumed to be bounded. To smoothen out jitter, elastic buffers are required. Our scheme guarantees a smooth playback of the stream and has very low buffer requirements. Model 2 covers intra-stream synchronization as well as inter-stream synchronization.

For the proposed synchronization scheme, we assume that a client **D** is receiving sub-streams from different servers[3]. Client and servers are interconnected via a network (see figure 2).

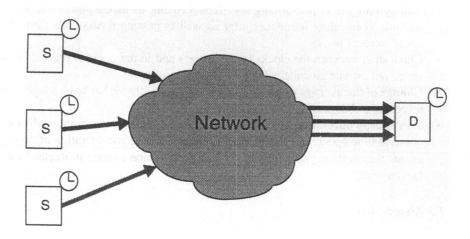

Fig. 2. Distributed Architecture for the Synchronization Scheme.

Each of the servers denoted by S delivers an independent **substream** of **media-units** (sometimes referred to as **frames** in the following). The production rate is driven by the server clock. Arriving media-units are buffered in FIFO queues at the destination D. The playout of the entire **stream**, composed of the substreams, is driven by the destination's clock.

---

[3] It is also possible that a *single* server sends *multiple* substreams to a client. Our model is more general and covers this case too.

While the use of globally synchronized clocks facilitates synchronization, our synchronization scheme does *not* assume the presence of a global time or synchronized clocks.

2.2 Sources of Asynchrony

Several sources of asynchrony exist in the configuration described in the previous section. These are:

- **Different delays**: the assumption of independent network connections imposes different delays. A synchronization scheme has to compensate for these differences in order to display the continuous media stream in a timely order.
  Beside the network delay, media-units experience a delay for the reasons of *packet-size/depacketizing*, the processing through the lower protocol layers, and the buffering on the client site.
  The variation of delay is defined as **jitter**.
- **Network jitter**: asynchronous transfer destroys synchrony. Jitter arises in intermediate nodes for the reason of buffering.
- **End-system jitter**: packetizing and depacketizing of media-units with different size due to encoding introduces jitter as well as passing media-units through the lower protocol layers.
- **Clock drift** between the clocks in the servers and in the client is present because we do not assume global clocks.
- **Change of the average delay**: the synchronization scheme has to be adaptive with respect to a change of the average delay.
- **Server drop outs** due to process scheduling are a realistic assumption when using non-real-time operating systems. At the same time, the consideration of drop outs covers the overload probability of statistical admission control strategies to a certain amount.

2.3 Assumptions

Our synchronization mechanism uses **time stamps**. Each time a media-unit[4] is scheduled by a server, it is stamped with the current local time. This enables the client to calculate statistics, such as for the roundtrip delay, jitter, or inter-arrival times. Moreover, we assume that each media-unit carries a **sequence number** for determining media-unit order.

In contrast to other approaches, buffer requirements or fill levels are always stated in terms of media-units or time, instead of the amount of allocated memory. This consideration is preferred because synchronization is a problem of time and for continuous media, time is represented implicitly by the media-units of a stream. This seems reasonable because media-unit sizes vary due to encoding algorithms like JPEG or MPEG [Koe94]. However, notice that a mapping of media-units to the allocation of bytes

---

[4] We will also use the abbreviation **mu** for media-unit.

must be carried out for implementation purposes. Taking the largest media-unit of a stream as an estimate wastes a lot of memory, especially when using MPEG compression. Sophisticated solutions of mapping are subject of future work. In the following, we will use the term **buffer slot** to denote the buffer space for one media-unit.

Since processing time, e.g. for protocol actions does not concern the actual synchronization problem we will neglect it whereas an implementation has to take it into account. Finally, we assume that control messages are reliably transferred.

Model Parameters.

n	number of server nodes in the server array	
N	number of media-units of a stream	
i, j, υ	media-unit index	$i, j, \upsilon = 0, ..., N\text{-}1$
k	server index	$k = 0, ..., n\text{-}1$
I_j	index set of n subsequent media-units starting with media-unit j	
S_k	denotes server node k providing substream k	
D	denotes the destination or client node	
s_i	initial sending time of media-unit i in server time	[sec]
s_i^c	synchronized sending time of media-unit i in server time	[sec]
a_i	arrival time of media-unit i in client time	[sec]
d_i	roundtrip delay[5] for media-unit i measured at client site	[sec]
d^{max}	maximum roundtrip delay	[sec]
$d^{max,j}$	maximum roundtrip delay for all j element of I_j	[sec]
t_{start}	starting time of the synchronization protocol	[sec]
t_{ref}	reference time for the start-up calculation	[sec]
t_{ref}^j	reference time regarding the set of media-units given by I_j	[sec]
t_i	expected arrival of the media-unit i at the client site	[sec]
δ_{ij}	arrival time difference between media-unit i and j	[sec]

A set of media-units that needs to be played out at the same time is referred to as **synchronization group**.

We assume that media-units are distributed in a *round robin fashion* across the involved server nodes. Hence, we can identify the storage location of a media-unit by its media-unit number[6], i.e.

$$\text{Server } S_{i \bmod n} \text{ stores the media-unit } i. \tag{1}$$

---

[5] The roundtrip delay comprises the delay for a control message that requests a media-unit and the delay for delivering the media-unit

[6] This implies that each substream will send media-units at the *same rate*. An extension of the scheme to different media-unit rate, each one being the integer multiple of a base rate is straight forward.

The leads to the following formulation of the **synchronization problem:**
The client must playout the media-units of all subsets I_j, with $j \bmod n = 0$, at the *same time*.

2.4 Model 1: Start-Up Synchronization

Introduction

Under the assumption of constant delay and zero jitter, we solve the synchronization problem by assuring that the first n media-units, which form a synchronization group, arrive at the *same time* at the client. We therefore need

$$t_i = t_0 \qquad \forall i \in I_0 \tag{2}$$

The major problem addressed by model 1 is the compensation for different delays due to the independence of the different substreams. For instance, the geographical distance from server to client may be different for each server. Thus, starting transmission of media-units in a synchronized order would lead to different arrival times at the client with the result of asynchrony. Usually, this is compensated by delaying media-units at the client site [Esc94]. Depending on the location of the sources large buffers may be required.

In order to avoid buffering to achieve the equalization of different delays, we take advantage of the fact that stored media offers more flexibility: The idea is to initiate playout at the servers such that media-units arrive at the sink site in a synchronous manner. This is performed by shifting the starting times of the servers on the time axis in correlation to the network delay of their connection to the client. The proposed start-up protocol consists of two phases.

- In the first phase, called *evaluation phase*, roundtrip delays for each substream are calculated, while
- In the second phase, called **synchronization phase**, the starting time for each server is calculated and transmitted back to the servers.

The model is based on the assumption of a constant end-to-end delay without any *jitter*. We further exclude *changing network conditions*, *server drop-outs*, and *clock drift*. In such a scenario, synchronization needs to be done once at the beginning and is maintained afterwards automatically.

We need to introduce some more notation to express interdependencies between the parameters of the model. We then give a description of the start-up protocol flow and prove its correctness. We close the section with an example for the protocol.

The starting time t_{start} of the protocol equals the beginning of the first phase. Without loss of generality let

$$t_{start} = 0 \tag{3}$$

To begin with, we regard the first n media-units of a stream given by I_0 that are distributed across the n servers. The roundtrip delay d_i for the media-unit i is given by the difference between its arrival time a_i and the starting time of the synchronization protocol

$$d_i = a_i - t_{start} \quad \forall i, j \in I_0 \tag{4}$$

Equation (5) computes the maximum of the roundtrip delay for all n substreams

$$d^{max} = max\{d_i | i \in I_0\} \tag{5}$$

The second phase of the protocol begins at time t_{ref}, which is determined by the last of the first n media-units that arrives.

$$t_{ref} = max\{a_i | i \in I_0\} \tag{6}$$

The difference between the arrival times of arbitrary media-units i and j is needed to calculate the starting times of the servers. We define the difference as follows.

$$\delta_{ij} = a_i - a_j \quad \forall i, j \tag{7}$$

Start-Up Protocol

The synchronization protocol for starting playback on the server sites is launched after all involved parties are ready for playback. It can be divided into two phases: *evaluation phase* and *synchronization phase*. The goal of the first phase is to compute the roundtrip delays $d_i \ \forall i \in I_0$ for each connection, while the second phase calculates the starting times and propagates them back to the servers. During start-up, the client sends two different kinds of control messages to the servers:

- *Eval_Request(i)*: Client D requests media-unit i from Server S_i, $\forall i \in I_0$.
- *Sync_Request(i, s_i^c)*: Client D transmits the starting time s_i^c to server S_i.

(a) Evaluation Phase

- At local time t_{start}, client D sends an *Eval_Request(i)* to Server S_i, $\forall i \in I_0$.
- Server S_i receives the *Eval_Request(i)* at local time s_i, $\forall i \in I_0$.
- Server S_i sends media-unit i time-stamped with s_i immediately back to client D, $\forall i \in I_0$.
- At local time a_i, client D receives media-unit i from Server S_i, $\forall i \in I_0$.
- At local time t_{ref}, client D has received the last media-unit.
  The roundtrip delay $d_i = a_i - t_{start} \ \forall i \in I_0$ and
  the relative distance between media-unit arrivals $\delta_{ij} = a_i - a_j \ \forall i, j \in I_0$ are computed.

(b) Synchronization Phase

- At local time t_{ref}, client D computes t_0 as $t_0 = max\{t_{ref} + d_i \mid i \in I_0\}$,
  the maximum round trip time as $d^{max} = max\{d_i \mid i \in I_0\}$,
  the index v that determines t_0 as $v = \{j \in I_0 \mid t_{ref} + d_j = t_0\}$, and
  the delay differences as $\delta_{vi} = a_v - a_i$, $\forall i \in I_0$
- With these results the starting time of Server S_i is calculated in server time
  $s_i^c = s_i + d^{max} + \delta_{vi}$, $\forall i \in I_0$.
- Client D sends a $Sync\_Request(i, s_i^c)$ to server S_i, $\forall i \in I_0$.
- At local time $s_i + d_i + (t_{ref} - a_i)$ server S_i receives the $Sync\_Request(i, s_i^c)$,
  $\forall i \in I_0$.
- At local time s_i^c, server S_i starts scheduling of the substream by sending media-
  unit i, $\forall i \in I_0$.
- At local time t_i, client D receives media-unit i, $\forall i \in I_0$.

At any time, only one synchronization group of n media-units must be buffered at the client; after the complete reception the media-units are played out immediately. To show the correctness of our mechanism we discuss the

- Calculation of t_0
- Calculation of s_i^c

(a) Calculation of the Earliest Possible Playout Time t_0 for the First Media-unit

We need to choose t_0 such that all media-units $i \in I_0$ can be delivered and played out in time, i.e they will arrive at their deadline t_i given by (2). It is obvious that media-unit $i \in I_0$ delivered by server S_i can not be expected earlier than $t_{ref} + d_i$. Hence, the substream with the largest delay determines t_0.

Theorem 1:   Let $t_0 = max\{t_{ref} + d_i \mid i \in I_0\}$.
     Then all media-units can be delivered and played out in time.
Proof: Since the earliest possible arrival time for media-unit $i \in I_0$ is $t_{ref} + d_i$ we
need to show that $t_i \geq t_{ref} + d_i$ $\forall i \in I_0$.
Let $t_0 = max\{t_{ref} + d_i \mid i \in I_0\}$
$\Rightarrow t_0 \geq t_{ref} + d_i$ $\forall i \in I_0$
(2) $\Rightarrow t_i = t_0 \geq t_{ref} + d_i$ $\forall i \in I_0$
$\Rightarrow t_i \geq t_{ref} + d_i$ $\forall i \in I_0$
$\Rightarrow t_0$ does not violate the arrival times of other substreams
To show that t_0 is minimal, we assume that $\exists \; \tilde{t}_0 < t_0$
$\Rightarrow \exists \; i_0 \in I_0$ with $\tilde{t}_0 < t_{ref} + d_{i_0}$
(2) $\Rightarrow$ $\tilde{t}_0 = t_{i_0} < t_{ref} + d_{i_0}$
$\Rightarrow$ contradiction to the earliest possible arrival time. ∎
     For the calculation of the future starting times s_i^c, $\forall i \in I_0$, we define the substream v determining t_0 as follows:

$$v = \{j \in I_0 | t_{ref} + d_j = t_0\} \tag{8}$$

(b) Calculation of the Synchronized Sending Time s_i^c of Media-unit i for Server S_i

Substream υ can be considered *critical* since it determines the starting times of all other initial substreams. It is therefore considered as a reference point to which all other substreams are adjusted. Clearly, the future starting time s_i^c of substream i is composed of the initial starting time s_i plus the maximum roundtrip delay d^{max}. This sum is corrected by the relative arrival time distance $\delta_{\upsilon i}$ between media-unit i and media-unit υ. This gives the starting time that provides a simultaneous arrival of the media-units of substream i and these of substream υ. The calculation based on (8), (7), (4) is stated in the following theorem.

Theorem 2: Let $s_i^c = s_i + d^{max} + \delta_{\upsilon i}, \ \forall \ i \in I_0$.
     Then media-unit $i \in I_0$ will arrive at client time t_i.
Proof: For each $i \in I_0$: At client time t_{ref}, s_i^c is sent back to server S_i which receives it at server time $s_i + d^{max}$ (see figure 3). If S_i sent media-unit i immediately back to D, it would arrive at client time $t_{ref} + d_i$. The term $s_i + d^{max}$ is corrected by $\delta_{\upsilon i}$.
Media-unit i will arrive at D at client time
$t_{ref} + d_i + \delta_{\upsilon i}$
$= t_{ref} + (a_i - t_{start}) + (a_\upsilon - a_i)$
$(3) = t_{ref} + a_\upsilon$
$= t_{ref} + d_\upsilon$
(theorem 1) $= t_0$
$(2) = t_i$ ∎

One can easily imagine situations where synchronization is needed not only at the beginning of a stream. A typical example is the VCR function *pause*. After having paused it becomes necessary to resynchronize again, starting with the media-unit subsequent to the last one displayed. The described scheme can be generalized to any series of subsequent media-units requested by the client.

Example of the Start-Up Protocol

The following example in figure 3 illustrates model 1. We assume $n = 3$, i.e. three servers, with one substream each. The calculated starting values are shown in table 1.

For each server and for the client D a time axis is provided. Arrows indicate control messages or media-units, respectively, that are transferred between client and servers.

With $t_0 = max\{t_{ref} + d_i \mid i \in I_0\} = max\{23, 18, 24\} = 24$ we get $\upsilon = 2$.

Substream 2 experiences the longest roundtrip delay d^{max} and determines therefore t_{ref}. Substream 2 is critical because it cannot be started earlier than $s_2 + 12$. As indicated on the time axis for server 0, substream 0 could be started earlier but is delayed to arrive at the same time as substream 2.

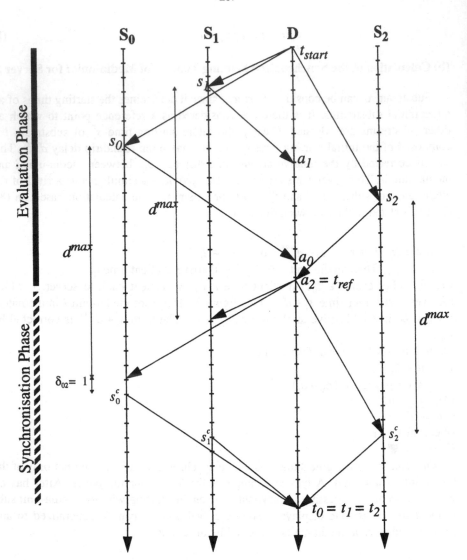

Fig. 3. Example of the Start-Up Synchronization Protocol Flow.

Server	a_i	d_i	t_{ref}	δ_{2i}	s_i^c
S_0	11	11	12	1	$s_0 + 13$
S_1	6	6	12	6	$s_1 + 18$
S_2	12	12	12	0	$s_2 + 12$

Table 1. Example for the Start-Up Calculations.

2.5 Model 2: Intra- and Inter-Stream Synchronization

Introduction

Model 1 shows how to cope with different delays for each substream. However, synchronization is performed under the assumption that jitter does not exist. Model 2 loosens this assumption and takes into account *end-system jitter* and *network jitter*. For our considerations, we regard the accumulated value of all sources of jitter described in section . Furthermore, we assume that the jitter is bounded.

When subject to jitter, media-units will not arrive in a synchronized manner although they have been sent in a correct timely order. The temporal relationship within one substream is destroyed and time gaps between arriving media-units vary according to the occurred jitter. Thus, an isochronous playback cannot be achieved if arriving media-units of a substream would be played out immediately. Furthermore, jitter may distort the relationship between media-units of a synchronization group. Hence, *intra-stream synchronization* as well as *inter-stream synchronization* is disturbed. To smoothen out the effects of jitter, media-units have to be delayed at the sink such that a continuous playback can be guaranteed. Consequently *playout buffers* corresponding to the amount of jitter are required.

The main point addressed by model 2 is intra- and interstream synchronization and the calculation of the required buffer space. First, we regard the synchronization of a single substream. Based on a rule of Santoso [San93] we formulate a theorem that states a well defined playout time for a substream such that intra-stream synchronization can be guaranteed. Using this so-called *playout deadline* we derive the required buffer space. Smooth playout cannot be guaranteed if starting before playout deadline. Starting at a later time would require more buffer space.

Afterwards, we will extend our considerations to the synchronization of multiple substreams. The main idea in order to achieve inter-stream synchronization is to maintain intra-stream synchronization for each substream [Ish95]. Each one of the substreams is assumed to have a different jitter bound. In this case, buffer reservation according to a single substream is not sufficient anymore as inter-stream synchronization will be disturbed for the reason of differences in the jitter bounds. Additional buffering is required to compensate for this. Furthermore, the playout deadline is modified with respect to multiple substreams.

Finally, we examine the effects of the start-up protocol (model 1) on buffer requirements in the case of jitter. The application of model 1 to initiate playback of the servers in a synchronized manner can introduce an error for the reason of jitter. We give a worst case estimate for the error and additional buffer requirements are computed accordingly.

We begin with an extension of the model parameters used so far.

Model Parameters

k	substream or server index,	$k = 0, \dots, n\text{-}1$
r	requested display rate of each substream at client site	[mu/sec]

d_k^{max}	maximum delay for substream k	[sec]
d_k^{min}	minimum delay for substream k	[sec]
$\bar{d}_k$	average delay for substream k	[sec]
Δ_k	jitter for substream k	[sec]
Δ^{max}	maximum jitter of all substreams	[sec]
Δ_k^+	maximum upper deviation from $\bar{d}_k$ due to jitter for substream k	[sec]
Δ_k^-	maximum lower deviation from $\bar{d}_k$ due to jitter for substream k	[sec]
Δ^{max+}	maximum upper deviation of all substreams	[sec]
b_k	buffer requirement for substream k on sink site	[mu]
b_k^S	buffer requirement for substream k on sink site with shifting	[mu]
b_k^M	buffer requirement for substream k on sink site with max. jitter	[mu]
B	total buffer requirement for a synchronization group	[mu]
B^S	total buffer requirement for a synchronization groupwith shifting	[mu]
B^M	total buffer requirement for a synchronization group with max. jitter	[mu]

Throughout this paper we assume *bounded* jitter and we use the definition of jitter given by Rangan et al. [Ran92] who define jitter as the difference between the maximum delay and the minimum delay[7].

$$\Delta_k = d_k^{max} - d_k^{min} \quad \forall k \tag{9}$$

$$\Delta^{max} = max\{\Delta_k | k \in \{0...n-1\}\} \tag{10}$$

In addition to this, we need a jitter bounds defined as the deviation from the average delay $\bar{d}_k$. Jitter is in general not distributed symmetrically. Thus, Δ_k^+ and Δ_k^- must not be equal. For further considerations, we assume interdependencies as follows.

$$\Delta_k = \Delta_k^+ + \Delta_k^- \quad \forall k \tag{11}$$

$$d_k^{max} = \bar{d}_k + \Delta_k^+ \quad \forall k \tag{12}$$

$$d_k^{min} = \bar{d}_k - \Delta_k^- \quad \forall k \tag{13}$$

$$\Delta^{max+} = max\{\Delta_k^+ | k \in \{0...n-1\}\} \tag{14}$$

Synchronized Playout for a Single Substream

To guarantee the timely presentation of a single stream subject to jitter, it is necessary to buffer arriving media-units at the sink to compensate the jitter. The buffer is emptied at a constant rate for displaying the media-units.

---

[7] Jitter is often defined as the *variation* of network delay.

Santoso [San93] has already shown that the temporal relationship within one continuous media stream can be preserved by delaying the output of the first media-unit for $d_k^{max} - d_k^{min}$ seconds. Based on this theorem, both the playout deadline and the buffer requirements are be derived. The deadline given by Santoso (case a) can be lowered in some situations (case b).

Theorem 3:   Smooth playout for a substream k can be guaranteed in case of bounded jitter whenever *either* one of the following two starting conditions holds true.
(a) $d_k^{max} - d_k^{min} = \Delta_k$ seconds elapsed after the arrival of the first media-unit, or
(b) the $(\lceil \Delta_k \cdot r \rceil + 1)$-*th* media-unit has arrived.

Proof: A proof for (a) can be found in [San93]. Condition (b) improves (a) in some cases, i.e. playout can start earlier without violating timeliness. Such a situation is shown in figure 4: the first media-unit experiences the maximum delay, subsequent media-units arrive in a burst (marked gray in figure (4)) such that after the arrival of the $(\lceil \Delta_k \cdot r \rceil + 1)$-*th* media-unit the elapsed time is less than $d_k^{max} - d_k^{min}$. The average delay of media-units is denoted by dotted lines.

Assuming that the $(\lceil \Delta_k \cdot r \rceil + 1)$-*th* media-unit just has arrived, we start the playout of the buffered media-units immediately. A number of $\lceil \Delta_k \cdot r \rceil + 1$ media-units is at least sufficient for a presentation period of $(\lceil \Delta_k \cdot r \rceil + 1) \cdot r^{-1} \geq \Delta_k + r^{-1}$ seconds. In the worst case, the $(\lceil \Delta_k \cdot r \rceil + 1)$-*th* media-unit experiences its minimum delay and the subsequent media-unit its maximum delay. Then the maximum period without any arrival is given by is $\Delta_k^- + r^{-1} + \Delta_k^+ = \Delta_k + r^{-1}$ seconds. $(\lceil \Delta_k \cdot r \rceil + 1) \cdot r^{-1}$ gives an upper bound for $\Delta_k + r^{-1}$. Consequently, the next media-unit arrives just in time. Following media-units will not arrive later because the last one has already experienced the largest delay. ∎

Theorem 4 enables us to calculate the required minimum buffer space for the synchronization of a single substream.

Theorem 4:   To guarantee intra-stream synchronization for a single substream by applying theorem 3, a minimum buffer space of $\lceil 2\Delta_k \cdot r \rceil$ media-units is required.
For a proof see [Gey95].

Synchronized Playout for Multiple Substreams

The basic idea of the synchronization scheme in model 2 is to achieve inter-stream synchronization between multiple substreams by intra-stream synchronization. Once the latter has been established by satisfying theorem 3 and 4 for each substream, inter-stream synchronization is attained [Ish95], [San93]. This holds true if each substream experiences the *same jitter*. In the following, we consider and examine the impact on buffer requirements for different jitter bounds for each substream . This reflects the

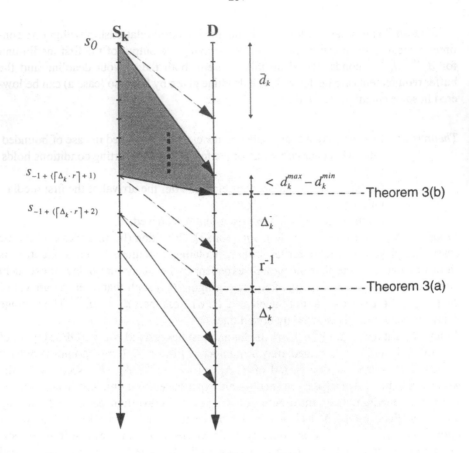

Fig. 4. Worst Case Scenario for a Single Substream.

case that the paths from sources to the destination are independent. We assume that media-units experience an average delay $\bar{d}$ on all substream connections. The following proofs can also carried out with different delays.

We present two methods to compute the buffer requirements for multiple substreams.

- The first approach estimates the jitter for all substreams with the maximum jitter value.
- The second strategy attempts to refine this coarse-grain estimation by shifting the starting times of each substream in correlation to their jitter values in order to save buffer space.

(a) Maximum Jitter Strategy

Obviously, playout can only start if theorem 3 is satisfied for *all* substreams. Thus, the playout deadline for a stream given by a *synchronization group* is defined by the latest substream that satisfies theorem 3. The situation is complicated by different jitter bounds for the corresponding substreams which lead to different playout deadlines and buffer requirements. We must avoid a situation where substreams with large jitter bounds still wait for their deadlines while the buffer of other substreams with small jitter bounds already overflows. To cope with this problem in a straight forward manner, Ishibashi et al. [Ish95] propose to allocate the buffer according to the substream with the largest jitter bound. Hence, the buffer requirement b_k^M for each substream of the group and B^M for the complete group are given as follows.

$$b_k^M = \left\lceil 2\Delta^{max} \cdot r \right\rceil \tag{15}$$

$$B^M = \sum_{k=0}^{n-1} b_k^M = n \cdot \left\lceil 2\Delta^{max} \cdot r \right\rceil \tag{16}$$

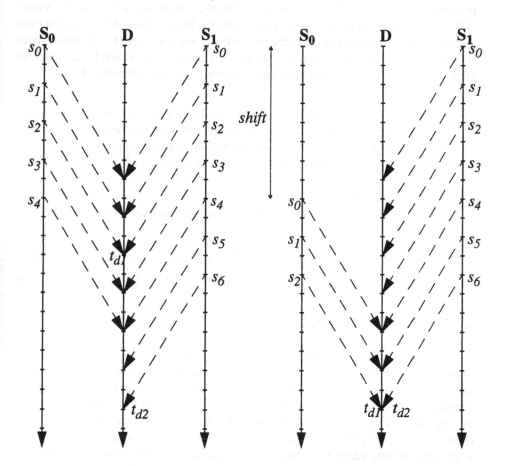

Fig. 5. Multiple Substreams without and with Shifting.

(b) Shifting Strategy

Depending on the differences in the jitter values for the substreams, the maximum jitter strategy might lead to a buffer waste. A more sophisticated way to handle this problem is to synchronize the different substreams such that they reach their playout deadline on average *at the same time*. This is done by shifting the starting points of all substreams according to the deadline of the substream, with the largest jitter bound. Figure 5 depicts such a scenario for two sources[8] where $\bar{d} = 3.5$, $\Delta_0 = 2$ and $\Delta_1 = 6$.

With theorem 4 we get buffer requirements of four media-units for substream 1 and twelve media-units for substream 2. Substream 1 reaches its playout deadline on average at t_{d1} and substream 2 at t_{d2}. Without shifting a buffer overflow occurs when receiving the 5th media-unit of substream 1 while substream 2 still has to wait two time units until playout can commence. By shifting, both substreams arrive at the same time. The amount of the forward shift can be easily derived from theorem 3. The k-th substream has to be shifted forward on time axis with the difference of its jitter to the maximum jitter, i.e. $\Delta^{max} - \Delta_k$ seconds. Clearly, substream k has to be started $\Delta^{max} - \Delta_k$ seconds later than the substream with the highest jitter. When applying that shift one might conclude that no further buffering is needed except for the buffer given by theorem 4. In fact, there exists a worst case that requires additional buffer space for each substream. The amount of additional buffering is stated in theorem 5.

Theorem 5: Applying a shift of $\Delta^{max} - \Delta_k$ to the *k-th* substream, $k = 0, \dots , n\text{-}1$, and having bounded jitter for each substream, inter-stream synchronization for multiple dependent substreams can be guaranteed if in addition to the buffer requirement of theorem 4, another $\lceil (\Delta^{max+} - \Delta_k^+) \cdot r \rceil$ buffer slots are allocated.

For a proof see [Gey95].

With the above theorems, the total buffer requirements can be computed as follows.

$$b_k^S = \left\lceil (2 \cdot \Delta_k + \Delta^{max+} - \Delta_k^+) \cdot r \right\rceil \tag{17}$$

$$B^S = \sum_{k=0}^{n-1} b_k^S = \sum_{k=0}^{n-1} \left\lceil (2 \cdot \Delta_k + \Delta^{max+} - \Delta_k^+) \cdot r \right\rceil \tag{18}$$

2.6 Start-up Protocol Influence

Until now, we have assumed that substreams are synchronized with respect to their average delay. Model 1 is based on the assumption of zero jitter. When we use the scheme in the case of bounded jitter, cannot guarantee the synchronization of the substreams with respect to their average delay since it is based on the roundtrip delay values *experienced* by the first n media-units. If this delay corresponds to the average delay, the start-up protocol works correctly. However, the observed delay can be altered due to jitter, hence the calculation introduces an error that must be considered.

The start-up protocol computation is based on a roundtrip delay for a request packet and one or several packets carrying a media-unit. However, the transmission of the request packet from sink to source and the sending of the media-unit back to the client are subject to jitter. Since the request message is a small packet made up of sev-

---

[8] In contrast to the definitions for model 1, each one of the depicted substreams delivers equal media-unit numbers.

eral bytes the following considerations we will neglect the jitter experienced by the request packet, supposing that the jitter bounds for the buffer calculations stated in theorem 4 and 5 have been chosen sufficiently large.

2.7 Exact Buffer Requirements

Model 2 gives us a framework to compute buffer requirements for multiple substreams with different jitter bounds to attain inter-stream synchronization by maintaining intra-stream synchronization. Buffer requirements are given by theorem 4 and 5. The error introduced by the start-up protocol is corrected by theorem 6. Throughout all theorems, we expressed the time we need to buffer in terms of media-units. The required buffer space can be optimized by summing up the time to buffer given by theorem 4 and 5 and by transforming the resulting sum into buffer slots. We can summarize the overall buffer requirements b_k for a substream k and B for a synchronization group consisting of n substreams as follows.

$$b_k = \left\lceil \left(2\Delta_k + (\Delta^{max+} - \Delta_k^+) + \right. \right. \tag{19}$$

$$\left. \left. max\{\Delta_m + \Delta_k^+ - \Delta^{max+} \mid m \neq k \wedge m = 0...n-1\} \right) \cdot r \right\rceil$$

$$B = \sum_{k=1}^{n} b_k =$$

$$\sum_{k=1}^{n} \left\lceil \left(2\Delta_k + \Delta^{max+} - \Delta_k^+ + max\{\Delta_m + \Delta_k^+ - \Delta^{max+} \mid m \neq k \wedge m = 0...n-1\} \right) \cdot r \right\rceil \tag{20}$$

3 Conclusion

We have presented a scheme for intra- and inter-stream synchronization of stored multimedia streams. The only assumption we make is that jitter is bounded, which is typically true in todays networks. Having presented a base-version of the synchronization scheme, we make enhancements such as shifting the start-up times in order to reduce the buffer requirements. At the end, we derived exact bounds for the buffer requirements.

Acknowledgment

The work described in this paper was supported by the Siemens Nixdorf AG, Munich.

4 References

[Aga94] N. Agarwal and S. Son. "Synchronization of Distributed Multimedia Data in an Application-specific Manner." In *2nd ACM International Conference on Multimedia*, pages 141–148, San Francisco, USA, October 1994.

[Ber95]   C. Bernhardt and E. Biersack. "The Server Array: A Novel Architecture for a Scalable Video Server." In *Proceedings of the Distributed Multimedia Conference*, pages 63–72, Stanford, USA, August 1995.

[Eff93]   W. Effelsberg, T. Meyer, and R. Steinmetz. "A Taxonomy on Multimedia-Synchronization." In *Proceedings of the Fourth Workshop on Future Trends of Distributed Computing Systems, Lisbon, Portugal, Sep. 1993*, pages 97–103. Eyrolles, 1993.

[Esc94]   J. Escobar, C. Patridge, and D. Deutsch. "Flow Synchronization Protocol." In *ACM Transactions on Networking*, volume 2, pages 111–121. IEEE, April 1994.

[Gey95]   W. Geyer. "Stream Synchronisation in a Scalable Video Server Array." Master's thesis, Institut Eurecom, Sophia Antipolis, France, September 1995.

[Ish95]   Y. Ishibashi and S. Tasaka. "A Synchronization Mechanism for Continuous Media in Multimedia Communications." In *IEEE Infocom'95*, volume 3, pages 1010–1019, Boston, Massachusetts, April 1995.

[Koe94]   D. Koehler and H. Mueller. "Multimedia Playout Synchronization Using Buffer Level Control." In *2nd International Workshop on Advanced Teleservices and High-Speed Communication Architectures*, pages 165–180, Heidelberg, Germany, September 1994.

[Ran92]   P. V. Rangan, H. M. Vin, and S. Ramanathan. "Designing an On-Demand Multimedia Service." *IEEE Communications Magazine*, 30(7):56–65, July 1992.

[Ran93]   P. Rangan, S. Ramanathan, H. M. Vin, and T. Kaeppner. "Techniques for Multimedia Synchronization in Network File Systems." *Computer Communications*, 16(3):168–176, March 1993.

[Rot95b]   K. Rothermel and T. Helbig. "An Adaptive Stream Synchronization Protocol." In *5th International Workshop on Network and Operating System Support for Digital Audio and Video*, Durham, New Hampshire, USA, April 1995.

[Rot95c]   K. Rothermel, T. Helbig, and S. Noureddine. "Activation Set: An Abstraction for Accessing Periodic Data Streams." In *Multimedia Computing and Networking*, volume 2417, San Jose, California, February 1995. IS&T/SPIE.

[San93]   H. Santoso, L. Dairaine, S. Fdida, and E. Horlait. "Preserving Temporal Signature: A Way to Convey Time Constrained Flows." In *IEEE Globecom*, pages 872 – 876, December 1993.

[Ste93a]   R. Steinmetz. *Multimedia-Technologie*. Springer Verlag, Heidelberg, Germany, 1993.

An Architecture for a
Distributed Stream Synchronization Service

Tobias Helbig, Kurt Rothermel

University of Stuttgart
Institute of Parallel and Distributed High-Performance Systems (IPVR)

Abstract: A stream synchronization service provides the basis for the efficient control and synchronization of continuous, time-dependent data streams in distributed environments. Together with resource management and application configuration, it is one of the core multimedia system services. The stream synchronization service may be realized by a three layer architecture consisting of an interface layer enabling distributed clients to access stream control interfaces, of the control and synchronization layer implementing alternative stream synchronization protocols to coordinate the flow of data units, and of the stream layer where data units of time-dependent streams are transferred and processed.

The proposed architecture supports the control of time-dependent data streams having arbitrarily distributed sources and sinks by clients which may be distributed themselves. The incorporation of alternative synchronization protocols offers the flexibility required to satisfy the wide range of requirements to control and synchronize data streams.

Keywords: Multimedia system services, stream control and synchronization, configurable implementation architecture, multi-threading, callback functions

1   Introduction

The efficient development and control of distributed applications is supported by middleware system services. They use basic functions provided by general purpose communication and operating systems, which they extend by special purpose functions and application-oriented service interfaces. A number of standardized middleware platforms for distributed applications are on the market, such as ODP [ISO91], OSF DCE [OSF91], and OMG [OMG91]. Within the frameworks of these platforms, multimedia system services are considered only slowly. However, the characteristics of distributed multimedia applications demand a sophisticated system support. Due to time-dependent data streams, large data quantities and challenging quality of service requirements, establishing and controlling distributed multimedia applications is difficult.

Several approaches have been made to provide appropriate system support for multimedia applications. For example, abstractions were proposed to extend the ANSA architecture by multimedia capabilities [CBDW92], to facilitate interoperability among stream handling devices of different vendors [IMA93], or to provide a development environment targeted at distributed multimedia applications (*CINEMA* [RBH94]).

The *CINEMA* environment (Configurable Integrated Multimedia Architecture) implements services to configure distributed processing topologies, to reserve resources and negotiate the quality of service of applications. Moreover, a stream synchronization service supports the control and synchronization of the flow of data units in end-to-end processing topologies. It frees a client from the ever recurring task of implementing flow control and synchronization algorithms as part of the development process of each multimedia application. By using the middleware service for stream synchronization, time-dependent data streams can easily be integrated into various applications, such as CSCW applications or tools to present multimedia documents. The focus of this paper is on the implementation architecture of *CINEMA*'s synchronization service.

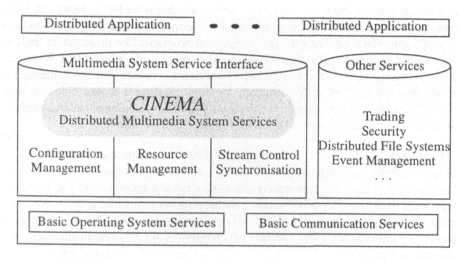

Fig. 1. System Services for Distributed Multimedia Applications

The architecture is open to integrate alternative synchronization protocols. The protocol implementations may be tailored to the specific characteristics of data streams and applications. An extensible architecture was chosen due to the fact that meeting the requirements of stream control and synchronization by a single, efficient protocol does not seem to be feasible. There is a wide range of requirements with regard to the quality of service and the structure of processing topologies (e.g., linear pipelines, multicast, mixing scenarios). Depending on the application scenario, sources and sinks of streams may be distributed in different ways. For example, a video may be played out from a CD-ROM on a stand-alone machine, a multimedia document may be retrieved from remote servers and presented locally, or there may be distributed output locations in a CSCW scenario. Further, media streams differ in their characteristics, e.g., the contents of stored streams can be played out forward or backward, whereas live streams only advance forward. In general, designing specialized protocols allows to use mechanisms optimally suited for specific requirements. This leads to shorter development times, better quality and lower run-time costs. The synchronization service architecture provides the framework to integrate and reuse these alternative protocol implementations.

In literature, several protocols to synchronize data streams may be found, such as the Flow Synchronization Protocol [EPD94], the Lancaster Orchestration Service [CCGH92], and the Adaptive Synchronization Protocol [RoHe95]. In some way, each approach defines an entity to coordinate the group of streams to be synchronized and an entity to control a stream's end-point. We term the former entity *controller*, the latter *agent*. By generalizing the abstractions, we make them the base concepts within our architecture. The key to "plug-in" alternative synchronisation protocols into the architecture is to define a uniform interface for accessing controllers and to enable agents to control the data flow as well as the stream end-points.

Although such an extensible architecture is a major step towards the implementation of a stream control and synchronization service, another issue has to be solved. Different applications have different requirements in terms of stream control. A low-level controller interface may be sufficient for system programs like presentation tools for multimedia documents. However, other applications (e.g., distributed CSCW applications) may need high-level abstractions for expressing synchronization relationships on application level as well as for achieving location transparent access to control interfaces. Hence, the synchronization service should be open to implement alternative high-level service interfaces on top of the uniform controller interface.

To meet the requirements of stream synchronization in distributed environments, we propose a three layer synchronization service architecture consisting of an interface layer providing high-level stream control abstractions, a control and synchronization layer implementing alternative stream synchronization protocols, and a stream layer where data units are transferred and stream handlers are activated. The core of the architecture is a uniform controller interface which provides for plugging in alternative synchronization protocols and is the base for alternative high-level abstractions.

The paper is structured as follows. In Section 2, we introduce the abstractions of the multimedia system service interface of *CINEMA*. Section 3 gives an overview of the base concepts of the architecture's layers and describes the so-called clock hierarchies as an example of high-level stream control abstractions. Section 4 introduces the uniform controller interface as well as the integration of controllers and agents into the *CINEMA* system. In Section 5, the use of callback function is shown as a way to control the periodic processing of data units by agents. The paper concludes with a short summary.

2 Abstractions of a Multimedia System Services Interface

In the following, we describe the main abstractions of the multimedia system services interface of *CINEMA*. For more details see [RBH94] and [RoHe96].

Time-dependent data streams consist of a sequence of data units. Each data unit is associated with a timestamp. The data units are processed by *components* which implement a specific stream handling function, e.g., to create, transform, or play-out data units. Components produce data units by writing to *ports*, respectively consume data units by reading from ports. Ports separate processing and transmission functions in multimedia systems. A *client* configures multimedia applications by defining *links* between input and output ports of components, hence establishing arbitrarily structured data flow graphs. Links may be realized locally by inter-process communication mechanisms or remotely by transport connections.

The abstractions of media clocks and clock hierarchies define the abstractions of the high-level service interface to control and synchronize the flow of data units. The temporal properties of an end-to-end data stream are defined by a *media clock*. A media clock is associated with a component where it defines the temporal properties of the stream that is processed. Additionally, it is the control interface to start and stop the flow of data units. By accessing a media clock associated with a sink component, not only the sink component is controlled, but all components contributing to the data stream. Accessing a single interface allows to control end-to-end data streams.

A *clock hierarchy* is the abstraction for grouping media streams, controlling groups of streams, and for specifying stream synchronization relationships. An operation called at a media clock is propagated in a root-to-leaf direction through the clock's subhierarchy and is performed at every clock reached. The relationships among clocks are expressed by the attributes of edges between them. Essential attributes of edges are the *reference point attribute* that relates media times to each other to describe synchronization relationships and the *skew attribute* to define the tolerance in the specified synchronization relationship. Additionally, we distinguish between *synchronization* and *control relationships*. While a synchronization relationship enforces data streams to be played out synchronously, the control relationship allows for a common control of streams without synchronizing them. A clock hierarchy may consist of multiple subhierarchies whose clocks are linked by synchronization relationships. Each of these subhierarchies may be controlled by a separate synchronization protocol. For further details about clock hierarchies, we refer to [RoHe96].

3 Architecture of the Stream Synchronization Service

The architecture of the synchronization service in the CINEMA platform consists of the Interface Layer, the Control and Synchronization Layer, and the Stream Layer.

The *Interface Layer* implements high-level, application-oriented interfaces to access the basic functions of the synchronization service. The interfaces are tailored to the needs of applications, e.g., they may support remote access of distributed clients to shared interface objects. Within the CINEMA system, the abstractions of media clocks and clock hierarchies are implemented by the Interface Layer's *Clock Management Module*. It provides an application programming interface to create, manage and access clock hierarchies in distributed environments. The Clock Management Module maps all operations of the application-oriented interface to the control interfaces of synchronization protocols, i.e., to the interfaces of controllers.

Clock hierarchies may be distributed among multiple end-systems of a computer network. The media clocks are objects in the sense of the object-oriented programming paradigm. They are identified by a globally unique name. Proxy objects [Shap86] offer the clients location transparent access to remote clocks. To control the flow of data units, a client calls clock operations at its local proxy objects. The proxy objects transparently forward the operations to local or remote instances of clock objects. Multiple clients may access the same clock instance when they cooperatively control common parts of applications. Concurrent access to shared clock objects has to be synchronized among the clients.

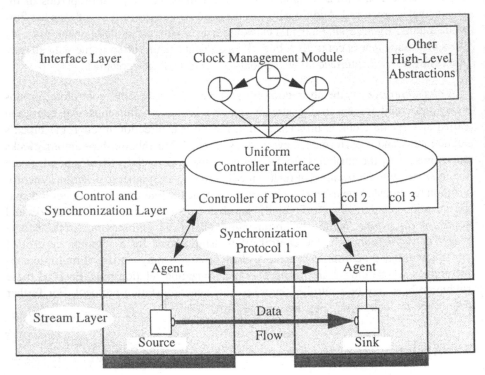

Fig. 2. Logical Structure of the Stream Synchronization Service

In a two-phase initialization protocol, the Clock Management Module analyzes clock hierarchies to assign media clocks to the controllers of synchronization protocols and to extract groups of streams to be synchronized. It propagates clock operations, such as starting or stopping of clocks, from a particular clock to all its descendents and forwards the resulting calls to synchronization protocols. Issuing a single clock operation may affect multiple independent synchronization protocols. For a detailed description of the implementation of distributed clock hierarchies, we refer to [RoHe96]. The focus of the remaining paper is on the integration of alternative synchronization protocols into a uniform architecture.

The *Control and Synchronization Layer* (CS-Layer) implements the protocols to control and synchronize the flow of data units. The major concepts are stream groups, controllers and agents. All data streams whose output is synchronized are grouped in a stream group. Each stream group is associated with a controller which is responsible for coordinating and synchronizing the streams of the group. On each end-system, exactly one controller is instantiated for each synchronization protocol. Multiple controllers for different synchronization protocols may coexist on a single end-system.

A controller is an object in the sense of the object-oriented programming paradigm. Each controller is accessed by a uniform controller interface which defines the basic set of methods of the controller object. The controller interface offers operations to create and delete stream groups as well as to add streams to or remove streams from stream groups. Sets of streams may be preloaded, started and stopped, their speed and play-back direction may be altered. Control operations may be used for individual streams as well as for whole groups.

Internally, the controller interacts with agents. Their pattern of communication is given by the synchronization protocol they implement. While the controller handles streams and groups of streams, the agents control the timing of data transfers and the data processing of individual components. Hence, agents are located on the same end-system as the end-points of streams. A detailed description of the integration of different synchronization protocols into the *CINEMA* system is given in Section 4.

The *Stream Layer* provides the basic mechanisms for transferring and processing the data units of time-dependent data streams including mechanisms for resource reservation, real-time scheduling, communication and buffer management. The processing of data units is performed by the stream handling code of components which is bound to threads of the end-system's operating system. Hence, the proposed architecture is a multi-threaded architecture. The concept chosen to control the timing of threads are well-defined callback-functions. They enable the agents to monitor buffer levels, control the processing by computing scheduling times and to release data units for processing by components. While the usage of callback functions is discussed in Section 5, issues of the interaction with a rate monotonic scheduling algorithm are described in [HNR95].

4 Control and Synchronization Layer

The *CINEMA* environment consists of a set of daemons. On each node of the distributed system, a single *CINEMA* daemon is running. Within each *CINEMA* daemon, a single controller is instantiated for each synchronization protocol. Controller of alternative synchronization protocols coexist without interacting with each other. They are addressed by an unique protocol identifier. A controller handler uses the protocol identifier to direct calls to the respective controller.

A controller creates and initializes agents to control the end-points of streams. The agents are located within the *CINEMA* daemon on the same end-system as the component they control. For each protocol, an agent handler holds the list of the protocol's agents.

Multiple agents coexist in a *CINEMA* daemon. They may be created by controllers implementing different protocols as well as by controllers implementing the same protocol but are located on different end-systems.

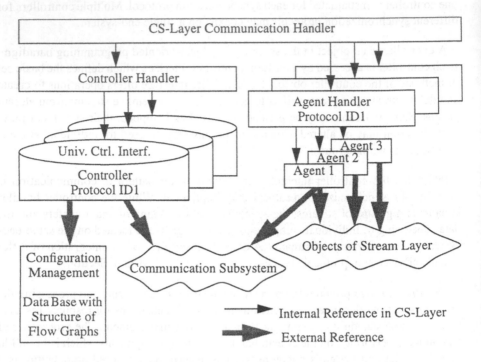

Fig. 3. Run-Time Structure of the CS-Layer in a *CINEMA* Daemon

After this brief overview, we will describe in detail the features of the uniform controller interface, the interactions between a controller and its agents, and the integration of a new synchronization protocol into the architecture.

4.1 Uniform Controller Interface to Access Alternative Protocols

The uniform controller interface offers generic functions to control data streams. By calling the respective operations, a controller is notified about the streams it controls, about their temporal properties, about groups of synchronized streams, about stream control operations to perform, and about the execution of blocks of operations. At the controller interface, addressing is based on identifiers of data stream end-points. The following list gives an overview of the essential operations and their main parameters:

ManagePort(Addr) notifies the controller about the address Addr of a stream end-point to be managed. This enables the controller to query the data base of the configuration management. The interface to the data base allows for traversing of the flow-graph information beginning at any node of the graph. Hence, the controller can determine the locations of components by traversing the logical structure of the flow-graph.

Based on this knowledge, it decides where agents are created to control the flow of data units.

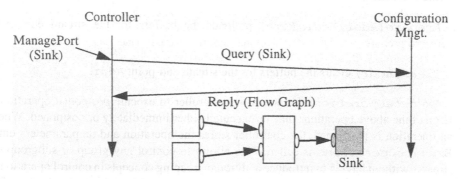

Fig. 4. Interactions between Controller and Configuration Management

UnManagePort(Addr) causes the controller to stop managing the stream end-point addressed by *Addr* and to remove the respective agents.

SetTiming(Addr,TimeSpec) sets the temporal parameters for the stream end-point addressed by *Addr*. The timing specification *TimeSpec* consists of the stream's rate in real-time and media time units as well as its play-out direction. The *TimeSpec* describes the time line of the stream.

CreateGroup(Addr,SyncSpec) creates a stream group containing the stream end-point addressed by *Addr*. It returns a group identifier. The *SyncSpec* describes the alignment of the stream's time line described by its *TimeSpec* to a normalized time line that begins with 0 and has the same scale as real-time. Additionally, it contains the tolerated skew between both time lines during run-time.

AddToGroup(Addr,GID,SyncSpec) adds the stream end-point identified by *Addr* to the stream group identified by *GID*. The semantics of the *SyncSpec* are the same as for creating a group. Hence, synchronization relationships among the streams of a group are expressed indirectly by means of the normalized time line.

Start(Addr,MediaTime) starts the flow of data units for the stream end-point *Addr* beginning with the data unit having the media time *MediaTime*.[1] Note that the operation not only starts the end-point *Addr*, but also the components that contribute to the stream.

Stop(Addr,MediaTime) stops the flow of data units for the stream end-point *Addr* when the media time *MediaTime* is reached.

Scale(Addr,MediaTime,TimeSpec) scales the timing for the stream end-

---

1. Besides specific values, media time may be set to values like "now" and "don't care", e.g. to enable immediate start-up of live streams or to add another stream to an active stream group without requiring knowledge about the actual position of the group's streams.

point Addr to the new timing specification TimeSpec when the media time Media-Time is reached.

Prepare(Addr,MediaTime) preloads the buffers for the stream end-point Addr to prepare for a later start with media time MediaTime.

Clear(Addr) clears the buffers for the stream end-point Addr.

ExecuteOperations() causes the controller to execute *postponed* operations. Each of the above operations may be executed either immediately or postponed. When an operation is postponed, the controller stores the operation and its parameters until ExecuteOperations is called. This allows to control any group or subgroup of streams without having to introduce additional grouping concepts in control operations. For example, starting two streams out of a stream group of five, the start operations for both streams are called in postponed mode, their synchronous execution is then caused by calling ExecuteOperations.

Further operations allow to query the actual state of streams and to execute control operations at a specific point in real-time. However, due to space limitations we do not discuss theses operations in detail.

4.2 Interaction of Controller and Agents

The interaction of a controller and its agents is discussed for the implementation of a particular synchronization protocol, the Adaptive Synchronization Protocol (ASP). ASP controls and synchronizes arbitrarily distributed stream groups, i.e., the streams may originate from sources residing on different nodes and may be played out at sinks on various nodes. The protocol adapts to changing transfer delays and regulates the play-out rate of sinks. To achieve inter-stream synchronization, the sink agents exchange messages among each other. For a detailed description of ASP's sub-protocols and a discussion of the cost of exchanges of messages between the controller and the agents we refer to [RoHe95].

Controller and agents consist of two major functional blocks. They implement the *protocol machine* and the *protocol management* of the given synchronization protocol. The controller's protocol management handles addresses of sources and sinks and the structure of stream groups. It coordinates creating and initializing of agents on the nodes of stream end-points. For the description of the initialization process, we assume a simple application scenario (see Figure 5). Two streams, stream S_1 and S_2, originate from host H_1. They are played out synchronously on host H_2 and host H_3, respectively. The controller coordinating the streams is located on host H_1.

The initialization of the given scenario begins with the notification of the controller to manage the stream end-points of $Sink_1$ and $Sink_2$ by calling Manage-Port(Sink$_1$) and ManagePort(Sink$_2$). For each stream, the protocol management of the ASP controller derives the complete structure of end-to-end stream by querying the configuration management's data base. In the case of stream S_1, it derives that the sink is located on host H_2 and that the stream originates from Source$_1$ on host H_1. With this information, a message can be sent to the agent handlers in the daemons on host H_1 and H_2, causing them to create Agent$_1$ and Agent$_2$. The agents are initialized to control the respective components. They connect themselves to the stream layer by hooking in callback functions (see Section 5).

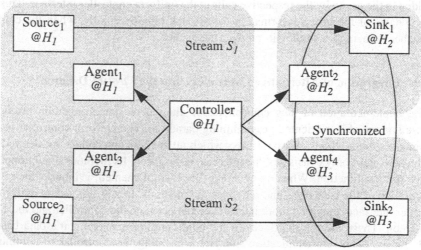

Fig. 5. Example Scenario

The timing for stream S_1 is set by calling SetTiming(Sink$_1$,TimeSpec). This causes the controller to notify Agent$_1$ and Agent$_2$ about the temporal parameters. The synchronization relationship among both streams is defined by creating a stream group. The call CreateGroup(Sink$_1$,SyncSpec) creates a trivial group containing stream S_1 and returns a group identifier GID. Stream S_2 is added to the group by calling AddToGroup(Sink$_2$,GID,SyncSpec). ASP requires the sinks of a stream group to know each other. This enables them to communicate directly. Hence, creating a stream group leads to the notification of all sink agents about the addresses of the other agents of the group. After creating the stream group, the initialization is finished and the data flow may be started.

For the sake of simplicity, we did not discuss postponed operations in the above description. Consequently, the initialization would lead to a lot of remote interactions. An optimization is achieved by postponing operations. If all operations were postponed and executed by calling ExecuteOperations, the initialization of a remote agent would lead to a single initialization message and the according acknowledgment.

The flow of data units is started for the whole group by calling Start(Sink$_1$,MediaTime) and Start(Sink$_2$,MediaTime) in postponed mode followed by ExecuteOperations. These requests cause the protocol machine to initiate the start-up for both streams by computing start-up times and propagating them to the agents of sources and sinks. While data units are transferred, inter-stream synchronization is achieved without involving the controller. Sink agents communicate directly with each other to coordinate changes in play-out rates while adapting to varying transfer delays (see [RoHe95] for a detailed description of the start-up and inter-stream synchronization protocols).

The stream group may be changed any time, i.e., streams may be removed from or added to the group by the respective calls at the uniform controller interface. This leads to updates of the group information for all sink clients. Finally, when the controller finishes to manage a stream, it removes the agents.

4.3 Integration of Alternative Controllers into the CINEMA Daemon

The implementation of new controllers for alternative synchronization protocols is based on the object-oriented programming paradigm. The uniform controller interface describes the methods of a base class which all specific controllers are derived from. The base class only consists of the interface description. Its methods do not implement any specific function. When a new controller is implemented, it inherits the interface definition of the base class and redefines the methods. In addition to the uniform controller interface, only two more interfaces exist between the controller and the CINEMA daemon. These are the interfaces to the configuration management's data base and, obviously, to the communication subsystem enabling the controller to communicate with other hosts (see Figure 3). Hence, the integration of a new controller may easily be achieved.

The implementation of a new agent follows the same paradigm: From a base class implementing the essential callback functions (see Figure 6), specific agents are derived. Protocol specific agents redefine the callback functions and add all methods required for protocol processing, i.e., for the interaction with the controller and other agents. Additionally, an agent can dynamically acquire references to instances of objects in the CINEMA daemon. It may call the object managing the control data of a thread to block or unblock the processing of a component. A call can be directed to the play-out buffer to mark data units for processing. The scheduler is accessed to set the scheduling times of activations.

The integration of a new synchronization protocol requires the code of controller and agents to be linked to the CINEMA daemon. Linking is performed either statically or dynamically. While the first requires all daemons to be stopped and to be restarted again after a recompilation, dynamic loading of controller and agents allows to extend the daemon without stopping it. The new protocol is assigned a unique protocol identifier to enable its selection. Controllers realizing identical protocols have the same identifier within each daemon.

The selection of a protocol to handle a stream group is based on the protocol identifier. A client may manually select the protocol by using the respective protocol identifier. We currently investigate an automatic selection of synchronization protocols. The selection is based on a matching of the application requirements and the capabilities of synchronization protocols in terms of the structure of the flow-graph and of the required quality of service.

5 Stream Layer

In the stream layer, data units of streams are transferred and processed. To this end, the stream layer implements data transfer functions to move data units from one component to another. The processing of data units is performed by components. The component's stream processing code is bound to a thread of the operating system where it is activated periodically in an *activation loop*. Assigning components to individual threads allows for parallel processing on multi-processor machines and pseudo-parallel processing on single-processor machines without the prohibiting costs of process switches incurred by assigning components to processes. Parallel processing simplifies the control of the component's timing. Furthermore, it is necessary to decouple data generation and play-out, which is prerequisite to equalizing end-to-end delays for inter-stream synchronization.

The timing of activation loops is controlled by agents. An agent object hooks in some of its methods as *callback functions* into activation loops where they are executed as part of the stream layer. A callback function (also referred to as *upcall* [Clar85]) is a function of a higher protocol layer that may be called by a lower protocol layer. It enables a very efficient interaction among the layers due to asynchronous upcalls and due to access to shared variables. Moreover, it offers a well-defined interface to plug-in the control code of different synchronization protocols into the stream layer. We first will show the assignment of processing and transport functions to threads. Then, we will identify the locations to hook-in callback functions and discuss the functions they implement in the context of the implementation of ASP.

The assignment of threads to processing and transfer functions is shown for a linear processing pipeline. Transfer and processing is realized by three threads when the pipeline consists of a source component, a transport link, a play-out buffer and a sink component (see Figure 6). Each thread executes an activation loop. The activation loop of the source thread calls the code of the source component which generates the next data unit and hands it over to the transport link. On the receiving end-system, arriving data units are read from the transport link's service access point and a reference to the data unit is written into the play-out buffer. The code is executed within the activation loop of the transport thread. The sink thread executes the stream handling function of the sink component which reads a data unit from the play-out buffer and presents it. Note that data units are transferred by passing a reference without copying them. Hence, data transfer on end-systems is very efficient.

The usage of separate threads for the source and the sink is needed to decouple data generation and play-out. Moreover, separate threads are inevitable when sources and sinks reside on different end-systems. While this separation is obvious, the usage of a transport thread is less so. Separating the data arrival and the data play-out process by assigning different threads is necessary due to the following reasons. Awaiting a data unit at the service access point of a transport system is a blocking call which is decoupled from real-time. On the contrary, the play-out process is periodic and real-time bound. Furthermore, the arrival time and the play-out time of a data unit are different points in time due to buffering and delay equalization. Hence, data arrival and play-out are independently timed and should be assigned to different threads.

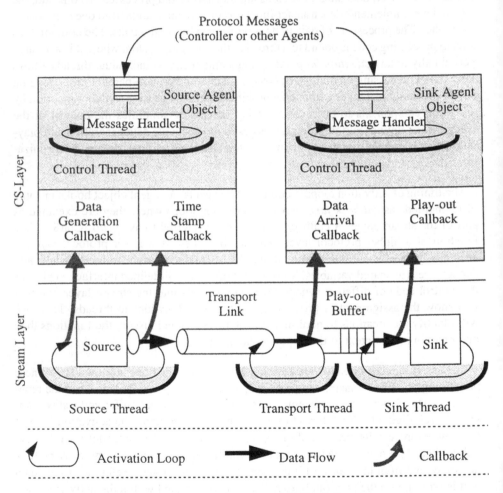

Fig. 6. Thread Assignment and Callback Functions

An agent hooks in a callback function into the activation loop of each thread either to monitor or to control the timing. The agents realize four types of callback functions: the *data generation* callback, the *time stamp* callback, the *data arrival* callback, and the *play-out* callback. The data generation and the time stamp callback are implemented by agents controlling a source. The data arrival and play-out callback are required to control sink components. Within the callback functions (which are methods of agent objects), the data structures of agents can be accessed directly without further communication overhead. The access to the data structures is exclusive to avoid inconsistencies. Hence, semaphores are used to guarantee mutual exclusion of the callback functions and the message handler executed in the control thread of an agent. It is made sure the real-time threads are not blocked by the non-real-time thread executing the agent's message handler. Figure 7 through Figure 9 show the activation loops of the source thread, the transport thread and the sink thread in a C++-like pseudo-code notation.

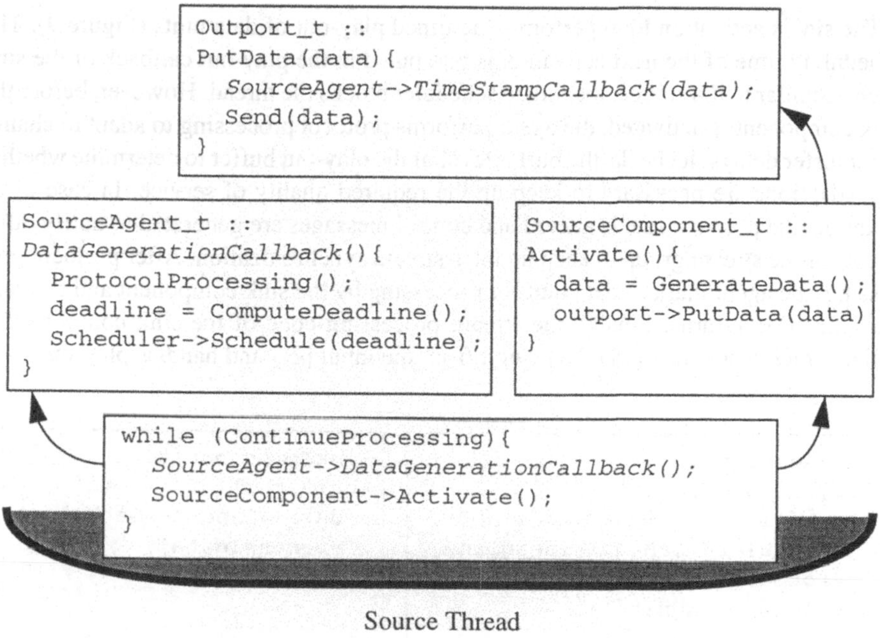

```
Outport_t ::
PutData(data){
    SourceAgent->TimeStampCallback(data);
    Send(data);
}
```

```
SourceAgent_t ::
DataGenerationCallback(){
    ProtocolProcessing();
    deadline = ComputeDeadline();
    Scheduler->Schedule(deadline);
}
```

```
SourceComponent_t ::
Activate(){
    data = GenerateData();
    outport->PutData(data)
}
```

```
while (ContinueProcessing){
    SourceAgent->DataGenerationCallback();
    SourceComponent->Activate();
}
```

Source Thread

Fig. 7. Activation Loop of the Source Thread

The data generation callback is called in the activation loop of the source thread (Figure 7). It times the generation of data units by computing scheduling times which are given to the thread scheduler. The scheduler blocks the thread until the given time. Consequently, the stream processing code of the component is activated when the callback returns. The component generates the next data unit and hands it over to its output port where the time stamp callback of the source agent is called. The agent is given a reference to the data unit enabling it to set a timestamp.

The activation loop of the transport thread reads incoming data units from the transport link where they are assembled from individual packets (Figure 8). Each time a data unit is completed, the data arrival callback is activated with the data unit's timestamp as parameter. The sink agent may evaluate the arrival time and the timestamp of the data unit before it is written into the play-out buffer of the sink. This provides the base for the determination of buffer levels and the estimation of transfer times.

```
while (ContinueProcessing){
  data = Link->Receive();
  SinkAgent->DataArrivalCallback(data->TS);
  PlayoutBuffer->Put(data);
}
```

Transport Thread

Fig. 8. Activation Loop of the Transport Thread

The sink's activation loop performs the timed play-out of data units (Figure 9). The scheduling time of the next activation is computed in the play-out callback of the sink agent. Similar to the source, the thread scheduler blocks the thread. However, before the sink component is activated, the agent performs protocol processing to adapt to changing transfer delays. It checks the buffer level of the play-out buffer to determine whether any adaptions are necessary to keep up the required quality of service. In case of an adaption, the play-out rate is altered and control messages are generated to notify other agents of the stream group to keep up inter-stream synchronization. After protocol processing, the agent marks a data unit for processing by the sink component and the callback function returns. Finally, the stream processing code of the sink component is called which reads the marked data unit from the input port and handles play-out.

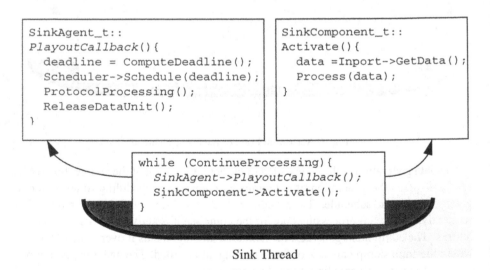

Sink Thread

Fig. 9. Activation Loop of the Sink Thread

Figure 10 shows some performance results of a 10 fps video transmission. A CellB-compressed video stream captured from a camera is transmitted over Ethernet from one Sun SPARCstation to another and played out in a window. The data flow is controlled by ASP, i.e. the configuration is the same as depicted in Figure 6. In Figure 10a, the distribution of transfer delays as seen by the data arrival callback is shown. The average transfer delay is approx. 25 msec. Some of the frames are delayed up to 0.5 sec mainly due to ressource shortages on the ethernet. Figure 10b evaluates the intra-stream quality: The difference between the actual inter-frame spacing of two succeeding frames and the nominal spacing of 100 msec (= 1/rate) is depicted. Only 40% of the frames differ less than 3 msec and 17 % differ by more than 5 msec. Figure 10c and d show the delays and spacing differences as seen by the play-out callback. For the measurement, ASP is tuned to hold on average half a data unit in the play-out buffer. This leads to a delay increase of 50 msec. Hence, the average end-to-end delay is about 70 msec. Intra-stream quality is significantly improved: 85% of all frames are spaced by 100 msec, i.e., they are played out on time. 95 % differ in their spacing by less then 3 msec. The overhead for monitoring delays and for timing activation loops is very low: It amounts to a single function call for each activation loop and each data unit (i.e., every 100 ms) and the execution of the instructions required for protocol processing.

Fig. 10a: Transfer Delay Distribution

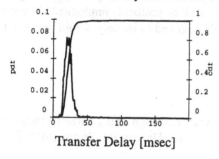

Transfer Delay [msec]

Fig. 10b: Interarrival Diffs. Distribution

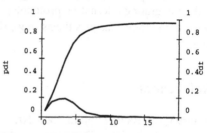

Interarrival Time Differences [msec]

Fig. 10c: End-to-End Delay Distribution

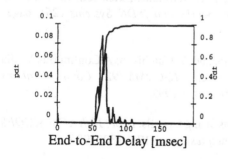

End-to-End Delay [msec]

Fig. 10d: Play-out Diffs Distribution

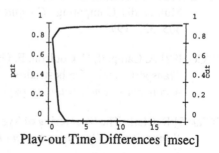

Play-out Time Differences [msec]

Fig. 10. Results of a Point-to-Point Video Transmission

By using callback functions, the timing of activation loops and, consequently, of complete processing topologies can be controlled. The approach allows for a clear separation of stream processing, data transfer and timing functions leading to a configurable architecture. Alternative synchronization protocols may be plugged in to control the stream processing in the stream layer. The execution of callback functions leads to efficient interactions between the stream layer and the control and synchronization layer.

6 Summary

We proposed an architecture for the implementation of a stream control and synchronization service in distributed environments. The architecture is open to integrate alternative synchronization protocols to handle the wide range of application requirements in terms of stream control. The integration of protocols is based on well-defined interfaces to access the controllers and to allow for the interaction of agents with the stream layer. The agents control activation loops by hooking in callback functions. Thus, the agents' code is executed directly in the stream layer leading to a very efficient interaction of the layers.

The major concepts of the architecture and several synchronization protocols were implemented in the prototype of the *CINEMA* environment. The prototype runs on Sun SPARCstations under Solaris and IBM RS/6000 machines under AIX. The workstations are interconnected by Ethernet as well as by FDDI or ATM, respectively. Practical experiences with our prototype are promising. We were able to implement demo multimedia applications in very short time by using the services of our prototype. Additionally, integrating alternative protocols, such as ASP or protocols implemented by students doing their master's thesis (e.g., [Baur95]), proved to be easy within reasonable time.

References

[Baur95] S. Baur: Diplomarbeit Nr. 1201: Synchronisation und Laufzeitverwaltung multimedialer Datenströme. Master's thesis, Universität Stuttgart/IPVR, 2 1995.

[CBDW92] G. Coulson, G. Blair, N. Davis, and N. Williams: Extensions to ANSA for Multimedia Computing. *Computer Networks and ISDN Systems (25)*, pages 305–323, 1992.

[CCGH92] A. Campell, G. Coulson, F. Garcia, and D. Hutchison: A Continuous Media Transport and Orchestration Service. *SIGCOMM'92 Communications Architectures and Protocols*, pages 99–110, 8 1992.

[Clar85] D. Clark: The Structuring of Systems Using Upcalls. *Proc. 10th ACM SIGOPS Symposium on Operating System Principles*, pages 171–180, 1985.

[EPD94] J. Escobar, C. Partridge, and D. Deutsch: Flow Synchronization Protocol. *IEEE Transactions on Networking*, 1994.

[HNR95] T. Helbig, S. Noureddine, and K. Rothermel: Activation Set: An Abstraction for Accessing Periodic Data Streams. *IS&T/SPIE Multimedia Computing and Networking '95, San Jose, USA*, pages 368–378, 2 1995.

[IMA93] IMA: *Multimedia System Services, Version 1.0, available via ftp from ibminet.awdpa.ibm.com.* Hewlett-Packard Company and International Business Machines Corporation and SunSoft Inc., 7 1993.

[ISO91] ISO: Basic Reference Model of Open Distributed Processing. *ISO/IEC JTC1/ SC21/WG7*, 12 1991.

[OMG91] OMG: Object Services - Request for Information. RfI 91.11.6, Object Management Group, 1991.

[OSF91] OSF: *OSF DCE Version 1.0, DCE Administration Guide, Module 4. DCE Distributed Time Service.* Open Software Foundation, Cambridge, USA, 1991.

[RBH94] K. Rothermel, I. Barth, and T. Helbig: CINEMA - An Architecture for Distributed Multimedia Applications. *Architecture and Protocols for High-Speed Networks*, pages 253–271, 1994.

[RoHe95] K. Rothermel and T. Helbig: An Adaptive Stream Synchronization Protocol. *5th International Workshop on Network and Operating System Support for Digital Audio and Video, Durham, New Hampshire, USA*, pages 189–202, 4 1995.

[RoHe96] K. Rothermel and T. Helbig: Clock Hierarchies: An Abstraction for Grouping and Controlling Media Streams. *IEEE Journal on Selected Areas in Communications - Synchronization Issues in Multimedia Communications*, 1996.

[Shap86] M. Shapiro: Structure and Encapsulation in Distributed Systems: The Proxy Principle. *6th International Conference on Distributed Computer Systems*, pages 198–204, 5 1986.

Comenius[1] - The Virtual Classroom

Christine Seidel
DeTeBerkom GmbH

Abstract: The media-educational project Comenius provides five Berlin schools with multimedia communication technology. Within the framework of the project students and teachers of these schools are enabled and fostered to conceive and carry out interdisciplinary and school spanning projects via data network, to communicate with each other, and to access multimedia databases. In each of the schools multimedia workstations were installed, which can be easily and intuitively operated by special software. Accompanying research will ensure that the new educational challenges will be documented and evaluated.

Keywords: Multimedia teleservices in education, challenges in scholastic learning, interdisciplinary projects, school spanning project, cooperative working, communicative learning, virtual classroom, broadband communication, three-dimensional navigation.

1 Introduction

The project Comenius is one of the first attempts to gather broad experience in the school environment with multimedia forms of education. It demonstrates how multimedia communications technology enriches teaching and learning in many subjects. Within the framework of the project students and teachers at five schools in Berlin are able to communicate with each other via data-networks.

The two project's main innovative chracteristics are:
- The use of a wide area network to enable joint class-projects in which the students, teachers and external users communicate and document the educational results of this process.
- Joint access to the multimedia resources made available by the central database and the utilisation of this source material to create their own individual multimedia productions.

---

[1] Comenius is a project within the R&D-program of DeTeBerkom GmbH. Involved in Comenius are the FWU (Institut für Film und Bild in Wissenschaft und Unterricht), the Condat DV-Beratung, Organisation und Software GmbH and PONTON European Media Art Lab.

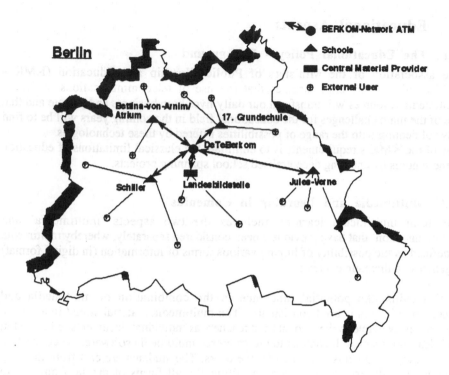

In Comenius the goals are:
- To investigate, how a network can enable teamwork in school spanning projects and the educational use of the multimedia resources.
- To research the new educational dimensions opened by the use of these telecommunication tools.
- To determine what practical educational problems and which limitations are associated with the use of this technology.
- To determine the requirements on networks and services for the use of telecommunication in the school's environment.

The communication tools are essential for cooperative work and learning in the network. The software generates a three-dimensional world, a so-called 'virtual classroom', in which all users move, and a space within this world, in which all partcipants cooperate on joint projects, called DisNet (Discoursive Networking).

Communication is always possible in Comenius. The user is in a 3D space and can contact others in writing, or by voice, or even video-conference. Thus, communications range from a brief conversation to cooperation on complex joint projects. These electronic communication options extend the student's world of learning and experience far outside the limits of the classroom and school, opening the classroom and school, helping to make the learning process increasingly action-oriented and socially responsible.

2 Educational Aspects

2.1 The Educational Policy - Background

The association of the Ministers of Public Worship and Education (KMK - Kultusministerkonferenz) assumes that the use of telecommunications to access multimedia resources will transform our daily lives both business and private and that one of the main challenges for the educational field in the coming years will be to find ways of dealing with the range of possibilities offered by these technologies.
One of the KMK's requirements is to eliminate the classical limitations of education in the schools by enabling decentralised school spanning projects.

2.2 Multimedia and Learning in Comenius

The term multimedia learning includes the two aspects 'multimedia' and 'communication' that have previously been considered separately, whereby multimedia is defined as the possibility of linking various forms of information (in digital format) together in a thematic context.

In Comenius, the potential inherence in the combination of multimedia and telecommunication is used consistently. The multimedia material stored in a central database is available to the students and teachers as individual documents to be used in their learning process. Incontrast to prestructured multimedia software, the connection between the documents is created by the users. The students are cast from the very beginning in the role of producers. Additionally, all forms of media, from text to moving pictures, are created and processed by the students themselves and are brought by them into a coherent presentation.

Comenius supports the three necessary telecommunication forms in different extensions:
- Conferencing, to support working at the same time at different places,
- Database access, to support individual or asynchronous working,
- Mail facilities, to support individual or asynchronous data exchange.

Thus, telecommunications delivers a variety of options to expand the world of the students far beyond the usual limits of a classroom or school:
- They open the class and the school
- Make the learning process both more action oriented and team-oriented, and at the same time more socially responsible.

Telecommunications is thus integrated into the communication in a manner that insures that the central role of scholastic communication in the learning group is not lost.

2.3 Scholastic Learning - Perspectives

It is expected that the Comenius project will show that, when multimedia communication forms are employed, scholastic learning gains new dimensions and or that the learning goals are better achieved. For the use of media technology in scholastic learning, the three primary goals are:

- To learn the capabilities of both, traditional and multimedia options, and to develop the awareness required to make a clear evaluation and selection.
- To develop a critical awareness of manipulation in presentation, thinking, and action.
- To expand the personal options for expression and creation, with increased capacity for precise perception, and dealing with media in socially responsible manner.

2.4 Pedagogical Content

Besides the planned teaching projects, an option has been kept open to incorporate offerings from the many varied areas within the schools (classes, recreation, and extra-curricular activities). The personal decision of the individual has been accorded a high value. New goals should develop freely in the course of teaching. Additionally, the placement of project workstations in public locations (school cafe, school library, etc.) should provide the students with the opportunity for independent participation.

Primarily , the pedagogical and the methodological didactic development and trials will occur in three interdisciplinary areas:

- Ecology
- Musical-Aesthetics
- Electronic Publishing

3 Graphical User Interface (GUI)

The user interface guides students of all ages through the use of the new media. The primary school students should not be overtasked nor should the older students be bored. Thus, the requirements that the user interface:

- be intuitive to use,
- leave room for personal creativity,
- adequately visualise the teaching and learning situation.

The operation of the interface is trimmed to the user group. Since the user group in Comenius consists of students, who are accustomed to playing with video games, the keyboard layout has been oriented to this standard. Initial trials showed a high degree of acceptance by the children and a quick achievement of proficiency.

Students, teacher, and parents or other guests move through an electronic world. Comenius is a three-dimensional communication space that may be entered and used every day around the clock from any location. Every user (after login) will be visible to the others as a geometrical form. Standard representations are: pyramids for students, cubes for teachers, and spheres for parents or guests. Additionally, the user name is displayed above each form so that one can easily identify the other.
The work takes place in houses with clearly defined functions:

- Schools, the five schools connected to the trial network with access to the user catalogue
- Conference Hall, for multimedia conferences
- Commons, for asynchronous communication between groups
- Project House, for school spanning projects handled in DisNet
- Media Center, for online research in the multimedia catalogue

Comenius uses the methaphor of a three-dimensional space. Every user is visible in, moves through, and can use the functions offered in this space. The paths between the locations are crossed as in the real world, so that this virtual world is experienced in its extent. There are private and public areas. Each user has his own 'private space', the virtual school satchel in which documents can be stored and processed with standard programs.

Multimedia conferences can be created with help of the media tools. E-Mail tools are available to enable sending and receiving private mail.

The acronym DisNet[2] stands for 'Discoursive Networking'. This term describes the public space within the Comenius network, in which students and teachers from different schools can cooperate on joint projects. The joint work is represented as a three-dimensional net structure. This web presents not only the relationship between the contents but also makes the creation process directly visible - the communication learning process.
The DisNet is thus a universal environment for cooperative work in projects.

4   Basic Technical System

The basic technical system links together five Berlin schools and the Landesbildstelle Berlin (content provider) via the Telekom's glass-fibre lines. Where fibre-optic lines are not available, the communication runs over bundled ISDN lines. The schools that are directly connected to the high-speed network can call up data from the Landesbildstelle at 155 Mbits/s, which is the equivalent of about 5000 text pages per second.

---

[2] DisNet is an argument link technology from Julean Simon and David Wohlhard.

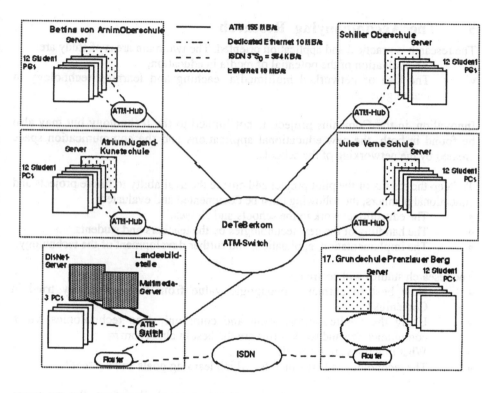

External users can also enter the Comenius network from the PC at home via ISDN. The system functionality is restricted by the low speed lines for these users.

Located in each school are twelve high performance Pcs. With these, the students gain access to the three-dimensional Comenius world, the GUI, and to DisNet. They can use the PC to call up (from the multimedia database) films, pictures, text, sound, or learning software. The PC can also be used to send the multimedia documents that they created themselves. For 'personal meetings' the Pcs are equipped with a video-conference system. Further, each PC has all usual PC application software. The student's Pcs have an access rate over the entire network of 10Mbits/s.

The Comenius participants can digitise, process, and cut video material on the PC. Each school has received a specially equipped PC for this purpose. These systems permit the creation of high quality video clips using a variety of special effects that can then be distributed to all Comenius partners.

5   The Accompanying Research

The research is practical and application oriented. The two main areas of study are:
*   An evaluation of the potential of media in education,
*   The Use of networked multimedia teaching and learning technology in learning psychology.

Innovation, in the Comenius project, is not limited to the technology but may also be found in both, the new educational applications and the communication space created by the networking of the schools.

To keep the results of the pilot project and ensure the availabilty to future projects and educational planners, the following must be documented and evaluated:
*   The educational work in the schools and classes,
*   The handling of the new technologies by the teachers and students
*   The implementation, application, and further development of the technology.

The research studies will centre on:
*   How best to extract a pedagogic value from the technology tried in Comenius?
*   Using the applied information and communication technologies which communication and work forms are the best in classroom?
*   What functions are fulfilled?
*   The technology is best suited for which learning goals and content?

The accompanying research is always school-oriented, therefore, the necessary observations and interviews are made on-location. An interdisciplinary steering committee is available to support the researchers.

The results of the project will be (with appropriate theoratical foundation) condensed into a model of Comenius. In particular, answers will be sought for the questions:
*   What contribution was made by the information and communications technology to the media an communication culture?
*   How might these results best be applied in other fields?

6   Conclusion

Comenius meets the recently formulated principles of the KMK. The project shows a way into new dimensions of teaching and learning. But, teaching and communication between the schools in the Comenius network presents the schools and teachers with new organisational tasks. The time, space, technical, and financial demands must be determined as well as the resulting changes in the school organisation, lesson prerequisites and realisation, as well as teacher and student behaviour.

Authors Index

Bansal, V.

C&C Research Laboratories,
NEC USA, Inc.
4 Independence Way
Princeton NJ 08540
USA

Bernhardt, Christoph

Institute Eurécom
2229 Route des Crêtes
B.P 193
F-06904 Sophia-Antipolis
France

Phone: +33 9300 2639, +33 9300 2664
Fax: +33 9300 2627
E-mail: bernhardt@eurecom.fr

Bettati, Riccardo

Texas A&M University
Dept. of Computer Science
301 H.R. Bright Building
College Station
TX 77843-3112
USA

Phone: +1 409 845 5469
Fax: +1 409 847 8578
E-mail: bettati@cs.tamu.edu
URL: http://www.cs.tamu.edu/faculty/bettati

Biersack, Ernst

Institute Eurécom
2229 Route des Crêtes
B.P. 193
F-06904 Sophia-Antipolis
France

Phone: +33 9300 2611, +33 9300 2664
Fax: +33 9300 2627
E-mail: erbi@eurecom.fr
URL: http://www.cica.fr/~erbi/

Dengler, Johannes

Institut Eurécom
2229 Routes des Crêtes
F-06904 Sophia Antipolis
France

Present address:
McKinsey & Company Inc.,
Taunusanlage 21,
D-60325 Frankfurt
Germany

Deterministic Admission Control Strategies in Video Servers with Variable Bit Rate Streams   245

Phone: +49 69 7162 700
Fax: +49 60 7162 305
E-mail: Johannes_Dengler@McKinsey.com

Froitzheim, Konrad

University of Ulm
Dept. for Distributed Systems
Oberer Eselsberg
D-89069 Ulm
Germany

Interactive Video and Remote Control via the World Wide Web   91

Phone: +49 731 502 4146
Fax: +49 731 502 4142
E-mail: frz@informatik.uni-ulm.de
URL: http://www-vs.informatik.uni-ulm.de/

García, Francisco J.

Hewlett-Packard Laboratories
Filton Road
Stoke Gifford
Bristol BS12 6QZ
UK

QoS Filters: Addressing the Heterogeneity Gap   227

Phone: +44 117 922 8817
Fax: +44 117 922 8972
E-mail: fg@hplb.hp.com

Georgiannakis, Giorgos

University of Crete
Dept. of Computer Science
and
Foundation for Research and
Technology-Hellas (FORTH)
Institute of Computer Science
Science and Technology Park
of Crete
Vassilika Vouton
PO Box 1385
GR 711 10 Heraklion
Crete, Greece

Design of an Immersive Teleconferencing Application   117

Phone: +30 81 391675, +30 81 391604, +30 81 391605
Fax: +30 81 391671, +30 81 391601
E-mail: georgian@ics.forth.gr
URL: http://www.ics.forth.gr/proj/pleiades

Geyer, Werner

Institute Eurécom
2229 Route des Crêtes
F-06904 Sophia-Antipolis
France

Present address:
University of Mannheim
Praktische Informatik IV
L 15,16
D-68131 Mannheim
Germany

A Synchronization Scheme for Stored Multimedia Streams 277

Phone: +49 621 292 3300
Fax: +49 621 292 5745
E-mail: geyer@pi4.informatik.uni-mannheim.de

Gupta, Amit

International Computer
Science Institute (ICSI)
1947 Center Street
Berkeley
CA 94704
USA

A Secure Architecture for Tenet Scheme 2 163

Phone: +1 510 642 4274 ext. 128
Fax: +1 510 643 7684
E-mail: amit@cs.berkeley.edu
URL: http://www.berkeley.edu/~amit

Helbig, Tobias

University of Stuttgart
Institute of Parallel and
Distributed High-Performance
Systems (IPVR)
Breitwiesenstraße 20-22
D-70565 Stuttgart
Germany

*An Architecture for a Distributed
Stream Synchronization Service* 297

Phone: +49 711 7816 275
Fax: +49 711 7816 424
E-mail: Tobias.Helbig@informatik.uni-stuttgart.de
URL: http://www.informatik.uni-stuttgart.de/ipvr/
vs/helbig/home.html

Hess, Robert

Dresden Univ. of Technology
Institute for Operating
Systems, Databases and
Computer Networks
D-01062 Dresden
Germany

*Video Communication and
Media Scaling System "Xnetvideo": Design and
Implementation* 195

Phone: +49 351 4575 457
Fax: +49 351 4575 251
E-mail: hess@ibc.inf.tu-dresden.de
URL: http://www.inf.tu-dresden.de/~rh6/

Heumann, Brian

Softadweis AG
Laufengasse 18
CH-8212 Neuhausen/Rhf.
Switzerland

*GLASS-Studio: An Open Authoring Environment for
Distributed Multimedia Applications* 45

Phone: +41 53 211181
E-mail: heumann@saw.ch

Hinsch, Elfriede

*The Secure Conferencing User Agent: A Tool to
Provide Secure Conferencing with MBONE
Multimedia Conferencing Applications* 131

GMD Darmstadt
Rheinstraße 75
D-64295 Darmstadt
Germany

Phone: +49 6151 869249
Fax: +49 6151 869224
E-mail: hinsch@gmd.de
URL: http://www.darmstadt.gmd.de/TKT

Hofrichter, Klaus

*MHEG 5 - Standardized Presentation Objects for the
Set Top Unit Environment* 33

GMD-FOKUS
Hardenbergplatz 2
D-10623 Berlin
Germany

Phone: +49 30 25499 211
Fax: +49 30 25499 202
E-mail: hofrichter@fokus.gmd.de
URL: http://www.fokus.gmd.de/ovma/
            employees/hofrichter/

Hutchison, David

QoS Filters: Addressing the Heterogeneity Gap 227

Lancaster University
Computing Department
Lancaster
LA1 4YR
UK

Phone: +44 1524 65201 ext. 3798/3802
Fax: +44 1524 593608
E-mail: dh@comp.lancs.ac.uk
URL: http://www.comp.lancs.ac.uk/computing/
            staff/dh.html

Hutschenreuther, Tino

*Video Communication and
Media Scaling System "Xnetvideo": Design and
Implementation* 195

Dresden Univ. of Technology
Institute for Operating
Systems, Databases and
Computer Networks
D-01062 Dresden
Germany

Phone: +49 351 4575 213
Fax: +49 351 4575 251
E-mail: tino@ibc.inf.tu-dresden.de
URL: http://www.inf.tu-dresden.de/~th8/

Jaegemann, Annemarie

*The Secure Conferencing User Agent: A Tool to Provide
Secure Conferencing with MBONE Multimedia
Conferencing Applications* 131

GMD
Rheinstraße 75
D-64295 Darmstadt
Germany

Phone: + 49 6151 869248
Fax: + 49 6151 869224
E-mail: jaegemann@gmd.de
URL: http://www.darmstadt.gmd.de/TKT

Leidig, Torsten

GLASS-Studio: An Open Authoring Environment for Distributed Multimedia Applications　　　45

Digital Equipment GmbH
European Applied Research
Center
CEC Karlsruhe
Vincenz-Prießnitz-Straße 1
D-76131 Karlsruhe
Germany

Phone:　+49 721 6902 30
Fax:　　+49 721 6968 16
E-mail:　leidig@nestvx.enet.dec.com

Mathy, Laurent

Features of the ACCOPI Multimedia Transport Service　　175

University of Liège
Service de Systemes et
Automatique
Institut d'electricite Montefiore,
B28
B-4000 Liège
Belgium

Phone:　+32 41 662691
Fax:　　+32 41 662989
E-mail:　mathy@montefiore.ulg.ac.be

URL: http://www-run.montefiore.ulg.ac.be

Present address:
Univ. of British Columbia
Dept. of Computer Science
#201 - 2366 Main Mall
V6T 1Z4
Vancouver BC
Canada

Phone:　+1 604 822 3123
Fax:　　+1 604 822 5485
E-mail:　mathy@cs.ubc.ca

Mauthe, Andreas

QoS Filters: Addressing the Heterogeneity Gap　　227

Lancaster University
Computing Department
Distributed Multimedia
Research Group
Lancaster
LA1 4YR
UK

Phone:　+44 1524 65201 ext. 4332
Fax:　　+44 1524 593608
E-mail:　andreas@comp.lancs.ac.uk
URL:　　http://www.comp.lancs.ac.uk/computing/
　　　　staff/andreas.html

Michelitsch, G.

Heidi-II: A Software Architecture for ATM Network Based Distributed Multimedia Systems　　1

C&C Research Laboratories,
NEC USA, Inc.
4 Independence Way
Princeton
NJ 08540
USA

Moran, Mark   *A Security Architecture for Tenet Scheme 2*   163

International Computer
Science Institute (ICSI)
1947 Center Street
Berkeley
CA 94704
USA

Phone: +1 510 642 4274 ext. 193
Fax: +1 510 643 7684
E-mail: moran@cs.berkeley.edu

Nikolaou, Christos   *Design of an Immersive Teleconferencing Application*   117

University of Crete
Dept. of Computer Science
and
Foundation for Research and
Technology-Hellas (FORTH)
Institute of Computer Science
Science and Technology Park
of Crete
Vassilika Vouton
P.O. Box 1385
GR 711 10 Heraklion
Crete, Greece

Phone: +30 81 391676, +30 81 391604, +30 81 391605
Fax: +30 81 391671, +30 81 391601
E-mail: nikolau@ics.forth.gr
URL: http://www.ics.forth.gr/proj/pleiades

Oppliger, Rolf   *A Security Architecture for Tenet Scheme 2*   163

University of Berne
Institute for Computer Science
and Applied Mathematics (IAM)
Neubrückstraße 10
CH-3012 Berne
Switzerland

Phone: +41 31 631 89 57
Fax: +41 31 631 33 55
E-mail: oppliger@iam.unibe.ch
URL: http://iamwww.unibe.ch/~oppliger

Orphanoudakis, Stelios   *Design of an Immersive Teleconferencing Application*   117

University of Crete
Dept. of Computer Science
and
Foundation for Research and
Technology-Hellas (FORTH)
Institute of Computer Science
Science and Technology Park
of Crete
Vassilika Vouton
P.O. Box 1385
GR 711 10 Heraklion
Crete, Greece

Phone: +30.81.391600, +30.81.391604, +30.81.391605
Fax: +30.81.391601
E-mail: orphanou@ics.forth.gr
URL: http://www.ics.forth.gr/proj/cvrl

Ott, Maximilian

Heidi-II: A Software Architecture for ATM Network Based Distributed Multimedia Systems   1

C&C Research Laboratories,
NEC USA, Inc.
4 Independence Way
Princeton
NJ 08540
USA

Phone: +1 609 951 2469
E-mail: max@ccrl.nj.nec.com

Rautenberg, Mathias

A Control System for an Interactive Video on Demand Server Handling Variable Data Rates   265

University of the Federal
Armed Forces Munich
Werner-Heisenberg-Weg 39
D-85577 Neubiberg
Germany

Phone: +49 89 6004 2254
Fax: +49 89 6004 3560
E-mail: mathias@informatik.unibw-muenchen.de
URL: http://www.informatik.unibw-muenchen.de/inst33/mr.html

Raychaudhuri, D.

Heidi-II: A Software Architecture for ATM Network Based Distributed Multimedia Systems   1

C&C Research Laboratories,
NEC USA, Inc.
4 Independence Way
Princeton
NJ 08540
USA

Reimann, K.

Radio On Demand   105

Technical University Berlin
FSP-PV/PRZ
Office HE104, Sekr. MA073
Straße des 17. Juni 136
D-10623 Berlin
Germany

Phone: +4930 314 26715
Fax: +4930 314 21114
E-mail: reimann@prz.tu-berlin.de

Reininger, D.

Heidi-II: A Software Architecture for ATM Network Based Distributed Multimedia Systems   1

C&C Research Laboratories,
NEC USA, Inc.
4 Independence Way
Princeton
NJ 08540
USA

Schill, Alexander

Video Communication and Media Scaling System "Xnetvideo": Design and Implementation   195

Dresden Univ. of Technology
Inst. for Operating Systems,
Databases and Computer
Networks
D-01062 Dresden
Germany

Phone: +49 351 4575 261
Fax: +49 351 4575 251
E-mail: schill@ibc.inf.tu-dresden.de
URL: http://www.inf.tu-dresden.de/~as2/

Schulzrinne, Henning

Personal Mobility for Multimedia Services in the Internet   143

GMD-FOKUS
Hardenbergplatz 2
D-10623 Berlin
Germany

Phone: +49 30 25499 182
Fax: +49 30 25499 202
E-mail: schulzrinne@fokus.gmd.de
URL: http://www.fokus.gmd.de/step/hgs

Seidel, Christine

COMENIUS - The Virtual Classroom   315

DeTeBerkom GmbH
Voltastraße 5
D-13355 Berlin
Germany

Phone: +49 30 467 01 221
Fax: +49 30 467 01 444
E-mail: seidel@deteberkom.de

Sellis, T.

Event and Action Representation and Composistion for Multimedia Application Scenario Modelling   71

Dept. of Electr. Engineering
Devision of Computer Science
National Technical Univ.
of Athens
Zographou 157 73
Athens
Greece

Phone: +301 7721 601
Fax: +301 7722 459
E-mail: timos@cs.ntua.gr

Siracusa, R.J.

Heidi-II: A Software Architecture for ATM Network Based Distributed Multimedia Systems   1

C&C Research Laboratories,
NEC USA, Inc.
4 Independence Way
Princeton
NJ 08540
USA

Smith, Jeffrey D.

Multimedia Architecture to Support Requirements Analysis   15

Nippon Telegraph and
Telephone Corporation
Software Laboratories
Palo Alto
250 Cambridge Ave., Suite 205
CA 94306
USA

Phone: +1 415 833 3605
Fax: +1 415 326 1878
E-mail: sumisu@nttlabs.com

Weber, Michael

University of Ulm
Dept. of Distributed Systems
Computer Science Faculty
Oberer Eselsberg
D-89069 Ulm
Germany

*Interactive Video and Remote Control via the
World Wide Web* 91

Phone: +49 731 502 4143
Fax: +49 731 502 4142
E-mail: weber@informatik.uni-ulm.de
URL: http://www-vs.informatik.uni-ulm.de/

Werner, Jörg

Technical University of
Chemnitz-Zwickau
Fakultät für Informatik
Lehrstuhl Betriebssysteme
D-09107 Chemnitz
Germany

*Scheduling Mechanisms Reducing
Contentation Situations in Multimedia Systems* 211

Phone: +49 371 531 1759
Fax: +49 371 531 1530
E-mail: j.werner@informatik.tu-chemnitz.de
URL: http://www.tu-chemnitz.de/home/
        informatik/osg/

Wolf, Klaus H.

University of Ulm
Dept. for Distributed Systems
Oberer Eselsberg
D-89069 Ulm
Germany

*Interactive Video and Remote Control via the
World Wide Web* 91

Phone: +49 731 502 4145
Fax: +49 731 502 4142
E-mail: wolf@informatik.uni-ulm.de
URL: http://www-vs.informatik.uni-ulm.de/

Wolf, Lars C.

IBM European Networking
Center
Vangerowstraße 18
D-69115 Heidelberg
Germany

*Scheduling Mechanisms Reducing
Contentation Situations in Multimedia Systems* 211

Phone: +49 6221 594515
Fax: +49 6221 593300
E-mail: lars@heidelbg.ibm.com
URL: http://www.ibm.com/

Yeadon, Nicholas

Lancaster University
Computing Department
Distributed Multimedia
Research Group
Lancaster LA1 4YR
UK

QoS Filters: Addressing the Heterogeneity Gap 227

Phone: +44 1524 65201 ext. 4539
Fax: +44 1524 593608
E-mail: njy@comp.lancs.ac.uk
URL: http://www.lancs.ac.uk/computing/
        staff/njy.html

Springer-Verlag
and the Environment

We at Springer-Verlag firmly believe that an international science publisher has a special obligation to the environment, and our corporate policies consistently reflect this conviction.

We also expect our business partners – paper mills, printers, packaging manufacturers, etc. – to commit themselves to using environmentally friendly materials and production processes.

The paper in this book is made from low- or no-chlorine pulp and is acid free, in conformance with international standards for paper permanency.

Lecture Notes in Computer Science

For information about Vols. 1–975

please contact your bookseller or Springer-Verlag

Vol. 1011: T. Furuhashi (Ed.), Advances in Fuzzy Logic, Neural Networks and Genetic Algorithms. Proceedings, 1994. (Subseries LNAI).

Vol. 1012: M. Bartošek, J. Staudek, J. Wiedermann (Eds.), SOFSEM '95: Theory and Practice of Informatics. Proceedings, 1995. XI, 499 pages. 1995.

Vol. 1013: T.W. Ling, A.O. Mendelzon, L. Vieille (Eds.), Deductive and Object-Oriented Databases. Proceedings, 1995. XIV, 557 pages. 1995.

Vol. 1014: A.P. del Pobil, M.A. Serna, Spatial Representation and Motion Planning. XII, 242 pages. 1995.

Vol. 1015: B. Blumenthal, J. Gornostaev, C. Unger (Eds.), Human-Computer Interaction. Proceedings, 1995. VIII, 203 pages. 1995.

VOL. 1016: R. Cipolla, Active Visual Inference of Surface Shape. XII, 194 pages. 1995.

Vol. 1017: M. Nagl (Ed.), Graph-Theoretic Concepts in Computer Science. Proceedings, 1995. XI, 406 pages. 1995.

Vol. 1018: T.D.C. Little, R. Gusella (Eds.), Network and Operating Systems Support for Digital Audio and Video. Proceedings, 1995. XI, 357 pages. 1995.

Vol. 1019: E. Brinksma, W.R. Cleaveland, K.G. Larsen, T. Margaria, B. Steffen (Eds.), Tools and Algorithms for the Construction and Analysis of Systems. Selected Papers, 1995. VII, 291 pages. 1995.

Vol. 1020: I.D. Watson (Ed.), Progress in Case-Based Reasoning. Proceedings, 1995. VIII, 209 pages. 1995. (Subseries LNAI).

Vol. 1021: M.P. Papazoglou (Ed.), OOER '95: Object-Oriented and Entity-Relationship Modeling. Proceedings, 1995. XVII, 451 pages. 1995.

Vol. 1022: P.H. Hartel, R. Plasmeijer (Eds.), Functional Programming Languages in Education. Proceedings, 1995. X, 309 pages. 1995.

Vol. 1023: K. Kanchanasut, J.-J. Lévy (Eds.), Algorithms, Concurrency and Knowlwdge. Proceedings, 1995. X, 410 pages. 1995.

Vol. 1024: R.T. Chin, H.H.S. Ip, A.C. Naiman, T.-C. Pong (Eds.), Image Analysis Applications and Computer Graphics. Proceedings, 1995. XVI, 533 pages. 1995.

Vol. 1025: C. Boyd (Ed.), Cryptography and Coding. Proceedings, 1995. IX, 291 pages. 1995.

Vol. 1026: P.S. Thiagarajan (Ed.), Foundations of Software Technology and Theoretical Computer Science. Proceedings, 1995. XII, 515 pages. 1995.

Vol. 1027: F.J. Brandenburg (Ed.), Graph Drawing. Proceedings, 1995. XII, 526 pages. 1996.

Vol. 1028: N.R. Adam, Y. Yesha (Eds.), Electronic Commerce. X, 155 pages. 1996.

Vol. 1029: E. Dawson, J. Golić (Eds.), Cryptography: Policy and Algorithms. Proceedings, 1995. XI, 327 pages. 1996.

Vol. 1030: F. Pichler, R. Moreno-Díaz, R. Albrecht (Eds.), Computer Aided Systems Theory - EUROCAST '95. Proceedings, 1995. XII, 539 pages. 1996.

Vol.1031: M. Toussaint (Ed.), Ada in Europe. Proceedings, 1995. XI, 455 pages. 1996.

Vol. 1032: P. Godefroid, Partial-Order Methods for the Verification of Concurrent Systems. IV, 143 pages. 1996.

Vol. 1033: C.-H. Huang, P. Sadayappan, U. Banerjee, D. Gelernter, A. Nicolau, D. Padua (Eds.), Languages and Compilers for Parallel Computing. Proceedings, 1995. XIII, 597 pages. 1996.

Vol. 1034: G. Kuper, M. Wallace (Eds.), Constraint Databases and Applications. Proceedings, 1995. VII, 185 pages. 1996.

Vol. 1035: S.Z. Li, D.P. Mital, E.K. Teoh, H. Wang (Eds.), Recent Developments in Computer Vision. Proceedings, 1995. XI, 604 pages. 1996.

Vol. 1036: G. Adorni, M. Zock (Eds.), Trends in Natural Language Generation - An Artificial Intelligence Perspective. Proceedings, 1993. IX, 382 pages. 1996. (Subseries LNAI).

Vol. 1037: M. Wooldridge, J.P. Müller, M. Tambe (Eds.), Intelligent Agents II. Proceedings, 1995. XVI, 437 pages. 1996. (Subseries LNAI).

Vol. 1038: W: Van de Velde, J.W. Perram (Eds.), Agents Breaking Away. Proceedings, 1996. XIV, 232 pages. 1996. (Subseries LNAI).

Vol. 1039: D. Gollmann (Ed.), Fast Software Encryption. Proceedings, 1996. X, 219 pages. 1996.

Vol. 1040: S. Wermter, E. Riloff, G. Scheler (Eds.), Connectionist, Statistical, and Symbolic Approaches to Learning for Natural Language Processing. Proceedings, 1995. IX, 468 pages. 1996. (Subseries LNAI).

Vol. 1041: J. Dongarra, K. Madsen, J. Waśniewski (Eds.), Applied Parallel Computing. Proceedings, 1995. XII, 562 pages. 1996.

Vol. 1042: G. Weiß, S. Sen (Eds.), Adaption and Learning in Multi-Agent Systems. Proceedings, 1995. X, 238 pages. 1996. (Subseries LNAI).

Vol. 1043: F. Moller, G. Birtwistle (Eds.), Logics for Concurrency. XI, 266 pages. 1996.

Vol. 1044: B. Plattner (Ed.), Broadband Communications. Proceedings, 1996. XIV, 359 pages. 1996.

Vol. 1045: B. Butscher, E. Moeller, H. Pusch (Eds.), Interactive Distributed Multimedia Systems and Services. Proceedings, 1996. XI, 333 pages. 1996.

Vol. 1046: C. Puech, R. Reischuk (Eds.), STACS 96. Proceedings, 1996. XII, 690 pages. 1996.

Vol. 1047: E. Hajnicz, Time Structures. IX, 244 pages. 1996. (Subseries LNAI).

Vol. 1048: M. Proietti (Ed.), Logic Program Syynthesis and Transformation. Proceedings, 1995. X, 267 pages. 1996.

Vol. 1049: K. Futatsugi, S. Matsuoka (Eds.), Object Technologies for Advanced Software. Proceedings, 1996. X, 309 pages. 1996.

Vol. 1050: R. Dyckhoff, H. Herre, P. Schroeder-Heister (Eds.), Extensions of Logic Programming. Proceedings, 1996. VII, 318 pages. 1996. (Subseries LNAI).

Vol. 1051: M.-C. Gaudel, J. Woodcock (Eds.), FME '96: Industrial Benefit of Formal Methods. Proceedings, 1996. XII, 704 pages. 1996.